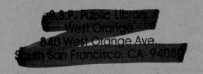

THE EASY PRESSURE COOKER COOKBOOK

BY Diane Phillips | MORE THAN **300** RECIPES FOR SOUPS, SIDES, MAIN DISHES, SAUCES, DESSERTS & BABY FOOD |

THE
Easy
PRESSURE
COOKER
Cookbook

CHRONICLE BOOKS

SAN FRANCISCO

Library of Congress Cataloging-in-Publication Data available.

ISBN 978-0-8118-7256-0

Manufactured in China

Designed by Alice Chau
Cover photograph by Yvonne Duivenvoorden
Typesetting by Helen Lee

10 9 8 7 6 5 4 3

Chronicle Books
680 Second Street
San Francisco, California 94107
www.chroniclebooks.com

To Poppy Sagan Sparrow Mand, who fills our lives with joy.

ACKNOWLEDGMENTS

No one writes a cookbook by themselves; we are joined in the kitchen and at our computers by our family, friends, and colleagues who give support to and nurture our work.

At home, my husband Dr. Chuck is always ready to sample a new recipe and give me encouragement when something isn't quite a home run; I'm so grateful to share my life and our adventures together. Our children Carrie, Eric, and Ryan are all such great cheerleaders when I begin a new project; Carrie and Eric are sold on the pressure cooker and have given me lots of great feedback about different recipes. Thanks to our son Ryan for encouraging me to start a blog and for always being a support when I'm in the throws of writing. Our granddaughter Poppy gave me the idea of using the pressure cooker to make baby food, and she is a source of constant joy to us all. I am so blessed to have you all in my life.

My agent Susan Ginsburg is not only the best agent on the face of the earth but also a dear friend, and I'm blessed to have her in my corner; thanks Susan for always knowing what's best for me, and for going the extra distance to get it done. Thanks also to her able assistants Bethany Strout and Carrie Pestritto for having answers to my questions every time I called.

I am indebted to Bill LeBlond at Chronicle Books for having faith in me and once again bringing me into the Chronicle family to write this book; my editor Amy Treadwell kept me on course and was open to my suggestions—thanks Amy for all your hard work on this monster project! I'm especially grateful to Amy for sending me copy editor Deborah Kops, whose sharp eye and attention to detail made my instructions simple and direct. Thanks, Deborah; it's been a pleasure to work with you again. Thanks also to all the hard-working people at Chronicle who shaped and finalized the book while in production, managing editor Doug Ogan, designer Alice Chau, and production coordinator Tera Killip.

And a huge load of gratitude to David Hawk and Peter Perez, in the marketing and sales department, for their hard work on my behalf; you two are a joy to work with.

Thanks also to the manufacturers who supplied products for me to test with: Cuisinart, Dan Kulp from Rachel Litner Associates for the electric pressure cooker, Rudy Keller of Kuhn Rikon and Linda Field of Field and Associates, and Sara de la Hera, VP of sales and marketing for Fagor America were more than generous with their support of this cookbook and my endeavors, and I am grateful to work with you all.

I would also like to thank the students and cooking schools who have welcomed me into their kitchens to teach over the years; I'm fortunate to teach all over this country and in Europe surrounded by professionals who make my job a joy each time I pick up a spatula.

Lastly, to you, dear reader, thank you for taking the time to pick up this book and to try out this piece of equipment. If you have any questions, please feel free to visit me at my Web site, www.dianephillips.com or my blog www.cucinadiva.blogspot.com. Now, let's put the pressure on and celebrate at the table!

CONTENTS

INTRODUCTION

For the home cook, the task of producing a meal at the end of the day can be overwhelming. The desire is there. But preparing a simple and delicious meal in under an hour may seem like an elusive dream, especially if the cook has put in a full workday or spent the afternoon chauffeuring children. Sadly, take-out pizza or a flat-tasting boxed, canned, or frozen dinner is often the *plat du jour*.

With a pressure cooker, the home cook can have it all: full-flavored dinners that are ready in minutes—that's right, a stew that is fork-tender and meltingly delicious within forty-five minutes; creamy risottos ready in less than ten minutes without stirring; and to soothe a cold or flu, comforting chicken soup to rival Mom's in less than an hour.

Pressure cookers have been around for a long time. Home cooks have used them to can vegetables and fruits from the garden or to make soup. More recently, we've seen chefs on competition reality shows using the pressure cooker to speed up the cooking process so their dishes are finished on time.

My first experience with a pressure cooker was at my mother-in-law's home, where she treated the cooker with the respect one might reserve for a nuclear missile. And I can't tell you the number of "oh my mom's split pea soup exploded and we never used it again" stories I heard when I told friends and students I was writing this book. But those stories are based on the type of pressure cooker my mother-in-law had, with a jiggly top and a lid that weighed about ten pounds. The pressure cooker would come to high pressure, hiss, steam, and frighten small children, until the food was ready. But, in fact, if you were reasonably careful, you could actually coax a delicious meal out of the pot.

These days, you won't see those pressure cookers for sale except at garage and tag sales. The new pressure cookers are gleaming, sleek, stainless-steel models, including the electric ones. They are perfectly safe to use and don't produce that hissing and steaming that made the old models seem so terrifying. Today's cookers have so many built-in safety features that a pressure cooker is a no-brainer for the home cook who wants to put a great meal on the table in minutes. There are even electric pressure cookers that do all the monitoring for you. This doesn't mean that you can skip the prep steps (which should only take fifteen minutes for the recipes in this book) or that you can leave the house while the cooker is on the stove. But it does mean that you can prepare delicious food in a quarter to half the time it would take to prepare the same meal in a conventional way.

The pressure cooker is one of those pieces that I would not be without. In addition to saving you cooking time, the cooker seals its lid while it operates, keeping all the goodies in the pot—the important vitamins and minerals in the foods and the ingredients' flavors. Pressure cookers have still another advantage: They are dual-purpose pots. The pot (without the lid) is terrific to use all by itself, eliminating the need to buy a 6- or 8-quart saucepan. And many come with an additional glass lid for conventional cooking.

The pressure cooker isn't reserved for cooking the main course. Grilling a porterhouse on the barbecue and want to serve steamed artichokes on the side? Pop those babies into the cooker, lock the lid, and in eleven minutes—the time it takes to preheat the grill—you will have perfectly steamed artichokes. For me, potato salads used to be an endless job, boiling whole potatoes for almost an hour, waiting for them to cool, and then making the salad. With a pressure cooker, the potatoes are cooked in less than twenty minutes. The potatoes are chilled quickly in the fridge, and in less than an hour, my salad is prepared and waiting for the barbecue to begin.

Desserts can also be made in a flash in the pressure cooker. Your family will be giving you standing ovations for bread puddings, rice puddings, and cheesecakes in all flavors. If you use fresh fruits at their peak, pressure cookers also make terrific fruit sauces and fruit butters. Homemade baby food is another task that is very well suited to the pressure cooker because, as noted earlier, the fresh taste and nutrients remain in the food. Making it from scratch is not only satisfying but also better for the baby.

So come along for an adventure in cooking under pressure, where the only steam you will feel is that rising from the delicious food served from your pressure cooker.

GETTING STARTED

Choosing Your Pot

Pressure cookers all work on the same principle of high-pressure cooking, ending with a release of the pressure. No matter which type you decide to buy, they all do the same thing. Your choice will depend on your budget and which cooker seems to be the best fit for your kitchen.

A well-stocked cookware store will have a selection of gorgeous stainless steel pressure cookers for the stove top as well as a few that are electric. Your choices here are size, style, and type of lid. Basically they are all safe, so that isn't an issue. Some cookers have a manual quick-release feature, which I like; it eliminates the need to run cold water over the top of the cooker to release the pressure. If you have a small kitchen with only one sink, this is a great feature.

I recommend a stainless steel pressure cooker with a three- to five-ply bottom for even heat. There are many European brands that are exceptional, turning out perfect dishes every time. Some of these cookers have a handle that is actually the pressure regulator, and some have a pressure regulator built into the lid. Cookers with aluminum interiors tend to pit, and they discolor when you cook foods containing acid, like tomatoes. A stainless interior is nonreactive and will also allow you to brown meats in the pressure cooker, creating one more layer of flavor before the lid is locked into place.

The shape of these cookers can vary; some are low and wide, while others are tall and deep. Your choices come down to how large a pressure cooker you want and whether you prefer a sauté type or a deeper one. If you think you will be making large quantities of soups, stocks, and stews, the taller pot may be the best choice for you. If, on the other hand, you will use the pot primarily for vegetables, risotto, and grains, then the shallower pot would be a good option. Regardless of which style you choose, I recommend that you buy a 4- to 6-quart pressure cooker for a family of two to four. An 8-quart size is ideal for larger families, or if you like to cook large quantities of food and freeze them.

An electric pressure cooker takes a lot of the guesswork out of pressure cooking. It automatically gets the food to the desired temperature, keeps the temperature constant, and then automatically reduces the pressure when the food has finished cooking. It also has a nonstick interior for easy cleanup.

Most of the better cookers come with a trivet and basket for steaming; these are used for keeping food out of the liquid in the bottom of the pan. They are essential if you want to make desserts or cook something in ramekins inside the pressure cooker. So keep them in mind when you are shopping.

Be sure to read your manufacturer's instruction booklet before getting started with pressure cooking. Many manufacturers include CDs with instructions for locking the lid into place, releasing pressure, and unlocking the lid.

Understanding Your Pressure Cooker

There is no way of actually seeing what is happening inside the pot once the lid has been locked down. Basically, liquid comes to a boil to produce steam, and the airtight seal keeps the steam trapped inside, which results in an increase in pressure in the pot—about fifteen pounds of pressure. As a result of the extra pressure, the liquid boils at 250 degrees F, rather than the standard 212 degrees. Because of the higher boiling point, the food fibers break down in a third to half of the time it would take them in a conventional pan.

The time it takes the pressure cooker to come to pressure will depend on the density of the food inside and how full the pot is. Generally, it will take between five and twenty minutes. Once the pot comes to your desired pressure, set your timer and then lower the heat on your stove-top burner to maintain the pressure level.

If your food isn't quite done after you have released the pressure, either by the quick-release method or naturally, you can return the pot to the stove top without the pressure lid for a few more minutes of cooking time. Or you can lock the lid on and allow the steam formed inside the pot to cook the ingredients for a few more minutes without bringing the pot back up to pressure. Undercooked food can happen for a few reasons. Most of the time it is because your pressure was not constant, probably because you weren't watching the regulator on your pressure cooker. And remember that foods aren't always predictable. An ingredient may take longer to cook for a variety of reasons, including size, density, and freshness. Sometimes old beans will take forever to cook in a pressure cooker. Be sure to check the expiration date on packaged beans.

All the recipes in this book were tested in the 6-quart-size pressure cooker. The recipes can be easily halved for a 3½- to 4-quart size. If you have an 8-quart pressure cooker, the recipes can be made in your pot without any adjustments.

Safety

Old pressure cookers had a weight that sat on the top of the lid, holding it in place; the pressure would push up on the lid and move the weight. If something got under the weight, it would fall off and the pot would literally explode into a shower of split peas or marinara. Today, pressure cookers have a built-in safety feature. If the pressure becomes too high, one or more safety vents will automatically release the pressure. This doesn't mean you should go out on the deck and drink coffee while the pressure cooker is on the stove. What it does mean is that you will get a warning (a whistling sound) if there is too much pressure building up. It's important to figure out how high you want the heat on your burner in order to obtain high pressure; so experiment, and find the sweet spot. A flame tamer can help to maintain an even heat on a gas stove.

Releasing Pressure

Pressure can be released either quickly or naturally. The are two ways to release it quickly: The first is the manual quick release, which is achieved by simply pulling back on the locking handle. Not all pressure cooker models have this feature, but it's one I recommend. The second quick method is to put the cooker under cold running water to allow the pressure to drop.

Pressure is released naturally by letting the pressure cooker sit after taking it off the heat. Depending on the amount of food in the cooker, this could take from 5 to 20 minutes. Safety mechanisms in the pressure cooker will keep you from opening the lid until the pressure has been released.

Each recipe is different. Some foods, risotto for example, benefit from a quick release, while others, such as stews, will produce a better result with a natural release. When removing the lid, after you have released the pressure, be sure to tilt the cooker away from you, so that any steam that escapes doesn't burn you.

A Baker's Dozen Tips for Successful Pressure Cooking

1 Read the **directions** that come with your pressure cooker. Although I developed the recipes using eight different brands, including an electric pressure cooker, the user's guide for yours will give you tips and timing for your cooker.

2 Never fill the pressure cooker more than **two-thirds full**.

3 Be sure you have **at least 1 cup** of cooking liquid.

4 Flavors tend to intensify in the pressure cooker, so use **half the amount of herbs and spices** that you normally do.

5 Make sure that the food going into the pressure cooker **isn't frozen**, as it will take forever to get up to pressure. It is better to microwave the vegetables or meat to defrost them than to waste the time with the pressure cooker.

6 Check the **gasket** to make sure that it fits snugly. It will wear out after prolonged use, so if it isn't snug, order a replacement.

7 Be careful when cooking **high-sugar foods**, which sometimes scorch. Add them last and watch the pressure regulator to be sure the pressure doesn't get higher than recommended.

8 The cooking time at **high pressure** doesn't include the time it takes to get to high pressure, which will depend on how full the pressure cooker is.

9 Once high pressure is reached, **lower the heat** and keep the heat high enough to maintain the pressure.

10 When the lid is unlocked after cooking, stir the food in the pressure cooker, and **allow to rest for 3 to 5 minutes** to let the flavors get to know each other.

11 Always **taste the food** before you serve it. Since pressure cooking can intensify the flavors, salt and pepper to taste are added at the end of many of the recipes in this book. If you are using broth that is already seasoned, you may not need any salt or pepper.

12 **Clean the vents** after every use.

13 To remove the steamer basket from the pressure cooker, use a pair of **silicone-tipped locking tongs**. The silicone will grip the stainless steel and stabilize the steamer as you remove it from the pot.

Pressure Cooker Lingo

LOCK THE LID IN PLACE

This sounds self-explanatory, but it's important to check a couple of things before you lock the lid: Make sure the valve is clear and check that the gasket, a rubber ring in the lid, fits there snugly. Each manufacturer will have a different method for locking the lid in place; it's important to check that the lid is sealed completely once the lid is locked down.

COOK AT HIGH PRESSURE

Once you have locked the lid in place and set the pot on the heat, you will need to wait while the pressure regulator comes up to pressure. On some pressure cookers, the pressure is indicated by a series of red rings on the lid. On others, the gauge registers the pressure, which is 15 psi (pounds per square inch) for high pressure.

COOK AT LOW PRESSURE

Low pressure is achieved in the same way as high pressure. The first red ring to emerge at the top of the regulator indicates low pressure on some cookers, while the gauge registers low pressure (5 pounds psi) on others. Turn down the heat to maintain low pressure and begin to time your dish.

RELEASE THE PRESSURE NATURALLY

After the food has cooked for its specified time, pressure is released naturally by taking the pan off the heat and allowing the pressure to drop.

QUICK RELEASE THE PRESSURE

There are two ways to do a quick release. The first is to manually release the pressure. The second is to remove the pressure cooker from the heat and run cold water over the lid.

PSST

Throughout this book, you will find notes labeled "Psst"—the sound your slow cooker makes when it comes to pressure. These notes are helpful hints about pressure cooking in general or about a particular recipe. You'll also find suggestions for alternative ingredients that work well with the recipe and those you should avoid.

PANTRY

These are just a few items in my pantry that you may want to stock in yours. I'm assuming that you have flour, sugar, peanut butter, and chocolate chips. Choose well. Remember that the quality of your ingredients will be reflected in the finished dish; if you use ingredients of inferior quality, chances are your dish will not be at its best.

Beans and legumes: Buy from health food markets, where you can scoop them from bins, rather than getting them in bags at your supermarket. The fresher the beans, the better they will taste, and the more accurate your timing will be when cooking them. Old beans take forever to cook.

Broth, stock, or reconstituted soup base: Everyone has a favorite broth that comes in a can or box, or is reconstituted. This is a matter of personal preference, and you should use one that works for you and your family. If you want to make your own stock with a pressure cooker (see pages 19, 20, 21, and 22), then by all means use it in any of the dishes in this book. After you see how easy it is to do, you will probably want to make extra and freeze it. Soup bases are jars of very thick reductions that are reconstituted with water; don't confuse these with bouillon cubes, which are mostly salt and a few seasonings. The first ingredient on a jar of soup base should be chicken or beef or whatever the soup base will become, and not salt.

Butter: Always use unsalted butter so that you can control the amount of salt in your dishes. Salted butter tends to retain moisture and will water down most dishes.

Canola oil: Find a brand that you like and stick with it. Canola has a neutral taste.

Extra-virgin olive oil: This is where I get a little militant. Buy a good-quality cold-pressed olive oil. Most gourmet stores will let you taste their oils, and you should find one you like, rather than buy blindly in the supermarket. The flavor of the olive oil will permeate everything you sauté in it.

Garlic: Use fresh garlic and peel it yourself. Garlic that is already peeled or processed loses its potency and gives dishes an odd flavor. Make sure each head is tightly closed and the cloves are firm when you press on them.

Herbs, fresh: Most fresh herbs lose their flavor and potency in the pressure cooker. Two exceptions are sprigs of thyme and branches of rosemary. Both of these herbs have a woodsy quality and tend to hold up well under pressure. In general, add fresh herbs at the end of the cooking time to refresh the flavors in your dishes.

Herbs and spices, dried: How do you know if they are still potent? I use the sniff test: If they have no aroma, chances are they won't impart any aroma or flavor to your finished dish. I recommend Penzeys Spices (www.penzeys.com) for freshness and a good selection.

Lemon or lime juice: Always buy a lemon or lime and squeeze it yourself. The juice in those little plastic lemons bears no resemblance to the real thing.

Nonstick cooking spray: Your best friend when making sticky dishes in the pressure cooker or elsewhere.

Parmigiano-Reggiano cheese: The undisputed king of cheeses, this aged Parmesan from Parma lends nuance and complex flavor to a dish. If you have leftover rinds, save them in zipper-top plastic bags in your freezer and use them in soups and sauces. They become soft and pliable and add a rich flavor.

Prosciutto di Parma: Imported from northern Italy, this is the finest of Italy's salt-cured hams, with an outstanding flavor. The ham is made according to traditional methods, and that is why it is expensive, but definitely worth the price.

Shallots: A member of the onion family, a shallot gives you a lot of great flavor in a small package.

Sweet yellow onions: Vidalia, Texas and Mayan Sweets, Walla Wallas, Maui, and Texas 1015s are all deemed "sweet" because they contain 6 percent sugar. They balance spicy, hot, and strong flavors, melding them and adding sweetness.

Tomatoes: I recommend San Marzano or organic canned tomatoes. Of course, use fresh tomatoes from your garden if you have some; just remove the skins and chop the tomatoes before adding to the pressure cooker.

Vanilla bean paste: If you love the flavor of vanilla, chances are you've been disappointed when you cook with vanilla extract, which has a high alcohol content. Vanilla bean paste is an emulsion packed with vanilla beans that gives your cooked desserts a great big punch of vanilla. It keeps in the pantry for up to a year.

SOUPS & CHILIES

Warm, comforting, full of flavor, and with good-for-you ingredients—no wonder everyone loves a well-made bowl of soup. Home-cooked soup can appear on your table often with the help of the pressure cooker. Instead of having to mind a pot on your stove top for hours, you'll get the same deeply flavored soup in a matter of minutes. And the best news is that the pressure cooker makes enough for dinner and then some, so you can make the soup and refrigerate or freeze any leftovers! From golden CHICKEN STOCK (page 19) to spins on old favorites like split pea with ham (see page 48), and everything in between, there is something for everyone in this chapter—even a delicious BLT SOUP (page 32).

Chili, that spicy and hearty dinner in a bowl, is ready in less than an hour in the pressure cooker, with the same slow-cooked, intense flavor that makes chili such a family favorite. Whether you like your chili with beef, poultry, or veggies, you'll find just the right recipe in this chapter, and it will be ready in no time.

Soups and chilies depend on the first ingredients to layer flavor for the finished dish. Be sure to use a good-quality extra-virgin olive oil when sautéing. Sauté dried herbs, onions, and garlic before adding liquids. And check to see that the dried herbs and spices are aromatic before adding them to the pot. If your dried herbs don't have much aroma, chances are your soup won't have much flavor. To refresh the taste of your soups, stir in fresh herbs at the end of the cooking time for a delicious fresh burst of flavor.

Most of the recipes in this chapter include salt and pepper at the end of the ingredients list. You will be using broth in each recipe rather than water, and since the pressure cooker intensifies flavors, there may be enough salt and pepper in the finished soup without your adding more. So I recommend correcting the seasoning at the end of the cooking time.

CHICKEN STOCK

Chicken stock is fast and incredibly delicious when made in the pressure cooker. The flavor of the chicken infuses the broth so deeply, you will probably rethink that can or box of broth that you buy in the store. And it's less expensive than store-bought, too. On the stove top, this same stock would take up to four hours; under pressure, it takes less than an hour. Use the stock to make a pot of soothing CHICKEN NOODLE SOUP (page 26). Or strain it into airtight containers and use it later.

MAKES ABOUT **8** CUPS

2 TABLESPOONS EXTRA-VIRGIN OLIVE OIL

2½ POUNDS CHICKEN BACKS AND NECKS, OR 1 WHOLE 2½-POUND CHICKEN, CUT UP

1 LARGE ONION, QUARTERED, SKIN LEFT ON

3 MEDIUM CARROTS, CUT INTO 2-INCH LENGTHS

4 CELERY STALKS (INCLUDING THE LEAVES), CUT INTO 2-INCH LENGTHS

½ CUP PACKED FRESH FLAT-LEAF PARSLEY, COARSELY CHOPPED

1 BAY LEAF

1 SPRIG FRESH THYME

4 BLACK PEPPERCORNS

1 TEASPOON SALT, PLUS MORE IF NEEDED

8 CUPS WATER

1 Heat the oil in the pressure cooker over high heat. Add the chicken parts and brown them on all sides, removing them to a plate as they brown. Add the onion, carrots, celery, and parsley and toss them in the oil to coat. Return the chicken to the pot and add the bay leaf, thyme, peppercorns, salt, and water. Lock the lid in place, and cook at high pressure for 45 minutes.

2 Release the pressure naturally and remove the lid, tilting the pot away from you to avoid the escaping steam. Strain the stock through a fine-mesh strainer and discard the solids. Taste for seasoning and add more salt if necessary. Cool the stock completely, skim off any fat that may have risen to the surface, and transfer to airtight containers. Stock keeps in the freezer for up to 6 months and in the refrigerator for up to 4 days.

PSST

Why leave the skin on the onion? First, for the nutrients it adds to the stock, and second, for the golden color it lends. Try it; you'll be amazed!

Ask the meat manager at your supermarket for necks and backs. If they aren't available, use chicken wings, which are usually less expensive than other parts. Most full-service meat markets will have necks and backs, and you can usually call to reserve them.

BEEF STOCK

Canned beef broth or stock is a poor relation to the real thing, and I urge you to try making your own with your pressure cooker. In forty-five minutes, you will have a stock that has a deep, beefy flavor, which will enhance all manner of delicious creations. Beef shanks are large, but any good butcher will go in the back room and saw them into manageable pieces for you. They can also be hard to find, though. If necessary, an equivalent amount of beef ribs will work in this recipe.

MAKES ABOUT **8** CUPS

....

2 GARLIC CLOVES, MINCED

2 TEASPOONS SALT, PLUS MORE IF NEEDED

1 TEASPOON FRESHLY GROUND BLACK PEPPER, PLUS MORE IF NEEDED

2½ POUNDS MEATY BEEF SHANKS OR BEEF RIBS, CUT INTO 1-INCH PIECES

2 TABLESPOONS EXTRA-VIRGIN OLIVE OIL

1 LARGE ONION, QUARTERED, SKIN LEFT ON

3 MEDIUM CARROTS, CUT INTO 2-INCH LENGTHS

4 CELERY STALKS (INCLUDING THE LEAVES), CUT INTO 2-INCH LENGTHS

2 TABLESPOONS TOMATO PASTE

1 BAY LEAF

2 SPRIGS FRESH THYME

8 CUPS WATER

1 Press the garlic through a garlic press and combine it with the salt and pepper to make a paste. Rub it onto the meat and bones. Heat the oil in the pressure cooker over medium-high heat. Brown the bones in the hot oil, turning to cook them evenly. Add the remaining ingredients and stir up any browned bits on the bottom of the pot. Lock the lid in place and cook at high pressure for 45 minutes.

2 Release the pressure naturally and remove the lid, tilting the pot away from you to avoid the escaping steam. Strain the stock through a fine-mesh strainer, discarding the solids. Taste for seasoning and add more salt and pepper if necessary. Cool the stock completely and skim off any fat that may have floated to the surface. Transfer to airtight containers and store in the refrigerator for up to 4 days or in the freezer for up to 6 months.

VEGETABLE STOCK

Vegetable stocks provide a delicious base for soups, casseroles, and other dishes. When made in the pressure cooker, they are especially fragrant and tasty because the pressure cooker coaxes every bit of flavor from the vegetables. Use this stock for any recipe that calls for chicken or beef stock or broth.

MAKES ABOUT 8 CUPS

2 TABLESPOONS EXTRA-VIRGIN OLIVE OIL

4 GARLIC CLOVES, MINCED

3 MEDIUM ONIONS, QUARTERED, SKIN LEFT ON

3 MEDIUM CARROTS, COARSELY CHOPPED

4 CELERY STALKS (INCLUDING THE LEAVES), COARSELY CHOPPED

2 MEDIUM YUKON GOLD POTATOES, SCRUBBED AND CUT INTO 1-INCH CHUNKS

½ POUND CREMINI MUSHROOMS, QUARTERED

1 TABLESPOON TOMATO PASTE

2 SPRIGS FRESH THYME

4 BLACK PEPPERCORNS

1½ TEASPOONS SALT, PLUS MORE IF NEEDED

7 CUPS WATER

1 Heat the oil in the pressure cooker over medium-high heat. Add the garlic and sauté for 1 minute, or until fragrant. Add the remaining ingredients, lock the lid in place, and cook at high pressure for 12 minutes.

2 Release the pressure naturally and remove the lid, tilting the pot away from you to avoid the escaping steam. Strain the stock through a fine-mesh strainer, discarding the solids. Taste the stock for seasoning and add more salt if necessary. Cool, then transfer to airtight containers and store in the refrigerator for up to 4 days or in the freezer for up to 6 months.

SEAFOOD STOCK

Good seafood stock made from fish trimmings and crustacean shells is hard to find in the supermarket, but you can have homemade seafood stock in your freezer in less than one hour, from start to finish. Be sure to use the trimmings from fish that have a mild flavor, such as halibut, snapper, or sea bass, rather than stronger oily fish like salmon or swordfish. Many fish markets will gladly give you the trimmings at no charge, but some will charge a nominal fee.

MAKES ABOUT **8** CUPS

....

2 POUNDS FISH TRIMMINGS, INCLUDING FISH HEADS (GILLS REMOVED), BONES, AND TAILS

3 LEEKS (WHITE AND TENDER GREEN PARTS), CLEANED AND COARSELY CHOPPED

2 MEDIUM CARROTS, COARSELY CHOPPED

3 CELERY STALKS (INCLUDING THE LEAVES), COARSELY CHOPPED

5 BLACK PEPPERCORNS

1 TEASPOON SALT

2 CUPS WHITE WINE, SUCH AS SAUVIGNON BLANC OR PINOT GRIGIO, OR DRY VERMOUTH

6 CUPS WATER

1 Combine all the ingredients in the pressure cooker. Lock the lid in place and cook at high pressure for 10 minutes.

2 Release the pressure naturally and remove the lid, tilting the pot away from you to avoid the escaping steam. Strain the stock through a fine-mesh strainer, discarding the solids. Cool and store in airtight containers in the refrigerator for up to 2 days or in the freezer for up to 2 months.

PARMESAN BROTH

This full-flavored broth is another vegetarian option, in addition to **VEGETABLE STOCK** (page 21). It uses up all those Parmigiano-Reggiano rinds that you might otherwise toss. The broth has the sweet, nutty flavor of Parmigiano, as well as the flavors of the vegetables. It's a great way to perk up mild-flavored soups like potato soup and give them a lot of personality. Be sure to layer the cheese rinds on top of the vegetables; otherwise, they may stick to the bottom of the pot during cooking.

MAKES ABOUT **8** CUPS

2 TABLESPOONS EXTRA-VIRGIN OLIVE OIL

2 LEEKS (WHITE AND TENDER GREEN PARTS), CLEANED AND COARSELY CHOPPED

3 MEDIUM CARROTS, COARSELY CHOPPED

3 CELERY STALKS (INCLUDING THE LEAVES), COARSELY CHOPPED

½ CUP CHOPPED PARMIGIANO-REGGIANO CHEESE RINDS

2 BLACK PEPPERCORNS

6 CUPS WATER

1 In the pressure cooker, heat the oil over medium-high heat. Add the leeks, carrots, and celery and cook for about 3 minutes, until the vegetables are coated with the oil. Add the cheese and peppercorns and carefully pour the water over the contents of the pot. Lock the lid in place and cook at high pressure for 10 minutes.

2 Release the pressure naturally and remove the lid, tilting the pot way from you to avoid the escaping steam. Strain the soup through a fine-mesh strainer, discarding the solids. Cool the stock completely, skim off any fat that may have accumulated on top of the stock (see the Psst), and transfer to airtight containers. Store the stock in the refrigerator for up to 4 days or in the freezer for up to 4 months.

PSST

This stock will not have much fat on the surface, and you can remove it easily with a paper towel. Fold a sheet into a square and skim the paper towel over the surface of the stock. You can use this trick to skim any soup or stew that doesn't have much fat.

FRENCH ONION SOUP

French onion soup is a guilty pleasure for me. What's not to love? Caramelized onions; beefy, thyme-flavored broth; and then the whole thing is covered with melted cheese. Life doesn't get much better than this! The soup is easily prepared in the pressure cooker, giving you a meal in a bowl for a cold winter's night in less than thirty minutes. The onions will take up to ten minutes to properly caramelize, but that is the only labor-intensive step in this heavenly dish.

SERVES 6

....

4 TABLESPOONS UNSALTED BUTTER

1 TABLESPOON EXTRA-VIRGIN OLIVE OIL

4 LARGE SWEET ONIONS, SUCH AS VIDALIA, HALVED AND THINLY SLICED

1 TEASPOON DRIED THYME

2 TEASPOONS SALT, PLUS MORE IF NEEDED

½ TEASPOON FRESHLY GROUND BLACK PEPPER

2 TEASPOONS SUGAR

1 CUP DRY WHITE WINE, SUCH AS SAUVIGNON BLANC OR PINOT GRIGIO, OR DRY VERMOUTH

6 CUPS BEEF STOCK (PAGE 20) OR STORE-BOUGHT BEEF BROTH

SIX ¾-INCH SLICES FRENCH BREAD, TOASTED

1 CUP FINELY SHREDDED GRUYÈRE CHEESE

½ CUP FRESHLY GRATED PARMIGIANO-REGGIANO CHEESE

1 Preheat the broiler unless you're planning to use a kitchen torch to melt the cheese.

2 In the pressure cooker, melt the butter with the oil over medium-high heat. Add the onions, thyme, salt, pepper, and sugar. Sauté for about 10 minutes, or until the onions begin to turn golden brown. Add the wine and stock. Lock the lid in place and cook at high pressure for 7 minutes.

3 Quick release the pressure and remove the lid, tilting the pot away from you to avoid the escaping steam. Taste the soup for seasoning and add more salt if necessary.

4 Arrange six heat-proof soup bowls on a work surface or, if using the broiler, on a baking sheet. Ladle the soup into the bowls and float a slice of bread on top of the soup in each bowl. Combine the cheeses and sprinkle evenly over the bread. If using the broiler, place the baking sheet under the preheated broiler about 6 inches from the heat for 7 to 10 minutes, or until the cheese is bubbling and golden brown. If using a kitchen torch, hold the torch 8 inches away from each bowl until the cheese is bubbling and golden brown. Serve immediately.

CREAMY CHICKEN AND WILD RICE SOUP

This hearty but elegant soup is thick with succulent bits of chicken, crunchy vegetables, and chewy wild rice. It's a crowd-pleaser and so simple to make in the pressure cooker.

SERVES **6** TO **8**

2 TABLESPOONS UNSALTED BUTTER

1 TABLESPOON EXTRA-VIRGIN OLIVE OIL

2 BONELESS, SKINLESS CHICKEN BREAST HALVES, CUT INTO BITE-SIZE PIECES

1 TEASPOON SALT, PLUS MORE IF NEEDED

½ TEASPOON FRESHLY GROUND BLACK PEPPER, PLUS MORE IF NEEDED

1 MEDIUM SWEET ONION, SUCH AS VIDALIA, FINELY CHOPPED

3 MEDIUM CARROTS, COARSELY CHOPPED

4 CELERY STALKS (INCLUDING THE LEAVES), COARSELY CHOPPED

1 TEASPOON DRIED THYME

1 CUP WILD RICE

6 CUPS CHICKEN STOCK (PAGE 19) OR STORE-BOUGHT CHICKEN BROTH

1 CUP HEAVY CREAM

1 Melt the butter with the oil in the pressure cooker over medium-high heat. Sprinkle the chicken evenly with the salt and pepper and cook in the butter and oil until it turns white on all sides. Add the onion, carrots, celery, and thyme and stir to combine. Stir in the wild rice and stock. Lock the lid in place and cook at high pressure for 10 minutes.

2 Release the pressure naturally and remove the lid, tilting the pot away from you to avoid the escaping steam. Stir in the cream, taste for seasoning, and add more salt and pepper if needed. Warm the soup and serve.

CHICKEN NOODLE SOUP

Nothing says "comfort" like chicken noodle soup—a steaming, rich broth filled with tender chunks of chicken and vegetables and a tangle of noodles. There is no better cure for a cold, the blues, or a bad day, and this chicken soup is ready in less than twenty minutes.

SERVES **6** TO **8**

2 TABLESPOONS UNSALTED BUTTER

1 TABLESPOON EXTRA-VIRGIN OLIVE OIL

4 BONELESS, SKINLESS CHICKEN BREAST HALVES, CUT INTO BITE-SIZE PIECES

1½ TEASPOONS SALT, PLUS MORE IF NEEDED

½ TEASPOON FRESHLY GROUND BLACK PEPPER, PLUS MORE IF NEEDED

4 MEDIUM CARROTS, COARSELY CHOPPED

4 CELERY STALKS (INCLUDING THE LEAVES), COARSELY CHOPPED

1 CUP GREEN BEANS, TRIMMED AND CUT INTO 1-INCH LENGTHS

1 CUP CORN KERNELS, FRESHLY CUT FROM THE COB, OR FROZEN CORN, DEFROSTED

1 TEASPOON DRIED THYME

8 CUPS CHICKEN STOCK (PAGE 19) OR STORE-BOUGHT CHICKEN BROTH

6 OUNCES FINE EGG NOODLES

1 Melt the butter with the olive oil in the pressure cooker over medium-high heat. Sprinkle the chicken evenly with the salt and pepper and sauté in the butter and oil until the chicken is white on all sides. Add the carrots, celery, green beans, corn, thyme, and stock. Lock the lid in place and cook at high pressure for 8 minutes.

2 Quick release the pressure and remove the lid, tilting the pot away from you to avoid the escaping steam. Add the noodles to the soup, bring to a boil, uncovered, and cook for 5 minutes, or until the noodles are al dente (barely tender). Season the soup with more salt and pepper and serve.

PSST

This soup is also great when made with leftover cooked pasta. Cut long strands of spaghetti or fettuccine into 1-inch lengths and add to the soup after it has finished pressure cooking. Rewarm the soup before serving.

IRISH CHICKEN SOUP

Chicken, potatoes, and mild savoy cabbage in a savory broth make for a satisfying meal—perfect for a weeknight or a Sunday afternoon while you're watching sports on television. Yukon Gold potatoes give this soup a lovely golden tint, but if they're not available, white creamers or red-skinned potatoes work just as well.

SERVES **6** TO **8**

2 TABLESPOONS UNSALTED BUTTER

1 TABLESPOON EXTRA-VIRGIN OLIVE OIL

4 BONELESS, SKINLESS CHICKEN BREAST HALVES, CUT INTO BITE-SIZE PIECES

1 TEASPOON SALT, PLUS MORE IF NEEDED

½ TEASPOON FRESHLY GROUND BLACK PEPPER

1 SMALL HEAD SAVOY CABBAGE, TOUGH OUTER LEAVES REMOVED, CORED, AND COARSELY CHOPPED

4 MEDIUM YUKON GOLD POTATOES, SCRUBBED AND CUT INTO ½-INCH CUBES

1 TEASPOON FINELY CHOPPED FRESH THYME

7 CUPS CHICKEN STOCK (PAGE 19) OR STORE-BOUGHT CHICKEN BROTH

1 CUP HEAVY CREAM

¼ CUP FINELY CHOPPED FRESH CHIVES FOR GARNISH

1 Melt the butter with the oil in the pressure cooker over medium-high heat. Sprinkle the chicken evenly with the salt and pepper and sauté in the butter and oil until the chicken is white on all sides. Add the cabbage, potatoes, thyme, and stock. Lock the lid in place and cook at high pressure for 20 minutes.

2 Quick release the pressure and remove the lid, tilting the pot away from you to avoid the escaping steam. Add the cream, taste the soup for seasoning, and add more salt if necessary. Warm the soup and serve, garnished with the chopped chives.

CURRIED CHICKEN AND POTATO SOUP

Curried soups are a nice change of pace from the usual weeknight fare. Brimming with succulent chicken, golden potatoes, yellow lentils, and a touch of coconut milk, this one will have your family lining up in the kitchen for second and third helpings.

SERVES **6** TO **8**

3 TABLESPOONS CANOLA OIL

4 BONELESS, SKINLESS CHICKEN BREAST HALVES, CUT INTO BITE-SIZE PIECES

2 TEASPOONS CURRY POWDER

1 MEDIUM ONION, FINELY CHOPPED

2 MEDIUM YUKON GOLD POTATOES, PEELED AND CUT INTO ½-INCH PIECES

1 CUP YELLOW LENTILS

6 CUPS CHICKEN STOCK (PAGE 19) OR STORE-BOUGHT CHICKEN BROTH

½ CUP COCONUT MILK

SALT AND FRESHLY GROUND BLACK PEPPER (OPTIONAL)

½ CUP MANGO CHUTNEY (PAGE 428) OR STORE-BOUGHT CHUTNEY, SUCH AS MAJOR GREY'S, FOR GARNISH

½ CUP FINELY CHOPPED ROASTED PEANUTS

3 GREEN ONIONS (WHITE AND GREEN PARTS), FINELY CHOPPED, FOR GARNISH

1 Heat the oil in the pressure cooker over medium-high heat. Sprinkle the chicken evenly with the curry powder and sauté in the oil until the chicken is white all over. Add the onion and stir to coat with some of the oil and spices. Add the potatoes, lentils, and stock. Lock the lid in place and cook at high pressure for 15 minutes.

2 Quick release the pressure and remove the lid, tilting the pot away from you to avoid the escaping steam. Stir in the coconut milk, taste the soup for seasoning, and add salt and pepper if necessary. Warm the soup and serve each portion topped with a dollop of chutney and sprinkle with some of the peanuts and green onions.

CREAMY ARTICHOKE SOUP WITH CRISPY PROSCIUTTO

An elegant first course for a special-occasion dinner, this creamy soup tastes like the essence of artichokes, with a salty, crispy garnish of sautéed prosciutto for contrast. Although the soup is a bit labor-intensive, you can serve it anytime. It's especially good when artichokes are in season. Make a double batch and freeze some for later use.

SERVES 6

....

4 LARGE ARTICHOKES

4 TABLESPOONS EXTRA-VIRGIN OLIVE OIL

1 GARLIC CLOVE, MINCED

¼ CUP FRESH LEMON JUICE

1 SPRIG FRESH THYME

1 BAY LEAF

4 CUPS CHICKEN STOCK (PAGE 19) OR STORE-BOUGHT CHICKEN BROTH

6 THIN SLICES PROSCIUTTO DI PARMA, FINELY CHOPPED, FOR GARNISH

1½ CUPS HEAVY CREAM

SALT (OPTIONAL)

1 OR 2 DROPS OF TABASCO OR ANOTHER HOT SAUCE (OPTIONAL)

1 Cut off the stems and the tough outer leaves of the artichokes with kitchen shears, until you reach the lighter green, tender leaves. Slice off about 1 inch from the top of each artichoke and cut the artichoke in half lengthwise. Remove the fuzzy choke and coarsely chop the artichoke heart.

2 Heat 2 tablespoons of the oil in the pressure cooker over medium-high heat. Add the artichokes and sauté with the garlic for 2 minutes, to coat them with the oil. Add the lemon juice, thyme, bay leaf, and stock. Lock the lid in place and cook at high pressure for 4 minutes.

3 While the soup is cooking, heat the remaining 2 tablespoons oil in a skillet over medium-low heat. Add the prosciutto and sauté until crisp. Remove from the pan and drain on paper towels.

4 When the soup is ready, release the pressure naturally and remove the lid, tilting the pot away from you to avoid the escaping steam. Remove the thyme and bay leaf and purée the soup with an immersion blender (or cool, transfer to a blender, and purée). Add the cream, taste for seasoning, and add salt if needed. Add the Tabasco (if desired), warm the soup, and serve, garnished with some of the crispy prosciutto.

SWEET PEA, ARTICHOKE, AND FAVA BEAN SOUP

This lovely spring-green soup is bursting with tender sweet peas, fava beans, and artichoke slices. A dollop of thick Greek yogurt at the end adds another tart note to the lemony broth. Fresh fava beans come in long green pods and are only available in the spring.

SERVES **6**

3 LARGE ARTICHOKES

3 TABLESPOONS EXTRA-VIRGIN OLIVE OIL

2 LEEKS (WHITE PARTS ONLY), FINELY CHOPPED

1 CUP SHELLED FAVA BEANS (SEE PSST)

¼ CUP FRESH LEMON JUICE

5 CUPS CHICKEN STOCK (PAGE 19) OR STORE-BOUGHT CHICKEN BROTH

½ CUP HEAVY CREAM

1 CUP FRESH PETITE PEAS OR FROZEN PEAS, DEFROSTED

SALT AND FRESHLY GROUND BLACK PEPPER (OPTIONAL)

½ CUP GREEK-STYLE YOGURT FOR GARNISH

¼ CUP FINELY CHOPPED FRESH CHIVES FOR GARNISH

1 Cut off the stems and the tough outer leaves of the artichokes with kitchen shears, until you reach the lighter green, tender leaves. Slice off about 1 inch from the top of each artichoke and cut the artichoke in half lengthwise. Remove the fuzzy choke and slice the artichoke heart ¼ inch thick.

2 Heat the oil in the pressure cooker over medium-high heat. Add the leeks and artichoke slices and sauté for 2 minutes to soften the leeks. Add the beans, lemon juice, and stock. Lock the lid in place and cook at high pressure for 10 minutes.

3 Quick release the pressure and remove the lid, tilting the pot away from you to avoid the escaping steam. Add the cream and peas, taste for seasoning, and add salt and pepper if necessary. Warm the soup and serve with a dollop of yogurt and a sprinkling of chopped chives.

PSST

If the fava beans are the size of a small white bean, their membrane (a thin white covering) doesn't need to be removed. But if the beans are larger, say the size of a thumbnail, you will need to soak the beans in boiling water for 1 minute and slip off the membrane.

SPINACH AND CORN SOUP WITH BACON

Flecked with bright green spinach and yellow corn, this colorful, bacon-infused soup delights the eye and the taste buds.

SERVES 6

....

8 BACON STRIPS, CUT CROSSWISE INTO PIECES ½ INCH WIDE FOR GARNISH

½ CUP FINELY CHOPPED SWEET ONION, SUCH AS VIDALIA

3 MEDIUM CARROTS, FINELY CHOPPED

ONE 10-OUNCE BAG BABY SPINACH, FINELY CHOPPED, OR ONE 1-POUND PACKAGE FROZEN CHOPPED SPINACH, DEFROSTED AND SQUEEZED DRY

2 CUPS CORN KERNELS, FRESHLY CUT FROM THE COB, OR FROZEN CORN, DEFROSTED

6 CUPS CHICKEN STOCK (PAGE 19) OR STORE-BOUGHT CHICKEN BROTH

1 CUP HEAVY CREAM

SALT AND FRESHLY GROUND BLACK PEPPER (OPTIONAL)

1 Cook the bacon in the pressure cooker over medium heat until it is crisp. Remove from the pan, drain on paper towels, and set aside. Drain off all but 2 tablespoons of the bacon drippings from the pan. Add the onion, carrots, spinach, and corn and sauté for about 5 minutes, or until the onion and carrots begin to soften. Add the stock. Lock the lid in place and cook at high pressure for 5 minutes.

2 Quick release the pressure and remove the lid, tilting the pot away from you to avoid the escaping steam. Add the cream, taste the soup for seasoning, and add salt and pepper if necessary. Warm the soup and crumble the bacon. Serve the soup garnished with the bacon.

BLT SOUP

Everyone loves a BLT, that classic sandwich of bacon, lettuce, and tomato on toast. This soup is a takeoff on that idea, but it's made with escarole rather than iceberg lettuce. Serve it with a sprinkling of croutons to give it a nice crunch.

SERVES **6**

2 TABLESPOONS UNSALTED BUTTER

1 CUP FINELY CHOPPED SWEET ONION, SUCH AS VIDALIA

TWO 14-OUNCE CANS TOMATO PURÉE

1 LARGE HEAD ESCAROLE, TOUGH STEMS TRIMMED AND LEAVES CHOPPED

3 CUPS CHICKEN STOCK (PAGE 19) OR STORE-BOUGHT CHICKEN BROTH

1 CUP HEAVY CREAM (SEE PSST)

SALT AND FRESHLY GROUND BLACK PEPPER (OPTIONAL)

8 SLICES BACON, COOKED UNTIL CRISP AND CRUMBLED FOR GARNISH

GARLIC CROUTONS FOR GARNISH (FACING PAGE)

1 Melt the butter in the pressure cooker over medium-high heat. Add the onion and sauté for 2 minutes, or until it begins to soften. Add the tomato purée, escarole, and stock. Lock the lid in place and cook at high pressure for 10 minutes.

2 Quick release the pressure and remove the lid, tilting the pot away from you to avoid the escaping steam. Stir in the cream, taste the soup for seasoning, and add salt and pepper if necessary. Warm the soup and serve garnished with the bacon and croutons.

PSST

If you would like to omit the heavy cream in this dish, you can add another cup of chicken stock. The soup won't be nearly as luxuriously creamy, but it will still be delicious.

GARLIC CROUTONS

Terrific for garnishing soups or salads, these simple croutons are a great way to use up not-so-fresh baguettes.

MAKES ABOUT **6** CUPS

....

6 CUPS FRENCH BREAD
CUBES (¾-INCH CUBES;
1 OR 2 BAGUETTES)

½ CUP EXTRA-VIRGIN OLIVE OIL

½ TEASPOON GARLIC SALT

½ TEASPOON DRIED OREGANO

½ TEASPOON DRIED BASIL

PINCH OF CAYENNE PEPPER

½ TEASPOON FRESHLY GROUND
BLACK PEPPER

½ TEASPOON SWEET PAPRIKA

1 Preheat the oven to 350 degrees F and line a baking sheet with parchment paper, aluminum foil, or a silicone baking liner. Spread out the bread on the baking sheet in one layer.

2 In a 2-cup measuring cup, stir together the oil, garlic salt, oregano, basil, cayenne, black pepper, and paprika. Pour the mixture over the bread and toss to coat. Bake the croutons for 20 minutes, turning them halfway through the cooking time. The croutons should be firm and golden brown.

CREAMY TOMATO AND FENNEL SOUP

This is a lovely soup to serve as a first course or as a Saturday-night supper with grown-up grilled cheese sandwiches made with sharp white cheddar, smoked mozzarella, sharp provolone, fresh Asiago, pepper Jack, or smoked Gouda. It takes no time to make in the pressure cooker, and the results are delectable.

SERVES **6** TO **8**

2 TABLESPOONS UNSALTED BUTTER

1 MEDIUM SWEET ONION, SUCH AS VIDALIA, FINELY CHOPPED

1 FENNEL BULB, FRONDS REMOVED AND ROOT END TRIMMED, FINELY CHOPPED

TWO 28-OUNCE CANS PLUM TOMATOES, DRAINED

6 CUPS CHICKEN STOCK (PAGE 19) OR STORE-BOUGHT CHICKEN BROTH

1½ CUPS HEAVY CREAM

SALT AND FRESHLY GROUND BLACK PEPPER (OPTIONAL)

1 Melt the butter in the pressure cooker over medium-high heat. Add the onion and fennel and cook for 2 minutes, or until the onion begins to soften. Add the tomatoes and stock. Lock the lid in place and cook at high pressure for 10 minutes.

2 Release the pressure naturally and remove the lid, tilting the pot away from you to avoid the escaping steam. Using an immersion blender, purée the soup (or transfer to a blender and purée). Add the cream and warm the soup. Taste for seasoning and add salt and pepper if needed.

TOMATO BASIL SOUP WITH TORTELLINI

This is one of my favorite winter soups. Redolent of basil and filled with tomatoes, chunky vegetables, and cheese tortellini, it is a meal in a bowl. The soup actually improves with age, and you can refrigerate it for up to three days or freeze it for up to three months.

SERVES 6 TO 8

3 TABLESPOONS EXTRA-VIRGIN OLIVE OIL

1 LARGE SWEET ONION, SUCH AS VIDALIA, FINELY CHOPPED

3 MEDIUM CARROTS, COARSELY CHOPPED

4 CELERY STALKS (INCLUDING THE LEAVES), COARSELY CHOPPED

ONE 28-OUNCE CAN TOMATO PURÉE

6 CUPS CHICKEN STOCK (PAGE 19) OR STORE-BOUGHT CHICKEN BROTH

2 CUPS FRESH CHEESE TORTELLINI

1 CUP PACKED FRESH BASIL, FINELY CHOPPED

SALT AND FRESHLY GROUND BLACK PEPPER (OPTIONAL)

½ TO ¾ CUP FRESHLY GRATED PARMIGIANO-REGGIANO CHEESE FOR GARNISH

1 Heat the oil in the pressure cooker over medium-high heat. Add the onion, carrots, and celery and sauté for 2 minutes, or until the onion begins to soften. Add the tomato purée, stock, and tortellini. Lock the lid in place and cook at high pressure for 5 minutes.

2 Release the pressure naturally and remove the lid, tilting the pot away from you to avoid the escaping steam. Stir in the basil, taste the soup for seasoning, and add salt and pepper if necessary. Serve each portion garnished with Parmigiano-Reggiano cheese.

CASBAH CARROT SOUP

Aromatic with the spices of the casbah—turmeric, cinnamon, and paprika—this simple Moroccan soup is a riff on a salad that I had in a Moroccan restaurant. The secret to this great soup is caramelizing the carrots a bit before putting the pressure on in order to bring out their sweetness.

SERVES 6

....

2 TABLESPOONS CANOLA OIL

2 GARLIC CLOVES, MINCED

½ TEASPOON GROUND TURMERIC

¼ TEASPOON GROUND CINNAMON

½ TEASPOON SWEET PAPRIKA

4 CUPS COARSELY CHOPPED CARROTS (1-INCH CHUNKS)

4 CUPS CHICKEN STOCK (PAGE 19) OR STORE-BOUGHT CHICKEN BROTH

SALT AND FRESHLY GROUND BLACK PEPPER (OPTIONAL)

¼ CUP FINELY CHOPPED FRESH CILANTRO FOR GARNISH

1 Heat the oil in the pressure cooker over medium-high heat. Add the garlic, turmeric, cinnamon, and paprika and cook for 1 minute, being careful not to burn the spices. Add the carrots and cook for 5 minutes, or until the carrots begin to color. Pour in the stock. Lock the lid in place and cook at high pressure for 7 minutes.

2 Quick release the pressure and remove the lid, tilting the pot away from you to avoid the escaping steam. Using an immersion blender, purée the soup (or cool, transfer to a blender, and purée). Season with salt and pepper if necessary and serve the soup garnished with the cilantro.

ORANGE-GINGER CARROT SOUP

This bright-orange soup makes a beautiful first course for any dinner, and it cooks up in less than ten minutes. The aromatic garnish of orange zest, basil, and parsley gives it a vibrant finish.

SERVES 6

2 TABLESPOONS UNSALTED BUTTER

1 TABLESPOON CANOLA OIL

1 SHALLOT, FINELY CHOPPED

1 TEASPOON GROUND GINGER

⅛ TEASPOON FRESHLY GROUND NUTMEG

4 CUPS COARSELY CHOPPED CARROTS (1-INCH CHUNKS)

1 CUP ORANGE JUICE

4 CUPS CHICKEN OR VEGETABLE STOCK (PAGE 19 OR 21) OR STORE-BOUGHT CHICKEN OR VEGETABLE BROTH

SALT AND FRESHLY GROUND BLACK PEPPER (OPTIONAL)

GRATED ZEST OF 1 LARGE ORANGE

¼ CUP FINELY CHOPPED FRESH FLAT-LEAF PARSLEY

¼ CUP FINELY CHOPPED FRESH BASIL

1 Melt the butter with the oil in the pressure cooker over medium-high heat. Add the shallot, ginger, and nutmeg and cook for 2 minutes, or until the shallot begins to soften. Add the carrots, orange juice, and stock. Lock the lid in place and cook at high pressure for 7 minutes.

2 Quick release the pressure and remove the lid, tilting the pot away from you to avoid the escaping steam. Using an immersion blender, purée the soup (or cool, transfer to a blender, and purée). Taste for seasoning and add salt and pepper if necessary. In a small bowl, combine the orange zest, parsley, and basil. Serve the soup in bowls and garnish with a bit of the zest mixture.

CREAMY BUTTERNUT SQUASH AND CARAMELIZED ONION SOUP

Here's a riff on traditional French onion soup. This time, the onions are added to butternut squash to make a deliciously smoky and luxurious soup. Serve this at the holidays, with a dollop of lump crabmeat to send it over the top!

SERVES **6** TO **8**

4 TABLESPOONS UNSALTED BUTTER

1 TABLESPOON CANOLA OIL

3 LARGE SWEET ONIONS, SUCH AS VIDALIA, COARSELY CHOPPED

2 TEASPOONS FINELY CHOPPED FRESH THYME

3 TABLESPOONS LIGHT BROWN SUGAR

2½ TO 3 POUNDS BUTTERNUT SQUASH, PEELED, SEEDED, AND CUT INTO 1-INCH CHUNKS (6 CUPS)

5 CUPS CHICKEN STOCK (PAGE 19) OR STORE-BOUGHT CHICKEN BROTH

1 CUP HEAVY CREAM

SALT AND FRESHLY GROUND BLACK PEPPER (OPTIONAL)

1 Melt the butter with the oil in the pressure cooker over medium-high heat. Add the onions, thyme, and sugar and cook, stirring frequently, for 10 minutes, or until the onions are golden brown. Add the squash and stock. Lock the lid in place and cook at high pressure for 10 minutes.

2 Quick release the pressure and remove the lid, tilting the pot away from you to avoid the escaping steam. Purée the soup with an immersion blender (or cool, transfer to a blender, and purée). Add the cream, season the soup with salt and pepper if necessary, and warm before serving.

CURRIED BUTTERNUT SQUASH SOUP

Everyone has a favorite butternut squash soup recipe, and this is mine. It's so simple to make, yet it has a complex flavor. The curry powder adds a nice bit of spice to the sweet squash, giving the soup a lovely balance of hot and sweet. If you would prefer a lower-fat version, replace the cream with more stock.

SERVES **6** TO **8**

3 TABLESPOONS UNSALTED BUTTER

1 MEDIUM SWEET ONION, SUCH AS VIDALIA, FINELY CHOPPED

2 MEDIUM GRANNY SMITH APPLES, PEELED, CORED, AND FINELY CHOPPED

2 TEASPOONS CURRY POWDER

2½ TO 3 POUNDS BUTTERNUT SQUASH, PEELED, SEEDED, AND CUT INTO 1-INCH CHUNKS (6 CUPS)

5 CUPS CHICKEN STOCK (PAGE 19) OR STORE-BOUGHT CHICKEN BROTH

1 CUP HEAVY CREAM

SALT AND FRESHLY GROUND BLACK PEPPER (OPTIONAL)

½ CUP FINELY CHOPPED FRESH CHIVES FOR GARNISH

1 Melt the butter in the pressure cooker over medium-high heat. Add the onion, apples, and curry powder and sauté for 2 minutes, or until the onion begins to soften. Add the squash and stock. Lock the lid in place and cook at high pressure for 5 minutes.

2 Quick release the pressure and remove the lid, tilting the pot away from you to avoid the escaping steam. Using an immersion blender, purée the soup. Add the cream, taste for seasoning, and add salt and pepper if needed. Warm the soup and serve, garnished with the chopped chives.

PSST

Don't have an immersion blender? A blender or food processor will work just fine. Remember to let the soup cool first; otherwise, the hot soup will blow right out of the blender or food processor and land all over you and your kitchen. If you aren't "plugged in," a good potato masher will do the trick.

CURRIED SWEET POTATO SOUP WITH COCONUT MILK

This was the soup of the day at a small bistro in the Midwest where I stopped during a cooking school tour. The soup was comforting after a long day of driving and teaching. Jalapeño corn bread makes a great accompaniment, balancing the complex character of the soup with the heat of the jalapeños and the sweetness of corn bread.

SERVES **6**

2 TABLESPOONS CANOLA OIL

2 MEDIUM SHALLOTS, FINELY CHOPPED

2 TEASPOONS CURRY POWDER

4 MEDIUM SWEET POTATOES, PEELED AND CUT INTO 1-INCH CHUNKS

6 CUPS VEGETABLE STOCK (PAGE 21) OR STORE-BOUGHT VEGETABLE BROTH

1½ CUPS COCONUT MILK

SALT AND FRESHLY GROUND BLACK PEPPER (OPTIONAL)

¼ CUP FINELY CHOPPED FRESH CHIVES FOR GARNISH

1 Heat the oil in the pressure cooker over medium-high heat. Add the shallots and curry powder and cook for 2 minutes, or until the shallots have softened. Add the sweet potatoes and stock. Lock the lid in place and cook at high pressure for 7 minutes.

2 Quick release the pressure and remove the lid, tilting the pot away from you to avoid the escaping steam. Using an immersion blender, purée the soup (or cool, transfer to a blender or food processor, and purée). Add 1¼ cups of the coconut milk, taste for seasoning, and add salt and pepper if necessary. Warm the soup and drizzle a bit of the remaining coconut milk in a spiral over each serving. Garnish with a sprinkling of chives.

SWEET POTATO SOUP WITH BUTTERED PECANS

Sweet potatoes tend to be overlooked in the market, except during the holidays, and that's a shame because they are a good-for-you food loaded with vitamin A and more fiber than oatmeal. This thyme-scented, cayenne-spiked soup, with its delicious garnish of buttered pecans coated in fleur de sel, is another great example of sweet and savory flavors coming together with a terrific result. The garnish also makes a tasty nibble by itself.

SERVES 6 TO 8

BUTTERED FLEUR DE SEL PECANS

4 TABLESPOONS UNSALTED BUTTER

1 TEASPOON SUGAR

⅛ TEASPOON CAYENNE PEPPER

2 CUPS PECAN HALVES

1 TABLESPOON FLEUR DE SEL OR ANOTHER COARSE SALT

SWEET POTATO SOUP

2 TABLESPOONS UNSALTED BUTTER

1 TABLESPOON CANOLA OIL

1 LEEK (WHITE PART ONLY), CLEANED, HALVED LENGTHWISE, AND FINELY CHOPPED

2 TEASPOONS FINELY CHOPPED FRESH THYME

⅛ TEASPOON CAYENNE PEPPER

4 MEDIUM SWEET POTATOES, PEELED AND CUT INTO 1-INCH CHUNKS

7 CUPS CHICKEN OR VEGETABLE STOCK (PAGE 19 OR 21) OR STORE-BOUGHT CHICKEN OR VEGETABLE BROTH

1 CUP HEAVY CREAM

SALT AND FRESHLY GROUND BLACK PEPPER (OPTIONAL)

1 **To make the pecans:** Preheat the oven to 400 degrees F. Line a baking sheet with parchment paper, aluminum foil, or a silicone baking liner. Melt the butter in a large skillet over medium heat. Add the sugar and cayenne and stir to dissolve. Add the pecans to the pan and stir to coat with the butter mixture.

2 Spread out the pecans on the prepared baking sheet and bake for about 10 minutes, turning once during the cooking time. The pecans are done when they are fragrant and begin to turn a shiny, darker shade of brown. Remove from the oven and sprinkle the pecans evenly with the fleur de sel. Allow to cool completely before using. (You should have about 2 cups.) Store the leftovers in airtight containers at room temperature for up to 4 days or in the freezer for up to 6 months.

3 **To make the soup:** Melt the butter with the oil in the pressure cooker over medium-high heat. Add the leek, thyme, and cayenne and sauté for 2 minutes to soften the leek. Add the sweet potatoes and stock. Lock the lid in place and cook at high pressure for 7 minutes.

4 Quick release the pressure and remove the lid, tilting the pot away from you to avoid the escaping steam. Using an immersion blender, purée the soup (or cool, transfer to a blender or food processor, and purée). Add the cream, taste for seasoning, and add salt and pepper if necessary. Warm the soup and serve garnished with the pecans.

BACON AND POTATO SOUP

Smoky bacon flavors this creamy soup filled with tender potatoes. It's like a loaded baked potato, only it takes about a third of the time to prepare. Jazz it up with your favorite garnishes—more bacon (yes!), extra chives, a dollop of sour cream, and a sprinkling of sharp cheddar are my faves.

SERVES 6

8 BACON STRIPS, CUT CROSSWISE INTO PIECES ½ INCH WIDE, FOR GARNISH

½ CUP FINELY CHOPPED SWEET ONION, SUCH AS VIDALIA

5 MEDIUM YUKON GOLD OR RED-SKINNED POTATOES, PEELED AND CUT INTO ½-INCH DICE

4 CUPS CHICKEN OR VEGETABLE STOCK (PAGE 19 OR 21) OR STORE-BOUGHT CHICKEN OR VEGETABLE BROTH

3 TABLESPOONS ALL-PURPOSE FLOUR

1½ CUPS HEAVY CREAM

6 DROPS OF TABASCO OR ANOTHER HOT SAUCE

SALT (OPTIONAL)

⅓ CUP FINELY CHOPPED FRESH CHIVES

1 Cook the bacon in the pressure cooker over medium-high heat until it is crisp. Remove half of the bacon and set aside. Drain off all but 2 tablespoons of the bacon drippings in the pan. Add the onion and sauté for 2 minutes to soften. Add the potatoes and stock. Lock the lid in place and cook at high pressure for 6 minutes.

2 Quick release the pressure and remove the lid, tilting the pot away from you to avoid the escaping steam. In a small bowl, whisk together the flour and ½ cup of the cream until smooth. Add the mixture to the soup and bring the soup to a boil. Add the remaining cup of cream and Tabasco, taste for seasoning, and add salt if necessary. Serve the soup garnished with the reserved bacon and the chives.

BISTRO LEEK AND POTATO SOUP

Leek and potato soup puréed and served cold is an elegant soup called vichyssoise. When it's served hot, with chunks of potato, it's more rustic fare, and may be the *potage du jour* (soup of the day) at any bistro. This version has a colorful sprinkling of chopped chives and crispy bacon for garnish. Serve in hollowed-out bread bowls for a quick cleanup!

SERVES **4** TO **6**

4 TABLESPOONS UNSALTED BUTTER

2 MEDIUM LEEKS (WHITE AND TENDER GREEN PARTS), CHOPPED

4 MEDIUM RUSSET POTATOES, PEELED AND CUT INTO ½-INCH DICE

3 CUPS CHICKEN STOCK (PAGE 19) OR STORE-BOUGHT CHICKEN BROTH

1 TEASPOON FINELY CHOPPED FRESH THYME

1 CUP HEAVY CREAM

SALT AND FRESHLY GROUND BLACK PEPPER (OPTIONAL)

2 TABLESPOONS FINELY CHOPPED FRESH CHIVES FOR GARNISH

6 BACON STRIPS, COOKED UNTIL CRISP AND CRUMBLED, FOR GARNISH

1 Melt the butter in the pressure cooker over medium-high heat. Add the leeks and cook for 2 minutes to coat with the butter. Add the potatoes, stock, and thyme. Lock the lid in place and cook at high pressure for 5 minutes.

2 Quick release the pressure and remove the lid, tilting the pot away from you to avoid the escaping steam. Stir in the cream, taste for seasoning, and add salt and pepper as needed. Warm the soup and serve garnished with the chives and bacon.

TORTILLA SOUP

Tortilla soup is on most menus here in San Diego. It can range from a thick, cheesy soup to a thin version heaped with limp tortilla chips. This vegetarian recipe is thick and cheesy. I love the addition of black beans and corn, which contribute to the soup's bold flavor. The salsa garnish is a real crowd-pleaser, too!

SERVES **8**

2 TABLESPOONS CANOLA OIL

4 GARLIC CLOVES, MINCED

2 LARGE ONIONS, FINELY CHOPPED

2 YELLOW BELL PEPPERS, SEEDED, DERIBBED, AND FINELY CHOPPED

1 RED BELL PEPPER, SEEDED, DERIBBED, AND FINELY CHOPPED

1 GREEN BELL PEPPER, SEEDED, DERIBBED, AND FINELY CHOPPED

1 TEASPOON ANCHO CHILE POWDER

½ TEASPOON GROUND CUMIN

½ CUP TEQUILA

6 CUPS CHICKEN OR VEGETABLE STOCK (PAGE 19 OR 21) OR STORE-BOUGHT CHICKEN OR VEGETABLE BROTH

2 CUPS COOKED BLACK BEANS

1 CUP CORN KERNELS, FRESHLY CUT FROM THE COB, OR FROZEN CORN, DEFROSTED

½ CUP FINELY CHOPPED FRESH CILANTRO

SALT AND FRESHLY GROUND BLACK PEPPER (OPTIONAL)

2 CUPS CRUMBLED FRIED TORTILLA CHIPS

2 CUPS FINELY SHREDDED MILD CHEDDAR OR MONTEREY JACK CHEESE, OR A COMBINATION, FOR GARNISH

1 CUP ROASTED VEGETABLE SALSA (FACING PAGE) FOR GARNISH

1 Heat the oil in the pressure cooker over medium-high heat. Add the garlic and onions and sauté for 2 minutes to soften the onion. Add the bell peppers, chile powder, and cumin and sauté for another 2 minutes. Add the tequila and cook until most of the tequila evaporates and there are only about 2 tablespoons in the bottom of the pot. Add the stock. Lock the lid in place and cook at high pressure for 6 minutes.

2 Quick release the pressure and remove the lid, tilting the pot away from you to avoid the escaping steam. Stir in the beans, corn, and cilantro. Cook over medium heat, uncovered, for about 2 minutes to bring the soup to serving temperature. Taste the soup for seasoning and add salt and pepper if needed. Arrange some tortilla chips in the bottom of each soup bowl, ladle the soup over the chips and garnish with the cheese and salsa.

ROASTED VEGETABLE SALSA

This spicy roasted salsa is delicious dolloped onto tortilla soup or tucked into tacos or burritos. Roasting the vegetables gives them a sweet flavor, which balances the spiciness of the jalapeño.

MAKES **2½** TO **3** CUPS

2 TABLESPOONS EXTRA-VIRGIN OLIVE OIL

1 CUP CORN KERNELS, FRESHLY CUT FROM THE COB, OR FROZEN CORN, DEFROSTED

2 GARLIC CLOVES, SLICED

1 MEDIUM ONION, FINELY CHOPPED

1 JALAPEÑO PEPPER, SEEDED, DERIBBED, AND FINELY CHOPPED

2 PLUM TOMATOES, FINELY CHOPPED

1½ TEASPOONS SALT

¼ TEASPOON CHILI POWDER

2 AVOCADOS, FINELY CHOPPED

2 TABLESPOONS FRESH LIME JUICE

SALT AND FRESHLY GROUND BLACK PEPPER (OPTIONAL)

1 Preheat the oven to 400 degrees F. Line a baking sheet with parchment paper, aluminum foil, or a silicone baking liner. In a mixing bowl, combine the oil, corn, garlic, onion, jalapeño, tomatoes, salt, and chili powder, tossing gently to mix. Spread out the mixture on the baking sheet and roast for 15 minutes, or until the vegetables are golden and tender. Cool completely and transfer to a glass mixing bowl.

2 Add the avocados and lime juice, stirring gently to combine. Taste for seasoning and add salt and black pepper if needed. Press plastic wrap onto the salsa and store in the refrigerator for up to 12 hours, or serve immediately.

PSST

If you have any leftover salsa, stir it into an omelet or create a dip by combining the salsa with sour cream. Serve with chips or fresh veggies.

MUSHROOM AND BARLEY SOUP

Thick with mushrooms and barley and fragrant with thyme and sage, this stick-to-your-ribs soup is especially welcome on cold nights. Or enjoy it as a lunchtime treat after playing in the snow. No matter when you make this classic, you'll have a satisfying home-cooked meal in less than thirty minutes. Serve it in hollowed-out bread bowls.

SERVES **6** TO **8**

3 TABLESPOONS EXTRA-VIRGIN OLIVE OIL

½ CUP FINELY CHOPPED ONION

2 GARLIC CLOVES, MINCED

1 TEASPOON DRIED THYME

1 POUND MIXED MUSHROOMS (SUCH AS WHITE BUTTON, CREMINI, SHIITAKE, OYSTER, TRUMPET, AND CHANTERELLE)

2 TABLESPOONS SOY SAUCE

1 CUP PEARL BARLEY, RINSED

8 CUPS BEEF OR VEGETABLE STOCK (PAGE 20 OR 21) OR STORE-BOUGHT BEEF OR VEGETABLE BROTH

2 FRESH SAGE LEAVES, FINELY CHOPPED (ABOUT ½ TEASPOON)

SALT AND FRESHLY GROUND BLACK PEPPER (OPTIONAL)

⅓ CUP FINELY CHOPPED FRESH FLAT-LEAF PARSLEY FOR GARNISH

1 Heat 2 tablespoons of the oil in the pressure cooker over medium-high heat. Add the onion, garlic, and thyme and cook for 2 minutes, or until the onion begins to soften. Add the mushrooms and sauté for another 3 minutes. Stir in the soy sauce, barley, and stock and drizzle with the remaining tablespoon of oil. Lock the lid in place and cook at high pressure for 8 minutes.

2 Release the pressure naturally and remove the lid, tilting the pot away from you to avoid the escaping steam. Stir in the sage, taste for seasoning, and add salt and pepper if needed. Garnish each serving with chopped parsley.

BEEF AND BARLEY SOUP

This soup is a meal in itself. The barley thickens the rich, beefy broth, and the beef becomes succulent as it cooks under high pressure. Serve this on a night when you want something hearty to ward off the chill.

SERVES **6** TO **8**

2 TABLESPOONS EXTRA-VIRGIN OLIVE OIL

1½ TEASPOONS SALT, PLUS MORE IF NEEDED

½ TEASPOON FRESHLY GROUND BLACK PEPPER, PLUS MORE IF NEEDED

1½ POUNDS BONELESS CHUCK ROAST, TRIMMED OF FAT AND CUT INTO ½-INCH PIECES

2 MEDIUM SWEET ONIONS, SUCH AS VIDALIA, FINELY CHOPPED

4 MEDIUM CARROTS, COARSELY CHOPPED

3 CELERY STALKS (INCLUDING THE LEAVES), COARSELY CHOPPED

1 TEASPOON DRIED THYME

1 BAY LEAF

½ CUP DRY RED WINE

¾ CUP PEARL BARLEY, RINSED

6 CUPS BEEF STOCK (PAGE 20) OR STORE-BOUGHT BEEF BROTH

2 MEDIUM ZUCCHINI, FINELY CHOPPED

1 CUP FROZEN PETITE PEAS, DEFROSTED

1 Heat the oil in the pressure cooker over high heat. Sprinkle the salt and pepper evenly over the beef and brown the beef, a few pieces at a time, removing them to a plate after they are browned. Add the onions, carrots, celery, thyme, and bay leaf to the pot and sauté for 2 minutes to soften the onions. Add the wine, return the beef to the pot, and bring to a boil. Add the barley and stock. Lock the lid in place and cook at high pressure for 20 minutes.

2 Quick release the pressure and remove the lid, tilting the pot away from you to avoid the escaping steam. Remove the bay leaf, add the zucchini and peas, and simmer for 5 minutes, uncovered. Taste the soup and season with more salt and pepper if necessary.

PSST

Leftover cooked vegetables can be added at the end of the cooking time along with the zucchini and peas.

FOOTBALL SUNDAY SPLIT PEA AND SAUSAGE SOUP

Late on a rainy and cold Sunday night, I asked my husband if he'd like some split pea soup for dinner. Knowing that it normally took about two hours to cook, he asked if we'd be having it out of a can. I replied that it would be ready in less than half an hour from prep to finish in the pressure cooker. This is the type of meal that makes this pot one of my favorite pieces of equipment in the kitchen. You can produce soothing soup to cure your ills or help you get over your favorite football team's loss in less than thirty minutes.

SERVES 8

....

¾ POUND SMOKED SAUSAGE, SUCH AS KIELBASA, CUT INTO ½-INCH ROUNDS

1 CUP FINELY CHOPPED ONION

3 MEDIUM CARROTS, COARSELY CHOPPED

3 CELERY STALKS (INCLUDING THE LEAVES), COARSELY CHOPPED

1 TEASPOON FRESH THYME LEAVES

1 POUND GREEN SPLIT PEAS, OR A COMBINATION OF ½ CUP YELLOW SPLIT PEAS AND ½ CUP GREEN SPLIT PEAS, RINSED

5 CUPS CHICKEN OR VEGETABLE STOCK (PAGE 19 OR 21) OR STORE-BOUGHT CHICKEN OR VEGETABLE BROTH

SALT AND FRESHLY GROUND BLACK PEPPER (OPTIONAL)

1 Heat the pressure cooker over medium-high heat and brown the sausage in the pot. Add the onion, carrots, celery, and thyme and cook for 2 to 3 minutes to soften the onion. Add the peas and stock. Lock the lid in place and cook at high pressure for 10 minutes.

2 Release the pressure naturally and remove the lid, tilting the pot away from you to avoid the escaping steam. Stir the soup, taste for seasoning, and add salt and pepper as needed. Serve immediately.

PSST

If you would like to make a vegetarian version of this soup, omit the sausage, add another carrot, and use vegetable stock.

CONFETTI CURRIED LENTIL SOUP

In this colorful soup, the red and brown lentils and yellow split peas contribute their unique tastes, resulting in an exceptionally flavorful mix. And you will love how simple this is to make; it cooks up in less than ten minutes. I like to serve this on a bed of basmati rice with a dollop of chutney mixed with yogurt for a vegetarian meal.

SERVES **6** TO **8**

2 TABLESPOONS CANOLA OIL

½ CUP FINELY CHOPPED ONION

1½ TEASPOONS MILD CURRY POWDER

1 CUP RED LENTILS, RINSED

1 CUP BROWN LENTILS, RINSED

1 CUP YELLOW SPLIT PEAS, RINSED

6 CUPS CHICKEN OR VEGETABLE STOCK (PAGE 19 OR 21) OR STORE-BOUGHT CHICKEN OR VEGETABLE BROTH

½ CUP NONFAT YOGURT

2 TABLESPOONS MANGO CHUTNEY (PAGE 428)

1 TABLESPOON FINELY CHOPPED FRESH CILANTRO

SALT AND FRESHLY GROUND BLACK PEPPER (OPTIONAL)

1 Heat the oil in the pressure cooker over medium-high heat. Add the onion and curry powder and sauté for 1 minute, or until the curry powder is fragrant. Add the lentils, split peas, and stock. Lock the lid in place and cook at high pressure for 5 minutes.

2 While the soup is cooking, stir together the yogurt, chutney, and cilantro in a small bowl and cover and refrigerate until ready to use.

3 Release the pressure naturally and remove the lid, tilting the pot away from you to avoid the escaping steam. Stir the soup, taste for seasoning, and add salt and pepper if needed. Serve the soup garnished with a dollop of the yogurt and chutney mixture.

TUSCAN LENTIL AND BARLEY SOUP WITH PANCETTA

This lovely thick soup is flavored with pancetta (Italian bacon) and rosemary and filled with vegetables, lentils, and tender barley. It makes a perfect dinner any time of the year, but I like it best when the weather turns crisp in the fall. Serve it with a rustic focaccia on the side.

SERVES **8**

....

4 TABLESPOONS EXTRA-VIRGIN OLIVE OIL

2 PANCETTA SLICES, FINELY CHOPPED

1 LARGE SWEET ONION, SUCH AS VIDALIA, FINELY CHOPPED

4 CELERY STALKS (INCLUDING THE LEAVES), COARSELY CHOPPED

2 TEASPOONS FINELY CHOPPED FRESH ROSEMARY

1½ CUPS BROWN LENTILS, RINSED

½ CUP PEARL BARLEY, RINSED

8 CUPS CHICKEN OR VEGETABLE STOCK (PAGE 19 OR 21) OR STORE-BOUGHT CHICKEN OR VEGETABLE BROTH

¼ CUP CHOPPED PARMIGIANO-REGGIANO CHEESE RIND (OPTIONAL)

SALT AND FRESHLY GROUND BLACK PEPPER (OPTIONAL)

1 Heat 2 tablespoons of the oil in the pressure cooker over medium-high heat. Add the pancetta and sauté until it is crispy and has rendered some fat. Add the onion, celery, and rosemary and cook for 2 minutes to soften the onion. Add the lentils, barley, stock, and rind (if using) and drizzle with the remaining 2 table-spoons oil. Lock the lid in place and cook at high pressure for 15 minutes.

2 Release the pressure naturally and remove the lid, tilting the pot away from you to avoid the escaping steam. Taste the soup, season with salt and pepper if necessary, and serve.

TUSCAN BEAN SOUP

This Italian soup has many iterations within the region of Tuscany. The basics are great olive oil, garlic, pancetta, thyme, and creamy white beans, which thicken and flavor the soup. Sometimes called *ribollita*, which means "twice cooked," the soup usually has bread added to it to thicken it. This version is cooked only once. It's made without bread, but I've added garlicky croutons for a crunchy garnish.

SERVES **6** TO **8**

4 TABLESPOONS EXTRA-VIRGIN OLIVE OIL

2 PANCETTA SLICES, FINELY CHOPPED

4 GARLIC CLOVES, MINCED

1 TEASPOON DRIED THYME

2 CUPS SMALL WHITE BEANS, PRESOAKED (SEE PAGE 151) AND DRAINED

8 CUPS CHICKEN OR VEGETABLE STOCK (PAGE 19 OR 21) OR STORE-BOUGHT CHICKEN OR VEGETABLE BROTH

SALT AND FRESHLY GROUND BLACK PEPPER (OPTIONAL)

GARLIC CROUTONS (PAGE 33) FOR GARNISH

1 Heat 2 tablespoons of the oil in the pressure cooker over medium heat. Add the pancetta, garlic, and thyme and cook until the pancetta renders some fat. Add the beans and stock. Lock the lid in place and cook at high pressure for 12 minutes.

2 Release the pressure naturally and remove the lid, tilting the pot away from you to avoid the escaping steam. Taste the soup for seasoning and add salt and pepper if needed. Drizzle each serving with some of the remaining 2 tablespoons of olive oil and scatter the croutons on top.

BEANS AND GREENS SOUP

I'm not sure where it originated, but in most Italian American neighborhoods, you can find a version of this hearty bean and chard soup. Some include sausage or pork or even ham hocks, but the basics are white beans, a green, a bit of tomato, and broth. The soup is terrific garnished with grated sharp Pecorino Romano cheese.

SERVES **6** TO **8**

4 TABLESPOONS EXTRA-VIRGIN OLIVE OIL

3 GARLIC CLOVES, MINCED

1 LARGE SWEET ONION, SUCH AS VIDALIA, FINELY CHOPPED

2 TEASPOONS FINELY CHOPPED FRESH ROSEMARY

3 MEDIUM CARROTS, FINELY CHOPPED

4 CELERY STALKS (INCLUDING THE LEAVES), FINELY CHOPPED

ONE 15-OUNCE CAN PLUM TOMATOES, DRAINED

2 CUPS SMALL WHITE BEANS, PRESOAKED (SEE PAGE 151) AND DRAINED

8 CUPS FINELY CHOPPED SWISS CHARD LEAVES (ABOUT 2 BUNCHES)

8 CUPS CHICKEN OR VEGETABLE STOCK (PAGE 19 OR 21) OR STORE-BOUGHT CHICKEN OR VEGETABLE BROTH

SALT AND FRESHLY GROUND BLACK PEPPER (OPTIONAL)

⅓ CUP FRESHLY GRATED PECORINO ROMANO CHEESE FOR GARNISH

1 Heat 2 tablespoons of the olive oil in the pressure cooker over medium-high heat. Add the garlic, onion, and rosemary and sauté for 2 minutes, or until the onion begins to soften. Add the carrots and celery, stirring to combine. Add the tomatoes, beans, chard, and stock. Drizzle with the remaining 2 tablespoons of oil. Lock the lid in place and cook at high pressure for 12 minutes.

2 Release the pressure naturally and remove the lid, tilting the pot away from you to avoid the escaping steam. Taste the soup for seasoning and add salt and pepper if necessary. Serve the soup garnished with the grated cheese.

HAM AND BEAN SOUP

Small white beans become tender and smoky in this stick-to-your-ribs soup. It's the perfect dish to make when you have a ham bone or leftover ham from a holiday dinner.

SERVES 6 TO 8

2 TABLESPOONS EXTRA-VIRGIN OLIVE OIL

½ CUP FINELY CHOPPED SWEET ONION, SUCH AS VIDALIA

3 CELERY STALKS, FINELY CHOPPED

3 MEDIUM CARROTS, FINELY CHOPPED

1 TEASPOON DRIED THYME

1 BAY LEAF

½ TEASPOON FRESHLY GROUND BLACK PEPPER, PLUS MORE IF NEEDED

2 CUPS SMALL WHITE BEANS, PRESOAKED (SEE PAGE 151) AND DRAINED

1 HAM BONE, WITH SOME MEAT ATTACHED, OR 2 CUPS DICED HAM

6 CUPS CHICKEN STOCK (PAGE 19) OR STORE-BOUGHT CHICKEN BROTH

SALT (OPTIONAL)

1 Heat the oil in the pressure cooker over medium-high heat. Add the onion, celery, carrots, thyme, bay leaf, and pepper and sauté until the onion begins to soften. Add the beans and stir to coat with the oil. Add the ham bone and stock. Lock the lid in place and cook at high pressure for 20 minutes.

2 Release the pressure naturally and remove the lid, tilting the pot away from you to avoid the escaping steam. Stir the soup, taste for seasoning, and add salt and more pepper if necessary. Discard the bay leaf. Remove the ham bone and cut any ham attached to the bone into bite-size pieces. Return the ham pieces to the pot and serve the soup immediately.

PSST

For a vegetarian soup, leave out the ham and substitute vegetable broth for the chicken broth.

PINTO BEAN SOUP WITH CHORIZO AND TORTILLAS

Hearty, spicy, and crowned with crunchy tortilla chips, this soup is a great Saturday-night supper. Serve it with lots of condiments and some Mexican beer to make it a fiesta.

SERVES **6** TO **8**

2 TABLESPOONS CANOLA OIL

½ POUND MEXICAN CHORIZO, CASING REMOVED (SEE PSST)

1 MEDIUM RED ONION, FINELY CHOPPED

1 ANAHEIM CHILE PEPPER, SEEDED, DERIBBED, AND FINELY CHOPPED

1 MEDIUM RED BELL PEPPER, SEEDED, DERIBBED, AND COARSELY CHOPPED

1 TEASPOON GROUND CUMIN

½ TEASPOON DRIED OREGANO

2 CUPS PINTO BEANS, PRESOAKED (SEE PAGE 151) AND DRAINED

7 CUPS CHICKEN STOCK (PAGE 19) OR STORE-BOUGHT CHICKEN BROTH

SALT AND FRESHLY GROUND BLACK PEPPER (OPTIONAL)

2 CUPS TORTILLA CHIPS, CRUSHED, FOR GARNISH

¼ CUP FINELY CHOPPED FRESH CILANTRO FOR GARNISH

1 Heat 1 tablespoon of the oil in the pressure cooker over medium-high heat. Add the chorizo and sauté, stirring and breaking it up, until it is no longer pink. Remove all but 1 tablespoon of the fat from the pan. Add the onion, chile and bell peppers, cumin, and oregano and sauté for 2 minutes to soften the onion. Add the beans and stock and drizzle with the remaining tablespoon of oil. Lock the lid in place and cook at high pressure for 10 minutes.

2 Quick release the pressure and remove the lid, tilting the pot away from you to avoid the escaping steam. Taste the soup for seasoning and add salt and pepper if necessary. Serve the soup garnished with tortilla chips and chopped cilantro.

PSST

Mexican chorizo is a sausage made with fresh pork. It comes in a casing, which you can easily remove. Spanish chorizo is made with smoked pork and is hard, like salami or pepperoni. Make sure you buy the right type.

CARIBBEAN BLACK BEAN SOUP

Black beans are a staple in the Caribbean, and this soup is one of my favorite iterations. The jalapeño gives it a bit of heat, and a splash of rum adds a smoky note.

SERVES **8**

....

4 TABLESPOONS CANOLA OIL

1 LARGE RED ONION, FINELY CHOPPED

3 GARLIC CLOVES, MINCED

1 MEDIUM RED BELL PEPPER, SEEDED, DERIBBED, AND CHOPPED

1 MEDIUM YELLOW BELL PEPPER, SEEDED, DERIBBED, AND COARSELY CHOPPED

1 SMALL JALAPEÑO PEPPER, SEEDED, DERIBBED, AND FINELY CHOPPED

1 TEASPOON GROUND CUMIN

1 TEASPOON DRIED OREGANO

¼ CUP DARK RUM

2 CUPS BLACK BEANS, PRESOAKED (SEE PAGE 151) AND DRAINED

ONE 15-OUNCE CAN CHOPPED TOMATOES, DRAINED

8 CUPS CHICKEN OR VEGETABLE STOCK (PAGE 19 OR 21) OR STORE-BOUGHT CHICKEN OR VEGETABLE BROTH

SALT AND FRESHLY GROUND BLACK PEPPER (OPTIONAL)

1 Heat 2 tablespoons of the oil in the pressure cooker over medium-high heat. Add the onion, garlic, bell peppers, jalapeño, cumin, and oregano and sauté for 4 minutes, or until the vegetables begin to soften. Stir in the rum and bring to a boil. Add the black beans, tomatoes, and stock and drizzle with the remaining 2 tablespoons of oil. Lock the lid in place and cook at high pressure for 20 minutes.

2 Release the pressure naturally and remove the lid, tilting the pot away from you to avoid the escaping steam. Taste the soup for seasoning, add salt or pepper if necessary, and serve.

PARSNIP SOUP WITH CARAMELIZED PEARS

This elegant soup is a good example of sweet and savory balanced to perfection. The garnish of caramelized pears makes a tasty counterpoint for the parsnips' rugged flavor. The combination is sure to please your friends and family. The garnish would also be delicious with roasted or grilled pork tenderloin or with a cheese tray of salty cheeses like Roquefort.

SERVES 6

CARAMELIZED PEAR GARNISH

4 TABLESPOONS UNSALTED BUTTER

4 LARGE RED PEARS, SUCH AS ANJOU OR BARTLETT, PEELED, CORED, AND FINELY CHOPPED

⅔ CUP FIRMLY PACKED LIGHT BROWN SUGAR

1 TEASPOON GROUND CINNAMON

¼ TEASPOON GROUND GINGER

⅛ TEASPOON FRESHLY GROUND NUTMEG

2 TABLESPOONS FRESH LEMON JUICE

PARSNIP SOUP

2 TABLESPOONS UNSALTED BUTTER

1 TABLESPOON CANOLA OIL

2 LEEKS (WHITE AND TENDER GREEN PARTS), CLEANED AND FINELY CHOPPED

6 PARSNIPS, PEELED AND CUT INTO ½-INCH PIECES

6 CUPS CHICKEN STOCK (PAGE 19) OR STORE-BOUGHT CHICKEN BROTH

½ CUP HEAVY CREAM

SALT AND FRESHLY GROUND BLACK PEPPER (OPTIONAL)

1 **To make the pear garnish:** Melt the butter in a large skillet over medium-high heat. Add the remaining ingredients, stirring to combine, and cook for 15 to 20 minutes, or until the mixture has thickened and the liquid in the pan has almost evaporated. Remove the pan from the heat and allow the mixture to cool completely. (You should have about 2 cups.) Store any leftover garnish in airtight containers in the refrigerator for up to 1 week or in the freezer for up to 3 months. Allow to come to room temperature before serving.

2 **To make the soup:** Melt the butter with the oil in the pressure cooker over medium-high heat. Add the leeks and parsnips and cook for 2 minutes, or until the leeks have softened. Add the stock. Lock the lid in place and cook at high pressure for 7 minutes.

3 Release the pressure naturally and remove the lid, tilting the pot away from you to avoid the escaping steam. Using an immersion blender, purée the soup (or cool, transfer to a blender, and purée). Add the cream, taste the soup for seasoning, and add salt and pepper if needed. Warm the soup and garnish each bowl with 1 tablespoon of the caramelized pears.

MINESTRA DI CECI

Sometimes the simplest preparations yield the most delicious results, and this chickpea-filled soup, flavored with prosciutto and rosemary, fills the bill. Add a bit of pasta at the end to make it a more substantial offering. Or omit the pasta and serve the soup with crusty bread and a salad.

SERVES **6** TO **8**

4 TABLESPOONS EXTRA-VIRGIN OLIVE OIL

4 PROSCIUTTO DI PARMA SLICES, FINELY CHOPPED

2 TEASPOONS FINELY CHOPPED FRESH ROSEMARY

ONE 15-OUNCE CAN CHOPPED TOMATOES WITH THEIR JUICE

2 CUPS CHICKPEAS, PRESOAKED (SEE PAGE 151) AND DRAINED

6 CUPS CHICKEN OR VEGETABLE STOCK (PAGE 19 OR 21) OR STORE-BOUGHT CHICKEN OR VEGETABLE BROTH

SALT AND FRESHLY GROUND BLACK PEPPER (OPTIONAL)

2 CUPS COOKED SMALL PASTA, SUCH AS DITALI, ORZO, OR SMALL SHELLS

1 Heat 2 tablespoons of the oil in the pressure cooker over medium-high heat. Add the prosciutto and sauté until it becomes crispy. Add the rosemary and the tomatoes and sauté for 2 minutes, stirring to blend with the prosciutto. Add the chickpeas and stock and drizzle with 1 tablespoon of the oil. Lock the lid in place and cook at high pressure for 17 minutes.

2 Release the pressure naturally and remove the lid, tilting the pot away from you to avoid the escaping steam. Taste the soup for seasoning and add salt and pepper if necessary. Add the pasta to the soup and warm over medium-high heat for 4 to 5 minutes, or until heated through. Serve drizzled with the remaining 1 tablespoon olive oil.

MINESTRONE

Minestrone means "big soup" in Italian. We need to pull all the flavor out of the vegetables and seasonings in this hearty soup, and that is just what the pressure cooker does best. Every Italian household has a version of this soup, whether it includes meat or poultry, or pasta added at the end. You'll find it in every region of the boot. My secret seasoning is the rind from the Parmigiano-Reggiano cheese, cut into tiny pieces to flavor the pot.

SERVES 6 TO 8

3 TABLESPOONS EXTRA-VIRGIN OLIVE OIL

1 LARGE SWEET ONION, SUCH AS VIDALIA, COARSELY CHOPPED

3 MEDIUM CARROTS, COARSELY CHOPPED

4 CELERY STALKS (INCLUDING THE LEAVES), COARSELY CHOPPED

2 TEASPOONS FINELY CHOPPED FRESH ROSEMARY

ONE 15-OUNCE CAN CHOPPED TOMATOES WITH THEIR JUICE

4 CUPS COARSELY CHOPPED SWISS CHARD (ABOUT 1 BUNCH)

¼ CUP COARSELY CHOPPED PARMIGIANO-REGGIANO CHEESE RIND (OPTIONAL, BUT OH SO GOOD!)

3 MEDIUM ZUCCHINI, HALVED LENGTHWISE AND CUT INTO ¾-INCH PIECES

1 CUP GREEN BEANS, TRIMMED AND CUT INTO ½-INCH PIECES

1 CUP BROWN LENTILS, RINSED

8 CUPS CHICKEN OR VEGETABLE STOCK (PAGE 19 OR 21) OR STORE-BOUGHT CHICKEN OR VEGETABLE BROTH

SALT AND FRESHLY GROUND BLACK PEPPER (OPTIONAL)

2 CUPS COOKED SMALL PASTA, SUCH AS DITALI, SMALL SHELLS, OR ORZO

⅓ CUP FRESHLY GRATED PARMIGIANO-REGGIANO CHEESE FOR GARNISH

1 Heat 2 tablespoons of the oil in the pressure cooker over medium-high heat. Add the onion, carrots, celery, and rosemary and sauté for 3 to 4 minutes, until the vegetables are softened. Add the tomatoes and cook for 2 minutes, stirring to incorporate them. Add the chard, cheese rind (if using), zucchini, green beans, lentils, and stock. Drizzle with the remaining tablespoon of oil. Lock the lid in place and cook at high pressure for 10 minutes.

2 Quick release the pressure and remove the lid, tilting the pot way from you to avoid the escaping steam. Taste for seasoning and add salt and pepper if necessary. Stir in the pasta and heat, uncovered, over medium-high heat, until the soup is at serving temperature. Serve sprinkled with the Parmigiano-Reggiano cheese.

MINESTRONE DI FARRO

My family in Spello, Italy, serves a version of this soup in their *enoteca* (wine bar) at lunchtime. Thick, hearty, and slightly chewy, this dish reminds me of the simple pleasures back home. Serve it with crusty breads, a salumi platter, pecorino cheese, and a hearty Italian red wine, such as Sagrantino.

SERVES **8**

3 TABLESPOONS EXTRA-VIRGIN OLIVE OIL

1 LARGE SWEET ONION, SUCH AS VIDALIA, FINELY CHOPPED

3 MEDIUM CARROTS, COARSELY CHOPPED

4 CELERY STALKS (INCLUDING THE LEAVES), COARSELY CHOPPED

3 FRESH SAGE LEAVES, FINELY CHOPPED

1½ CUPS FARRO

8 CUPS CHICKEN OR VEGETABLE STOCK (PAGE 19 OR 21) OR STORE-BOUGHT CHICKEN OR VEGETABLE BROTH

SALT AND FRESHLY GROUND BLACK PEPPER (OPTIONAL)

1 Heat 2 tablespoons of the oil in the pressure cooker over medium-high heat. Add the onion, carrots, celery, and sage and sauté for 2 minutes to soften the onion. Stir in the farro and toss to combine with the vegetables. Stir in the stock and drizzle with the remaining tablespoon of oil. Lock the lid in place and cook at high pressure for 12 minutes.

2 Release the pressure naturally and remove the lid, tilting it away from you to avoid the escaping steam. Taste the soup for seasoning and add salt and pepper to taste. Serve immediately.

HARIRA

This thick Moroccan soup is traditionally served during the holy month of Ramadan, when Muslims fast during the day and break their fast each night with harira. It is thick with lentils, chickpeas, and tomatoes and fragrant with saffron and ginger. In many homes, the soup is made with lamb or chicken, which gives it extra flavor and heartiness. Flour is traditionally used to thicken the soup, but I like to serve it with cooked rice, which helps to balance the spices. The pressure cooker makes short work of the dried chickpeas, which most Moroccans feel are far superior to those found in a can, and I heartily agree with that! If you are looking for a warming, exotic soup on a cold night, this is just the ticket.

SERVES **8**

3 TABLESPOONS EXTRA-VIRGIN OLIVE OIL

1 LARGE SWEET YELLOW ONION SUCH AS VIDALIA, FINELY CHOPPED

3 MEDIUM CARROTS, FINELY CHOPPED

3 CELERY STALKS (INCLUDING THE LEAVES), FINELY CHOPPED

¼ TEASPOON SAFFRON THREADS, CRUSHED IN THE PALM OF YOUR HAND

⅛ TEASPOON GROUND GINGER

2 CUPS DRIED CHICKPEAS, PRESOAKED (SEE PAGE 151) AND DRAINED

1 CUP BROWN LENTILS, RINSED

ONE 28-OUNCE CAN TOMATO PURÉE

8 CUPS CHICKEN OR VEGETABLE STOCK (PAGE 19 OR 21) OR STORE-BOUGHT CHICKEN OR VEGETABLE BROTH

SALT AND FRESHLY GROUND BLACK PEPPER (OPTIONAL)

½ CUP FINELY CHOPPED FRESH CILANTRO

½ CUP FINELY CHOPPED FRESH FLAT-LEAF PARSLEY

3 CUPS COOKED LONG-GRAIN RICE, SUCH AS BASMATI FOR SERVING

1 Heat 2 tablespoons of the oil in the pressure cooker over medium-high heat. Add the onion, carrots, celery, saffron, and ginger and sauté for 4 to 5 minutes to soften the vegetables. Add the chickpeas, lentils, tomato purée, and stock and drizzle with the remaining tablespoon of oil. Lock the lid in place and cook at high pressure for 17 minutes.

2 Release the pressure naturally and remove the lid, tilting the pot away from you to avoid the escaping steam. Taste the soup for seasoning and add salt and pepper if needed. Stir in the cilantro and parsley and serve the soup over rice in large bowls.

BEEF BORSCHT

Borscht is a traditional soup served in central and Eastern European countries and in American homes with roots in that part of the world. This version is hearty, stick-to-your-ribs fare. The main ingredient—beets—balances the strong flavor of the beef. Borscht has many variations, including hot ones made with cabbage and cold ones that contain very little except for beets.

SERVES 8

2 TABLESPOONS EXTRA-VIRGIN OIL

1 POUND BONELESS CHUCK ROAST, TRIMMED OF FAT AND CUT INTO ½-INCH PIECES

1½ TEASPOONS SALT, PLUS MORE IF NEEDED

½ TEASPOON FRESHLY GROUND BLACK PEPPER, PLUS MORE IF NEEDED

1 LARGE RED ONION, FINELY CHOPPED

3 GARLIC CLOVES, MINCED

3 MEDIUM CARROTS, COARSELY CHOPPED

1 TEASPOON DRIED THYME

1 BAY LEAF

2 TABLESPOONS TOMATO PASTE

3 LARGE BEETS, PEELED AND CUT INTO ½-INCH CUBES

8 CUPS BEEF STOCK (PAGE 20) OR STORE-BOUGHT BEEF BROTH

1 CUP SOUR CREAM FOR GARNISH

1 Heat the oil in the pressure cooker over medium-high heat. Sprinkle the meat evenly with the salt and pepper and brown in the oil, a few pieces at a time, removing the meat to a plate when done. Add the onion, garlic, carrots, thyme, bay leaf, and tomato paste and sauté for 3 minutes, or until the onion begins to soften. Add the beets and stock and return the beef to the pot. Lock the lid in place and cook at high pressure for 30 minutes.

2 Release the pressure naturally and remove the lid, tilting the pot away from you to avoid the escaping steam. Skim off any excess fat from the top of the soup and discard the bay leaf. Taste for seasoning and add more salt and pepper if needed. Serve the soup garnished with a dollop of sour cream.

MANHATTAN-STYLE CLAM CHOWDER

Even though I grew up in the Boston area, I still prefer the spicy flavor of a Manhattan clam chowder to the creamy New England version any day of the week. Brimming with clams and vegetables in a thick, thyme-flavored tomato broth, Manhattan chowder is a huge hit at our house. We love it on a cold winter's night and eat it in hollowed-out-bread bowls. If you can't get freshly shucked clams, canned clams will work. See the Psst.

SERVES 6 TO 8

6 BACON STRIPS, CUT CROSSWISE INTO PIECES ½ INCH WIDE

1½ CUPS FINELY CHOPPED SWEET ONION, SUCH AS VIDALIA (ABOUT 2 LARGE OR 3 MEDIUM)

4 CELERY STALKS (INCLUDING THE LEAVES), COARSELY CHOPPED

1 MEDIUM GREEN BELL PEPPER, SEEDED, DERIBBED, AND COARSELY CHOPPED

1 MEDIUM RED BELL PEPPER, SEEDED, DERIBBED, AND COARSELY CHOPPED

2 GARLIC CLOVES, MINCED

2 TEASPOONS DRIED THYME

1 TEASPOON DRIED OREGANO

1 BAY LEAF

PINCH OF CAYENNE PEPPER

6 MEDIUM YUKON GOLD OR RED-SKINNED POTATOES, SCRUBBED AND CUT INTO ½-INCH DICE

ONE 28-OUNCE CAN CHOPPED TOMATOES WITH THEIR JUICE

1 QUART SHUCKED CHERRYSTONE CLAMS, CHOPPED, WITH THEIR JUICE (SEE PSST)

CLAM JUICE AS NEEDED (SEE PSST)

2 CUPS CHICKEN STOCK (PAGE 19) OR STORE-BOUGHT CHICKEN BROTH

SALT

1 OR 2 DROPS TABASCO SAUCE

1 Cook the bacon in the pressure cooker over medium-high heat until crisp. Remove all but 2 tablespoons of the bacon drippings. Add the onion, celery, bell peppers, garlic, thyme, oregano, bay leaf, and cayenne and sauté for 3 to 4 minutes to soften the onion. Add the potatoes, tomatoes and their juice, clams and juice, and stock. Lock the lid in place and cook at high pressure for 7 minutes.

2 Release the pressure naturally and remove the lid, tilting the pot away from you to avoid the escaping steam. Remove the bay leaf, taste the chowder for seasoning, and add salt and Tabasco to taste.

PSST

If you are unable to get freshly shucked clams in your area, substitute an equal quantity of canned clams. Regardless of whether you are using fresh or canned, you will need 4 cups of their juice. If you don't have that much, add enough bottled clam juice to get 4 cups. You'll find the clam juice in your supermarket near the canned clams and tuna.

SMOKED TURKEY AND CORN CHOWDER

Thick with vegetables and smoky chunks of turkey, this meal in a bowl is a real crowd-pleaser any night of the week. It's a great way to get rid of a few leftovers, and it's ready in less than ten minutes.

SERVES 6 TO 8

2 TABLESPOONS CANOLA OIL

2 MEDIUM SHALLOTS, FINELY CHOPPED

3 CELERY STALKS (INCLUDING THE LEAVES), FINELY CHOPPED

3 MEDIUM CARROTS, FINELY CHOPPED

1 TEASPOON DRIED THYME

2 CUPS DICED SMOKED TURKEY (½-INCH DICE; ABOUT ⅓ POUND)

2 CUPS CORN KERNELS, FRESHLY CUT FROM THE COB, OR FROZEN CORN, DEFROSTED

2 CUPS DICED YUKON GOLD POTATOES (½-INCH DICE)

5 CUPS CHICKEN OR VEGETABLE STOCK (PAGE 19 OR 21) OR STORE-BOUGHT CHICKEN OR VEGETABLE BROTH

1 CUP MILK

SALT AND FRESHLY GROUND BLACK PEPPER (OPTIONAL)

1 Heat the oil over medium-high heat in the pressure cooker. Add the shallots, celery, carrots, and thyme and sauté for 2 minutes to soften the vegetables. Add the turkey, corn, potatoes, and stock. Lock the lid in place and cook at high pressure for 6 minutes.

2 Quick release the pressure and remove the lid, tilting the pot away from you to avoid the escaping steam. Stir in the milk, taste for seasoning, and add salt and pepper if necessary. Warm the soup and serve.

PSST

If you have any leftover cooked legumes, like black beans or small white beans, they are a great add-in at the end of the pressure cooking time.

SWEET CORN BISQUE

The crispy bacon garnish accents the creamy sweetness of this beautiful soup. Bisques are usually made with seafood, but corn makes a fine substitute. This is a great make-ahead soup to have on hand in the freezer for unexpected company. Serve with homemade biscuits or focaccia.

SERVES **6**

2 TABLESPOONS UNSALTED BUTTER

1 CUP FINELY CHOPPED SWEET ONION, SUCH AS VIDALIA

6 CUPS CORN KERNELS, FRESHLY CUT FROM THE COB, OR FROZEN CORN, DEFROSTED

3 CUPS CHICKEN OR VEGETABLE STOCK (PAGE 19 OR 21) OR STORE-BOUGHT CHICKEN OR VEGETABLE BROTH

½ CUP HEAVY CREAM

6 DROPS OF TABASCO OR ANOTHER HOT SAUCE

8 BACON STRIPS, COOKED UNTIL CRISP AND CRUMBLED FOR GARNISH

¼ CUP FINELY CHOPPED FRESH CHIVES FOR GARNISH

1 In the pressure cooker, melt the butter over medium-high heat. Add the onion and corn and sauté for 4 to 5 minutes, until softened. Add the stock, lock the lid in place, and cook at high pressure for 5 minutes.

2 Quick release the pressure and remove the lid, tilting the pot away from you to avoid the escaping steam. Stir in the cream and Tabasco. Use an immersion blender to purée the soup (or cool, transfer to a food processor or blender, and purée). Warm the soup and serve, garnished with the bacon and chives.

BEAN AND VEGGIE CHILI

A hill of beans and crunchy vegetables make this thick and savory chili a winner with both vegetarians and meat-eaters.

SERVES 8

4 TABLESPOONS CANOLA OIL

2 LARGE SWEET ONIONS, SUCH AS VIDALIA, COARSELY CHOPPED

1 TEASPOON ANCHO CHILE POWDER

1 TEASPOON GROUND CUMIN

½ TEASPOON DRIED OREGANO

1 MEDIUM GREEN BELL PEPPER, SEEDED, DERIBBED, AND COARSELY CHOPPED

1 MEDIUM RED BELL PEPPER, SEEDED, DERIBBED, AND COARSELY CHOPPED

1 MEDIUM YELLOW OR ORANGE BELL PEPPER, SEEDED, DERIBBED, AND COARSELY CHOPPED

1 CUP PINTO BEANS, PRESOAKED (SEE PAGE 151) AND DRAINED

1 CUP KIDNEY BEANS, PRESOAKED (SEE PAGE 151) AND DRAINED

1 CUP BLACK BEANS, PRESOAKED (SEE PAGE 151) AND DRAINED

1 CUP RED BEANS, PRESOAKED (SEE PAGE 151) AND DRAINED

ONE 28-OUNCE CAN CHOPPED TOMATOES WITH THEIR JUICE

7 CUPS CHICKEN OR VEGETABLE STOCK (PAGE 19 OR 21) OR STORE-BOUGHT CHICKEN OR VEGETABLE BROTH

2 CUPS CORN KERNELS, FRESHLY CUT FROM THE COB, OR FROZEN CORN, DEFROSTED

SALT AND FRESHLY GROUND BLACK PEPPER (OPTIONAL)

1 Heat 2 tablespoons of the oil in the pressure cooker over medium-high heat. Add the onions, chile powder, cumin, and oregano and sauté for 2 minutes, or until the onions begin to soften. Add the bell peppers, beans, tomatoes, and stock, and drizzle with the remaining 2 tablespoons of oil. Lock the lid in place and cook at high pressure for 20 minutes.

2 Release the pressure naturally and remove the lid, tilting the pot away from you to avoid the escaping steam. Stir in the corn, taste the chili for seasoning, and add salt and pepper if needed. Serve immediately.

CHICKEN AND BLACK BEAN CHILI

Chock-full of black beans, vegetables, and tender chunks of chicken, this chili will satisfy even the most devoted meat-and-potatoes fan.

SERVES 8

4 TABLESPOONS CANOLA OIL

3 BONELESS, SKINLESS CHICKEN BREAST HALVES, CUT INTO 1-INCH PIECES

1½ TEASPOONS SALT, PLUS MORE IF NEEDED

½ TEASPOON FRESHLY GROUND BLACK PEPPER, PLUS MORE IF NEEDED

1 LARGE ONION, FINELY CHOPPED

3 GARLIC CLOVES, MINCED

1 TEASPOON GROUND CUMIN

½ TEASPOON ANCHO CHILE POWDER

1 MEDIUM GREEN BELL PEPPER, SEEDED, DERIBBED, AND COARSELY CHOPPED

1 MEDIUM RED BELL PEPPER, SEEDED, DERIBBED, AND COARSELY CHOPPED

ONE 28-OUNCE CAN CHOPPED TOMATOES WITH THEIR JUICE

1½ CUPS BLACK BEANS, PRESOAKED (SEE PAGE 151) AND DRAINED

7 CUPS CHICKEN STOCK (PAGE 19) OR STORE-BOUGHT CHICKEN BROTH

2 CUPS CORN KERNELS, FRESHLY CUT FROM THE COB, OR FROZEN CORN, DEFROSTED

1 Heat 2 tablespoons of the oil in the pressure cooker over medium-high heat. Sprinkle the chicken evenly with the salt and pepper, add to the pan, and sauté until white on all sides. Add the onion, garlic, cumin, and chile powder and sauté for 2 minutes, or until the onion begins to soften. Add the bell peppers, tomatoes, black beans, and stock and drizzle with the remaining 2 tablespoons of oil. Lock the lid in place and cook at high pressure for 20 minutes.

2 Release the pressure naturally and remove the lid, tilting the pot away from you to avoid the escaping steam. Stir in the corn, taste for seasoning, and add more salt and pepper if needed. Serve immediately.

TURKEY AND WHITE BEAN CHILI

Thick with creamy white beans and chunks of turkey, this spicy chili is a winner anytime. Garnish it with diced avocados, shredded cheese, sour cream, and crushed tortilla chips.

SERVES 8

4 TABLESPOONS CANOLA OIL

2 POUNDS GROUND TURKEY

1½ TEASPOONS SALT, PLUS MORE IF NEEDED

½ TEASPOON FRESHLY GROUND BLACK PEPPER, PLUS MORE IF NEEDED

1 LARGE SWEET ONION, SUCH AS VIDALIA, FINELY CHOPPED

1 MEDIUM RED BELL PEPPER, SEEDED, DERIBBED, AND COARSELY CHOPPED

1 MEDIUM YELLOW BELL PEPPER, SEEDED, DERIBBED, AND COARSELY CHOPPED

1 ANAHEIM CHILE PEPPER, SEEDED, DERIBBED, AND COARSELY CHOPPED

½ TEASPOON ANCHO CHILE POWDER

½ TEASPOON GROUND CUMIN

2 TABLESPOONS CORNMEAL

1½ CUPS SMALL WHITE BEANS, PRE-SOAKED (SEE PAGE 151) AND DRAINED

8 CUPS CHICKEN STOCK (PAGE 19) OR STORE-BOUGHT CHICKEN BROTH

CONDIMENTS

2 HASS AVOCADOS, DICED AND TOSSED WITH 1 TABLESPOON FRESH LIME JUICE

1 TO 2 CUPS SOUR CREAM

2 TO 3 CUPS FINELY SHREDDED MILD CHEDDAR CHEESE, OR A COMBINATION OF MONTEREY JACK AND MILD CHEDDAR

3 TO 4 CUPS CORN TORTILLA CHIPS, CRUSHED

ASSORTED HOT SAUCES, SUCH AS TABASCO, CHOLULA, AND A CHIPOTLE HOT SAUCE

1 Heat 2 tablespoons of the oil in the pressure cooker over medium-high heat. Sprinkle the turkey evenly with the salt and pepper, add to the pot, and sauté until it is no longer pink. Add the onion, bell peppers, chile pepper, chile powder, cumin, and cornmeal and sauté for 3 minutes, or until the onion is softened. Add the beans and stock and drizzle with the remaining 2 tablespoons of oil. Lock the lid in place and cook the chili at high pressure for 25 minutes.

2 Quick release the pressure and remove the lid, tilting the pot away from you to avoid the escaping steam. Taste the chili for seasoning and add more salt and pepper if necessary. Serve the chili with the condiments.

SMOKY BRISKET CHILI

Succulent pieces of brisket infused with smoky chipotle chile form the base for this thick and spicy bowl of red. Serve the chili with condiments and pinto beans on the side. True chili, according to the International Chili Society and other chili aficionados, does not contain beans.

SERVES 8

2 TABLESPOONS CANOLA OIL

2 POUNDS BEEF BRISKET, TRIMMED OF FAT AND CUT INTO 1-INCH PIECES

1½ TEASPOONS SALT, PLUS MORE IF NEEDED

½ TEASPOON FRESHLY GROUND BLACK PEPPER, PLUS MORE IF NEEDED

2 LARGE RED ONIONS, FINELY CHOPPED

4 GARLIC CLOVES, MINCED

3 CHIPOTLE CHILES IN ADOBO SAUCE, FINELY CHOPPED

1 TEASPOON GROUND CUMIN

ONE 28-OUNCE CAN CHOPPED TOMATOES WITH THEIR JUICE

6 CUPS BEEF STOCK (PAGE 20) OR STORE-BOUGHT BEEF BROTH

2 TABLESPOONS CORNMEAL

¼ CUP WATER

1 Heat the oil in the pressure cooker over medium-high heat. Sprinkle the meat evenly with the salt and pepper and brown in the oil, a few pieces at a time. Remove the browned meat to a plate as it's done. Add the onions, garlic, chipotles, and cumin to the pot and sauté for 2 minutes to soften the onions. Add the tomatoes and stock and return the beef to the pot. Lock the lid in place and cook at high pressure for 30 minutes.

2 Release the pressure naturally and remove the lid, tilting the pot way from you to avoid the escaping steam. In a small bowl, combine the cornmeal and water, stirring to blend. Bring the chili to a boil, uncovered, and add the cornmeal mixture, stirring to combine. Return the chili to a boil, taste for seasoning, and add more salt and pepper if necessary. This chili is delicious the day after it's made so that the flavors have a chance to get to know each other.

TEX-MEX SIRLOIN CHILI

A marriage of traditional beef chili with pinto beans in a thick, spicy sauce is my idea of a great meal in a bowl. This is our house chili. We eat it when we are watching sports on TV or when we just feel like a hearty, spicy bowl full. Condiments are required for this dish, so plan to dice up onions, avocado, jalapeños, and tomatoes. Shred some cheese and be sure to have lots of beer on hand to wash this down!

SERVES 8

4 TABLESPOONS CANOLA OIL

2 POUNDS GROUND BEEF (85% LEAN)

1½ TEASPOONS SALT, PLUS MORE IF NEEDED

1 TEASPOON ANCHO CHILE POWDER

2 CUPS FINELY CHOPPED SWEET ONION, SUCH AS VIDALIA

ONE 28-OUNCE CAN TOMATO PURÉE

1½ CUPS PINTO BEANS, PRESOAKED (SEE PAGE 151) AND DRAINED

7 CUPS BEEF STOCK (PAGE 20) OR STORE-BOUGHT BEEF BROTH

FRESHLY GROUND BLACK PEPPER (OPTIONAL)

CONDIMENTS

1 CUP FINELY CHOPPED RED ONION

2 HASS AVOCADOS, DICED AND TOSSED WITH 1 TABLESPOON FRESH LIME JUICE

½ CUP PICKLED JALAPEÑOS

1 TO 2 CUPS FINELY CHOPPED TOMATOES

2 TO 3 CUPS FINELY SHREDDED MIXED CHEESES, SUCH AS MILD CHEDDAR, MONTEREY JACK, AND PEPPER JACK

ASSORTED HOT SAUCES, SUCH AS TABASCO, CHOLULA, AND A CHIPOTLE HOT SAUCE

1 Heat 2 tablespoons of the oil in the pressure cooker over medium-high heat. Add the beef and sauté until it loses its pink color. Add the salt, chile powder, and onion and sauté for 2 minutes, or until the onion begins to soften. Add the tomato purée, beans, and stock and drizzle with the remaining 2 tablespoons of oil. Lock the lid in place and cook at high pressure for 20 minutes.

2 Release the pressure naturally and remove the lid, tilting the pot away from you to avoid the escaping steam. Taste the chili for seasoning and add more salt and some pepper if needed. Serve immediately with the condiments.

VEGETABLES

My students often complain that their families don't eat enough vegetables, and they are constantly challenging me to come up with new and inventive ways to serve great vegetable side dishes the entire family will eat. From my point of view, the pressure cooker is a great place to start. Many vegetables are done in less than 10 minutes. Others, like root vegetables, will take a bit longer, but never more than 20 minutes. And the best part is that all the flavor and nutrients are locked into the food, rather than getting cooked away. When you're not cooking the main course in your pressure cooker, use it to create great vegetable dishes for your weeknight meals. If you would like to serve artichokes with that grilled steak, it will only take 12 minutes to have them perfectly steamed. Mashed potatoes (including sweet potatoes) can be made in less than 10 minutes. Slow-cooked green beans, pressure roasted beets, and honey-glazed steamed baby carrots can cook alongside your entrée and appear on the table in less than 20 minutes.

I find that pressure steaming vegetables in water usually works as well or better than steaming them in broth or in an aromatic mixture (which doesn't seem to enhance the flavors of vegetables). When I steam vegetables in a pressure cooker, I use a steamer basket. Most pressure cookers come with a basket, and some have a trivet for the basket to sit on. If your cooker didn't come with a steamer basket, a small collapsible metal steamer will work just fine in the bottom of your pressure cooker. (Silicone steamer baskets are not recommended for pressure cookers.) Or you can simply crumple aluminum foil, poke vent holes into it, and set it on the bottom of the pressure cooker. Add water and arrange vegetables on the foil. It works in a pinch.

VEGETABLE	COOKING TIME AT HIGH PRESSURE
Artichokes	12 minutes
Beets (baby)	12 minutes
Beets (medium)	15 minutes
Broccoli rabe	5 minutes
Brussels sprouts	4 minutes
Butternut squash (½-inch pieces)	3 to 4 minutes
Butternut squash (1-inch chunks)	5 minutes
Cabbage	3 minutes
Cauliflower (whole)	5 minutes
Cauliflower (florets)	3 minutes
Carrots (baby)	5 minutes
Carrots (½-inch slices)	4 minutes
Chard	2 to 3 minutes
Collard greens (coarsely chopped)	4 minutes
Corn on the cob	1 to 2 minutes
Eggplant (1½-inch chunks)	2 to 3 minutes
Green beans	2 to 3 minutes
Kale (coarsely chopped)	4 minutes
Parsnips (½-inch rounds)	2 minutes
Potatoes (small whole)	7 minutes
Potatoes (medium whole)	10 minutes
Potatoes (1-inch chunks)	8 minutes
Potatoes (½-inch-thick slices)	2 to 3 minutes
Sweet potatoes (1-inch pieces)	7 minutes

These cooking times are based on a quick release of pressure for steaming individual vegetables.

SMOKY EGGPLANT

A whiff of garlic, cumin, and smoked paprika emerges when you uncover this savory mélange. Serve it as a relish or as a topping for grilled chicken or fish. It's also terrific as a side dish for a vegetarian feast.

SERVES **6**

2 TABLESPOONS EXTRA-VIRGIN OLIVE OIL

4 GARLIC CLOVES, MINCED

½ CUP FINELY CHOPPED WHITE ONION

6 SMALL JAPANESE EGGPLANTS, STEM ENDS REMOVED, CUT INTO 1-INCH CHUNKS (SEE PSST)

2 TEASPOONS SPANISH SMOKED PAPRIKA

¾ TEASPOON GROUND CUMIN

ONE 14½-OUNCE CAN CHOPPED TOMATOES WITH THEIR JUICE

¼ CUP FINELY CHOPPED FRESH CILANTRO

¼ CUP FINELY CHOPPED FRESH FLAT-LEAF PARSLEY

1 Heat the oil in the pressure cooker over medium-high heat. Add the garlic and onion and sauté for 2 minutes, or until the onion begins to soften. Add the eggplant, paprika, and cumin and sauté for 2 minutes. Add the tomatoes. Lock the lid in place and cook at high pressure for 6 minutes.

2 Quick release the pressure and remove the lid, tilting the pot away from you to avoid the escaping steam. Stir the mixture and add the cilantro and parsley. Let rest for about 5 minutes and transfer to a serving bowl. The eggplant can be served warm or at room temperature.

PSST

The tender skin on Japanese eggplants is delicious and it helps to keep the flesh intact, but if you prefer, peel the eggplant and reduce the cooking time by 2 minutes.

RATATOUILLE

From the French region of Provence, this eggplant dish is flavored with a traditional bouquet of herbs and garlic and, for a change of pace, the zest of an orange, added at the end. Serve this with grilled or roasted entrées or as a topping for poached chicken or seafood. Or spoon some onto crusty bread and top with Brie, Gruyère, Parmigiano, or goat cheese.

SERVES 6 TO 8

2 TABLESPOONS EXTRA-VIRGIN OLIVE OIL

1 LARGE RED ONION, THINLY SLICED

2 GARLIC CLOVES, MINCED

1 MEDIUM YELLOW BELL PEPPER, SEEDED, DERIBBED, AND COARSELY CHOPPED

1 MEDIUM RED BELL PEPPER, SEEDED, DERIBBED, AND COARSELY CHOPPED

2 MEDIUM EGGPLANTS, STEM END CUT OFF, AND CUT INTO 1-INCH CHUNKS

1 TEASPOON DRIED THYME (SEE PSST)

½ TEASPOON DRIED ROSEMARY, CRUSHED BETWEEN YOUR FINGERS

½ TEASPOON DRIED SAVORY

½ TEASPOON FENNEL SEEDS

1½ TEASPOONS SALT, PLUS MORE IF NEEDED

½ TEASPOON FRESHLY GROUND BLACK PEPPER, PLUS MORE IF NEEDED

2 TEASPOONS SUGAR

2 CUPS CRUSHED TOMATOES WITH THEIR JUICE

½ CUP FINELY CHOPPED FRESH FLAT-LEAF PARSLEY

GRATED ZEST OF 1 ORANGE

1 Heat the oil in the pressure cooker over medium-high heat. Add the onion, garlic, and bell peppers and sauté for 3 to 4 minutes, or until the vegetables begin to soften. Add the eggplant, herbs, salt, pepper, and sugar and toss the mixture until the eggplant is coated with the oil and herbs. Add the tomatoes. Lock the lid in place and cook at high pressure for 6 minutes.

2 Quick release the pressure and remove the lid, tilting the pot away from you to avoid the escaping steam. Stir in the parsley and orange zest, taste for seasoning, and add more salt and pepper if needed. Let the ratatouille rest for at least 10 minutes before serving to let the flavors mellow a bit. Serve hot, warm, or at room temperature.

PSST

Herbes de Provence is sold in gourmet shops and includes a variety of herbs, including lavender. If you have herbes de Provence on your spice shelf, use 2½ teaspoons and omit the thyme, rosemary, savory, and fennel seeds.

CAPONATA

Caponata is a sweet and savory chunky eggplant relish that originated in Sicily. It is served with antipasti or as a condiment to accompany grilled fish, steak, or chicken. The pressure cooker will bring it to the table in less than ten minutes.

MAKES ABOUT **6** CUPS

2 TABLESPOONS EXTRA-VIRGIN OLIVE OIL

2 LARGE SWEET ONIONS, SUCH AS VIDALIA, FINELY CHOPPED

3 GARLIC CLOVES, MINCED

⅛ TEASPOON RED PEPPER FLAKES

4 CELERY STALKS, FINELY CHOPPED

2 MEDIUM EGGPLANTS, PEELED, STEM ENDS REMOVED, AND CUT INTO ½- TO ¾-INCH DICE

ONE 28-OUNCE CAN TOMATO PURÉE

¼ CUP BALSAMIC VINEGAR

1 CUP GOLDEN RAISINS

2 TABLESPOONS SUGAR

¼ CUP BRINE-CURED CAPERS, CHOPPED IF LARGE

1 CUP KALAMATA OLIVES, PITTED AND COARSELY CHOPPED

¼ CUP FINELY CHOPPED FRESH FLAT-LEAF PARSLEY

1 Heat the oil in the pressure cooker over medium-high heat. Add the onions, garlic, and red pepper flakes and sauté for 2 minutes, or until the onions begin to soften. Add the celery, eggplant, tomato purée, vinegar, raisins, sugar, capers, and olives. Lock the lid in place and cook at high pressure for 5 minutes.

2 Quick release the pressure and remove the lid, tilting the pot away from you to avoid the escaping steam. Stir in the parsley and transfer the caponata to a bowl to cool. Serve warm or at room temperature.

PRESSURE-ROASTED GARLIC

You can roast up to six bulbs of garlic in your pressure cooker in less than fifteen minutes. You may wonder why this method is better than roasting garlic in the oven. In the middle of the summer, I prefer to use the pressure cooker rather than heat up the kitchen. Plus the garlic cooks in a quarter of the time, and the results are terrific!

MAKES 6 BULBS

....

1 CUP WATER

6 GARLIC BULBS

¼ TO ⅓ CUP EXTRA-VIRGIN OLIVE OIL

1 TABLESPOON COARSE SALT

1 Pour the water into the pressure cooker. Make squares of aluminum foil that are three times the size of the garlic bulbs, so they will seal the garlic completely. Arrange each garlic bulb in the center of a square, drizzle with oil, and sprinkle with a bit of salt. Wrap the garlic in the foil. Arrange the trivet and steamer basket in the pressure cooker and transfer the garlic packets to the steamer basket. Lock the lid in place and cook at high pressure for 10 minutes.

2 Release the pressure naturally and remove the lid, tilting the pot away from you to avoid the escaping steam. Remove the packets from the steamer basket and allow them to cool for about 10 minutes. Remove the aluminum foil and squeeze the garlic out of its papery skin into a bowl. Pour any remaining olive oil over the roasted garlic, cover, and refrigerate for up to 5 days.

PSST

Here's a great trick for getting roasted garlic out of its skin: Put the garlic bulbs into a potato ricer and press the garlic through the ricer. It does a phenomenal job!

EDAMAME

Edamame is the Japanese word for green soybeans. They make a great nibble before dinner, and they are so good for you—packed with fiber and protein. Usually sold vacuum sealed or frozen in their pods, edamame are also a terrific snack for kids. The pressure cooker will steam them in about three minutes; then a sprinkling of coarse salt is all that's needed. Edamame are usually served in their pods, for diners to shell themselves, but you can shell them if you prefer (see the Psst). They make great additions to stir-fries and salads, or you can mash them up and make guacamole.

SERVES **6**

1 CUP WATER OR CHICKEN OR VEGETABLE STOCK (PAGE 19 OR 21) OR STORE-BOUGHT CHICKEN OR VEGETABLE BROTH

2 CUPS FRESH OR FROZEN EDAMAME IN THEIR PODS (DEFROST IF FROZEN)

1 TEASPOON COARSE SALT

1 Pour the water into the pressure cooker. Arrange the trivet and steamer basket in the bottom and spread out the edamame in the basket in an even layer. Lock the lid in place and cook at high pressure for 3 minutes.

2 Quick release the pressure and remove the lid, tilting the pot away from you to avoid the escaping steam. Transfer the edamame to a serving bowl and sprinkle with coarse salt.

PSST

If you would like to shell the edamame, wait for them to cool first.

GARLIC ASIAN BEANS

Asian long beans seem to take forever to cook on the stove top, and they are invariably tough, but the pressure cooker takes on the beans and cooks them perfectly in less than ten minutes. This recipe includes garlic, ginger, soy, and broth to bring out the flavors of the beans. Serve this dish either hot or cold—it will be a hit either way.

SERVES **4** TO **6**

....

2 TABLESPOONS CANOLA OIL

3 GARLIC CLOVES, MINCED

1 TEASPOON GRATED FRESH GINGER

½ CUP CHICKEN STOCK (PAGE 19) OR STORE-BOUGHT CHICKEN BROTH

¼ CUP SOY SAUCE

1 POUND ASIAN LONG BEANS, TIPS TRIMMED, AND CUT INTO 1-INCH LENGTHS

2 TEASPOONS TOASTED SESAME OIL

2 TABLESPOONS TOASTED SESAME SEEDS

1 Heat the oil in the pressure cooker over medium-high heat. Add the garlic and ginger and sauté for 1 minute. Add the stock, soy sauce, and beans. Lock the lid in place and cook the beans at high pressure for 3 minutes.

2 Quick release the pressure and remove the lid, tilting the pot away from you to avoid the escaping steam. Stir the beans and transfer them to a serving dish. Drizzle with the sesame oil and sprinkle with the sesame seeds before serving. Serve the beans hot or at room temperature.

GREEN BEANS, SOUTHERN STYLE

Green beans cooked with bacon are a staple of Southern cooking, and they usually take an hour or so to prepare. Ready in just ten minutes, these green beans have a smoky flavor and go perfectly with comfort foods like meat loaf and fried chicken.

SERVES **6**

4 THICK-CUT BACON STRIPS, CUT CROSSWISE INTO PIECES ½ INCH WIDE

1 CUP FINELY CHOPPED SWEET ONION, SUCH AS VIDALIA

1 CUP CHICKEN STOCK (PAGE 19) OR STORE-BOUGHT CHICKEN BROTH

2 POUNDS GREEN BEANS, TRIMMED AND CUT INTO 1-INCH LENGTHS

1 Cook the bacon in the pressure cooker over medium-high heat until it begins to render its fat and becomes crispy. Add the onion and sauté for 2 minutes. Pour in the stock and add the green beans. Lock the lid in place and cook at high pressure for 10 minutes.

2 Quick release the pressure and remove the lid, tilting the pot away from you to avoid the escaping steam. Using a slotted spoon, transfer the green beans to a serving bowl.

Artichokes

Artichokes are the flower buds of a large thistle plant. The tough outer leaves and meaty heart require a long cooking time on the stove top, but with the pressure cooker, that changes. You can have perfectly steamed artichokes in about 12 minutes. After the artichokes have cooked, remove the leaves and finish up the recipe. If you decide that steamed artichokes would be the perfect vegetable side dish for your grilled steak, then by all means, put them in the pressure cooker and steam away. Stuffed artichokes—which we often ate when I was growing up—take even longer on the stove top than steamed artichokes. But with the pressure cooker, they are ready in less than thirty minutes and make a delicious dish to nibble before dinner.

STEAMED ARTICHOKES WITH DILL AIOLI

Plain steamed artichokes cry out for a delicious sauce, and this aioli is the perfect accompaniment. Aioli is a garlicky mayonnaise that is usually made from scratch with raw eggs. Here, I've streamlined the recipe by using prepared mayonnaise as the base for this luscious sauce. You can also pair the sauce with other cooked vegetables, seafood, or poultry. You can definitely swap herbs here and use tarragon, lemon thyme, or chervil in place of the dill.

SERVES **4**

DILL AIOLI
1⅔ CUPS MAYONNAISE
4 GARLIC CLOVES, MINCED
2 TABLESPOONS FINELY CHOPPED FRESH DILL WEED
6 DROPS OF TABASCO OR ANOTHER HOT SAUCE
1 TEASPOON DIJON MUSTARD
2 TABLESPOONS FRESH LEMON JUICE

ARTICHOKES
1 CUP WATER
2 GARLIC CLOVES, MINCED
1 TEASPOON DRIED THYME
1 BAY LEAF
2 LEMONS, QUARTERED
4 MEDIUM ARTICHOKES

1 **To make the aioli:** Whisk together all the ingredients in a small bowl. (You should have about 2 cups.) Cover and refrigerate for up to 5 days.

2 **To prepare the artichokes:** Pour the water into the pressure cooker and add the garlic, thyme, and bay leaf. Squeeze the lemons into the water and drop them in. Using a chef's knife, cut off the top inch of each artichoke, remove the stem, and dip the artichokes into the lemon water. Using a pair of kitchen shears, cut off the tough outer leaves. Arrange the trivet and steamer basket in the bottom of the pot and put the artichokes in the steamer basket, stacking them if necessary. Lock the lid in place and cook at high pressure for 12 minutes.

3 Quick release the pressure and remove the lid, tilting the pot away from you to avoid the escaping steam. Test the artichokes with the sharp tip of a knife to make sure they are cooked all the way through. If they require a bit more time, put the lid back on the pot and allow them to steam for 5 minutes more off the heat. Remove the artichokes from the pressure cooker and serve with ramekins of aioli on the side.

STUFFED ARTICHOKES PROVENÇAL

The flavors of Provence remind me of one of its famous residents: Julia Child. Julia had a home in Provence, and the regional cuisine really does match her personality—big and bold. Sunny Mediterranean vegetables and liberal amounts of thyme, rosemary, lavender, and chervil are Provençal trademarks. This is a terrific dish to serve as a nibble before dinner. I usually set the artichokes out, and we graze on them while we are sipping wine and chatting. Don't be put off by the anchovies. They add a salty, rather than fishy, flavor to this dish.

SERVES 4

1 CUP WATER

5 GARLIC CLOVES, MINCED

1 TEASPOON DRIED THYME

1 BAY LEAF

2 LEMONS, QUARTERED

3 TABLESPOONS EXTRA-VIRGIN OLIVE OIL

½ CUP FINELY CHOPPED SHALLOTS (2 MEDIUM)

2 WHOLE ANCHOVIES, FINELY CHOPPED, OR 1 TABLESPOON ANCHOVY PASTE

1 CUP CHERRY TOMATOES, QUARTERED

2 TEASPOONS CHOPPED FRESH THYME

1 TEASPOON FINELY CHOPPED FRESH ROSEMARY

1 TABLESPOON FINELY CHOPPED FRESH FLAT-LEAF PARSLEY

½ CUP OIL-CURED BLACK OLIVES, PITTED AND CHOPPED (SEE PSST)

¼ CUP BRINE-CURED CAPERS, DRAINED AND CHOPPED IF LARGE

SALT AND FRESHLY GROUND BLACK PEPPER (OPTIONAL)

2 CUPS FRESH BREAD CRUMBS

4 MEDIUM ARTICHOKES

1 Pour the water into the pressure cooker and add two-fifths of the garlic, the dried thyme, and bay leaf. Squeeze the lemons into the water and drop them in. Arrange the trivet and steamer basket in the bottom of the pressure cooker.

2 In a sauté pan over medium-high heat, heat 2 tablespoons of the oil. Add the remaining garlic and the shallots and sauté for 2 minutes, or until fragrant. Add the anchovies and sauté for another minute. Add the tomatoes, fresh thyme, rosemary, and parsley and sauté until the tomatoes are softened. Stir in the olives and capers. Taste for seasoning and add salt and pepper if necessary. Allow to cool a bit. Meanwhile, heat the remaining tablespoon of oil in a skillet and toss the bread crumbs in the oil. Cook, stirring, until they become golden brown. Remove from the pan and stir into the tomato mixture.

3 Using a chef's knife, cut off the top inch of an artichoke and remove the stem. Pulling the outer leaves apart, stuff some of the mixture between the outer leaves with a spoon. Work your way around the artichoke through the layers of leaves and stop when you get to the leaves that are tightly bound in the center. Repeat with the remaining artichokes. Put the artichokes in the steamer basket. Lock the lid in place and cook at high pressure for 13 minutes.

4 Quick release the pressure and remove the lid, tilting the pot away from you to avoid the escaping steam. Remove the steamer basket. Allow the artichokes to rest in the basket for about 5 minutes and transfer them to a serving platter. Provide a plate for the discarded leaves.

PSST

One easy way to pit olives is to press down on them with the blade of your chef's knife or santoku until the pit releases. Or you can use a cherry pitter.

Picholine olives, which are native to Provence, are brine cured and usually flavored with herbes de Provence. If you have trouble locating them, Lucques olives will work well, or you can substitute the more readily available green Manzanilla olives and toss them with some herbes de Provence.

SAUSAGE-STUFFED ARTICHOKES

My grandmother's stuffed artichoke recipe gets an infusion of spicy Italian sausage, making it a terrific starter, side dish, or lunch entrée. The artichokes are cut in half and stuffed, rather than left whole. Serve them with grilled seafood, chicken, or beef.

SERVES 6

1 CUP WATER

2 GARLIC CLOVES, MINCED

1 TEASPOON DRIED THYME

1 BAY LEAF

2 LEMONS, QUARTERED

3 MEDIUM ARTICHOKES

½ POUND BULK ITALIAN SAUSAGE

½ CUP FINELY CHOPPED RED ONION

½ CUP FINELY CHOPPED OIL-PACKED SUN-DRIED TOMATOES, DRAINED

2 TABLESPOONS FINELY CHOPPED FRESH FLAT-LEAF PARSLEY

2 CUPS FRESH BREAD CRUMBS

⅔ CUP FINELY GRATED PECORINO ROMANO CHEESE

4 TABLESPOONS EXTRA-VIRGIN OLIVE OIL

1 Pour the water into the pressure cooker and add the garlic, thyme, and bay leaf. Squeeze the lemons into the water and drop them in. Using a chef's knife, cut off the top inch of each artichoke and remove the stem. Cut the artichokes in half lengthwise and discard the fuzzy choke in the center. Dip the cut sides of the artichoke into the lemon water. Arrange the trivet and steamer basket in the bottom of the pressure cooker.

2 In a medium sauté pan over medium-high heat, sauté the sausage, stirring and breaking it up until it is no longer pink. Remove all but 1 teaspoon of the fat from the pan. Add the onion and sun-dried tomatoes and sauté until the onion begins to soften, about 2 minutes. Transfer to a bowl and allow to cool. Add the parsley, bread crumbs, and cheese to the sausage mixture and toss to combine. Drizzle 2 tablespoons of the oil over the mixture and stir. Stuff each artichoke half with one-sixth of the mixture and drizzle with the remaining 2 tablespoons of oil. Stack the artichokes in the steamer basket, placing squares of aluminum foil between them to prevent them from sticking together. Lock the lid in place and cook at high pressure for 13 minutes.

3 Quick release the pressure and remove the lid, tilting the pot away from you to avoid the escaping steam. Allow the artichokes to rest for 5 minutes before removing the basket. Separate the artichokes, remove the foil, and replace any stuffing that may have stuck to the foil. Transfer to a serving platter and serve warm or at room temperature.

CORN BREAD—STUFFED ARTICHOKES WITH PROSCIUTTO

I can make a meal of these artichokes, which are stuffed with corn bread and studded with prosciutto, sage, golden raisins, and shallots. The raisins add a delicious sweetness to the salty prosciutto and give the whole dish a sweet-and-savory flavor. Many markets sell freshly baked corn bread, in case you don't have time to make your own. In a pinch, packaged corn bread stuffing crumbs work, too. Add ½ cup chicken or vegetable broth to moisten them.

SERVES 4

4 MEDIUM ARTICHOKES

1 CUP WATER

2 GARLIC CLOVES, MINCED

1 BAY LEAF

2 LEMONS, QUARTERED

6 FRESH SAGE LEAVES, FINELY CHOPPED

4 TABLESPOONS EXTRA-VIRGIN OLIVE OIL

6 THIN SLICES PROSCIUTTO DI PARMA, FINELY CHOPPED

½ CUP FINELY CHOPPED SHALLOTS (2 SMALL)

2 CUPS CORN BREAD, CRUMBLED

½ CUP GOLDEN RAISINS, FINELY CHOPPED

1 Cut off the top inch of each artichoke and remove the stem. Pour the water into the pressure cooker and add the garlic and bay leaf. Squeeze the lemons into the water and drop them in. Dip the cut ends of the artichokes into the lemon water and set aside. Arrange the trivet and steamer basket in the bottom of the pressure cooker.

2 In a medium skillet over medium-high heat, sauté the sage in 1 tablespoon of the oil for 1 minute, or until fragrant. Add the prosciutto and cook until crispy. Add the shallots and cook for another 2 to 3 minutes, until the shallots are softened. Transfer to a bowl and allow the mixture to cool. Add the crumbled corn bread, raisins, and the remaining 3 tablespoons of oil, tossing the crumbs until coated with oil. Beginning with the outer leaves, carefully separate the leaves and spoon some of the stuffing between them. Work your way around the artichoke through the layers of leaves and stop when you get to the leaves that are tightly bound in the center. Repeat with the remaining artichokes. Put the artichokes in the steamer basket; it's fine to stack them on top of each other if your pressure cooker is tall and narrow. Lock the lid in place and cook at high pressure for 13 minutes.

3 Quick release the pressure and remove the lid, tilting the pot away from you to avoid the escaping steam. Allow the artichokes to rest for 5 minutes. Remove them carefully from the steamer basket and transfer to a serving platter. Serve warm or at room temperature.

ARTICHOKE AND GOAT CHEESE SOUFFLÉS

These custards make a delicious side dish or even a brunch entrée. A blend of smooth fresh goat cheese, eggs, garlic, and artichokes bakes in the pressure cooker to give you a creamy dish with lots of flavor.

SERVES 4

4 TABLESPOONS UNSALTED BUTTER, SOFTENED

1 SMALL SHALLOT, FINELY CHOPPED

2 GARLIC CLOVES, MINCED

ONE 10-OUNCE BAG FROZEN ARTICHOKE HEARTS, DEFROSTED AND COARSELY CHOPPED; OR 3 FRESH ARTICHOKE HEARTS, COARSELY CHOPPED

1½ TEASPOONS SALT

6 DROPS OF TABASCO OR ANOTHER HOT SAUCE

3 LARGE EGGS

1 CUP HEAVY CREAM

1 CUP FRESH BREAD CRUMBS

¼ POUND CRUMBLED FRESH GOAT CHEESE

2 CUPS WATER

1 Coat the insides of four 4-ounce ramekins with 2 tablespoons of the butter. Melt the remaining 2 tablespoons of butter in a medium skillet over medium-high heat. Add the shallot and garlic and sauté for 2 to 3 minutes, until the shallot is softened. Add the artichoke hearts, season with the salt, and continue sautéing until the artichokes are dry and begin to turn golden. Transfer to a bowl and allow to cool.

2 In a mixing bowl, whisk together the Tabasco, eggs, and cream. Add the cooled artichoke mixture and bread crumbs, pressing down on the crumbs so they absorb the custard. Spoon into the ramekins, which should be three-quarters full. Sprinkle the goat cheese over the tops and cover each ramekin tightly with aluminum foil. Pour the water into the pressure cooker, arrange the trivet and steamer basket in the bottom, and stack the ramekins in the basket. Lock the lid in place and cook at high pressure for 9 minutes.

3 Quick release the pressure and remove the lid, tilting the pot away from you to avoid the escaping steam. Carefully remove the ramekins from the steamer basket, leaving the foil in place. Allow to cool for 10 minutes to let the soufflés set up. Remove the foil and serve warm.

Greens

Greens are healthful food. Filled with vitamins, minerals, and great flavor, they generally require a long conventional cooking time. Within five minutes, though, kale, Swiss chard, beet tops, collards, and broccoli rabe all pressure cook into tender and flavorful side dishes. And the good news is they retain their beautiful colors along with their robust flavors and nutrients.

Look for healthy leaves with vibrant color and stems that are rigid, rather than spongy. Wash the greens several times in cold water to remove any sand or grit that may cling to them.

SPINACH AND BACON SOUFFLÉS

Here, ramekins are lined with crispy bacon and filled with a creamy Gruyère and egg mixture studded with bright green spinach. These make a terrific brunch entrée, or you can serve the soufflés as a side dish for an elegant dinner. The ramekins can be assembled ahead of time, then all they need are 8 minutes at high pressure and they're on the table.

SERVES 6

6 BACON STRIPS, COOKED UNTIL CRISP AND DRAINED

2 TABLESPOONS UNSALTED BUTTER

1 MEDIUM SHALLOT, FINELY CHOPPED

ONE 10-OUNCE BAG BABY SPINACH, CHOPPED

⅛ TEASPOON FRESHLY GRATED NUTMEG

1 TEASPOON SALT, PLUS MORE IF NEEDED

½ TEASPOON FRESHLY GROUND BLACK PEPPER, PLUS MORE IF NEEDED

3 LARGE EGGS PLUS 1 LARGE EGG YOLK

½ CUP HEAVY CREAM

1 CUP FINELY SHREDDED GRUYÈRE CHEESE

2 CUPS WATER

1 Coat the insides of six 4-ounce ramekins with nonstick cooking spray. Arrange a strip of bacon in each ramekin so that it fits right up against the sides. The bacon may need to be trimmed a bit.

2 In a sauté pan over medium-high heat, melt the butter. Add the shallot and cook for 2 minutes, or until the shallot is softened. Add the spinach, nutmeg, salt, and pepper and cook for 2 to 3 minutes, or until the spinach is wilted. Taste for seasoning and add more salt and pepper if necessary. Allow the mixture to cool.

3 In a mixing bowl, whisk together the eggs and cream and stir in the spinach mixture. Using a ⅓-cup measure, pour the mixture into the bacon-lined ramekins. Sprinkle each one with a sixth of the cheese and cover tightly with aluminum foil. (At this point, the ramekins can be refrigerated overnight.)

4 Pour the water into the pressure cooker. Arrange the trivet and steamer basket in the bottom and stack the ramekins in the basket. Lock the lid in place and cook at high pressure for 8 minutes.

5 Release the pressure naturally and remove the lid, tilting the pot away from you to avoid the escaping steam. Remove the ramekins carefully, remove the foil, and allow the ramekins to rest for 5 minutes. Loosen the sides with an offset spatula, tip out the soufflés onto plates, and serve.

CREAMY SPINACH CUSTARDS

Spinach is so delicate that it doesn't benefit from pressure cooking. But creamy spinach custards cook perfectly in the pressure cooker, and they make an elegant side dish. The custards can be made ahead and pressure cooked just before serving.

SERVES **6**

4 TABLESPOONS UNSALTED BUTTER

¼ CUP FRESHLY GRATED PARMIGIANO-REGGIANO CHEESE

2 TABLESPOONS FINELY CHOPPED SHALLOT

TWO 10-OUNCE BAGS BABY SPINACH, CHOPPED

¼ TEASPOON FRESHLY GRATED NUTMEG, PLUS MORE IF NEEDED

1½ TEASPOONS SALT, PLUS MORE IF NEEDED

½ TEASPOON FRESHLY GROUND BLACK PEPPER, PLUS MORE IF NEEDED

2 TABLESPOONS ALL-PURPOSE FLOUR

1½ CUPS HALF-AND-HALF

3 LARGE EGG YOLKS, LIGHTLY BEATEN

2 CUPS WATER

1 Butter six 4-ounce ramekins with 2 tablespoons of the butter, sprinkle the insides of the ramekins with half of the cheese, and set aside. Melt the remaining 2 tablespoons of butter in a large sauté pan over medium-high heat. Add the shallot and sauté for 2 minutes, or until it begins to soften. Add the spinach, nutmeg, salt, and pepper and sauté until the spinach is wilted. Add the flour and cook for 2 to 3 minutes, until the flour begins to bubble. Add the half-and-half and bring to a boil. Remove from the heat, taste for seasoning, and add more salt, pepper, and nutmeg if needed. Allow to cool slightly. Beat the egg yolks lightly in a small bowl and stir some of the cooled spinach mixture into the yolks. Stir the egg mixture into the spinach in the pan, stirring to blend. Spoon ⅓ to ½ cup of the spinach mixture into each prepared ramekin and sprinkle the tops with the remaining Parmigiano. Cover the ramekins tightly with aluminum foil. (At this point, the ramekins can be refrigerated for up to 2 days.)

2 When ready to cook, bring the ramekins to room temperature if chilled. Pour the water into the pressure cooker. Arrange the trivet and steamer basket in the bottom and stack the ramekins in the basket. Lock the lid in place and cook at high pressure for 8 minutes.

3 Allow the pressure to drop naturally for 5 minutes before releasing the pressure manually. Remove the lid, tilting the pot away from you to avoid the escaping steam. Carefully remove the ramekins and allow to rest for 5 minutes to set up. Remove the aluminum foil, blotting any excess moisture from the surface of the custards with a paper towel. If you would like to unmold the custards onto plates, run an offset spatula around the inside of each ramekin to loosen the custard, then tip out onto a plate. Serve immediately.

COLLARD GREENS, SOUTHERN STYLE

Down home and downright delicious, these greens and smoked ham hocks make a great side dish to serve with other homey favorites like fried chicken or pork chops.

SERVES 6

8 CUPS COARSELY CHOPPED COLLARD GREENS (ABOUT 3 BUNCHES)

2 CUPS CHICKEN STOCK (PAGE 19) OR STORE-BOUGHT CHICKEN BROTH

1 SMOKED HAM HOCK OR HAM BONE

1 BAY LEAF

6 DROPS OF TABASCO OR ANOTHER HOT SAUCE

SALT AND FRESHLY GROUND BLACK PEPPER (OPTIONAL)

1 Combine all the ingredients but the salt and pepper in the pressure cooker, lock the lid in place, and cook at high pressure for 15 minutes.

2 Quick release the pressure and remove the lid, tilting the pot away from you to avoid the escaping steam. Remove the ham hock and cut the meat from the bone into bite-size pieces. Return the ham to the pot. Remove the bay leaf, taste the collards, and add salt and pepper if needed. With a slotted spoon, transfer the collards and ham to a serving bowl and serve immediately.

PSST

Southern cooks save the liquid in the pan for sopping up with bread or using in other dishes. It is smoky and delicious. Freeze the liquid for up to 4 months and use it in split pea soup.

COLLARDS WITH HAM AND POTATOES

A little more refined than the **COLLARD GREENS, SOUTHERN STYLE** (facing page), this dish is almost a one-pot meal. Serve it with corn bread for a simple supper. The potatoes and collards really soak up the flavor of the ham. This is a terrific way to use up leftover ham from a holiday dinner.

SERVES 6

8 CUPS COARSELY CHOPPED COLLARD GREENS (ABOUT 3 BUNCHES)

4 MEDIUM YUKON GOLD OR RED-SKINNED POTATOES, QUARTERED (PEEL IF THE SKINS AREN'T PERFECT)

1 SWEET ONION, SUCH AS VIDALIA, FINELY CHOPPED

2 CUPS DICED HAM

1 HAM BONE (OPTIONAL)

2 CUPS CHICKEN STOCK (PAGE 19) OR STORE-BOUGHT CHICKEN BROTH

1 BAY LEAF

6 DROPS OF TABASCO OR ANOTHER HOT SAUCE

SALT AND FRESHLY GROUND BLACK PEPPER (OPTIONAL)

1 Combine all the ingredients but the salt and pepper in the pressure cooker. Lock the lid in place and cook at high pressure for 10 minutes.

2 Release the pressure naturally and remove the lid, tilting the pot away from you to avoid the escaping steam. Remove the ham bone (if using), cut the meat from the bone into bite-size pieces, and return the meat to the pot. Remove the bay leaf, taste the collards, and add salt and pepper if necessary. Using a slotted spoon, transfer the collards to a serving dish and serve immediately.

BRAISED KALE WITH BACON AND GOLDEN RAISINS

Sweet and smoky, this dish is not only scrumptious but good for you, too! Kale is delicious when braised until tender and flavored with bacon and sweet golden raisins. This is terrific served with grilled chicken or fish.

SERVES **6** TO **8**

4 BACON STRIPS, CUT CROSSWISE INTO PIECES ½ INCH WIDE

6 CUPS CHOPPED KALE (ABOUT 3 BUNCHES)

½ CUP VEGETABLE STOCK (PAGE 21) OR STORE-BOUGHT VEGETABLE BROTH

2 TABLESPOONS RICE VINEGAR

½ CUP GOLDEN RAISINS

1 Cook the bacon in the pressure cooker over medium heat until crisp. Remove from the pan, drain on paper towels, and set aside. Remove all but 2 tablespoons of the bacon drippings from the pan. Add the kale, stock, vinegar, and raisins. Lock the lid in place and cook at high pressure for 4 minutes.

2 Quick release the pressure and remove the lid, tilting the pot away from you to avoid the escaping steam. Add the reserved bacon to the pot and stir to combine. Using a slotted spoon, transfer the kale to a bowl and serve.

BROCCOLI RABE AND ROSEMARY WHITE BEAN RAGU

This hearty dish flavored with garlic, rosemary, and a bit of lemon makes a terrific side dish for lamb or beef.

SERVES **6** TO **8**

4 TABLESPOONS EXTRA-VIRGIN OLIVE OIL

2 GARLIC CLOVES, MINCED

2 TEASPOONS FINELY CHOPPED FRESH ROSEMARY

PINCH OF RED PEPPER FLAKES

3 BUNCHES BROCCOLI RABE, TRIMMED AND COARSELY CHOPPED

3 CUPS CHICKEN STOCK (PAGE 19) OR STORE-BOUGHT CHICKEN BROTH

1 CUP SMALL WHITE BEANS, PRESOAKED (SEE PAGE 151) AND DRAINED

GRATED ZEST OF 1 LEMON

SALT AND FRESHLY GROUND BLACK PEPPER (OPTIONAL)

1 Heat 2 tablespoons of the oil in the pressure cooker over medium-high heat. Add the garlic, rosemary, and red pepper flakes and sauté for 1 minute. Add the broccoli rabe and stir to coat with the oil mixture. Add the stock and beans, stirring to blend, and drizzle with 1 tablespoon of the oil. Lock the lid in place and cook at high pressure for 10 minutes.

2 Release the pressure naturally and remove the lid, tilting the pot away from you to escape the steam. Stir in the lemon zest. Taste for seasoning and add salt and pepper if necessary. Using a slotted spoon, transfer the beans and greens to a serving bowl and drizzle with the remaining tablespoon of oil. Serve the dish warm or at room temperature.

GARLIC SWISS CHARD

My grandmother made a version of this garlic oil–infused Swiss chard that was so delicious I would eat it hot or cold (it's good at room temperature, too). Simple to prepare, the chard makes a great bed for serving grilled chicken or fish. And it's ready in less than five minutes. Try the varicolored chard available in most markets; the deep green leaves set against bright yellow and red stems makes a beautiful presentation on the dinner plate.

SERVES **4** TO **6**

¼ CUP EXTRA-VIRGIN OLIVE OIL

6 GARLIC CLOVES, SLICED

PINCH OF RED PEPPER FLAKES

½ CUP CHICKEN STOCK (PAGE 19) OR STORE-BOUGHT CHICKEN BROTH

6 CUPS COARSELY CHOPPED SWISS CHARD (ABOUT 2 BUNCHES)

SALT AND FRESHLY GROUND BLACK PEPPER (OPTIONAL)

1 Heat the oil in the pressure cooker over medium-high heat. Add the garlic and red pepper flakes and sauté for 1 minute, or until fragrant. Add the stock and chard, stirring to coat the chard. Lock the lid in place and cook at high pressure for 3 minutes.

2 Quick release the pressure and remove the lid, tilting the pot away from you to avoid the escaping steam. Stir the chard and remove the garlic cloves. Taste for seasoning and add salt or pepper if needed. Serve the chard warm or at room temperature.

PSST

The smaller the pieces of garlic in a dish, the more intense the flavor. Here, since you want just a hint of garlic in the oil, you slice it rather than mince it and then remove the garlic before serving.

You can substitute chopped broccoli rabe for the Swiss chard.

Cabbage

Cabbage cooks rapidly in the pressure cooker, which yields lovely side dishes for your dinner table. When fresh, cabbage is naturally sweet. It is also very nutritious, since it's high in potassium and folic acid, which is a vitamin. There are lots of great cabbage dishes that pair well with main courses. I've included the ones I enjoy the most, such as **SWEET-AND-SOUR RED CABBAGE** (page 99). I urge you to try cabbage as a side dish for your dinner table; you will be amazed at the difference pressure cooking can make.

BASIC STEAMED CABBAGE

A whole cabbage, quartered and steamed in the pressure cooker, takes three minutes to cook to perfection. Still crisp, yet tender, all it needs is a little salt, pepper, and olive oil or butter. Serve it with corned beef or with roast beef, lamb, or pork entrées.

SERVES 6

1 CUP WATER

1 LARGE HEAD CABBAGE, CORED AND QUARTERED

1½ TEASPOONS SALT

½ TEASPOON FRESHLY GROUND BLACK PEPPER

2 TABLESPOONS EXTRA-VIRGIN OLIVE OIL, OR 2 TABLESPOONS UNSALTED BUTTER, MELTED

1 Pour the water into the pressure cooker. Arrange the trivet and steamer basket in the bottom and put the cabbage in the basket. Lock the lid in place and cook at high pressure for 3 minutes.

2 Quick release the pressure and remove the lid, tilting the pot away from you to avoid the escaping steam. Arrange the cabbage in a serving dish and sprinkle with the salt and pepper. Drizzle with the oil and serve immediately.

PSST

Add a bit of Tabasco or your favorite hot sauce to the olive oil or butter; it will add flavor, not heat.

SWEET-AND-SOUR RED CABBAGE

Brightly colored, piquant, and scrumptious alongside poultry or pork, this is one of my favorite side dishes. Not only is it delicious, it also elicits oohs and aahs from my guests. Think about arranging the cabbage on a serving platter as a bed for roast pork or turkey. Or use it as a dramatic stuffing for a crown roast of pork.

SERVES **8**

2 TABLESPOONS CANOLA OIL

2 CUPS THINLY SLICED RED ONION

1 LARGE RED CABBAGE, CORED AND SLICED ¼ INCH THICK (6 TO 8 CUPS)

2 LARGE BRAEBURN APPLES, PEELED, CORED, AND SLICED ¼ INCH THICK (SEE PSST)

1 CUP APPLE JUICE

½ CUP POMEGRANATE JUICE

2 TABLESPOONS APPLE CIDER VINEGAR

½ CUP FIRMLY PACKED LIGHT BROWN SUGAR

SALT AND FRESHLY GROUND BLACK PEPPER (OPTIONAL)

1 Heat the oil in the pressure cooker over medium-high heat. Add the onion and sauté for 2 to 3 minutes, until it begins to soften. Add the cabbage, apples, apple juice, pomegranate juice, vinegar, and sugar and stir to blend. Lock the lid in place and cook at high pressure for 5 minutes.

2 Quick release the pressure and remove the lid, tilting the pot away from you to avoid the escaping steam. Stir the cabbage, taste for seasoning, and add salt and pepper if necessary. Serve the cabbage hot, warm, or at room temperature.

PSST

If Braeburns aren't available, substitute your favorite cooking apple.

BACON, POTATOES, AND CABBAGE

In this version of colcannon—a classic dish from Ireland—bacon and Yukon Gold potatoes are added to the cabbage. (Colcannon is made with kale, too.) The result is a golden, savory, comforting main dish for dinner, or a side dish for pork, beef, or poultry. It's also delightful as a stand-in for the usual boiled cabbage when you serve traditional corned beef and cabbage. Try this dish for St. Patty's Day!

SERVES 6

4 TABLESPOONS UNSALTED BUTTER

2 MEDIUM LEEKS (WHITE AND TENDER GREEN PARTS), CUT INTO ½-INCH ROUNDS

1 MEDIUM HEAD CABBAGE, CORED AND THINLY SLICED

6 MEDIUM YUKON GOLD POTATOES, PEELED AND CUT INTO 1-INCH CHUNKS

½ CUP CHICKEN STOCK (PAGE 19) OR STORE-BOUGHT CHICKEN BROTH

½ CUP HEAVY CREAM

1½ TEASPOONS SALT, PLUS MORE IF NEEDED

½ TEASPOON FRESHLY GROUND BLACK PEPPER, PLUS MORE IF NEEDED

¼ CUP FINELY CHOPPED FRESH CHIVES

6 THICK-CUT BACON STRIPS, COOKED UNTIL CRISP, AND CRUMBLED

1 Melt the butter in the pressure cooker over medium-high heat. Add the leeks and sauté for 2 to 3 minutes. Add the cabbage, potatoes, and stock. Lock the lid in place and cook at high pressure for 8 minutes.

2 Quick release the pressure and remove the lid, tilting the pot away from you to avoid the escaping steam. Return the pot to medium heat. Add the cream and stir to mash the potatoes into the cabbage mixture. Stir in the salt, pepper, chives, and bacon. Taste for seasoning and add more salt and pepper if needed. Transfer to a serving bowl and serve immediately.

PSST

If Yukon Gold potatoes aren't available, substitute red-skinned or white creamer potatoes.

ESTONIAN SAUERKRAUT WITH APPLES AND CABBAGE

My friend Martha Mand taught my daughter, Carrie, this dish many years ago. Although I've modified the recipe a bit for the pressure cooker, I know Martha would applaud the speed with which this dish comes together.

SERVES **6**

½ CUP (1 STICK) UNSALTED BUTTER

3 LARGE SWEET ONIONS, SUCH AS VIDALIA, THINLY SLICED

2 MEDIUM GRANNY SMITH APPLES, PEELED, CORED, AND THINLY SLICED

1½ MEDIUM HEADS GREEN CABBAGE, CORED AND THINLY SLICED (ABOUT 6 CUPS)

1 POUND FRESH SAUERKRAUT, RINSED AND DRAINED

½ CUP SUGAR

1 CUP APPLE JUICE

1 Melt the butter in the pressure cooker over medium-high heat. Add the onions and apples and sauté for 4 to 5 minutes, or until the onions begin to soften. Stir in the cabbage, sauerkraut, sugar, and apple juice, stirring to distribute the ingredients. Lock the lid in place and cook at high pressure for 8 minutes.

2 Quick release the pressure and remove the lid, tilting the pot away from you to avoid the escaping steam. Place the pot over high heat and cook the sauerkraut mixture for another 4 minutes, to let the juices evaporate. The dish can be served hot or warm.

Cauliflower

Cauliflower is on the delicate side. It requires a short cooking time with a quick release of pressure. Steaming a whole cauliflower or florets in the pressure cooker keeps the vegetable crisp and tender. There are new cauliflower hybrids popping up in farmers' markets, such as orange, which has high levels of vitamin A, and purple, which is rich in antioxidants. Their flavors are a bit stronger than the creamy white variety.

WHOLE STEAMED CAULIFLOWER

Whole cauliflower makes a spectacular side dish. Whether you cover it with toasted bread crumbs or an oozy, cheesy sauce, it's a showstopper on the dinner table. This is the basic recipe for cooking florets and whole cauliflower. You can use it as a springboard to make all manner of cauliflower dishes. Present the cauliflower simply with a sprinkling of salt and pepper and a drizzle of olive oil, or transform it into **WHOLE CAULIFLOWER AU GRATIN** (page 104).

SERVES **6**

2 CUPS WATER

1 LARGE HEAD CAULIFLOWER LEFT WHOLE (SEE PSST)

1 Pour the water into the pressure cooker. Arrange the trivet and steamer basket in the bottom and put the cauliflower in the basket. Lock the lid in place and cook at high pressure for 5 minutes.

2 Quick release the pressure and remove the lid, tilting the pot away from you to avoid the escaping steam. Carefully remove the steamer basket.

PSST

If you are preparing florets, cook at high pressure for 3 minutes and quick release the pressure.

WHOLE CAULIFLOWER AU GRATIN

A whole cauliflower makes a spectacular presentation for your dining table. Although this dish is usually reserved for holiday meals, it can be on your table in less than twenty minutes and will earn you applause from your family any old time. You can make the cheese sauce in advance if you like.

SERVES **6**

1 RECIPE WHOLE STEAMED CAULIFLOWER (PAGE 103)

3 TABLESPOONS UNSALTED BUTTER

1 MEDIUM SHALLOT, FINELY CHOPPED

1 GARLIC CLOVE, MINCED

2 TABLESPOONS ALL-PURPOSE FLOUR

2 CUPS MILK

1½ TEASPOONS SALT

5 DROPS OF TABASCO OR ANOTHER HOT SAUCE

1½ CUPS FINELY SHREDDED SHARP WHITE CHEDDAR CHEESE (ABOUT 6 OUNCES)

1 Preheat the broiler. Cook the cauliflower and set it aside while you make the cheese sauce.

2 Melt the butter in a small saucepan over medium-high heat. Add the shallot and garlic and sauté for 2 to 3 minutes until softened. Add the flour and cook, whisking, for 3 minutes. Add the milk, salt, and Tabasco and continue whisking until the mixture comes to a boil. Remove the saucepan from the heat, whisk in the cheese a bit at a time, and continue whisking until the cheese has melted. (At this point, the cheese sauce can be refrigerated for up to 3 days.)

3 Put the cauliflower in a gratin dish or another heat-proof serving dish and pour the sauce over it. Run the dish under the preheated broiler until the sauce is bubbling and golden brown, or use a kitchen torch to brown the sauce.

PSST

Change the cheese and give yourself a new dish. Some great choices are smoked Gouda, imported Swiss (Emmentaler or Gruyère), yellow cheddar, Havarti (plain or with dill), smoked mozzarella, Provolone, Parmigiano-Reggiano, blue, Monterey Jack (aged or not), or Boursin. You can also toast some fresh bread crumbs in a little olive oil and sprinkle the bread crumbs over the cheese sauce before putting the cauliflower under the broiler.

CAULIFLOWER WITH CRUNCHY BREAD CRUMBS

Showered with crispy, cheesy bread crumbs, this dish is a winner any night of the week.

SERVES **6**

2 CUPS WATER OR CHICKEN OR VEGETABLE STOCK (PAGE 19 OR 21) OR STORE-BOUGHT CHICKEN OR VEGETABLE BROTH

1 LARGE HEAD CAULIFLOWER, CUT INTO LARGE FLORETS (ABOUT 6 CUPS)

1½ TEASPOONS SALT

½ TEASPOON FRESHLY GROUND BLACK PEPPER

4 TABLESPOONS EXTRA-VIRGIN OLIVE OIL

1 CUP FRESH BREAD CRUMBS

2 TABLESPOONS FRESHLY GRATED PARMIGIANO-REGGIANO

1 TABLESPOON FINELY CHOPPED FRESH FLAT-LEAF PARSLEY

1 Pour the water into the pressure cooker. Place the trivet and steamer basket in the bottom and put the cauliflower in the basket. Lock the lid in place and cook at high pressure for 3 minutes.

2 Quick release the pressure and remove the lid, tilting the pot away from you to avoid the escaping steam. Carefully remove the basket, transfer the cauliflower to a serving platter, and sprinkle with the salt, pepper, and 2 tablespoons of the oil, tossing to coat.

3 In a small skillet, heat the remaining 2 tablespoons of oil over high heat and add the bread crumbs. Toast them by tossing them in the oil until they become golden brown. Remove from the heat and add the cheese and parsley. Sprinkle the bread crumb mixture over the cauliflower and serve hot, warm, or at room temperature.

PSST

You can also sprinkle these cheesy crumbs over a whole cauliflower or almost any steamed vegetable. Leftover crumbs can be stored in zipper-top plastic bags in the freezer for up to 6 months.

CURRIED CAULIFLOWER AND POTATOES

This is a standard dish in many Indian restaurants, and you can easily make it at home. The pressure cooker seals in the flavors of the vegetables, and in three minutes, you have a lovely dish with crisp cauliflower and flavorful cubes of potatoes. Sweet petite peas balance the flavor of the curry.

SERVES 6

2 TABLESPOONS CANOLA OIL

1 CUP FINELY CHOPPED SWEET ONION, SUCH AS VIDALIA

1 GARLIC CLOVE, MINCED

1 TEASPOON GRATED FRESH GINGER

2 TEASPOONS MADRAS CURRY POWDER (SEE PSST)

4 MEDIUM YUKON GOLD POTATOES, CUT INTO ½-INCH CUBES (ABOUT 2 CUPS)

1 LARGE HEAD CAULIFLOWER, CUT INTO LARGE FLORETS (ABOUT 6 CUPS)

1½ CUPS CHICKEN STOCK (PAGE 19) OR STORE-BOUGHT CHICKEN BROTH

1 CUP FROZEN PETITE PEAS, DEFROSTED

SALT AND FRESHLY GROUND BLACK PEPPER (OPTIONAL)

1 CUP NONFAT YOGURT (OPTIONAL)

1 CUP FRUIT CHUTNEY (OPTIONAL)

1 Heat the oil in the pressure cooker over medium-high heat. Add the onion, garlic, ginger, and curry powder, stirring to blend, and sauté for about 2 minutes, until fragrant. Add the potatoes and stir until they are coated with the spices. Add the cauliflower and stock, stirring to blend. Lock the lid in place and cook at high pressure for 3 minutes.

2 Quick release the pressure and remove the lid, tilting the pot away from you to avoid the escaping steam. Stir in the peas and cook for another minute over medium heat to warm the peas. Using a slotted spoon, transfer the vegetables to a serving bowl and cover with aluminum foil to keep warm. Bring the sauce to a boil, taste for salt and pepper, and adjust the seasoning if needed. Spoon some of the sauce over the vegetables and, if you like, serve with nonfat yogurt and your favorite sweet chutney.

PSST

Many people use this dish as a stuffing for pita bread. It makes a great snack or luncheon dish.

Madras curry is what I call the Goldilocks of curry powder. Not too spicy and not too bland, it's just right. If you prefer a spicier curry, use it sparingly, because cooking under pressure tends to increase the heat.

CURRIED CAULIFLOWER WITH TOMATOES AND APRICOTS

Vegetarian dishes are some of my favorites, especially when I'm in the mood to create something different for dinner. This dish came about after I finished reading a travel book about India and its cuisine. I had noted the different types of curry and the use of cauliflower in so many recipes. Cauliflower can be strong in flavor and aroma, but this dish has a pleasing sweet and savory taste, thanks to the dried apricots and curry powder. Your family will love it served alongside grilled chicken or seafood or as a main dish served with rice.

SERVES **6** to **8**

2 TABLESPOONS CANOLA OIL

1 CUP FINELY CHOPPED RED ONION

2 GARLIC CLOVES, MINCED

2 TEASPOONS MADRAS CURRY POWDER

ONE 14½-OUNCE CAN CHOPPED TOMATOES WITH THEIR JUICE

½ CUP DRIED APRICOTS (ABOUT 8), COARSELY CHOPPED

1 LARGE HEAD CAULIFLOWER, CUT INTO FLORETS (ABOUT 6 CUPS)

1½ CUPS VEGETABLE STOCK (PAGE 21) OR STORE-BOUGHT VEGETABLE BROTH

2 TABLESPOONS ORANGE JUICE

SALT AND FRESHLY GROUND BLACK PEPPER (OPTIONAL)

1 Heat the oil in the pressure cooker over medium-high heat. Add the onion, garlic, and curry powder and sauté until the onion is fragrant, 2 to 3 minutes. Add the tomatoes, apricots, cauliflower, and stock, stirring to blend. Lock the lid in place and cook at high pressure for 4 minutes.

2 Quick release the pressure and remove the lid, tilting the pot away from you to avoid the escaping steam. Stir in the orange juice, taste for seasoning, and add salt and pepper if needed. Serve as a side dish or over rice.

Corn

Corn on the cob cooked under pressure comes out tender and sweet, without losing any of its fresh-picked taste. I like to wrap the corn in aluminum foil with a favorite butter. That way it's ready to go when it emerges from the pressure cooker, perfectly tender and dripping with flavor. If you had an abundance of corn during the summer and froze the corn kernels, or if you want to cook packaged frozen corn, the pressure cooker will do this very well, without any loss of flavor or texture. Frozen corn kernels should steam in the pressure cooker for 5 minutes.

SUGAR SNAP PEA AND CORN SUCCOTASH

This bright green and yellow side dish is brimming with crisp, fresh flavors, accented by smoky bacon and a garnish of fresh chives. It's terrific served with grilled or roasted entrées and makes a beautiful bed for grilled seafood or chicken.

SERVES **4** TO **6**

....

6 THICK-CUT BACON STRIPS, CUT CROSSWISE INTO PIECES ½ INCH WIDE

1 CUP FINELY CHOPPED SWEET ONION, SUCH AS VIDALIA

6 CUPS FRESH CORN KERNELS, CUT FROM THE COB (ABOUT 8 LARGE OR 10 MEDIUM EARS OF CORN)

3 CUPS SUGAR SNAP PEAS, TRIMMED AND TOUGH STRINGS REMOVED

½ CUP CHICKEN STOCK (PAGE 19) OR STORE-BOUGHT CHICKEN BROTH

2 TEASPOONS SUGAR

1 TEASPOON SALT

½ TEASPOON FRESHLY GROUND BLACK PEPPER

2 TABLESPOONS FINELY CHOPPED FRESH CHIVES FOR GARNISH

1 Cook the bacon in the pressure cooker over medium-high heat until crisp. Remove the bacon, drain on paper towels, and set aside. Remove all but 2 tablespoons of the fat from the pan. Add the onion and cook for 2 minutes, or until it begins to soften. Add the corn, snap peas, stock, sugar, salt, and pepper and toss to combine. Lock the lid in place and cook at high pressure for 2 minutes.

2 Quick release the pressure and remove the lid, tilting the pot away from you to avoid the escaping steam. Stir the bacon into the vegetables. Using a slotted spoon, transfer to a serving bowl and garnish with the chives before serving.

CORN ON THE COB WITH CHIPOTLE BUTTER

Try this recipe with the Chipotle Butter, or choose another flavored butter (see the variations on the facing page). This recipe can be used to cook fresh corn or frozen corn that has been defrosted. If the ears of corn are too large to fit into the steamer basket (you will have to do a little measuring), cut them in half and stack them. You can cook up to six full ears of corn (twelve halves) using this method. But it's a fast process, so if you are serving a crowd, you can definitely keep on going, reloading the cooker after one batch is cooked. You can keep the corn warm in a warming drawer in your oven or in a slow cooker set on warm.

SERVES 4 TO 6

1 CUP WATER

6 EARS CORN, ENDS TRIMMED, HUSKS AND SILK REMOVED

CHIPOTLE BUTTER (FACING PAGE)

1 Pour the water into the pressure cooker and arrange the trivet and steamer basket in the bottom. Cut 6 pieces of aluminum foil large enough to wrap a whole ear of corn. Lay each ear in the middle of an aluminum foil sheet and spread with about 2 table-spoons of the butter. Wrap up the corn in the foil and put in the steamer basket. Lock the lid in place and cook at high pressure for 2 minutes.

2 Quick release the pressure and remove the lid, tilting the pot away from you to avoid the escaping steam. Remove the steamer basket and allow the corn to rest for 3 minutes. Remove the foil and serve the corn with the remaining 4 tablespoons of flavored butter.

CHIPOTLE BUTTER

MAKES 1 CUP

1 CUP (2 STICKS) UNSALTED
BUTTER, SOFTENED

2 CHIPOTLE CHILES IN ADOBO
SAUCE, FINELY CHOPPED

1 TABLESPOON FINELY CHOPPED
FRESH CILANTRO

1 TEASPOON FINELY CHOPPED
GREEN ONIONS (GREEN AND
WHITE PARTS)

In a small bowl, stir together all the ingredients until blended. Store the butter in an airtight container and refrigerate for up to 1 month or freeze for up to 3 months.

VARIATIONS

Garlic Parmesan Butter: Omit the adobo sauce, cilantro, and green onions and combine the butter with 3 minced garlic cloves, ¼ cup of freshly grated Parmigiano-Reggiano cheese, and 1 teaspoon of dried oregano.

Sun-Dried Tomato Butter: Omit the adobo sauce, cilantro, and green onions and combine the butter with ¼ cup of sun-dried tomatoes packed in oil, drained and finely chopped; 2 tablespoons of finely chopped fresh flat-leaf parsley; 2 minced garlic cloves; and 2 tablespoons of finely chopped fresh basil.

Tarragon Dijon Butter: Omit the adobo sauce, cilantro, and green onions and combine the butter with 2 tablespoons of finely chopped fresh tarragon, 1 tablespoon of finely chopped shallot, and 1 tablespoon of Dijon mustard.

Butternut Squash

The bulbous butternut hides luscious flesh under-neath its plain manila skin. Once the flesh is cooked, your possibilities for serving are endless. Sweet and creamy, butternut squash has a lovely consistency, but it can take more than forty-five minutes to become tender with conventional cooking. The pressure cooker, on the other hand, cooks the squash in less than ten minutes. From there, you can make any number of delicious side dishes or fantastic soups. Always cut the pieces into uniform size to ensure even cooking.

BASIC BUTTERNUT SQUASH

I follow this simple recipe if I have a squash that I'm not ready to use. Then I store the cooked squash in the freezer and eventually I turn it into a side dish or soup. This is a great way to take advantage of the produce from your garden, the farmers' market, or a sale at your local market. Always peel the squash and seed it before pressure cooking; and discard the peels and seeds in the garbage or compost and not down the disposal, as they will clog it.

SERVES 6

1 CUP WATER, OR CHICKEN OR VEGETABLE STOCK (PAGE 19 OR 21) OR STORE-BOUGHT CHICKEN OR VEGETABLE BROTH

4 CUPS CHOPPED BUTTERNUT SQUASH (1-INCH CHUNKS)

1½ TEASPOONS SALT

½ TEASPOON FRESHLY GROUND BLACK PEPPER

3 TABLESPOONS EXTRA-VIRGIN OLIVE OIL

1 Pour the water into the pressure cooker. Arrange the trivet and steamer basket in the bottom and put the squash in the basket. Lock the lid in place and cook at high pressure for 5 minutes.

2 Quick release the pressure and remove the lid, tilting the pot away from you to avoid the escaping steam. Test the squash with the tip of a sharp knife to make sure it is tender. If it is still hard, return the lid to the pressure cooker but don't lock it. Let the squash steam for about 5 minutes off the heat. Remove the steamer basket. Transfer the squash to a serving bowl, season with the salt and pepper, and drizzle with the olive oil. Or, if preparing in advance, cool and store in airtight containers in the refrigerator for up to 2 days or in the freezer for up to 2 months.

PSST

Sometimes vegetables don't cook all the way through during the suggested cooking time, which can happen for a variety of reasons. The best way to finish the vegetable is to put the lid back on the pot and allow the vegetable to continue steaming without pressure.

BUTTERNUT SQUASH WITH GOLDEN RAISINS, CINNAMON, AND ALMONDS

Here, the cinnamon-infused squash is studded with nuggets of golden raisins and crunchy almonds, which make a delicious counterpoint to the creamy texture of the squash. This makes a terrific side dish to accompany poultry or pork.

SERVES 6

4 TABLESPOONS UNSALTED BUTTER

½ CUP FINELY CHOPPED SWEET ONION, SUCH AS VIDALIA

1 TEASPOON GROUND CINNAMON

¼ TEASPOON FRESHLY GRATED NUTMEG

4 CUPS CHOPPED BUTTERNUT SQUASH (1-INCH CHUNKS)

½ CUP CHICKEN OR VEGETABLE STOCK (PAGE 19 OR 21) OR STORE-BOUGHT CHICKEN OR VEGETABLE BROTH

¼ TO ⅓ CUP HEAVY CREAM

1 CUP GOLDEN RAISINS

½ CUP FINELY CHOPPED TOASTED ALMONDS (SEE PSST)

1 Melt 2 tablespoons of the butter in the pressure cooker over medium-high heat. Add the onion, cinnamon, and nutmeg and cook for 2 minutes, or until the onion begins to soften. Add the squash and stock. Lock the lid in place and cook at high pressure for 5 minutes.

2 Quick release the pressure and remove the lid, tilting the pot away from you to avoid the escaping steam. Mash the squash, incorporating the remaining 2 tablespoons of butter and the cream. Stir in the raisins and almonds, transfer to a serving dish, and serve immediately.

PSST

Chopped toasted walnuts, pecans, or macadamia nuts are all terrific in this dish instead of the almonds.

To toast nuts: Preheat the oven to 350 degrees F. Arrange the nuts in one layer on a baking sheet covered with parchment paper or a silicone baking liner. Sliced almonds are very thin, and will only take about 7 minutes to toast. Other nuts, like pecans, walnuts, and macadamia nuts, will take about 15 minutes. About halfway through the baking time, shake the pan to turn the nuts. Your cue that they're done will be their aroma as they begin to release their natural oils. Immediately transfer the nuts to a bowl to stop them from toasting further.

MASHED BUTTERNUT SQUASH WITH SAGE AND PANCETTA

In this lovely dish from Italy, the squash cooks with sage and pancetta, which enliven the sweet squash, giving it a smoky, woodsy flavor. Serve this with the Sunday roast chicken or Thanksgiving turkey for an extraordinary side.

SERVES **6**

....

2 TABLESPOONS EXTRA-VIRGIN OLIVE OIL

2 PANCETTA SLICES, CUT INTO SMALL DICE

6 FRESH SAGE LEAVES, THINLY SLICED

½ CUP CHICKEN OR VEGETABLE STOCK (PAGE 19 OR 21) OR STORE-BOUGHT CHICKEN OR VEGETABLE BROTH

4 CUPS CHOPPED BUTTERNUT SQUASH (1-INCH CHUNKS)

2 TABLESPOONS UNSALTED BUTTER

¼ TO ⅓ CUP HEAVY CREAM

1 Heat the oil in the pressure cooker over medium-high heat. Add the pancetta and cook until it renders some fat and begins to crisp. Add the sage and sauté for another minute, or until it is fragrant. Add the stock and squash. Lock the lid in place and cook at high pressure for 5 minutes.

2 Quick release the pressure and remove the lid, tilting the pot away from you to avoid the escaping steam. Add the butter and cream to the pot and mash the squash. Transfer the squash to a serving dish and serve immediately.

ORANGE AND FIVE-SPICE BUTTERNUT SQUASH

Squash with a bit of an Asian twist is just the right side dish to serve with grilled chicken or pork skewers. Flavored with orange, a bit of soy, five-spice powder, and a finish of sesame oil, this squash could end up on your list of family favorites.

SERVES 6

½ CUP ORANGE JUICE

2 TABLESPOONS SOY SAUCE

1 TEASPOON FIVE-SPICE POWDER (SEE PSST)

2 TABLESPOONS UNSALTED BUTTER, MELTED

4 CUPS CHOPPED BUTTERNUT SQUASH (1-INCH CHUNKS)

1 TABLESPOON TOASTED SESAME OIL

1 LARGE NAVEL ORANGE, SKIN LEFT ON, SLICED ½ INCH THICK

¼ CUP TOASTED SESAME SEEDS

1 Pour the orange juice and soy sauce into the pressure cooker and stir to combine. Stir the five-spice powder into the butter. Put the squash in a mixing bowl, add the butter mixture, and toss the squash to coat. Transfer to the pressure cooker. Lock the lid in place and cook at high pressure for 5 minutes.

2 Quick release the pressure and remove the lid, tilting the pot away from you to avoid the escaping steam. Using a slotted spoon, transfer the squash to a serving dish. Drizzle with the sesame oil and arrange the orange slices around the squash. Sprinkle the squash with the sesame seeds and serve.

PSST

Five-spice powder is a blend of star anise, cinnamon, cloves, fennel, and Szechuan pepper. Sometimes ground ginger or anise seeds are included, too. The powder is sold in the Asian or spice section of most supermarkets.

AMARETTO-GLAZED BUTTERNUT SQUASH AND PEARS

Amaretto liqueur glazes this squash and pear duet, lending the dish an almond flavor with a hint of apricot, for a scrumptious side dish. A sprinkling of crushed amaretti cookies over the top give it a nice crunch. You'll never put marshmallows on top of squash again! I love to serve this in the fall with a roast chicken or pork dish.

SERVES **6**

4 TABLESPOONS UNSALTED BUTTER

¼ CUP AMARETTO DI SARRONO

½ CUP CHICKEN OR VEGETABLE STOCK (PAGE 19 OR 21) OR STORE-BOUGHT CHICKEN OR VEGETABLE BROTH

2 TABLESPOONS LIGHT BROWN SUGAR

2 CUPS CHOPPED BUTTERNUT SQUASH (1-INCH CHUNKS)

3 MEDIUM FIRM RED PEARS, SUCH AS ANJOU OR BARTLETT, PEELED, CORED, AND CUT INTO 1-INCH CHUNKS

4 AMARETTI COOKIES, CRUSHED, FOR GARNISH (ABOUT ½ CUP; OPTIONAL)

1 Melt 2 tablespoons of the butter in the pressure cooker over medium-high heat. Add the Amaretto, stock, and sugar, stirring to blend. Add the squash and pears to the pot. Lock the lid in place and cook at high pressure for 4 minutes.

2 Quick release the pressure and remove the lid, tilting the pot away from you to avoid the escaping steam. Using a slotted spoon, transfer the squash and pears to a serving bowl and cover with aluminum foil to keep warm. Add the remaining 2 table-spoons of butter to the liquid in the pressure cooker and bring to a boil over medium-high heat. Continue boiling to reduce the liquid in the pot to a glaze, 5 to 7 minutes. Pour the glaze over the squash and garnish with the crushed amaretti (if using).

APPLE CIDER–GLAZED BUTTERNUT SQUASH

Dried apples and squash are a terrific combination. The sweet squash soaks up the flavor of the apples, resulting in a side dish that is almost like dessert, and that's a good thing when you are feeding fussy children! This is another great dish for the holidays or to serve alongside your favorite pork or poultry entrée.

SERVES **6**

4 TABLESPOONS UNSALTED BUTTER

1 CUP APPLE CIDER

2 TABLESPOONS LIGHT BROWN SUGAR

1 CUP DRIED APPLES, COARSELY CHOPPED

3 CUPS CHOPPED BUTTERNUT SQUASH (1-INCH CHUNKS)

½ CUP FINELY CHOPPED TOASTED PECANS FOR GARNISH (OPTIONAL; SEE PSST ON PAGE 114)

1 Melt 2 tablespoons of the butter in the pressure cooker over medium-high heat. Add the cider and sugar and stir to blend. Add the apples and squash. Lock the lid in place and cook at high pressure for 4 minutes.

2 Quick release the pressure and remove the lid, tilting the pot away from you to avoid the escaping steam. Using a slotted spoon, transfer the apples and squash to a serving dish and cover with foil to keep warm. Add the remaining 2 tablespoons of butter to the liquid in the pressure cooker and bring the sauce to a boil over high heat. Continue boiling until you've reduced the sauce to a syrupy consistency, 5 to 7 minutes. Pour the sauce over the warm squash and garnish with the pecans (if using).

Potatoes

Versatile, inexpensive, and simple to prepare, potatoes are a popular starch. They are available in a variety of colors (golden, purple, white, and red), sizes, and types (for example, russet and Yukon Gold). You'll find a good assortment in most supermarkets, and if you are lucky enough to have a local farmers' market, you will find even more variety when potatoes come into season.

Mashed potatoes are one of the most popular sides for the dinner table, but because of their twenty- to thirty-minute cooking time, they don't seem to make it to the table all that often, or a powdered imitation takes their place. The pressure cooker makes short work of steaming or boiling potatoes, and within ten minutes, you can be mashing them and turning out terrific dishes.

I love to vary the flavor and texture, so I've included lots of ways to mash your potatoes. The best type of potato for mashing is the russet, or baking potato. High in starch, it has a dry, mealy flesh, which is easily transformed into the ethereal, creamy mashed potato dish we all love. That being said, Yukon Gold, red-skinned, and other waxy, low-starch potatoes are also good mashed. They really shine, though, in potato salads and gratins because they tolerate dressings well and absorb liquids readily.

How Much Is Enough

Since potatoes are not uniform in size, it may be difficult to figure out how much will serve your family and friends. As a general rule, 1 pound of potatoes will yield 2 to 2½ cups of mashed potatoes, which should feed 4 to 5 people (½ cup of mashed potatoes per person). But if you are having the frat boys for dinner, plan on a *lot* of potatoes! Here's another way to calculate the number of potatoes you need: Use 1 medium to large baking potato for each person when mashing, and 1 medium Yukon Gold per person for salads and gratins. But, of course, if you have big eaters or potato lovers in your family, adjust the amounts accordingly.

Potatoes are a tuber. They are the underground stem of the potato plant, and since they're dug out of the ground, they will have some grit and dirt on them when you buy them. So scrub them with a vegetable brush before using.

What to Look For

If you would like to use the potato skins, choose ones that are smooth and unblemished, with no wrinkles. Avoid potatoes with sprouts starting to grow from the "eyes" or pockets of the potatoes. This means they have been stored for too long, and will be mushy or fall apart when cooked.

Beware of a green tinge on potato skins. It comes from exposure to light, which can happen in the store or in your kitchen if you leave them on the counter. The green color is a toxin called solanine, which develops when the eyes begin to sprout. Solanine will give you a stomachache if you eat it, but you can safely peel away all the green and use the rest of the potato.

How to Store Potatoes

Store your spuds in a cool, dry, dark place, such as a cupboard or under a counter. Or keep them in a paper bag on the counter; that way they won't be exposed to light. Don't keep the potatoes in the fridge. And don't store them near onions or other root vegetables, as they tend to sprout rapidly when they hang around other roots.

BASIC STEAMED POTATOES

This simple method for steaming potatoes will allow you to make any number of potato dishes. These side dishes won't disappoint, and you will love how quickly they come together. For steamed potatoes, it's best to use a low-starch potato. You can use those potatoes you've been admiring in the farmers' market—Peruvian purple, fingerling, Yellow Finn, White Rose, banana, and Russian Red—for this recipe and for any of the steamed potato recipes that follow. The more common Yukon Gold and Red Bliss will work, too. I really don't recommend high-starch baking potatoes for these recipes; they tend to disintegrate. Peeling the potatoes before steaming is optional. If the peels are pristine—not wrinkled or green—then go ahead and keep them. But if the skin is not beautiful, peel them before steaming.

SERVES **4** TO **6**

1½ CUPS WATER

2½ POUNDS SMALL LOW-STARCH POTATOES, SUCH AS FINGERLING, YUKON GOLD, OR RED BLISS, SCRUBBED, PEELED IF NECESSARY, AND HALVED

2 TEASPOONS COARSE SALT

½ TEASPOON FRESHLY GROUND BLACK PEPPER

2 TABLESPOONS EXTRA-VIRGIN OLIVE OIL

1 Pour the water into the pressure cooker. Arrange the trivet and steamer basket in the bottom and stack the potatoes in the basket. Lock the lid in place and cook at high pressure for 5 minutes.

2 Quick release the pressure and remove the lid, tilting the pot away from you to avoid the escaping steam. Drain the potatoes and transfer to a serving bowl.

3 Sprinkle with the salt and pepper, drizzle with the oil, and toss to coat. Serve the potatoes immediately.

PARSLEY AND CHIVE STEAMED POTATOES

Fresh chives and parsley in a lemony butter sauce gives these potatoes a zesty kick. Serve them with poultry or seafood for a change of pace.

SERVES **4** TO **6**

....

2½ POUNDS SMALL LOW-STARCH POTATOES, SUCH AS FINGERLING, YUKON GOLD, OR RED BLISS, SCRUBBED, PEELED IF NECESSARY, HALVED, AND STEAMED (SEE FACING PAGE)

½ CUP (1 STICK) UNSALTED BUTTER, MELTED

6 DROPS OF TABASCO OR ANOTHER HOT SAUCE

GRATED ZEST OF 1 LEMON

¼ CUP FINELY CHOPPED FRESH FLAT-LEAF PARSLEY

2 TABLESPOONS FINELY CHOPPED FRESH CHIVES

1 TEASPOON SALT

¼ TEASPOON SWEET PAPRIKA

Drain the steamed potatoes and return them to the pot. Place over medium heat. Add the butter, Tabasco, lemon zest, parsley, chives, salt, and paprika, shaking to coat the potatoes. Cook for 2 minutes and then transfer to a serving dish and serve hot.

GOAT CHEESE AND HERB STEAMED POTATOES

These potatoes are a little fancy but well worth the extra work. They're steamed and then baked with garlic, herbs, and goat cheese, which give the potatoes a delicious crust. Serve with pork, lamb, or beef.

SERVES **4** TO **6**

2½ POUNDS SMALL LOW-STARCH POTATOES, SUCH AS FINGERLING, YUKON GOLD, OR RED BLISS, SCRUBBED, PEELED IF NECESSARY, HALVED, AND STEAMED (SEE PAGE 120)

½ CUP EXTRA-VIRGIN OLIVE OIL

2 GARLIC CLOVES, MINCED

2 TEASPOONS FINELY CHOPPED FRESH THYME

1 TEASPOON FINELY CHOPPED FRESH CHIVES

1 TEASPOON FINELY CHOPPED FRESH FLAT-LEAF PARSLEY

ONE 11-OUNCE LOG GOAT CHEESE, CUT INTO ROUNDS ½ INCH THICK

1 Preheat the oven to 400 degrees F. Coat the inside of a 13-by-9-inch baking dish with nonstick cooking spray and set aside. Drain the steamed potatoes and transfer to the prepared baking dish.

2 In a small saucepan, heat the oil over medium-high heat. Add the garlic and sauté for 1 minute. Remove from the heat and add the herbs. Pour the herb mixture evenly over the potatoes. Top with the goat cheese and bake for 10 to 15 minutes, until the cheese is melted. Serve immediately.

POTATOES BOULANGERIE

French villagers would place a gratin of thinly sliced potatoes under roasting meat to flavor the potatoes with the meat juices. Inspired by that dish, we make steamed potatoes into something special to serve on the side for dinner. But instead of the meat juices, we use cream.

SERVES 4 TO 6

....

1½ CUPS WATER

2½ POUNDS SMALL LOW-STARCH POTATOES, SUCH AS FINGERLING, YUKON GOLD, OR RED BLISS, SCRUBBED, PEELED IF NECESSARY, AND HALVED

2 MEDIUM LEEKS (WHITE AND TENDER GREEN PARTS), CLEANED AND CUT INTO ½-INCH ROUNDS

1 CUP HEAVY CREAM

2 TEASPOONS DRIED THYME

1½ TEASPOONS SALT

1 TEASPOON TABASCO OR ANOTHER HOT SAUCE

6 BACON STRIPS, COOKED UNTIL CRISP, AND CRUMBLED

1 Pour the water into the pressure cooker. Arrange the trivet and steamer basket in the bottom and stack the potatoes in the basket. Arrange the leeks on top of the potatoes. Lock the lid in place and cook at high pressure for 5 minutes.

2 Quick release the pressure and remove the lid, tilting the pot away from you to avoid the escaping steam. Drain the potatoes and leeks and return them to the pot over medium-high heat. Add the cream, thyme, salt, and Tabasco and cook for 5 minutes to reduce the cream. Stir in the bacon, transfer to a serving dish, and serve immediately.

MASHED POTATOES

Unbelievably creamy, these potatoes are what you want when there is gravy around. But they are also scrumptious without gravy, and you can serve them with just about any entrée. This basic recipe is followed by an assortment of tasty variations. Think about your favorite flavor combinations and come up with your own!

SERVES 6 TO 8

1½ CUPS WATER

6 MEDIUM RUSSET POTATOES, SCRUBBED, PEELED, AND QUARTERED

⅓ TO ½ CUP HEAVY CREAM, WARMED

3 TABLESPOONS UNSALTED BUTTER

1½ TEASPOONS SALT, PLUS MORE IF NEEDED

½ TEASPOON FRESHLY GROUND BLACK PEPPER, PLUS MORE IF NEEDED

1 Pour the water into the pressure cooker. Arrange the trivet and steamer basket in the bottom and stack the potatoes in the basket. Lock the lid in place and cook at high pressure for 5 minutes.

2 Quick release the pressure and remove the lid, tilting the pot away from you to avoid the escaping steam. Drain the potatoes and return to the pot, shaking it to dry the potatoes. Mash in ⅓ cup of the cream and 2 tablespoons of the butter. Continue mashing until the potatoes are smooth, adding more cream if necessary. Stir in the salt and pepper and taste for seasoning. Add more salt and pepper if necessary and stir in the remaining tablespoon of butter. Serve the potatoes immediately.

PSST

Warming the cream helps to create a fluffier potato. When the cream is cold, it has a tendency to work the gluten in the potatoes, resulting in a stickier potato.

VARIATIONS

Smoked Gouda Mashed Potatoes: Smoked Gouda cheese adds a mellow, smoky quality when stirred into mashed potatoes. After you mash the cream and 2 tablespoons of butter into the cooked potatoes, stir in 1 cup of shredded smoked Gouda cheese, only ½ teaspoon of salt, the pepper, and the remaining tablespoon of butter.

Garlic Mashed Potatoes: Here, sliced garlic steams along with the potatoes. Sprinkle 6 sliced garlic cloves over the raw potatoes in the pressure cooker and proceed with the recipe.

Gorgonzola Mashed Potatoes: Gorgonzola blue cheese gives these potatoes a lot of personality. Mash the cream and only 1 tablespoon of butter into the cooked potatoes and then stir in 1 cup of crumbled Gorgonzola cheese, 1 teaspoon of salt, and the pepper. Garnish with 6 bacon strips, cooked until crisp, and crumbled.

Garlic and Herb Mashed Potatoes: Boursin cheese is delicately flavored with garlic and herbs, and it gives the potatoes a luxurious quality. Mash the cooked potatoes with only 3 tablespoons of cream, 1 tablespoon of butter, and one 5.2-ounce package of softened Boursin cheese. Stir in just ½ teaspoon of salt and ¼ teaspoon of freshly ground black pepper.

Sun-Dried Tomato and Pesto Mashed Potatoes: Dotted with sun-dried tomatoes and swirled with garlicky basil pesto, these are addictive. Mash the cream and ¼ cup of finely chopped sun-dried tomatoes packed in oil into the cooked potatoes. Stir in ¼ cup of homemade (see page 335) or store-bought basil pesto, ¼ cup of finely grated Parmigiano-Reggiano, ½ teaspoon of salt, and ¼ teaspoon of freshly ground black pepper.

Bacon, White Cheddar, and Scallion Mashed Potatoes: These are as good as a loaded baked potato! Mash ¼ cup of cream, ¼ cup of sour cream (at room temperature), 1½ cups of shredded sharp white Cheddar cheese, and 2 tablespoons of butter into the cooked potatoes. Stir in 3 tablespoons of finely chopped scallions (white and light green parts), ¼ teaspoon of salt, ¼ teaspoon of freshly ground black pepper, and 8 bacon strips, cooked until crisp, and crumbled. Stir in another tablespoon of butter.

CARAMELIZED ONION AND GRUYÈRE MASHED POTATOES

Caramelized onions are like gold in your freezer. They are great to have on hand to stir into dishes like this one, which tastes like French onion soup and Gruyère cheese mashed into potatoes. This recipe will give you leftover onions. If you want to make less, see the Psst.

SERVES 6 TO 8

CARAMELIZED ONIONS
½ CUP (1 STICK) UNSALTED BUTTER

2 TABLESPOONS EXTRA-VIRGIN OLIVE OIL

4 LARGE SWEET ONIONS, SUCH AS VIDALIA, HALVED AND CUT INTO ½-INCH-THICK HALF-MOONS

1½ TEASPOONS SALT

½ TEASPOON FRESHLY GROUND BLACK PEPPER

1 TEASPOON DRIED THYME

2 TABLESPOONS SUGAR

POTATOES
1½ CUPS WATER

6 MEDIUM RUSSET POTATOES, SCRUBBED, PEELED, AND QUARTERED

⅓ CUP HEAVY CREAM, WARMED

1½ CUPS SHREDDED GRUYÈRE OR EMMENTALER CHEESE

SALT AND FRESHLY GROUND BLACK PEPPER (OPTIONAL)

1 To make the onions: Melt the butter with the oil in a large skillet over medium-high heat. Add the onions, salt, pepper, thyme, and sugar. Stir the mixture to coat the onions and cook over medium heat for 30 minutes, or until the onions are golden. Remove from the heat and cool. You should have about 2 cups. Set aside ½ cup of the onions for the mashed potatoes. Cool the remainder completely and save for another use. (The onions will keep in airtight containers in the freezer for up to 3 months.)

2 To make the potatoes: Pour the water into the pressure cooker. Arrange the trivet and steamer basket in the bottom and stack the potatoes in the basket. Lock the lid in place and cook at high pressure for 5 minutes.

3 Quick release the pressure and remove the lid, tilting the pot away from you to avoid the escaping steam. Drain the potatoes and return to the pot, shaking it to dry the potatoes. Mash in the cream and continue mashing until the potatoes are smooth. Add the reserved ½ cup of caramelized onions and the cheese, stirring until blended. Taste for seasoning and add salt and pepper if necessary. Serve the potatoes immediately.

PSST

If you would like to make just half a recipe of caramelized onions, simply halve the quantities of the ingredients. You end up with 1 cup of caramelized onions. Use ½ cup for the potatoes and save the remaining ½ cup for another dish.

MOM'S OLD-FASHIONED POTATO SALAD

My mom's potato salad recipe appears on our table during the summer months for barbecues and on the Fourth of July. The pressure cooker helps make potato salad a reality even when your time is short. Give the potatoes eight minutes to steam and a short time to cool down. Then just toss the ingredients together and enjoy the rest of your day.

SERVES **6** TO **8**

1½ CUPS WATER

8 MEDIUM RED BLISS POTATOES, SCRUBBED (SEE PSST)

2 TEASPOONS WHITE VINEGAR

1 TEASPOON SALT

½ TEASPOON FRESHLY GROUND BLACK PEPPER

½ TEASPOON CELERY SEEDS

2 SCALLIONS (WHITE AND TENDER GREEN PARTS), FINELY CHOPPED

3 MEDIUM CELERY STALKS, FINELY CHOPPED

3 SWEET MIDGET PICKLES, FINELY CHOPPED

3 HARD-COOKED EGGS, DICED

1½ CUPS MAYONNAISE (LOW-FAT IS FINE)

1 TEASPOON PREPARED YELLOW MUSTARD

2 TEASPOONS MILK TO THIN THE MAYONNAISE

SWEET PAPRIKA FOR GARNISH (OPTIONAL)

1 Pour the water into the pressure cooker. Arrange the trivet and steamer basket in the bottom and stack the potatoes in the basket. Lock the lid in place and cook at high pressure for 10 minutes.

2 Quick release the pressure and remove the lid, tilting the pot away from you to avoid the escaping steam. Remove the potatoes and allow to cool completely.

3 When the potatoes are cool, peel them and cut into ¾-inch pieces, dropping them into a serving bowl as you work. Add the vinegar, salt, pepper, and celery seeds and toss to coat the potatoes. Stir in the scallions, celery, pickles, and eggs.

4 In a small mixing bowl, whisk together the mayonnaise, mustard, and milk until the mixture is well blended. Pour 1 cup of the dressing over the potatoes and toss until the potatoes are coated and the salad is well mixed. Cover the salad and remaining dressing and refrigerate for at least 2 hours and up to 12 hours. When ready to serve, remove the salad from the refrigerator and toss with some of the remaining dressing if the salad looks dry. Sprinkle with the paprika (if desired) before serving.

PSST

Even if the skins of the potatoes aren't perfect, steam the potatoes in their skins. Otherwise, the potatoes may become watery and disintegrate. Peeling the potatoes after cooking is much easier; the skins usually slip right off.

Hold back on the dressing. Since Red Bliss are low-starch potatoes, they tend to soak up the dressing quickly.

RED BLISS POTATO SALAD WITH LEMON-DILL DRESSING

Another potato salad for summertime parties, this one has a tangy, yogurt-based lemon-dill dressing with feta cheese. It's particularly delicious with burgers as well as with grilled chicken and lamb dishes. This is also a great side to take along to a potluck party.

SERVES **6** TO **8**

1½ CUPS WATER

8 MEDIUM RED BLISS POTATOES, SCRUBBED

1 RED BELL PEPPER

2 TEASPOONS WHITE VINEGAR

1 TEASPOON SALT

3 MEDIUM SCALLIONS (WHITE AND TENDER GREEN PARTS), FINELY CHOPPED

3 MEDIUM CELERY STALKS, FINELY CHOPPED

1½ CUPS GREEK-STYLE YOGURT

GRATED ZEST OF 1 LEMON

2 TEASPOONS FRESH LEMON JUICE

2 TEASPOONS FINELY CHOPPED FRESH DILL, PLUS ADDITIONAL SPRIGS FOR GARNISH

6 DROPS OF TABASCO OR ANOTHER HOT SAUCE

1 CUP CRUMBLED FETA CHEESE

2 TO 3 TABLESPOONS MILK TO THIN THE DRESSING (OPTIONAL)

1 Pour the water into the pressure cooker. Arrange the trivet and steamer basket in the bottom and stack the potatoes in the basket. Lock the lid in place and cook at high pressure for 8 minutes.

2 Quick release the pressure and remove the lid, tilting the pot away from you to avoid the escaping steam. Remove the potatoes and allow to cool completely. Meanwhile, halve the bell pepper lengthwise, seed, and derib. Finely chop half the pepper. Thinly slice the other half and set aside for a garnish.

3 Peel the cooled potatoes and cut into ¾-inch pieces. Transfer to a serving bowl and sprinkle with the vinegar and salt, tossing to coat. Add the scallions, celery, and chopped bell pepper, tossing to combine.

4 In a small bowl, whisk together the yogurt, lemon zest and juice, dill, Tabasco, and feta until blended. If the dressing is too thick, thin it with some milk. Pour half of the dressing over the potatoes and toss to coat. Cover the salad and remaining dressing and refrigerate for at least 2 hours and up to 12 hours. When ready to serve, toss the salad with as much of the reserved dressing as you need. Garnish with the dill sprigs and reserved strips of red bell pepper.

MOTHER LODE YUKON GOLD POTATO SALAD

We call this the mother lode salad because it's loaded with nuggets of scallion, bacon, and Cheddar cheese and bathed in a luscious, lemony sour cream dressing. The Yukon Gold potatoes give this salad a gorgeous golden color and lovely flavor. Serve it with grilled steaks or roasted pork or lamb.

SERVES **6** TO **8**

1½ CUPS WATER

8 MEDIUM YUKON GOLD POTATOES, SCRUBBED

2 TEASPOONS WHITE VINEGAR

2 TEASPOONS SALT

3 SCALLIONS (WHITE AND TENDER GREEN PARTS), FINELY CHOPPED

1 CUP SHREDDED SHARP CHEDDAR CHEESE (SEE PSST)

1 CUP SOUR CREAM

½ CUP MAYONNAISE

GRATED ZEST OF 1 LEMON

2 TEASPOONS FRESH LEMON JUICE

6 DROPS OF TABASCO OR ANOTHER HOT SAUCE

2 TO 3 TABLESPOONS MILK TO THIN THE DRESSING (OPTIONAL)

8 BACON STRIPS, COOKED UNTIL CRISP AND CRUMBLED (SEE PSST)

1 Pour the water into the pressure cooker. Arrange the trivet and steamer basket in the bottom and stack the potatoes in the basket. Lock the lid in place and cook at high pressure for 10 minutes.

2 Quick release the pressure and remove the lid, tilting the pot away from you to avoid the escaping steam. Remove the potatoes and allow to cool. Peel and cut into ¾-inch pieces. Sprinkle the potatoes with the vinegar and salt, tossing to coat the potatoes. Add the scallions and cheese.

3 In a small mixing bowl, whisk together the sour cream, mayonnaise, lemon zest and juice, and Tabasco. Thin the dressing with milk if needed. Pour half of the dressing over the potatoes and toss to coat. Cover the salad and remaining dressing and refrigerate for at least 2 hours and up to 12 hours. When ready to serve, sprinkle the bacon over the salad, and toss the salad with as much of the remaining dressing as you need. Serve immediately.

PSST

Yellow Cheddar shows up better in the salad, but white is also delicious.

Don't add the bacon until you are ready to serve the salad; the flavor tends to get lost in the salad if it's added ahead of time.

GERMAN POTATO SALAD

A favorite at tailgates and family picnics, this salad gets its pizzazz from a warm sweet-and-savory dressing and bits of bacon throughout. It can be made ahead and reheated before serving if you'd like.

SERVES 6 TO 8

1½ CUPS WATER

8 MEDIUM YUKON GOLD POTATOES, SCRUBBED AND CUT INTO ½-INCH PIECES

8 BACON STRIPS, CUT CROSSWISE INTO PIECES ½ INCH WIDE

1 CUP FINELY CHOPPED SWEET ONION, SUCH AS VIDALIA

2 TABLESPOONS LIGHT BROWN SUGAR

2 TABLESPOONS WHOLE-GRAIN MUSTARD

⅓ CUP CIDER VINEGAR

1 TABLESPOON CELERY SEEDS

6 DROPS OF TABASCO OR ANOTHER HOT SAUCE

SALT (OPTIONAL)

1 Pour the water into the pressure cooker. Arrange the trivet and steamer basket in the bottom and stack the potatoes in the basket. Lock the lid in place and cook at high pressure for 3 minutes.

2 Quick release the pressure and remove the lid, tilting the pot away from you to avoid the escaping steam. Remove the potatoes and set aside.

3 In a large nonreactive skillet over medium-high heat, cook the bacon until crisp. Remove all but 2 tablespoons of the fat from the skillet. Add the onion and sauté until it begins to soften, 2 to 3 minutes. Add the sugar, mustard, and vinegar and bring to a boil. Add the celery seeds and Tabasco and taste for seasoning. If the dressing is too acidic, add some salt or a teaspoon of water to balance the acid. Transfer the potatoes to the skillet and gently toss in the dressing. Serve the salad warm, at room temperature, or cool. (You can also refrigerate the salad for up to 12 hours, then rewarm in a skillet or in a slow cooker on low for 2 hours.)

PSST

I like to substitute hot sauce or Tabasco sauce for ground black pepper when the extra heat will benefit the finished dish. I particularly like Tabasco in creamy sauces and dressings.

POTATO SALAD NIÇOISE

This delicious salad is inspired by salade Niçoise, a French classic made famous in the United States by Julia Child. The salad usually includes green beans, potatoes, hard-cooked eggs, tuna, tomatoes, and olives, all of which are tossed in a vinaigrette dressing. The potato salad is a nice change of pace when paired with your favorite grilled entrée; I particularly like it with grilled fish. The dressing also makes a great marinade for chicken. Serve this salad at room temperature.

SERVES **6** TO **8**

1½ CUPS WATER

8 MEDIUM YUKON GOLD POTATOES, SCRUBBED

1 MEDIUM SHALLOT, FINELY CHOPPED

2 TABLESPOONS FINELY CHOPPED FRESH FLAT-LEAF PARSLEY

1 GARLIC CLOVE, MINCED

⅔ CUP EXTRA-VIRGIN OLIVE OIL

1 TABLESPOON DIJON MUSTARD

3 TABLESPOONS WHITE WINE VINEGAR

1 TEASPOON SALT

½ TEASPOON FRESHLY GROUND BLACK PEPPER

¼ CUP FINELY CHOPPED FRESH CHIVES FOR GARNISH

1 Pour the water into the pressure cooker. Arrange the trivet and steamer basket in the bottom and stack the potatoes in the basket. Lock the lid in place and cook at high pressure for 10 minutes.

2 Quick release the pressure and remove the lid, tilting the pot away from you to avoid the escaping steam. Remove the potatoes and allow to cool enough so you can handle them; they should still be warm. Peel the potatoes and slice ½ inch thick. Put them in a serving bowl.

3 In a small mixing bowl, whisk together the remaining ingredients except the chives and pour half of the dressing over the potatoes. Toss until the potatoes are coated with the dressing. Cover the salad and remaining dressing and refrigerate for at least 2 hours or overnight. One hour before serving, remove the salad and dressing from the refrigerator and allow to come to room temperature. Sprinkle the salad with as much of the reserved dressing as you need to moisten it and toss. Garnish with the chopped chives and serve.

Sweet Potatoes

Sweet potatoes are a delicious vegetable to eat year-round. Whether they are mashed or made into a sweet potato hash or braised, the pressure cooker makes short work of them, and the results are scrumptious. When you buy sweet potatoes at the market, look for unblemished skins that are tight, without any sprouting eyes. The potatoes should be firm, not spongy.

Red yams are a Southern cousin of the sweet potato. They are really a variety of sweet potato, usually from Louisiana, and they often show up on holiday tables. True yams have yellow flesh and are found mainly in Africa and Asia. Red yams and common sweet potatoes can be used in these recipes, since they will cook for the same amount of time.

ASIAN PEARS AND SWEET POTATO HASH

Sweet and smoky, this dish will pair beautifully with your favorite egg dish for brunch, or you can serve it on the side with pork or poultry.

SERVES **6** TO **8**

6 BACON STRIPS, CUT CROSSWISE INTO PIECES ½ INCH WIDE, FOR GARNISH

1 CUP FINELY CHOPPED RED ONION

1 TEASPOON DRIED THYME

PINCH OF CAYENNE PEPPER

2 MEDIUM ASIAN PEARS, PEELED, CORED, AND CHOPPED INTO ½-INCH PIECES

4 MEDIUM SWEET POTATOES, PEELED AND CUT INTO ½-INCH PIECES

1½ TEASPOONS SALT, PLUS MORE IF NEEDED

½ CUP APPLE CIDER

1 Cook the bacon in the pressure cooker over medium heat until it is crisp. Remove from the pan, transfer to paper towels to drain, and set aside. Remove all but 2 tablespoons of the fat from the pan. Add the onion, thyme, and cayenne and sauté for 2 minutes, or until the onion begins to soften. Add the pears, sweet potatoes, and salt, stirring to combine. Remove from the heat and add the apple cider. Lock the lid in place and cook at high pressure for 4 minutes.

2 Quick release the pressure and remove the lid, tilting the pot away from you to avoid the escaping steam. Stir the hash, taste for seasoning, and add more salt if needed. Using a slotted spoon, transfer the hash to a serving bowl, garnish with the reserved bacon, and serve immediately.

ORANGE SWEET POTATO MASH

These creamy sweet potatoes studded with nuggets of orange just might replace the marshmallow-capped ones on the Thanksgiving table. Flavored with ginger and nutmeg, they are a real crowd-pleaser. But you don't need to wait for Thanksgiving; serve these any night of the week.

SERVES 6 TO 8

1 CUP WATER

6 MEDIUM SWEET POTATOES, PEELED AND CUT INTO 1-INCH CHUNKS

1 NAVEL ORANGE

3 TABLESPOONS UNSALTED BUTTER

¼ TEASPOON GROUND GINGER

⅛ TEASPOON FRESHLY GROUND NUTMEG

⅓ TO ½ CUP ORANGE JUICE, AT ROOM TEMPERATURE

1½ TEASPOONS SALT

5 DROPS OF TABASCO OR ANOTHER HOT SAUCE

1 Pour the water into the pressure cooker. Arrange the trivet and steamer basket in the bottom and put the sweet potatoes in the basket. Lock the lid in place and cook at high pressure for 7 minutes. Meanwhile, peel the orange and remove the pith. Pull apart the orange segments and cut into ½-inch pieces.

2 Quick release the pressure and remove the lid, tilting the pot away from you to avoid the escaping steam. Carefully remove the steamer basket from the pressure cooker.

3 Melt the butter in a large skillet over medium heat. Add the ginger and nutmeg and cook for 1 minute. Add the sweet potatoes to the pan and mash them, adding as much of the orange juice as you need to make them smooth. Add the salt, Tabasco, and orange segments and stir until blended. Transfer the sweet potatoes to a serving bowl and serve immediately.

CINNAMON AND HONEY SWEET POTATOES

Here's another terrific treatment for sweet potatoes. This time, you steam them and finish them with a buttery cinnamon and honey sauce, which also works really well with carrots.

SERVES **6** TO **8**

....

1 CUP WATER

6 MEDIUM SWEET POTATOES, PEELED AND CUT INTO 1-INCH CHUNKS

½ CUP (1 STICK) UNSALTED BUTTER

1 TEASPOON GROUND CINNAMON

3 TABLESPOONS HONEY

1 Pour the water into the pressure cooker. Arrange the trivet and steamer basket in the bottom and put the sweet potatoes in the basket. Lock the lid in place and cook at high pressure for 7 minutes. While the sweet potatoes are cooking, melt the butter in a large skillet over medium-high heat. Stir in the cinnamon and honey and cook, stirring, for 3 to 4 minutes, until well blended. Remove from the heat, cover, and keep warm.

2 Quick release the pressure and remove the lid, tilting the pot away from you to avoid the escaping steam. Carefully remove the steamer basket and transfer the sweet potatoes to the skillet. Toss with the butter mixture and then transfer to a serving bowl. Serve hot.

SHERRIED APPLES AND SWEET POTATOES

This dish cooks in no time, and your family and friends will love the combination of apples, sweet potatoes, sherry, cinnamon, and nutmeg. It's a perfect side dish for a harvest dinner and goes well with both poultry and pork.

SERVES **6** TO **8**

2 CUPS WATER

4 LARGE SWEET POTATOES, PEELED AND CUT INTO 1-INCH CHUNKS

4 MEDIUM GRANNY SMITH APPLES, PEELED, CORED, AND CUT INTO 1-INCH CHUNKS

½ CUP (1 STICK) UNSALTED BUTTER, MELTED

½ CUP FIRMLY PACKED DARK BROWN SUGAR

3 TABLESPOONS CREAM SHERRY

1 TEASPOON GROUND CINNAMON

⅛ TEASPOON FRESHLY GRATED NUTMEG

1 Pour the water into the pressure cooker. Arrange the trivet and steamer basket in the bottom and stack the sweet potatoes and apples in the basket. Lock the lid in place and cook at high pressure for 7 minutes.

2 Quick release the pressure and remove the lid, tilting the pot away from you to avoid the escaping steam. Carefully transfer the sweet potatoes and apples to a mixing bowl. Mash the sweet potatoes and apples together and mash in the butter, sugar, sherry, cinnamon, and nutmeg. Transfer to a serving dish and serve hot.

Carrots

Carrots come in different colors, such as yellow, red, and purple. They range in size from baby carrots to the conventional ones you find in the market, which my family calls Bugs Bunny carrots. The baby carrots that are bagged and sold in the supermarket, though, aren't really babies at all. They are just larger carrots cut into smaller shapes. True baby carrots are quite expensive and can usually be found in gourmet markets or at your local farmers' market.

Whichever type you choose to use, the carrots will take less than ten minutes in the pressure cooker, and you will enjoy the full benefit of their nutrients, namely vitamin A and potassium. Carrots store their sugar in the core, so if a carrot is fat, it will probably be sweet all the way through. Avoid carrots that are split or cracked; they will be dry and unappetizing. If you like buying carrots with their tops still attached, make sure the tops are brilliant green and the end attached to the root isn't dark, which indicates the carrots are old.

STEAMED CARROTS

This basic recipe will get you started. You can use baby bagged carrots or the conventional ones.

SERVES **4** TO **6**

1½ CUPS WATER

1½ POUNDS CARROTS, PEELED AND CUT INTO 2-INCH LENGTHS, OR 1½ POUNDS BABY CARROTS

1½ TEASPOONS SALT

½ TEASPOON FRESHLY GROUND BLACK PEPPER

3 TO 4 TABLESPOONS EXTRA-VIRGIN OLIVE OIL

1 Pour the water into the pressure cooker. Arrange the trivet and steamer basket in the bottom and stack the carrots in the basket. Lock the lid in place and cook at high pressure for 5 minutes.

2 Quick release the pressure and remove the lid, tilting the pot away from you to avoid the escaping steam. Carefully remove the steamer basket and transfer the carrots to a serving dish. Season with the salt and pepper, drizzle with the olive oil, and stir to combine. Serve the carrots immediately.

GINGERED CARROTS

Braised in a sweet and savory broth, these ginger carrots will wake up the plainest rotisserie chicken or grilled pork chops. And they go from the stove top to the table in five minutes.

SERVES **4** TO **6**

2 TABLESPOONS UNSALTED BUTTER

1 TEASPOON GRATED FRESH GINGER

2 TABLESPOONS LIGHT BROWN SUGAR

½ CUP CHICKEN STOCK (PAGE 19) OR STORE-BOUGHT CHICKEN BROTH

1½ POUNDS CARROTS, PEELED AND CUT INTO ½-INCH ROUNDS

1 Melt the butter in the pressure cooker over medium-high heat. Add the ginger and sauté for 2 minutes, until fragrant. Add the sugar and stock, stirring to combine. Stir in the carrots. Lock the lid in place and cook at high pressure for 4 minutes.

2 Quick release the pressure and remove the lid, tilting the pot away from you to avoid the escaping steam. Transfer the carrots to a serving dish and serve immediately.

HONEYED CARROTS

This is one of my favorite carrot recipes because it is so simple to prepare and the braising liquid brings out the sweetness of the carrots. I serve this with poultry or pork, and it's terrific at Thanksgiving dinner in place of the ubiquitous yam casserole!

SERVES **4** TO **6**

2 TABLESPOONS UNSALTED BUTTER

1 SMALL SHALLOT, FINELY CHOPPED

½ TEASPOON DRIED THYME

2 TABLESPOONS HONEY

½ CUP ORANGE JUICE

½ CUP CHICKEN STOCK (PAGE 19) OR STORE-BOUGHT CHICKEN BROTH

1½ POUNDS CARROTS, PEELED AND CUT INTO 2-INCH LENGTHS

1 Melt the butter in the pressure cooker over medium-high heat. Add the shallot and thyme and sauté for 2 minutes, or until the shallot begins to soften. Add the honey, orange juice, and stock, stirring to combine. Add the carrots and toss them in the honey mixture. Lock the lid in place and cook at high pressure for 5 minutes.

2 Quick release the pressure and remove the lid, tilting the pot away from you to avoid the escaping steam. Using a slotted spoon, transfer the carrots to a serving dish and serve immediately.

CARROT PUDDING

Ramekins filled with a soufflé-like carrot mixture make a lovely addition to any special dinner, especially when poultry, pork, or seafood are on the table. Steam the carrots in the pressure cooker, prepare the pudding, and finish cooking it in ramekins in the pressure cooker, as you would any other pudding or crème brûlée.

SERVES **4** to **6**

1 RECIPE STEAMED CARROTS (PAGE 138), OLIVE OIL OMITTED

3 TABLESPOONS UNSALTED BUTTER, PLUS MORE FOR PANS

1 SMALL SHALLOT, FINELY CHOPPED

2 TABLESPOONS ALL-PURPOSE FLOUR

1½ CUPS MILK

⅛ TEASPOON FRESHLY GRATED NUTMEG

½ TEASPOON SALT

½ TEASPOON FRESHLY GROUND BLACK PEPPER

2 LARGE EGG YOLKS, LIGHTLY BEATEN

¼ CUP DEMERARA SUGAR

2 CUPS WATER

1 Mash the carrots in a large mixing bowl. In a small saucepan, melt the butter over medium-high heat. Add the shallot and sauté for 2 minutes, or until softened. Add the flour and cook for 2 to 3 minutes, whisking constantly. Add the milk and bring the sauce to a boil. Stir in the nutmeg, salt, and pepper. Whisk a bit of the sauce into the egg yolks and then transfer the egg mixture and the remaining sauce to the mashed carrots and stir to blend. Coat the insides of six 4-ounce ramekins with additional butter or nonstick cooking spray. Sprinkle with some of the sugar. Spoon the carrot pudding into the ramekins and cover each ramekin tightly with aluminum foil.

2 Pour the water into the pressure cooker. Arrange the trivet and steamer basket in the bottom and stack the ramekins in the basket. Lock the lid in place and cook at high pressure for 10 minutes.

3 Release the pressure naturally and remove the lid, tilting the pot away from you to avoid the escaping steam. Unwrap each ramekin and serve immediately. If you like, you can tip a pudding out onto each dinner plate.

Parsnips

Parsnips make a tasty substitute for carrots in many recipes, so do give them a try. They are delicious braised, mashed, or in gratins with other root veggies. Choose parsnips with a creamy white skin. They should feel rigid, like a fresh carrot, when you pick them up.

MASHED PARSNIPS AND CARROTS

Parsnips and carrots both have sweet flavors, and when mashed together, they are a treat. Try this recipe out on your family. The brown butter gives everything a nice smoky flavor, and your family may not even realize there are parsnips in the dish!

SERVES **4** TO **6**

1 CUP WATER

1 POUND CARROTS, PEELED AND SLICED ½ INCH THICK

1 POUND PARSNIPS, PEELED AND SLICED ½ INCH THICK

3 TABLESPOONS UNSALTED BUTTER

3 TABLESPOONS HEAVY CREAM

1½ TEASPOONS SALT

½ TEASPOON FRESHLY GROUND BLACK PEPPER

1 Pour the water into the pressure cooker. Arrange the trivet and steamer basket in the bottom and load the basket with the carrots and parsnips. Lock the lid in place and cook at high pressure for 2 minutes.

2 Quick release the pressure and remove the lid, tilting the pot away from you to avoid the escaping steam. Drain the water from the pot and return the vegetables to the pressure cooker.

3 In a small saucepan over medium heat, melt the butter and cook until it begins to turn golden brown. Remove the butter from the heat and pour it over the vegetables. Add the cream, sprinkle with the salt and pepper, and mash the vegetables with the butter. Transfer the mash to a serving bowl and serve immediately.

HERBED PARSNIPS

Braised with fresh herbs, these parsnips would make a nice side dish to serve alongside grilled chicken or seafood.

SERVES **4** TO **6**

....

½ CUP CHICKEN OR VEGETABLE STOCK
(PAGE 19 OR 21) OR STORE-BOUGHT
CHICKEN OR VEGETABLE BROTH

2 POUNDS PARSNIPS, PEELED AND CUT
INTO ½-INCH PIECES

3 TABLESPOONS UNSALTED BUTTER

2 TEASPOONS FINELY CHOPPED
FRESH THYME

½ TEASPOON FINELY CHOPPED
FRESH SAGE

1 TABLESPOON FINELY CHOPPED
FRESH CHIVES

1 TEASPOON SALT

½ TEASPOON FRESHLY GROUND BLACK
PEPPER

1 Combine all the ingredients in the pressure cooker. Lock the lid in place and cook at high pressure for 2 minutes.

2 Quick release the pressure and remove the lid, tilting the pot away from you to avoid the escaping steam. Transfer the parsnips to a serving bowl and spoon a bit of the braising liquid over them. Serve immediately.

PARSNIP AND POTATO MASH

Parsnips add sweetness to everyday mashed potatoes, transforming them into a new side dish to try on your family.

2 CUPS WATER

1 POUND RUSSET POTATOES, PEELED AND CUT INTO 2-INCH PIECES

1 POUND PARSNIPS, PEELED AND CUT INTO 2-INCH PIECES

⅓ CUP HEAVY CREAM, WARMED

2 TABLESPOONS UNSALTED BUTTER

1½ TEASPOONS SALT

½ TEASPOON FRESHLY GROUND BLACK PEPPER

1 Pour the water into the pressure cooker. Arrange the trivet and steamer basket in the bottom and load the potatoes and parsnips into the basket. Lock the lid in place and cook at high pressure for 5 minutes.

2 Quick release the pressure and remove the lid, tilting the pot away from you to avoid the escaping steam. Drain the vegetables and return them to the pot. Put the pot over low heat. Add the cream, butter, salt, and pepper and mash them into the vegetables until smooth. Transfer to a serving bowl and serve immediately.

Beets

It's a shame beets don't show up on the dinner table more often. They are rich in vitamins (folic acid and vitamin C), minerals (iron and potassium), and fiber. Naturally sweet, steamed beets are delicious cold in a salad with a good-quality olive oil. Or serve them warm with a nice sauce. Many markets now sell varicolored beets, and it's fun to mix the golden and orange beets in with the traditional red beets to introduce more colors and flavors. The gold and orange ones have a sweeter and more delicate flavor. If the beet greens are tender, you can cook them as you would collards or kale for a delicious side dish.

Large beets cook in about 20 minutes in the pressure cooker, which is about half the time they take with a conventional method. When trimming them, leave on about ¾ inch of the stem. To test for doneness, insert the tip of a sharp knife into the center of a beet; the knife should go all the way through without resistance.

Although the beet recipes that follow wrap up the root vegetables in this chapter, there are two more root vegetables you can try on your own: turnips and rutabagas. Both should be peeled and cut into 1-inch chunks. They cook at high pressure for 6 minutes. Give them a quick release and then mash them or serve with butter or olive oil, salt, and pepper.

BABY BEET AND GOAT CHEESE SALAD

Tiny beets, young greens, goat cheese, and toasted walnuts make an elegant salad, especially when tossed with a raspberry vinaigrette. Serve it for a special dinner.

SERVES 6

1 CUP WATER

16 BABY BEETS, PREFERABLY IN A VARIETY OF COLORS, TRIMMED AND SCRUBBED (SEE PSST)

1 CUP CANOLA OIL

½ CUP RASPBERRY VINEGAR

1 SMALL SHALLOT, FINELY CHOPPED

2 TABLESPOONS SUGAR

1 TEASPOON SALT

½ TEASPOON FRESHLY GROUND BLACK PEPPER

3 CUPS MESCLUN

1½ CUPS CRUMBLED GOAT CHEESE

1 CUP TOASTED WALNUTS (SEE PSST ON PAGE 114)

1 Pour the water into the pressure cooker. Arrange the trivet and steamer basket in the bottom and put the beets in the basket. Lock the lid in place and cook at high pressure for 12 minutes.

2 Quick release the pressure and remove the lid, tilting the pot away from you to avoid the escaping steam. Insert the sharp tip of a knife into the center of a beet to make sure it is cooked through; the knife should go all the way through without resistance. If they are not done, leave them in the steamer basket, replace the lid, and allow them to steam off the stove top for an additional 5 minutes. Let cool while you make the dressing.

3 In a small bowl, whisk together the oil, vinegar, shallot, sugar, salt, and pepper until blended. Peel the beets and quarter them. Pour some of the dressing over the beets and toss to coat. Arrange the salad greens in a large bowl, pour some of the dressing over the greens, and toss until the leaves are coated. Arrange salad greens on individual plates, top with the beets, and sprinkle with the crumbled goat cheese and walnuts. Serve any leftover dressing on the side.

PSST

If baby beets are not available, it's fine to use medium beets. Cook them at high pressure for 15 minutes.

BEET AND BARLEY SALAD

This beautifully colored, healthful salad involves a two-step process to cook the barley and then the beets in the pressure cooker. Both can be made ahead of time, though, and then tossed together when you are ready to serve the salad. Because the dish travels well, it's a great one to take to a friend's house for dinner. Or serve it at home with grilled or steamed fish or shellfish.

SERVES **6**

BARLEY

1 CUP PEARL BARLEY

4 CUPS VEGETABLE OR CHICKEN BROTH

1 TABLESPOON CANOLA OIL

BEETS

2 CUPS WATER

4 MEDIUM BEETS, TRIMMED AND SCRUBBED

4 SCALLIONS (WHITE AND TENDER GREEN PARTS), FINELY CHOPPED

2 TABLESPOONS FINELY CHOPPED FRESH FLAT-LEAF PARSLEY

2 TABLESPOONS THINLY SLICED FRESH BASIL

1 CUP CRUMBLED FETA CHEESE

1 CUP EXTRA-VIRGIN OLIVE OIL

½ CUP WHITE BALSAMIC VINEGAR

2 TEASPOONS SALT

½ TEASPOON FRESHLY GROUND BLACK PEPPER

1 **To make the barley:** Pour the barley and stock into the pressure cooker and float the oil on the top of the broth. Lock the lid in place and cook at high pressure for 15 minutes. Quick release the pressure and remove the lid, tilting the pot away from you to avoid the escaping steam. Drain the barley and transfer to a bowl to cool. The barley can be refrigerated in an airtight container for up to 4 days or frozen for up to 1 month.

2 **To make the beets:** Pour the water into the pressure cooker. Arrange the trivet and steamer basket in the bottom and put the beets in the basket. Lock the lid in place and cook at high pressure for 15 minutes. Quick release the pressure and remove the lid, tilting the pot away from you to avoid the escaping steam. Insert the sharp tip of a knife into the center of a beet to make sure it is tender. Allow the beets to cool, then peel and cut into ½-inch dice.

3 In a large bowl, combine the barley and beets with the scallions, parsley, basil, and feta. In a small mixing bowl, whisk together the oil, vinegar, salt, and pepper. Pour over the salad and toss until coated. The salad will keep, covered, at room temperature for up to 4 hours or refrigerated overnight. Remove from the refrigerator at least 1 hour before serving and toss again.

BEETS WITH POMEGRANATE GLAZE

This beet dish, with its sweet and spicy sauce, will give your dinner a lot of pizzazz. Serve it with grilled or roasted entrées, such as grilled chicken, lamb chops, pork chops, or grilled steak.

SERVES **6**

2 CUPS WATER

4 MEDIUM BEETS, TRIMMED AND SCRUBBED

1 CUP POMEGRANATE JUICE

½ CUP ORANGE JUICE

2 TABLESPOONS RED WINE VINEGAR

2 TABLESPOONS SUGAR

1 TEASPOON CORNSTARCH DISSOLVED IN 2 TABLESPOONS WATER

1 Pour the water into the pressure cooker. Arrange the trivet and steamer basket in the bottom and put the beets in the basket. Lock the lid in place and cook at high pressure for 15 minutes.

2 Quick release the pressure and remove the lid, tilting the pot away from you to avoid the escaping steam. Insert the sharp tip of a knife into the center of a beet to make sure it is done. Allow the beets to cool and then peel and cut into ½-inch slices or wedges. Set aside.

3 In a small saucepan, heat the pomegranate juice, orange juice, vinegar, and sugar until the liquid comes to a boil. Add the cornstarch slurry and return the mixture to a boil, whisking until it is no longer cloudy. Remove from the heat and drizzle over the beets.

LEGUMES

Beans, lentils, and peas are loaded with fiber, protein, and complex carbohydrates. People around the globe eat them daily, and for good reasons: They are a great way to stretch a food dollar, providing a filling and nutritious alternative to meat or poultry. The choices are endless for color, flavor, and texture—from tiny brown lentils to large white cannellini beans.

Beans benefit from presoaking before cooking. I have provided charts with presoaking times for the beans and cooking times for the beans and other legumes. If you don't have time to presoak the beans, just double the cooking time and release the pressure naturally.

I recommend that you buy your beans, lentils, and peas at a health food store or organic market where you can buy them in bulk from bins. This way you can be sure that the beans are replenished on a regular basis. The packages at your supermarket may not be fresh, and cooking old dried beans takes almost twice as long as cooking fresher ones.

Cooked legumes can be stored in the refrigerator for up to 4 days, and you can freeze them for up to 4 months in zipper-top plastic bags. Cooking them in the pressure cooker gives you a quick, simple way to serve them any day of the week.

Tips for Cooking Legumes

1 For each cup of beans, you will need 1½ cups of liquid for cooking.

2 Cook beans at high pressure.

3 Add salt after cooking the beans. Salt added to beans during cooking can slow the cooking process.

4 Always rinse dried beans to remove any grit or dirt from the outer skin.

5 Limit the number of cups of beans to 3 cups for a 6-quart pot.

6 Beans have a tendency to foam in the pressure cooker; a drizzle of oil over the liquid in the pressure cooker will keep the foam to a minimum.

Three Ways to Presoak Beans

Presoaking cleans the outer shell of the bean of any dirt or grit and also softens the shell, speeding up the cooking time and giving you creamier beans. Before you soak them, pick over the beans for stones and loose dirt. After you've soaked the beans, pour out the soaking liquid and use fresh cold water or broth to cook them. There are three different ways to presoak beans:

STEAMING IN THE PRESSURE COOKER Put the beans in the pressure cooker and cover with water by 1 inch. Lock the lid in place and cook at high pressure for 5 minutes. Release the pressure naturally and drain the beans. At this point, the beans are ready for your recipe.

BOILING ON THE STOVE TOP Put the beans in a large pot and cover with water by 2 inches. Bring the water to a boil, cover, and remove from the heat. Allow to sit for 2 hours. Drain the water and proceed with your recipe.

SOAKING ON THE COUNTERTOP Put the beans in a large mixing bowl and cover with water by 1 inch. Soak according to the time recommended on the chart on page 152. Drain the beans and use in your chosen recipe.

LEGUME	PRESOAKING TIME ON THE COUNTERTOP	COOKING TIME AT HIGH PRESSURE
Black beans	4 hours	20 minutes
Black-eyed peas	none	7 minutes
Cannellini beans	8 hours	15 minutes
Chickpeas (garbanzo beans)	8 hours	16 minutes
Cranberry beans	4 hours	12 minutes
Fava beans (dried)	12 hours	4 minutes
Great Northern beans	4 hours	14 minutes
Kidney beans	4 hours	14 minutes
Lima beans (large)	8 hours	8 minutes
Lima beans (baby)	8 hours	7 minutes
Lentils	none	6 minutes
Navy beans or other small white beans	4 hours	12 minutes
Pink beans	4 hours	12 minutes
Pinto beans	4 hours	10 minutes
Red beans	4 hours	20 minutes
Soybeans	8 hours	15 minutes
Split peas	none	10 minutes

Use a quick release if you've soaked the beans. If you haven't, double the cooking time and release the pressure naturally.

LENTIL AND FENNEL SALAD WITH WHITE WINE VINAIGRETTE

Lentils pack plenty of nutrition and flavor into a small package. And since they don't need to be presoaked, lentil dishes can be on the table in no time. This simple salad makes a good weeknight side dish or vegetarian main course. The tender lentils absorb the vinaigrette, while the crunchy fennel provides contrast. The result is a scrumptious salad, which can serve as a bed for grilled seafood, poultry, or lamb.

SERVES 6

2 CUPS DRIED LENTILS, RINSED

1½ CUPS CHICKEN OR VEGETABLE STOCK (PAGE 19 OR 21) OR STORE-BOUGHT CHICKEN OR VEGETABLE BROTH

1 BAY LEAF

1 FENNEL BULB, FRONDS REMOVED AND ROOT END TRIMMED

⅔ CUP EXTRA-VIRGIN OLIVE OIL

¼ CUP WHITE WINE VINEGAR

1 GARLIC CLOVE, MINCED

1 SMALL SHALLOT, FINELY CHOPPED

1½ TEASPOONS SALT, PLUS MORE IF NEEDED

½ TEASPOON FRESHLY GROUND BLACK PEPPER

1 Combine the lentils, stock, and bay leaf in the pressure cooker. Lock the lid in place and cook at high pressure for 5 minutes.

2 Quick release the pressure and remove the lid, tilting the pot away from you to avoid the escaping steam. Drain the lentils, remove the bay leaf, and transfer the lentils to a serving bowl to cool.

3 With a sharp knife, cut the fennel bulb in half lengthwise and wash thoroughly. Using a sharp knife or mandoline, shave the fennel into thin slices and add to the lentils. In a small mixing bowl, whisk together the oil, vinegar, garlic, shallot, salt, and pepper until blended. Taste the dressing for seasoning and add more salt if the dressing is too acidic.

4 Pour half of the dressing over the salad and toss. Taste the salad and add more dressing if needed. Serve the salad at room temperature. If you want to serve it later, refrigerate the salad and the remaining dressing. Remove them both from the refrigerator about 1 hour before serving and toss the salad with more dressing. The lentils will absorb all of the dressing, so it is important to save a bit when making it ahead of time.

WILD MUSHROOM AND LENTIL SALAD

When wild mushrooms appear in the farmers' market, I usually buy way too many. They are so fragrant with the scent of the woods and so delicious that I use them in lots of different dishes. This salad includes savory roasted mushrooms and lentils for a delicious vegetarian entrée or as a take-along for a picnic or tailgate.

SERVES **6** TO **8**

MUSHROOMS

½ CUP EXTRA-VIRGIN OLIVE OIL

¼ CUP BALSAMIC VINEGAR

1 TABLESPOON FINELY CHOPPED FRESH SAGE

¼ CUP FINELY CHOPPED SHALLOT (SEE PSST)

3 GARLIC CLOVES, MINCED

2 TEASPOONS SALT

1 TEASPOON FRESHLY GROUND BLACK PEPPER

1½ POUNDS ASSORTED WILD OR CULTIVATED MUSHROOMS (CREMINI, CHANTERELLE, OYSTER, MOREL, SHIITAKE, OR TRUMPET), TOUGH STEMS REMOVED, AND QUARTERED

2 CUPS CHICKEN OR VEGETABLE STOCK (PAGE 19 OR 21) OR STORE-BOUGHT CHICKEN OR VEGETABLE BROTH

2 CUPS LENTILS, RINSED

4 CELERY STALKS, FINELY CHOPPED

½ CUP FINELY CHOPPED RED ONION

¼ CUP FINELY CHOPPED FRESH FLAT-LEAF PARSLEY

1 Preheat the oven to 400 degrees F. Line a baking sheet with aluminum foil or a silicone baking liner.

2 To make the mushrooms: In a small mixing bowl, whisk together the oil, vinegar, sage, shallot, garlic, salt, and pepper until blended. Arrange the mushrooms on the baking sheet, pour half the dressing over the mushrooms, and toss to coat the mushrooms with the dressing. Refrigerate the remaining dressing.

3 Bake the mushrooms for 15 minutes, turning once halfway through the cooking time. The mushrooms should be turning golden brown when you remove them from the oven. With a slotted spoon, transfer the mushrooms to a large bowl and let cool to room temperature. In a small bowl, set aside about 2 tablespoons of the liquid from the pan and discard the rest.

4 Combine the stock and lentils in the pressure cooker and stir them together. Lock the lid in place and cook at high pressure for 6 minutes. Quick release the pressure and remove the lid, tilting the pot away from you to avoid the escaping steam. Drain the lentils and transfer them to a large salad bowl to cool.

5 Combine the celery, onion, and parsley with the lentils in the salad bowl. Add the mushrooms and toss. Whisk the reserved mushroom liquid into the reserved dressing, pour over the salad, and toss to coat. Serve the salad at room temperature.

PSST

Instead of the chopped shallot, you can substitute more red onion.

LENTILS, CASTELLUCCIO STYLE

Castelluccio, a hamlet in Italy's Monti Sibillini National Park, is famous for its tender lentils, which, like French green lentils, retain their shape when cooked. Celery and rosemary are the flavorings for this dish, which is usually served as a *contorno*, or side dish, with porchetta, Umbria's famous and spectacular roast pork dish.

SERVES 6

3 TABLESPOONS EXTRA-VIRGIN OLIVE OIL

1 MEDIUM SWEET ONION, SUCH AS VIDALIA, FINELY CHOPPED

4 CELERY STALKS (INCLUDING THE LEAVES), CHOPPED

1 TEASPOON FINELY CHOPPED FRESH ROSEMARY

2 CUPS LENTILS, PREFERABLY FRENCH OR ITALIAN, RINSED

2 CUPS CHICKEN OR VEGETABLE STOCK (PAGE 19 OR 21) OR STORE-BOUGHT CHICKEN OR VEGETABLE BROTH

1½ TEASPOONS SALT, PLUS MORE IF NEEDED

½ TEASPOON FRESHLY GROUND BLACK PEPPER, PLUS MORE IF NEEDED

1 Heat 2 tablespoons of the oil in the pressure cooker over medium-high heat. Add the onion, celery, and rosemary and sauté until the onion begins to soften, about 2 minutes. Add the lentils, stock, salt, and pepper and stir to combine. Drizzle with the remaining tablespoon of oil. Lock the lid in place and cook at high pressure for 6 minutes.

2 Quick release the pressure and remove the lid, tilting the pot away from you to avoid the escaping steam. Stir the lentils, taste for seasoning, and add more salt and pepper if necessary. Transfer to a serving dish and serve warm or at room temperature.

CURRIED LENTILS

In some Asian countries, the combination of lentils and curry is as common as fries and ketchup in the States. This version is made with coconut milk for a fresh twist. It makes a great vegetarian main dish to serve with rice and naan, an Indian flatbread. Or serve it as a tasty side dish to accompany grilled or roasted lamb, chicken, or beef.

SERVES **6**

....

2 TABLESPOONS CANOLA OIL

1 MEDIUM SWEET ONION, SUCH AS VIDALIA, FINELY CHOPPED

3 MEDIUM CARROTS, FINELY CHOPPED

2 TEASPOONS MADRAS CURRY POWDER, PLUS MORE IF NEEDED

2 CUPS LENTILS, RINSED

1 CUP CHICKEN OR VEGETABLE STOCK (PAGE 19 OR 21) OR STORE-BOUGHT CHICKEN OR VEGETABLE BROTH

1 CUP COCONUT MILK

SALT AND FRESHLY GROUND BLACK PEPPER (OPTIONAL)

1 Heat the oil in the pressure cooker over medium-high heat. Add the onion, carrots, and curry powder and sauté until the onion begins to soften, about 2 minutes. Add the lentils, stock, and coconut milk. Lock the lid in place and cook at high pressure for 6 minutes.

2 Quick release the pressure and remove the lid, tilting the pot away from you to avoid the escaping steam. Stir the lentils and taste for seasoning. Add more curry powder or salt and pepper if needed. Transfer the lentils to a serving dish and serve hot.

CHICKPEAS WITH ROSEMARY

Chickpeas, also known as garbanzo beans, are terrific cooked in the pressure cooker. They become creamy and flavorful and put their spongy canned counterparts to shame. This recipe, with its bits of pancetta, fragrant rosemary, garlic, and tomato, was a favorite at my grandmother's house. Nona would serve this as a side dish, one of many that would grace her table, no matter what the entrée was. I love it with pork or beef.

SERVES 6

4 TABLESPOONS EXTRA-VIRGIN OLIVE OIL

2 PANCETTA SLICES, FINELY CHOPPED

1 MEDIUM SWEET ONION, SUCH AS VIDALIA, FINELY CHOPPED

2 GARLIC CLOVES, MINCED

PINCH OF RED PEPPER FLAKES

2 TEASPOONS FINELY CHOPPED FRESH ROSEMARY

ONE 14½-OUNCE CAN CHOPPED TOMATOES WITH THEIR JUICE

1 CUP CHICKEN OR VEGETABLE STOCK (PAGE 19 OR 21) OR STORE-BOUGHT CHICKEN OR VEGETABLE BROTH

2 CUPS CHICKPEAS, PRESOAKED (SEE PAGE 151) AND DRAINED

SALT AND FRESHLY GROUND BLACK PEPPER (OPTIONAL)

1 Heat 2 tablespoons of the oil in the pressure cooker over medium-high heat. Add the pancetta and cook until crispy. Remove all but 2 tablespoons of the fat from the pot. Add the onion, garlic, red pepper flakes, and rosemary and sauté for 2 minutes, or until the onion begins to soften. Add the tomatoes, stock, and chickpeas, stirring to blend. Drizzle with the remaining 2 tablespoons of olive oil. Lock the lid in place and cook at high pressure for 16 minutes.

2 Quick release the pressure and remove the lid, tilting the pot away from you to avoid the escaping steam. Stir the beans, taste for seasoning, and add salt and black pepper if needed. Transfer to a serving dish and serve hot, warm, or at room temperature.

CHICKPEAS WITH BASIL AND CORN

Sweet corn and creamy curried chickpeas are a delightful combination. Enjoy them as a side dish or as a vegetarian entrée served over rice. The sweetness of the corn balances the spiciness of the curry, making this dish a winner any night of the week.

SERVES **6**

3 TABLESPOONS CANOLA OIL

1 MEDIUM SWEET ONION, SUCH AS VIDALIA, FINELY CHOPPED

3 MEDIUM CARROTS, FINELY CHOPPED

2 TEASPOONS MADRAS CURRY POWDER, PLUS MORE IF NEEDED

2 CUPS CHICKPEAS, PRESOAKED (SEE PAGE 151) AND DRAINED

2 CUPS CHICKEN OR VEGETABLE STOCK (PAGE 19 OR 21) OR STORE-BOUGHT CHICKEN OR VEGETABLE BROTH

2 CUPS CORN KERNELS, FRESHLY CUT FROM THE COB, OR FROZEN CORN, DEFROSTED

SALT AND FRESHLY GROUND BLACK PEPPER (OPTIONAL)

¼ CUP FINELY CHOPPED FRESH BASIL

1 Heat 2 tablespoons of the oil in the pressure cooker over medium-high heat. Add the onion, carrots, and curry powder and sauté for 2 minutes, or until the onion begins to soften. Add the chickpeas and stock and stir to combine. Drizzle with the remaining tablespoon of oil. Lock the lid in place and cook at high pressure for 16 minutes.

2 Quick release the pressure and remove the lid, tilting the pot away from you to avoid the escaping steam. Stir the corn into the bean mixture and cook over medium-high heat without pressure for 3 minutes, until the corn is cooked. Taste the mixture for seasoning and add more curry powder or salt or pepper if needed. Transfer to a serving bowl and stir in the basil. Serve the chickpeas hot, warm, or at room temperature.

PSST

Sometimes I serve these in pita bread with a dollop of plain yogurt and some mango salsa or chutney for a vegetarian snack before dinner.

NEW YEAR'S DAY BLACK-EYED PEAS AND RICE

On New Year's Day, black-eyed peas are served in many homes in the South, where they are considered good luck for the year ahead. These velvety beans, flavored with ham and a bit of cayenne pepper, can be addictive. Serve them over rice (it's mandatory). And for a truly Southern meal, offer your guests corn bread.

SERVES **6** TO **8**

2 TABLESPOONS EXTRA-VIRGIN OLIVE OIL

1 LARGE ONION, FINELY CHOPPED

1 BAY LEAF

2 SMOKED HAM HOCKS

2 CUPS BLACK-EYED PEAS, RINSED AND DRAINED

6 CUPS CHICKEN STOCK (PAGE 19) OR STORE-BOUGHT CHICKEN BROTH

TABASCO OR ANOTHER HOT SAUCE

SALT (OPTIONAL)

4 CUPS COOKED LONG-GRAIN RICE FOR SERVING

1 Heat the oil in the pressure cooker over medium-high heat. Add the onion and bay leaf and sauté for 2 minutes, or until the onion begins to soften. Add the ham hocks, peas, and stock, stirring to combine. Lock the lid in place and cook at high pressure for 7 minutes.

2 Quick release the pressure and remove the lid, tilting the pot away from you to avoid the escaping steam. Taste the beans for seasoning and add Tabasco to taste and some salt if needed. Remove the bay leaf. Remove the ham hocks from the pot and cut the meat from the bone, trimming off any fatty pieces. Dice the meat into bite-size pieces and return to the pot, stirring to combine them with the black-eyed peas. Serve over rice in bowls.

CANNELLINI BEANS OREGANATA

Cannellini are large white beans. They can take quite a bit of time to cook conventionally on the stove top, but with a pressure cooker, they are ready in less than thirty minutes. Garlic, oregano, and a hint of pancetta flavor the beans in this terrific side dish from Sicily. Serve it with roast lamb, beef, or pork.

SERVES 6

½ CUP EXTRA-VIRGIN OLIVE OIL

2 PANCETTA SLICES, FINELY CHOPPED

2 GARLIC CLOVES, SLICED

1 BAY LEAF

1 TEASPOON DRIED OREGANO

2 CUPS CANNELLINI BEANS, PRESOAKED (SEE PAGE 151) AND DRAINED

3 CUPS CHICKEN OR VEGETABLE STOCK (PAGE 19 OR 21) OR STORE-BOUGHT CHICKEN OR VEGETABLE BROTH

SALT AND FRESHLY GROUND BLACK PEPPER (OPTIONAL)

1 Heat the oil in the pressure cooker over medium-high heat. Add the pancetta and sauté until it renders its fat. Add the garlic, bay leaf, and oregano and sauté for 1 minute, or until the garlic is fragrant. Remove all but 2 tablespoons of the oil and set it aside. Add the beans and stock, stirring to combine. Lock the lid in place and cook at high pressure for 15 minutes.

2 Quick release the pressure and remove the lid, tilting the pot away from you to avoid the escaping steam. Remove the bay leaf, stir the reserved oil into the beans, and taste for seasoning. Add salt and pepper if needed and serve.

WHITE BEAN DIP WITH OLIVE OIL AND ROSEMARY

Using freshly cooked white beans gives you a creamier and fresher-tasting dish than if you use canned beans. This creamy dip, flavored with olive oil and rosemary, is similar in texture to hummus. It is terrific with toasted baguette slices, pita chips, or fresh veggies to serve before dinner.

SERVES 8

1 CUP SMALL WHITE BEANS, SUCH AS NAVY BEANS, PRESOAKED (SEE PAGE 151) AND DRAINED

3 CUPS VEGETABLE STOCK (PAGE 21) OR STORE-BOUGHT VEGETABLE BROTH

4 TABLESPOONS EXTRA-VIRGIN OLIVE OIL

1 TABLESPOON FINELY CHOPPED FRESH ROSEMARY

2 GARLIC CLOVES, MINCED

2 TEASPOONS RED WINE VINEGAR

1½ TEASPOONS SALT, PLUS MORE IF NEEDED

6 DROPS OF TABASCO OR ANOTHER HOT SAUCE, PLUS MORE IF NEEDED

1 Combine the beans and stock in the pressure cooker. Drizzle with 1 tablespoon of the oil. Lock the lid in place and cook at high pressure for 12 minutes.

2 Release the pressure naturally and remove the lid, tilting the pot away from you to avoid the escaping steam. Drain the beans, reserving the liquid. Transfer the beans to the work bowl of a food processor and set aside.

3 In a small skillet, heat the remaining 3 tablespoons of oil over low heat. Add the rosemary and garlic and sauté until the garlic is fragrant but not browned, about 3 minutes.

4 In the food processor, use on and off pulses to break up the beans. With the food processor running, add the rosemary-garlic oil, vinegar, salt, and Tabasco through the feed tube and process until the beans are smooth. Taste the dip for seasoning and add more salt or Tabasco if needed. Serve the dip immediately at room temperature or refrigerate in an airtight container for up to 3 days. Remove from the refrigerator at least 1 hour before serving.

PRESSURE COOKER–STYLE BOSTON BAKED BEANS

My Irish grandmother worked as a cook for wealthy Boston families when she arrived in this country, and learning how to prepare Boston baked beans was one of her first tasks. I've added a bit of pizzazz to her simple recipe by including thyme, ginger, Worcestershire, and brown sugar. The beans become creamy and soak up the molasses and tomato sauce. They make a satisfying main dish when accompanied by Boston brown bread, or a perfect side dish for burgers, sausages, or ham.

SERVES 6 TO 8

8 BACON STRIPS, CUT INTO ½-INCH DICE

1 LARGE SWEET ONION, SUCH AS VIDALIA, FINELY CHOPPED

1 TEASPOON DRIED THYME

½ TEASPOON GROUND GINGER

2 CUPS SMALL WHITE BEANS, PRESOAKED (SEE PAGE 151)

3 CUPS CHICKEN OR VEGETABLE STOCK (PAGE 19 OR 21) OR STORE-BOUGHT CHICKEN OR VEGETABLE BROTH

1 TABLESPOON CANOLA OIL

ONE 14½-OUNCE CAN TOMATO SAUCE

½ CUP MOLASSES

¼ CUP FIRMLY PACKED DARK BROWN SUGAR

1 TABLESPOON WORCESTERSHIRE SAUCE

½ CUP KETCHUP

2 TABLESPOONS DIJON MUSTARD

1 Fry the bacon in the pressure cooker over medium-high heat until crisp. Remove all but 2 tablespoons of the fat from the pot. Add the onion, thyme, and ginger and sauté for 2 to 3 minutes, or until the onion begins to soften. Add the beans and stock, stirring to combine. Drizzle with the oil. Lock the lid in place and cook at high pressure for 20 minutes.

2 Release the pressure naturally and remove the lid, tilting the pot away from you to avoid the escaping steam. Stir the beans and add the tomato sauce, molasses, sugar, Worcestershire sauce, ketchup, and mustard. Simmer on the stove top without pressure for 20 minutes. You can serve the beans immediately, or let cool, cover, and refrigerate for up to 3 days.

NEW ORLEANS—STYLE RED BEANS

Traditionally, Monday was wash day in New Orleans, and women would put a pot of Creole-flavored red beans on the stove top to simmer until dinnertime, while they tended to the laundry. These beans are still enjoyed in New Orleans on Mondays—with rice, the traditional accompaniment. With a pressure cooker, this meal is on the table in less than thirty minutes, and it has all the flavor and stick-to-your-ribs goodness of the original bean dish. The choice of meat that goes into the bean pot depends on the preferences of the cook. Some like a ham hock for its smoky qualities, while others prefer andouille, a spicy Creole sausage that perks up the flavor and gives the dish some sass. If you would like to use a less spicy sausage, Polish kielbasa works well, too. You can also omit the meat and use vegetable broth for a vegetarian dish.

SERVES 6 TO 8

3 TABLESPOONS CANOLA OIL

1 LARGE SWEET ONION, SUCH AS VIDALIA, FINELY CHOPPED

4 CELERY STALKS (INCLUDING THE LEAVES), FINELY CHOPPED

1 LARGE GREEN BELL PEPPER, SEEDED, DERIBBED, AND FINELY CHOPPED

3 GARLIC CLOVES, MINCED

1 TEASPOON DRIED THYME

½ TEASPOON CAYENNE PEPPER

1 POUND ANDOUILLE SAUSAGE OR POLISH KIELBASA, CUT INTO ½-INCH ROUNDS; OR 1 SMOKED HAM HOCK OR MEATY HAM BONE

2 CUPS RED BEANS, PRESOAKED (SEE PAGE 151) AND DRAINED

4 CUPS CHICKEN OR VEGETABLE STOCK (PAGE 19 OR 21) OR STORE-BOUGHT CHICKEN OR VEGETABLE BROTH

SALT AND FRESHLY GROUND BLACK PEPPER (OPTIONAL)

TABASCO OR ANOTHER HOT SAUCE FOR SERVING

LONG-GRAIN RICE FOR SERVING

½ CUP FINELY CHOPPED SCALLIONS (WHITE AND TENDER GREEN PARTS)

1 Heat 2 tablespoons of the oil in the pressure cooker over medium-high heat. Add the onion, celery, bell pepper, garlic, thyme, and cayenne and sauté for 2 minutes, stirring to prevent the spices from burning. Add the sausage and sauté to render some of the fat, about 3 minutes. Add the beans and stock, stirring to combine, and drizzle with the remaining tablespoon of oil. Lock the lid in place and cook at high pressure for 20 minutes. While the beans are cooking, start the rice in another pan.

2 Release the pressure naturally and remove the lid, tilting the pot away from you to avoid the escaping steam. If you used a ham hock or ham bone, remove it from the pressure cooker and cut the meat off the bone into bite-size pieces. Return the meat to the beans. Stir the beans, taste for seasoning, and add salt, pepper, or Tabasco if needed. Serve the beans over the rice, sprinkled with the scallions. Offer Tabasco or your favorite hot sauce on the side.

PINK AND RED BEANS

These ancho chile–spiked pink and red beans remind me of confetti. They make a delicious side dish to serve with grilled entrées, or you can spoon them onto crispy tortillas and top with salad and shredded cheese.

SERVES **6** TO **8**

....

3 CUPS CHICKEN OR VEGETABLE STOCK (PAGE 19 OR 21) OR STORE-BOUGHT CHICKEN OR VEGETABLE BROTH

1 CUP PINK BEANS, PRESOAKED (SEE PAGE 151) AND DRAINED

1 CUP RED BEANS, PRESOAKED (SEE PAGE 151) AND DRAINED

3 TABLESPOONS EXTRA-VIRGIN OLIVE OIL

2 GARLIC CLOVES, MINCED

1 TEASPOON ANCHO CHILE POWDER

½ CUP FINELY CHOPPED RED ONION

2 TEASPOONS FINELY CHOPPED FRESH OREGANO

1½ TEASPOONS SALT (OPTIONAL)

1 Combine the stock and beans in the pressure cooker, stirring to combine. Drizzle 1 tablespoon of the oil over the stock. Lock the lid in place and cook at high pressure for 20 minutes.

2 Release the pressure naturally and remove the lid, tilting the pot away from you to avoid the escaping steam. Drain the beans and set aside, reserving the bean liquid.

3 In a large skillet, heat the remaining 2 tablespoons of oil over medium-high heat. Add the garlic, chile powder, onion, and oregano and cook for 3 to 4 minutes, or until the onion is softened and the garlic is fragrant. Add the beans to the skillet and toss to coat with the oil and spices. Taste the beans for seasoning and add the salt if necessary. If the mixture seems dry, add up to ¼ cup of the bean liquid. Cook over medium heat without pressure for 3 to 4 minutes, until the beans are heated through. Transfer the beans to a serving bowl and serve warm.

BASIC PRESSURE COOKED PINTO BEANS

Pinto beans are sold here in San Diego in twenty-five pound bags; they are a part of the daily diet here and south of the border. Once these pintos have been cooked, you can serve them with just a sprinkling of salt and pepper or make them into soups, salads, burritos, refried beans, and bean dips. And the best part: They take less than half an hour from start to finish.

SERVES **6** (ABOUT **4** CUPS)

2 CUPS PINTO BEANS, PRESOAKED (SEE PAGE 151) AND DRAINED

6 CUPS CHICKEN OR VEGETABLE STOCK (PAGE 19 OR 21) OR STORE-BOUGHT CHICKEN OR VEGETABLE BROTH

2 TABLESPOONS CANOLA OIL

1½ TEASPOONS SALT (OPTIONAL)

½ TEASPOON FRESHLY GROUND BLACK PEPPER (OPTIONAL)

1 In the pressure cooker, combine the beans and stock, stirring to blend. Drizzle with the oil. Lock the lid in place and cook at high pressure for 10 minutes.

2 Release the pressure naturally and remove the lid, tilting the pot away from you to avoid the escaping steam. Drain the beans, sprinkle with the salt and pepper, and serve. If you are storing them to use later, do not season. Store the beans separately from the liquid, in zipper-top plastic bags or in an airtight storage container. (The beans will continue to absorb the liquid if you store them together.) The stock from the beans can be frozen for use in soups or sauces.

REFRIED BEANS

Refried beans are creamy and delicious, and freshly pressure cooked beans make them even better. This dish includes jalapeño and garlic to perk up the flavor and add a bit of heat. Serve refried beans with fajitas or any grilled entrée.

SERVES 6

3 TABLESPOONS EXTRA-VIRGIN OLIVE OIL

1 LARGE SWEET ONION, SUCH AS VIDALIA, FINELY CHOPPED

2 GARLIC CLOVES, MINCED

1 SMALL JALAPEÑO PEPPER, SEEDED, DERIBBED, AND FINELY CHOPPED

4 CUPS BASIC PRESSURE COOKED PINTO BEANS (FACING PAGE)

½ CUP COOKING LIQUID FROM THE BEANS, CHICKEN OR VEGETABLE STOCK (PAGE 19 OR 21) OR STORE-BOUGHT CHICKEN OR VEGETABLE BROTH, OR WATER

SALT

TABASCO OR ANOTHER HOT SAUCE

SHREDDED MILD CHEDDAR CHEESE FOR SERVING (OPTIONAL)

In a large skillet, heat the oil over medium-high heat. Add the onion, garlic, and jalapeño and sauté for 2 to 3 minutes, or until the onion and jalapeño begin to soften. Add the beans and mash them with a potato masher, adding some of the bean liquid to make them easier to mash. Continue to cook the beans over medium heat, stirring occasionally, until they become creamy, 30 to 45 minutes, adding more liquid as needed. Season the beans with salt and Tabasco to taste and serve hot. If you like, sprinkle the beans with shredded Cheddar cheese before serving.

Black Beans

Black beans, also called turtle beans, make a delicious addition to lots of meals, including your favorite south-of-the-border dishes. If you like, you can cook them in the pressure cooker ahead of time and then refrigerate them for up to four days or freeze them for up to two months for future use. After the beans get a quick twenty minutes in the pressure cooker, you're on your way to any number of dishes for a weeknight dinner or a potluck with friends.

SPICY REFRIED BLACK BEANS

A local restaurant makes a version of this spicy dish, and I can't seem to get enough of it. Don't let the amount of chipotle peppers steer you away from this dish. A chipotle is a smoked jalapeño, which adds a smoky note to the beans.

SERVES 6 TO 8

2 CUPS BLACK BEANS, PRESOAKED (SEE PAGE 151) AND DRAINED

6 CUPS CHICKEN OR VEGETABLE STOCK (PAGE 19 OR 21) OR STORE-BOUGHT CHICKEN OR VEGETABLE BROTH

4 TABLESPOONS EXTRA-VIRGIN OLIVE OIL

1 LARGE WHITE ONION, FINELY CHOPPED

1 MEDIUM RED BELL PEPPER, SEEDED, DERIBBED, AND FINELY CHOPPED

3 GARLIC CLOVES, MINCED

2 TO 3 CHIPOTLE CHILES IN ADOBO SAUCE (DEPENDING ON YOUR HEAT PREFERENCE), FINELY CHOPPED

1 TEASPOON GROUND CUMIN

¼ CUP TEQUILA

ONE 14½-OUNCE CAN FIRE-ROASTED TOMATOES (SEE PSST)

1 TEASPOON SALT, PLUS MORE IF NEEDED

FRESHLY GROUND BLACK PEPPER (OPTIONAL)

1 Combine the beans and stock in the pressure cooker, stirring to combine. Drizzle with 1 tablespoon of the oil. Lock the lid in place and cook at high pressure for 20 minutes. Release the pressure naturally and remove the lid, tilting the pot away from you to avoid the escaping steam. Drain the beans, reserving about 1 cup of the cooking liquid. Set the beans aside.

2 In a large skillet over medium-high heat, heat the remaining 3 tablespoons of oil. Add the onion, bell pepper, garlic, chiles, and cumin and sauté for about 4 minutes, or until the onion and bell pepper begin to soften. Add the tequila and bring to a boil. Stir in the tomatoes, salt, and beans, stirring to combine. Simmer the beans for 10 to 15 minutes, stirring occasionally, until they become creamy. Add some of the reserved cooking liquid from the beans if the mixture seems dry and sticks to the bottom of the pan. Taste the beans for seasoning and add more salt or some black pepper. Transfer the beans to a serving bowl and serve immediately.

PSST

You can find fire-roasted tomatoes at many markets. Muir Glen's and Trader Joe's brands are excellent.

BLACK BEAN SALSA

This smoky salsa gets its kick from chipotle chiles, cumin, and fresh lime juice. It's served in the Southwest as a side dish with grilled meats or as a dip with tortilla chips for a Cinco de Mayo celebration. The crunchy texture comes from jicama and bell peppers, which also add sweetness to the dip.

MAKES ABOUT **4** CUPS

2 CUPS BLACK BEANS, PRESOAKED (SEE PAGE 151) AND DRAINED

6 CUPS VEGETABLE STOCK (PAGE 21) OR STORE-BOUGHT VEGETABLE BROTH

½ CUP PLUS 2 TEASPOONS CANOLA OIL

½ CUP FINELY CHOPPED WHITE ONION

2 CHIPOTLE CHILES IN ADOBO SAUCE, FINELY CHOPPED

1 CUP FINELY CHOPPED JICAMA

1½ CUPS CORN KERNELS, FRESHLY CUT FROM THE COB, OR FROZEN CORN, DEFROSTED

1 CUP CHERRY TOMATOES, QUARTERED (SEE PSST)

2 GARLIC CLOVES, MINCED

½ CUP FINELY CHOPPED RED BELL PEPPER

¼ CUP FRESH LIME JUICE

½ TEASPOON GROUND CUMIN

1½ TEASPOONS SALT

¼ CUP FINELY CHOPPED FRESH CILANTRO

1 Combine the beans and stock in the pressure cooker and drizzle with 2 teaspoons of the oil. Lock the lid in place and cook at high pressure for 20 minutes.

2 Release the pressure naturally and remove the lid, tilting the pot away from you to avoid the escaping steam. Drain the beans and allow to cool.

3 In a large bowl, combine the cooled beans, onion, chiles, jicama, corn, tomatoes, garlic, and bell pepper, stirring to combine. In a small mixing bowl, whisk together the remaining ½ cup of oil, the lime juice, cumin, and salt until blended. Pour over the black bean mixture and toss to coat. Add the cilantro and toss again. Serve the salsa at room temperature.

PSST

Cherry tomatoes are flavorful all year round, which is why I use them in this recipe. But if you have a garden full of tomatoes, use a meaty tomato for this recipe and cut it into small dice.

BLACK BEAN, CORN, AND AVOCADO SALAD

Here's a great vegetable salad that you can take along to a picnic or serve at home. The avocado dressing gives it an elegant look and terrific flavor. If you would like to make this into an entrée salad, leftover chicken, beef, pork, or shrimp make great additions.

SERVES 6

1 CUP BLACK BEANS, PRESOAKED (SEE PAGE 151) AND DRAINED

3 CUPS VEGETABLE STOCK (PAGE 21) OR STORE-BOUGHT VEGETABLE BROTH

1 CUP PLUS 1 TABLESPOON CANOLA OIL

4 SCALLIONS (WHITE AND GREEN PARTS), FINELY CHOPPED

2 CUPS FROZEN CORN, DEFROSTED

1 MEDIUM YELLOW OR ORANGE BELL PEPPER, SEEDED, DERIBBED, AND FINELY CHOPPED

½ CUP CHERRY TOMATOES, QUARTERED

1 SMALL JALAPEÑO PEPPER, SEEDED, DERIBBED, AND FINELY CHOPPED

3 TEASPOONS SALT, PLUS MORE IF NEEDED

1 HEAD ROMAINE LETTUCE, FINELY CHOPPED

1 CUP SHREDDED SHARP CHEDDAR CHEESE

2 TABLESPOONS FRESH LIME JUICE

¼ CUP WHITE WINE VINEGAR

½ TEASPOON GROUND CUMIN

2 TABLESPOONS FINELY CHOPPED RED ONION

¼ CUP FINELY CHOPPED FRESH CILANTRO

6 DROPS OF TABASCO OR ANOTHER HOT SAUCE, PLUS MORE IF NEEDED

1 LARGE HASS AVOCADO, FINELY CHOPPED

1 Combine the beans and stock in the pressure cooker and drizzle with 1 tablespoon of the oil. Lock the lid in place and cook at high pressure for 20 minutes.

2 Release the pressure naturally and remove the lid, tilting the pot away from you to avoid the escaping steam. Drain the beans and allow to cool.

3 In a large bowl, combine the cooled black beans, scallions, corn, bell pepper, tomatoes, and jalapeño, tossing to combine. Sprinkle with 2 teaspoons of the salt and set aside. Put the lettuce and cheese in another large mixing bowl.

4 In a medium bowl, whisk together the remaining 1 cup of oil, the lime juice, vinegar, cumin, onion, cilantro, the remaining teaspoon of salt, and the Tabasco, stirring to blend. Taste the dressing for seasoning and add more salt and Tabasco if needed. Stir in the avocado and pour about ⅓ cup of the dressing over the romaine and cheese, tossing to blend. Arrange some of the lettuce mixture on each plate. Pour the remaining dressing over the bean mixture and toss to combine. Spoon over the lettuce and serve the salad cold.

POULTRY

Chicken, turkey, and Cornish game hens braise to perfection in the pressure cooker, emerging succulent and flavorful. Try making **PULLED CHICKEN FOR BARBECUE** (page 180) or **CHICKEN ENCHILADAS** (page 182). Chicken salads are simple when you cook boneless chicken breasts in less than five minutes and then cut them into bite-size pieces. Lots of choices and flavors await you when you use the pressure cooker for poultry.

CUT OF POULTRY	COOKING TIME AT HIGH PRESSURE
Chicken breast (bone in)	5 minutes
Chicken breast (boneless)	4 minutes
Chicken thigh (bone in)	8 minutes
Chicken thigh (boneless)	4 minutes
Cornish game hen (1 to 1½ pounds)	7 minutes
Turkey breast (bone in with stuffing, 4 pounds)	30 minutes
Turkey breast (boneless, 2 to 3 pounds)	22 minutes
Whole chicken (3 pounds)	16 to 18 minutes

These cooking times are based on a natural release of pressure. If your poultry weighs more, add 4 minutes of cooking time per pound.

COOKED CHICKEN

Cooking chicken breasts in the pressure cooker gives you instant morsels to use for casseroles and salads. Simple, quick, and easily stored for future meals, this is my go-to recipe when chicken is on sale and I can save a bit of money.

MAKES ABOUT **6** CUPS

1½ CUPS CHICKEN STOCK (PAGE 19) OR STORE-BOUGHT CHICKEN BROTH

8 SKINLESS, BONELESS CHICKEN BREAST HALVES

1 Combine the stock and chicken in the pressure cooker, stacking the chicken to fit. Lock the lid in place and cook at high pressure for 5 minutes.

2 Release the pressure naturally and remove the lid, tilting the pot away from you to avoid the escaping steam. Remove the chicken to a cutting board. Strain the broth and reserve for a later use (refrigerate for up to 4 days or freeze for up to 6 months). If using the chicken for a salad, chop into ½-inch dice. Or shred it for a Mexican dish. If not using right away, cool and refrigerate for up to 3 days or freeze in airtight containers for up to 3 months.

WALDORF SALAD

Said to have originated at the Waldorf-Astoria Hotel in New York City, the original salad combined juicy chunks of chicken with sweet apples, toasted walnuts, and celery, tossed in a mayonnaise-based dressing. This contemporary version with a sweet and savory poppy seed vinaigrette lightens things up. Serve the salad with Parker House rolls on the side.

SERVES 6 TO 8

1 RECIPE COOKED CHICKEN (FACING PAGE), CUT INTO BITE-SIZE PIECES

4 CELERY STALKS, FINELY CHOPPED

3 LARGE GALA APPLES, CORED AND FINELY CHOPPED

2 TABLESPOONS FINELY CHOPPED FRESH CHIVES

¼ CUP APPLE JUICE

2 TABLESPOONS CIDER VINEGAR

2 TABLESPOONS SUGAR

½ TEASPOON DRY MUSTARD

1 TEASPOON SALT

6 DROPS OF TABASCO OR ANOTHER HOT SAUCE

¾ CUP CANOLA OIL

1 TABLESPOON POPPY SEEDS

1 HEAD BIBB LETTUCE, SEPARATED INTO LEAVES

1 CUP CHOPPED WALNUTS, TOASTED (SEE PSST ON PAGE 114) FOR GARNISH

1 In a large mixing bowl, combine the chicken, celery, apples, and chives. In a small mixing bowl, whisk together the apple juice, vinegar, sugar, dry mustard, salt, Tabasco, oil, and poppy seeds until blended.

2 Pour some of the dressing over the chicken mixture and toss to coat. Add more dressing if necessary and toss again. Serve the chicken on Bibb lettuce leaves and garnish with the toasted walnuts. The salad can be refrigerated for up to 8 hours before serving. Take it out of the refrigerator 30 minutes before serving and retoss to blend.

MEDITERRANEAN CHICKEN AND PASTA SALAD

Boasting a Mediterranean flavor, this colorful pasta salad with bright red tomatoes, cucumbers, and Kalamata olives will cool you off on a hot summer day. Serve the salad with fresh fruit to keep the meal cool and refreshing.

SERVES **6** TO **8**

1 RECIPE COOKED CHICKEN (PAGE 174)

1 POUND FUSILLI OR SHELL PASTA, COOKED 2 MINUTES SHORT OF AL DENTE (SEE PSST)

1 CUP CHERRY TOMATOES, QUARTERED

1 ENGLISH CUCUMBER, FINELY CHOPPED

1 CUP KALAMATA OLIVES, DRAINED, PITTED, AND SLICED

½ CUP FINELY CHOPPED RED ONION

1½ CUPS CRUMBLED FETA CHEESE

1 CUP EXTRA-VIRGIN OLIVE OIL

½ CUP CANOLA OIL

½ CUP RED WINE VINEGAR

2 GARLIC CLOVES, MINCED

2 TABLESPOONS DRIED DILL WEED

1 TEASPOON SUGAR

1½ TEASPOONS SALT

1 TEASPOON FRESHLY GROUND BLACK PEPPER

1 In a large salad bowl, combine the chicken, pasta, tomatoes, cucumber, olives, onion, and feta, tossing to combine. In a small mixing bowl, whisk together the oils, vinegar, garlic, dill, sugar, salt, and pepper.

2 Pour the dressing over the salad and toss to combine. Serve the salad cold or at room temperature. It can be covered and refrigerated for up to 8 hours. Take it out of the refrigerator 30 minutes before serving and retoss to blend.

PSST

The reason for cooking the pasta 2 minutes short of al dente is that the acid in the dressing will soften the pasta.

CHICKEN AND DILL SALAD

Equally delicious served on lettuce leaves or in a sandwich on whole-grain bread, this salad is filled with the fresh flavor of dill. A lemony dressing gives it lots of character.

SERVES **6** TO **8**

1 RECIPE COOKED CHICKEN (PAGE 174)

2 CUPS FINELY CHOPPED CELERY

1 CUP SEEDLESS RED GRAPES, HALVED

4 SCALLIONS (WHITE AND TENDER GREEN PARTS), FINELY CHOPPED

1½ CUPS MAYONNAISE

2 TABLESPOONS FRESH LEMON JUICE

GRATED ZEST OF 1 LEMON

3 TABLESPOONS FINELY CHOPPED FRESH DILL

SALT AND FRESHLY GROUND BLACK PEPPER (OPTIONAL)

In a mixing bowl, combine the chicken, celery, grapes, and scallions. In a small mixing bowl, whisk together the mayonnaise, lemon juice and zest, and dill. Pour over the chicken mixture and toss to coat. Taste for seasoning and add salt and pepper if necessary before serving. Refrigerate the salad, covered, for up to 2 days.

BUFFALO CHICKEN SANDWICHES

Buffalo chicken wings are everyone's favorite. There is something so appealing about fried spicy wings served with cooling celery and blue cheese dressing. Although the pressure cooker won't deep-fry the chicken, it will infuse the meat with the spicy flavors that make Buffalo chicken so addictive.

SERVES 8

½ CUP (1 STICK) UNSALTED BUTTER

½ CUP CHICKEN STOCK (PAGE 19) OR STORE-BOUGHT CHICKEN BROTH

¼ CUP FRANK'S REDHOT SAUCE (SEE PSST), OR TABASCO

8 BONELESS SKINLESS CHICKEN BREAST HALVES

8 KAISER ROLLS

1 CUP BLUE CHEESE DRESSING, EITHER HOMEMADE (SEE FACING PAGE) OR STORE-BOUGHT

8 LEAVES BIBB LETTUCE

1 In the pressure cooker, melt the butter with the stock and hot sauce over medium-high heat. Coat the chicken with the mixture and stack in the pressure cooker. Lock the lid in place and cook at high pressure for 5 minutes.

2 Release the pressure naturally and remove the lid, tilting the pot away from you to avoid the escaping steam. Remove the chicken from the sauce and place each chicken breast on the bottom half of a kaiser roll. Top with a dollop of the blue cheese dressing and cover with a lettuce leaf. Drizzle a bit of the sauce on the other half of the kaiser roll and close the sandwich. Serve a small ramekin of sauce with each sandwich for dipping.

PSST

Frank's is the hot sauce used at the Anchor Bar in Buffalo, New York, where Buffalo wings were created. Frank's has more of a hot chile flavor than Tabasco sauce, which is a bit vinegary. The choice is yours.

BLUE CHEESE DRESSING

MAKES **2¼** CUPS

¾ CUP MAYONNAISE
(LOW-FAT IS FINE)

½ CUP SOUR CREAM

1 TABLESPOON WORCESTERSHIRE
SAUCE

1 TEASPOON FRESH LEMON JUICE

1 TEASPOON RED WINE VINEGAR

1 CUP CRUMBLED BLUE CHEESE
(SEE PSST)

In a mixing bowl, whisk together the ingredients until blended. Cover and refrigerate the dressing for at least 2 hours or up to 4 days.

PSST

Use your favorite blue. I love Maytag or Point Reyes.

PULLED CHICKEN FOR BARBECUE

A cayenne-spiked all-purpose barbecue rub gets these chicken breasts ready to be slathered with your favorite barbecue sauce. I like to tuck it into soft rolls (see the variation).

MAKES ENOUGH FOR 12 SANDWICHES

1 TEASPOON GARLIC SALT

2 TABLESPOONS FIRMLY PACKED LIGHT BROWN SUGAR

1 TABLESPOON SWEET PAPRIKA

½ TEASPOON CAYENNE PEPPER

2 TEASPOONS CELERY SEEDS

1 TEASPOON ONION SALT

8 BONELESS, SKINLESS CHICKEN BREAST HALVES

1½ CUPS CHICKEN STOCK (PAGE 19) OR STORE-BOUGHT CHICKEN BROTH

1 In a small bowl, combine the garlic salt, sugar, paprika, cayenne, celery seeds, and onion salt. Rub the mixture into the chicken. Pour the stock into the pressure cooker and stack the chicken to fit. Lock the lid in place and cook at high pressure for 5 minutes.

2 Release the pressure naturally and remove the lid, tilting the pot away from you to avoid the escaping steam. Remove the chicken from the pot and transfer to a cutting board. Strain the stock; it's terrific to add to barbecue sauce for extra flavor. Pull the chicken apart into shreds or cut into ½-inch dice. If not using the stock right away, refrigerate for up to 4 days or freeze in airtight containers for up to 6 months. Cool and refrigerate the chicken for up to 3 days or freeze for up to 3 months.

PULLED CHICKEN SANDWICHES

In a Dutch oven, combine the cooked chicken with 1 recipe of **ALABAMA-STYLE BBQ SAUCE** (page 201) and simmer over low heat for 1 hour. Serve the chicken on soft rolls with slaw or potato salad on the side.

PULLED CHICKEN FOR ENCHILADAS, TACOS, AND BURRITOS

Tender chunks of chicken cook in a salsa-flavored broth, which permeates the chicken. It's terrific for enchiladas, tacos, tostados, or any other south-of-the-border dish you would like to make. The sauce is perfect to spoon over enchiladas or quesadillas.

MAKES ENOUGH TO FILL
12 ENCHILADAS

2 TABLESPOONS CANOLA OIL

2 MEDIUM ONIONS, FINELY CHOPPED

1 MEDIUM RED BELL PEPPER, SEEDED, DERIBBED, AND COARSELY CHOPPED

1 MEDIUM GREEN BELL PEPPER, SEEDED, DERIBBED, AND COARSELY CHOPPED

1 TEASPOON GROUND CUMIN

2 TABLESPOONS FRESH LIME JUICE

THREE 8-OUNCE JARS MEDIUM-HOT SALSA

1½ CUPS CHICKEN STOCK (PAGE 19) OR STORE-BOUGHT CHICKEN BROTH

8 BONELESS, SKINLESS CHICKEN BREAST HALVES

1 Heat the oil in the pressure cooker over medium-high heat. Add the onions, peppers, and cumin and sauté for 2 to 3 minutes to soften the onions. Add the lime juice, salsa, and stock, stirring to combine. Put the chicken breasts in the sauce, stacking the chicken to fit. Lock the lid in place and cook at high pressure for 5 minutes.

2 Release the pressure naturally and remove the lid, tilting the pot away from you to avoid the escaping steam. Remove the chicken from the pot and transfer to a cutting board. Skim any excess fat from the sauce. Pull the chicken apart into shreds or cut into ½-inch dice. If not using right away, refrigerate the sauce for up to 4 days or freeze in airtight containers for up to 6 months. Cool the chicken and refrigerate for up to 3 days or freeze for up to 3 months.

CHICKEN ENCHILADAS

Succulent chicken enchiladas make for a simple weeknight supper or potluck take-along. To complete this one-dish meal, serve with a salad.

SERVES **6**

1 RECIPE PULLED CHICKEN FOR ENCHILADAS, TACOS, AND BURRITOS (PAGE 181), INCLUDING 4 TO 5 CUPS OF THE SAUCE

2 CUPS SHREDDED MONTEREY JACK CHEESE

2 CUPS SHREDDED MILD CHEDDAR CHEESE

2 CUPS SOUR CREAM

TWELVE 6-INCH CORN TORTILLAS

1 Preheat the oven to 350 degrees F. Coat the inside of a 13-by-9-inch pan with nonstick cooking spray.

2 In a large mixing bowl, combine the chicken, 1 cup of the Monterey Jack Cheese, 1 cup of the Cheddar cheese, and the sour cream, stirring to combine.

3 Heat the sauce in a skillet. Spread out about ½ cup in the prepared baking dish to cover the bottom. Dip a tortilla into the sauce in the skillet to soften it and transfer it to a flat work surface. Put 1 cup of the cheese mixture in the tortilla, roll it up, and place, seam-side down, in the prepared dish. Repeat with the remaining tortillas and filling. Cover the enchiladas with the remaining sauce in the skillet and the remaining cup of each cheese. Bake for 30 minutes, or until the sauce is bubbling and the cheese begins to turn golden brown. Allow the enchiladas to rest for 5 to 10 minutes before serving.

TROPICAL HAWAIIAN CHICKEN

Fragrant with garlic and ginger and flavored with soy sauce and pineapple juice, this dish will transport you to the islands. You might even find yourself singing "Tiny Bubbles," by the Hawaiian singer Don Ho, while it cooks. The chicken is equally good hot or cold. Serve it with sticky rice and stir-fried vegetables.

SERVES 6

¼ CUP CANOLA OIL

2 POUNDS BONE-IN CHICKEN PARTS, SKIN REMOVED

4 GARLIC CLOVES, MINCED

2 TEASPOONS GRATED FRESH GINGER

1 CUP PINEAPPLE JUICE

½ CUP SOY SAUCE

¼ CUP KETCHUP

2 TABLESPOONS SEASONED RICE VINEGAR

¼ CUP CHICKEN STOCK (PAGE 19) OR STORE-BOUGHT CHICKEN BROTH

1 TEASPOON CHILI GARLIC SAUCE

1 Heat the oil in the pressure cooker over medium-high heat. Add the chicken, a few pieces at a time, and brown, removing the browned pieces to a plate. Add the garlic and ginger and sauté for 1 minute. Add the pineapple juice, soy sauce, ketchup, vinegar, and stock. Return the chicken to the pot. Lock the lid in place and cook at high pressure for 15 minutes.

2 Release the pressure naturally and remove the lid, tilting the pot away from you to avoid the escaping steam. Carefully remove the chicken to a serving platter. Bring the sauce to a boil, add the chili garlic sauce, and boil the sauce until reduced by a quarter and slightly thickened. Pour some of it over the chicken and serve the rest on the side.

LEMON-GARLIC CHICKEN

This is similar to one of Frank Sinatra's favorites dishes, which he used to order from a restaurant in Palm Springs when he had a hankering for it. Ready in less than fifteen minutes, this simple, intensely flavored chicken is terrific served with mashed potatoes, rice, or pasta.

SERVES 6

3 TABLESPOONS EXTRA-VIRGIN OLIVE OIL

2 TEASPOONS SALT

2 POUNDS BONE-IN CHICKEN PARTS, SKIN REMOVED

4 GARLIC CLOVES, SLICED

PINCH OF RED PEPPER FLAKES

1 TEASPOON DRIED OREGANO

½ CUP DRY WHITE WINE, SUCH AS SAUVIGNON BLANC OR PINOT GRIGIO, OR DRY VERMOUTH

½ CUP FRESH LEMON JUICE (2 LEMONS)

½ CUP CHICKEN STOCK (PAGE 19) OR STORE-BOUGHT CHICKEN BROTH

1 TABLESPOON FINELY CHOPPED FRESH OREGANO

¼ CUP FINELY CHOPPED FRESH FLAT-LEAF PARSLEY

1 Heat the oil in the pressure cooker over medium-high heat. Sprinkle the salt evenly over the chicken. Add the chicken to the pot, a few pieces at a time, and brown, removing the browned pieces to a plate. Add the garlic, red pepper flakes, and oregano to the pot and cook for 1 minute, or until the garlic is fragrant. Add the wine, lemon juice, and stock to the pot and arrange the chicken in the pressure cooker. Lock the lid in place and cook at high pressure for 15 minutes.

2 Release the pressure naturally and remove the lid, tilting the pot away from you to avoid the escaping steam. Carefully remove the chicken to a serving platter, bring the sauce to a boil, and add the oregano and parsley. Pour the sauce over the chicken and serve.

PSST

If you choose to use boneless chicken parts, reduce the cooking time to 8 minutes.

CHICKEN WITH OLIVES AND LEMON

A tagine is a Moroccan cooking vessel with a vented conical top, and it's also the name of the type of dish that it's used for: a slowly simmered braise flavored with saffron, coriander, paprika, and other spices. Tagines are made with a variety of meats, including lamb (see page 239). Some have sweet sauces flavored with dried fruits, while others have more savory ingredients, such as olives and preserved lemons. This version was inspired by one from my favorite Moroccan restaurant in Paris, Le Table de Fès. Serve with couscous to soak up the delicious sauce.

SERVES 6

....

4 TABLESPOONS EXTRA-VIRGIN OLIVE OIL

1 TEASPOON SAFFRON THREADS, CRUSHED IN THE PALM OF YOUR HAND

1 TEASPOON GROUND CUMIN

½ TEASPOON GROUND CORIANDER

PINCH OF RED PEPPER FLAKES

PINCH OF GROUND CLOVES

PINCH OF GROUND CINNAMON

3 POUNDS CHICKEN LEGS AND THIGHS, SKIN REMOVED

2 LARGE ONIONS, FINELY CHOPPED

3 GARLIC CLOVES, MINCED

1½ CUPS CHICKEN STOCK (PAGE 19) OR STORE-BOUGHT CHICKEN BROTH

2 TABLESPOONS FRESH LEMON JUICE

½ CUP OIL-CURED GREEN OLIVES, PITTED

1 LEMON, THINLY SLICED

¼ CUP FINELY CHOPPED FRESH CILANTRO

1 In a large mixing bowl, combine 2 tablespoons of the oil with the saffron, cumin, coriander, pepper flakes, cloves, and cinnamon. Add the chicken to the bowl and toss to coat. Heat the remaining 2 tablespoons of oil in the pressure cooker over medium-high heat. Brown the chicken on all sides, a few pieces at a time, and transfer the browned pieces to a plate. Add the onions and garlic to the pot, and any spiced oil in the chicken bowl, and sauté for 2 minutes, or until the onions begin to soften. Return the chicken to the pot and pour in the stock and lemon juice. Lock the lid in place and cook at high pressure for 8 minutes.

2 Release the pressure naturally and remove the lid, tilting the pot away from you to avoid the escaping steam. Transfer the chicken to a serving platter and cover with aluminum foil to keep warm.

3 Bring the sauce to a boil, add the olives, lemon slices, and cilantro, and simmer for 10 minutes to concentrate the flavors. Spoon the sauce over the chicken and serve.

CHICKEN TIKKA MASALA

This is one of our favorite meals when we go to London. Some call it the national dish of Britain, having been brought from India by British officers who loved the tender, juicy chicken simmered in a spicy tomato cream sauce. After marinating for six hours, the chicken will be out of the pressure cooker in less than fifteen minutes. Serve it with basmati rice and a fruit salad.

SERVES **6**

MARINADE

2 CUPS PLAIN YOGURT

1 TEASPOON GROUND TURMERIC

1 TEASPOON SWEET PAPRIKA

1 TEASPOON GROUND CORIANDER

⅛ TEASPOON CAYENNE PEPPER

2 TABLESPOONS GRATED FRESH GINGER

2 GARLIC CLOVES, MINCED

8 BONELESS, SKINLESS CHICKEN THIGHS

2 TABLESPOONS CANOLA OIL

2 LARGE ONIONS, FINELY CHOPPED

3 GARLIC CLOVES, MINCED

1 TABLESPOON GRATED FRESH GINGER

2 TABLESPOONS GARAM MASALA

ONE 14-OUNCE CAN CHOPPED TOMATOES, DRAINED

½ CUP CHICKEN STOCK (PAGE 19) OR STORE-BOUGHT CHICKEN BROTH

1½ CUPS HEAVY CREAM

¼ CUP FINELY CHOPPED FRESH CILANTRO FOR GARNISH

1 **To make the marinade:** In a large mixing bowl, whisk together all the ingredients.

2 Put the chicken in a zipper-top plastic bag and pour the marinade over the chicken. Seal the bag and refrigerate for at least 6 hours or overnight.

3 Remove the chicken from the marinade and set aside. Discard the marinade. Heat the oil in the pressure cooker. Add the onions, garlic, ginger, and garam masala and sauté for 2 to 3 minutes to soften the onions. Add the tomatoes and stock and arrange the chicken in the pressure cooker. Lock the lid in place and cook at high pressure for 4 minutes.

4 Release the pressure naturally and remove the lid, tilting the pot away from you to avoid the escaping steam. Transfer the chicken to a bowl and cover loosely with aluminum foil.

5 Bring the sauce to a boil and add the cream, stirring to blend. Warm the sauce and pour over the chicken. Serve garnished with the cilantro.

TANDOORI-STYLE CHICKEN

A tandoor is a clay oven used in Indian cuisine. Tandoori chicken is marinated in a spicy yogurt blend, which turns the chicken red when it's cooked. Replicating this dish in the pressure cooker is simple. The result is tender chicken in a luscious sauce, ready to serve over basmati rice.

SERVES **6**

2 CUPS PLAIN YOGURT

1 TEASPOON GROUND TURMERIC

½ TEASPOON SALT

1 GARLIC CLOVE, MINCED

PINCH OF CAYENNE PEPPER

1 TEASPOON GARAM MASALA

1 TEASPOON FRESH LEMON JUICE

2 TEASPOONS SUGAR

8 BONELESS, SKINLESS CHICKEN BREAST HALVES

2 TABLESPOONS CANOLA OIL

½ CUP CHICKEN STOCK (PAGE 19) OR STORE-BOUGHT CHICKEN BROTH

1 In a large mixing bowl, whisk together the yogurt, turmeric, salt, garlic, cayenne, garam masala, lemon juice, and sugar. Put the chicken in a zipper-top plastic bag, and pour the marinade over the chicken. Seal the bag and refrigerate for at least 4 hours or overnight.

2 Remove the chicken from the marinade, reserving the marinade. Heat the oil in the pressure cooker over medium-high heat. Add the chicken and brown in the oil. Add the marinade to the pot and pour in the stock. Lock the lid in place and cook at high pressure for 5 minutes.

3 Release the pressure naturally and remove the lid, tilting the pot away from you to avoid the escaping steam. Remove the chicken from the sauce and set aside, covered with aluminum foil.

4 Bring the sauce to a boil, reduce the heat, and simmer until it is reduced and thickened, about 10 minutes. Return the chicken to the sauce and serve.

CURRIED CHICKEN WITH CHUTNEY MAYONNAISE

Lots of tender chicken is jumbled with chunks of cantaloupe, celery, apples, golden raisins, and salted cashews, giving you a different taste in every bite. The salad is terrific served in a hollowed-out pineapple or small melon.

SERVES 6

1 RECIPE COOKED CHICKEN (PAGE 174)

1 CUP FINELY CHOPPED CELERY

2 GALA APPLES, CORED AND CUT INTO ½-INCH DICE

1 CUP GOLDEN RAISINS

1 CUP CHOPPED CANTALOUPE

⅔ CUP MAYONNAISE

¼ CUP SOUR CREAM OR PLAIN YOGURT

¼ CUP FINELY CHOPPED MAJOR GREY'S CHUTNEY

1½ TEASPOONS MADRAS CURRY POWDER

1 CUP FINELY CHOPPED SALTED ROASTED CASHEWS FOR GARNISH

½ CUP DRIED BANANA CHIPS FOR GARNISH

¼ CUP TOASTED SWEETENED SHREDDED COCONUT (SEE PSST) FOR GARNISH

1 In a mixing bowl, combine the chicken, celery, apples, raisins, and cantaloupe. In a small bowl, whisk together the mayonnaise, sour cream, chutney, and curry powder until blended.

2 Pour the dressing over the chicken and toss to coat. Serve the salad garnished with cashews, banana chips, and toasted coconut. The salad can be refrigerated for up to 8 hours before serving. Take it out of the refrigerator 30 minutes before serving and retoss to blend.

PSST

To toast coconut, preheat the oven to 350 degrees F. Line a baking sheet with parchment paper or a silicone liner. Toast the coconut for 10 minutes, shaking the pan after 5 minutes to turn and redistribute the coconut. When the coconut has turned golden brown, remove from the oven and allow to cool completely.

CURRIED CHICKEN AND RICE WITH YOGURT CHUTNEY

I love the complex flavor of curry with chicken. Sweet, hot, and smoky, this one-pot meal features chicken in a coconut milk sauce and fragrant basmati rice, all ready in less than ten minutes.

SERVES **6**

2 TABLESPOONS CANOLA OIL

1 LARGE ONION, FINELY CHOPPED

2 LARGE GRANNY SMITH APPLES, PEELED, CORED, AND FINELY CHOPPED

1 GARLIC CLOVE, MINCED

1 TEASPOON GROUND GINGER

1½ TEASPOONS MADRAS CURRY POWDER

½ TEASPOON GARAM MASALA

6 BONELESS, SKINLESS CHICKEN BREAST HALVES, CUT INTO 1-INCH PIECES

4 CUPS CHICKEN STOCK (PAGE 19) OR STORE-BOUGHT CHICKEN BROTH

1 CUP COCONUT MILK

1 CUP BASMATI RICE

¼ CUP FINELY CHOPPED FRESH CILANTRO FOR GARNISH

1 CUP PLAIN YOGURT

½ CUP FINELY CHOPPED MANGO CHUTNEY (PAGE 428)

1 Heat the oil in the pressure cooker over medium-high heat. Add the onion, apples, garlic, ginger, curry powder, and garam masala and sauté for about 3 minutes, or until the spices are fragrant. Add the chicken and sauté for 1 minute to coat the chicken in the spices. Pour in the chicken stock and coconut milk and stir to blend. Add the rice to the pot and stir to submerge the rice. Lock the lid in place and cook at high pressure for 5 minutes.

2 Release the pressure naturally and remove the lid, tilting the pot away from you to avoid the escaping steam. Stir the chicken and rice and transfer to a serving bowl. Garnish the curry with the cilantro. In a small bowl, combine the yogurt and chutney and serve alongside the curry.

CHICKEN CACCIATORE WITH RED SAUCE

There really is no definitive answer about where this dish came from. *Cacciatore* means "hunter style." There are two versions in this chapter. This is the one you'll often find on the menus at casual Italian American red sauce restaurants. In addition to the tomatoes, it includes bell peppers, hearty cremini mushrooms, and a hint of spicy red pepper. It doesn't take long at all for the chicken to absorb the flavors of the sauce in the pressure cooker—about as long as it takes to boil water for pasta, which is the perfect side dish.

SERVES 6

2 TABLESPOONS EXTRA-VIRGIN OLIVE OIL

2 TEASPOONS SALT, PLUS MORE IF NEEDED

1 TEASPOON FRESHLY GROUND BLACK PEPPER, PLUS MORE IF NEEDED

4 BONE-IN CHICKEN THIGHS, SKIN REMOVED

4 BONE-IN CHICKEN BREAST HALVES, SKIN REMOVED

1 LARGE SWEET ONION, SUCH AS VIDALIA, COARSELY CHOPPED

2 GARLIC CLOVES, MINCED

1 TEASPOON DRIED OREGANO

PINCH OF RED PEPPER FLAKES

½ POUND CREMINI MUSHROOMS, QUARTERED

1 MEDIUM RED BELL PEPPER, SEEDED, DERIBBED, AND COARSELY CHOPPED

1 MEDIUM GREEN BELL PEPPER, SEEDED, DERIBBED, AND COARSELY CHOPPED

¼ CUP FULL-BODIED RED WINE, SUCH AS CHIANTI, ZINFANDEL, OR BAROLO

ONE 14-OUNCE CAN CRUSHED TOMATOES WITH THEIR JUICE

¼ CUP FINELY CHOPPED FRESH FLAT-LEAF PARSLEY

PASTA, SUCH AS LINGUINE, FARFALLE, OR PAPPARDELLE, FOR SERVING (OPTIONAL)

1 Heat the oil in the pressure cooker over medium-high heat. Sprinkle the salt and pepper evenly over the chicken and brown the chicken on all sides, a few pieces at a time, removing the browned pieces to a plate. Add the onion, garlic, oregano, and pepper flakes to the pot and sauté for 2 minutes to soften the onion. Add the mushrooms, bell peppers, wine, and tomatoes to the pot, stirring to combine. Return the chicken to the pot, lock the lid in place, and cook at high pressure for 8 minutes.

2 Release the pressure naturally and remove the lid, tilting the pot away from you to avoid the escaping steam. Carefully remove the chicken from the pot, transfer to a serving platter, and cover with aluminum foil to keep warm.

3 Bring the sauce to a boil, add the parsley, and remove from the heat. Taste the sauce for seasoning and add salt and pepper if necessary. Pour the sauce over the chicken and serve. Or pour half of the sauce over the chicken and toss the rest with pasta.

CHICKEN CACCIATORE WITH WHITE SAUCE

This is the cacciatore that I grew up with. My *nona* would make it and tell me the legends of her native town of Gubbio, including the story of the wolf that was tamed by one of Gubbio's most famous visitors, St. Francis. This cacciatore relies on ingredients a hunter might have carried with him to cook his dinner: a bit of lardo or salt pork, herbs, garlic, and vinegar. In the years since Nona has been gone, I've had the pleasure of roaming the streets and hills around Gubbio and Assisi, where the food reminds me of her.

SERVES 6

8 THICK-CUT BACON STRIPS, CUT CROSSWISE INTO PIECES ½ INCH WIDE

8 GARLIC CLOVES, SLICED

1 TABLESPOON FINELY CHOPPED FRESH ROSEMARY, PLUS EXTRA SPRIGS FOR GARNISH

8 BONE-IN CHICKEN THIGHS, SKIN REMOVED

1 TEASPOON SALT

1 TEASPOON FRESHLY GROUND BLACK PEPPER

⅔ CUP CHICKEN STOCK (PAGE 19) OR STORE-BOUGHT CHICKEN BROTH

½ CUP BALSAMIC VINEGAR

1 Cook the bacon in the pressure cooker until crisp, remove, and drain on paper towels. Remove all but 2 tablespoons of the bacon fat. Add the garlic and chopped rosemary and sauté for 1 minute, or until fragrant. Sprinkle the chicken evenly with the salt and pepper and brown on all sides, a few pieces at a time, removing the browned pieces to a plate. Return all the chicken to the pot and pour in the stock and vinegar. Lock the lid in place and cook at high pressure for 8 minutes.

2 Release the pressure naturally and remove the lid, tilting the pot away from you to avoid the escaping steam. Transfer the chicken to a serving platter and spoon the sauce over the chicken. Garnish with the reserved bacon and rosemary sprigs.

CHICKEN PROVENÇAL

Tarragon, artichoke hearts, a bit of tomato, and a finish of cream make this dish a winner. The fact that it's cooked in less than ten minutes gives it a gold star in my book! You can certainly make it with bone-in chicken parts (see the Psst), but I prefer to use boneless chicken breasts for easier serving.

SERVES 6

2 TABLESPOONS EXTRA-VIRGIN OLIVE OIL

6 BONELESS, SKINLESS CHICKEN BREAST HALVES (SEE PSST)

2 TEASPOONS SALT, PLUS MORE IF NEEDED

1 TEASPOON FRESHLY GROUND BLACK PEPPER, PLUS MORE IF NEEDED

2 MEDIUM SHALLOTS, FINELY CHOPPED

2 TEASPOONS DRIED THYME

1 BAY LEAF

1 CUP DRY WHITE WINE, SUCH AS SAUVIGNON BLANC OR PINOT GRIGIO, OR DRY VERMOUTH

ONE 14-OUNCE CAN CHOPPED TOMATOES, DRAINED

ONE 10-OUNCE PACKAGE FROZEN ARTICHOKE HEARTS, DEFROSTED

½ CUP HEAVY CREAM

¼ CUP FINELY CHOPPED FRESH FLAT-LEAF PARSLEY

1 Heat the oil in the pressure cooker over medium-high heat. Sprinkle the chicken breasts with the salt and pepper. Sauté the chicken, a few pieces at a time, until they turn white on all sides, removing the pieces to a plate when they're done. Add the shallots, thyme, and bay leaf and sauté for 2 minutes to soften the shallots. Add the wine and tomatoes to the pot and top with the artichokes and chicken. Lock the lid in place and cook at high pressure for 5 minutes.

2 Release the pressure naturally and remove the lid, tilting the pot away from you to avoid the escaping steam. With a slotted spoon, transfer the chicken and artichokes to a serving platter. Remove the bay leaf and bring the sauce to a boil. Stir in the cream and parsley and remove from the heat. Taste the sauce for seasoning and add more salt and pepper if necessary. Spoon some of the sauce over the chicken and artichokes and serve the rest on the side.

PSST

If you use bone-in chicken parts, remove the skin and cook the chicken for 10 minutes at high pressure.

BONELESS COQ AU VIN

I love this dish because it reminds me of the first time I saw Julia Child on her *French Chef* television show. Julia whacked the chicken apart with the skill of a surgeon and then proceeded to make the most magnificent chicken stew. As a teenager, I was game to try it, and it was love at first bite. The succulent chicken simmers in red wine with some smoky bacon. Sautéed onions and mushrooms are added to the sauce at the end and voilà, a dish you can enjoy with your family or dress up for company. I prefer boneless parts to cutting apart a chicken; boneless pieces cook faster and serve up neatly.

SERVES **6**

8 THICK-CUT BACON STRIPS, CUT CROSSWISE INTO PIECES ½ INCH WIDE

4 BONELESS, SKINLESS CHICKEN BREAST HALVES

4 BONELESS, SKINLESS CHICKEN THIGHS

3 TEASPOONS SALT, PLUS MORE IF NEEDED

2 TEASPOONS FRESHLY GROUND BLACK PEPPER, PLUS MORE IF NEEDED

2 SPRIGS FRESH THYME

2 BAY LEAVES

2 CUPS BURGUNDY WINE

1 CUP CHICKEN STOCK (PAGE 19) OR STORE-BOUGHT CHICKEN BROTH

6 TABLESPOONS UNSALTED BUTTER, SOFTENED

24 SMALL PEARL ONIONS, PEELED (SEE PSST ON PAGE 275)

1 POUND WHITE BUTTON MUSHROOMS, HALVED

2 TABLESPOONS ALL-PURPOSE FLOUR

1 Cook the bacon in the pressure cooker over medium-high heat until crisp, remove, and drain on paper towels. Skim off all but 2 tablespoons of the bacon fat. Sprinkle the chicken pieces evenly with 2 teaspoons of the salt and 1 teaspoon of the pepper. Sauté in the pressure cooker, a few pieces at a time, removing the browned pieces to a plate. Add the thyme, bay leaves, wine, and stock to the pot and stir to blend. Put the chicken pieces in the broth. Lock the lid in place and cook at high pressure for 10 minutes.

2 While the chicken is cooking, melt 4 tablespoons of the butter in a large skillet over medium-high heat. Sauté the onions for 5 minutes, or until they begin to turn golden. Add the mushrooms, season with the remaining 1 teaspoon of salt and 1 teaspoon of pepper, and sauté until the mushrooms begin to turn golden. Remove from the heat and set aside until the chicken is cooked.

3 Release the pressure naturally and remove the lid, tilting the pot away from you to avoid the escaping steam. Carefully remove the chicken pieces from the sauce, transfer to a serving platter, and cover loosely with aluminum foil.

4 Remove the bay leaves and thyme from the sauce. Bring the sauce to a boil and continue boiling for 5 minutes, to reduce the sauce and concentrate the flavor. Stir the remaining 2 tablespoons of butter with the flour in a small dish, whisk into the sauce, and continue whisking until the sauce returns to a boil and thickens. Add the mushrooms and onions, taste for seasoning, and add more salt and pepper if necessary. Pour the sauce over the chicken, sprinkle with the bacon, and serve.

POULET EN COCOTTE

A classic roast chicken in the pressure cooker? Yes, indeed, and this one is ready in half the usual time. It's intensely flavored, moist and tender, and surrounded by potatoes and carrots. And best of all, it comes with a luscious pan sauce to spoon over the chicken.

SERVES 4 to 6

ONE 3- TO 4-POUND CHICKEN

1 TEASPOON SALT, PLUS MORE IF NEEDED

1 TEASPOON FRESHLY GROUND BLACK PEPPER, PLUS MORE IF NEEDED

6 THICK-CUT BACON STRIPS, CUT CROSSWISE INTO PIECES ½ INCH WIDE

2 LEEKS (WHITE AND TENDER GREEN PARTS), CLEANED AND COARSELY CHOPPED

4 MEDIUM YUKON GOLD OR RED-SKINNED POTATOES, SCRUBBED AND QUARTERED

4 MEDIUM CARROTS, CUT INTO 2-INCH LENGTHS

2 SPRIGS FRESH THYME

1 BAY LEAF

1 CUP DRY WHITE WINE, SUCH AS SAUVIGNON BLANC OR PINOT GRIGIO, OR DRY VERMOUTH

1 CUP CHICKEN STOCK (PAGE 19) OR STORE-BOUGHT CHICKEN BROTH

2 TABLESPOONS UNSALTED BUTTER, SOFTENED

2 TABLESPOONS ALL-PURPOSE FLOUR

½ CUP FINELY CHOPPED FRESH FLAT-LEAF PARSLEY

1 Sprinkle the chicken evenly inside and out with the salt and pepper. In the pressure cooker, cook the bacon over medium-high heat until it is crisp. Remove and drain on paper towels. Discard all but 2 tablespoons of the bacon fat. Brown the chicken in the pressure cooker, breast-side down, being careful not to rip the skin. (If the chicken sticks to the pot, it's not ready to be turned.) Turn the chicken and brown on all sides. Lift the chicken out of the pot and arrange the leeks on the bottom of the pot. Top with the chicken and surround the chicken with the potatoes and carrots. Add the thyme, bay leaf, wine, and stock. Lock the lid in place and cook at high pressure for 18 minutes for a 3-pound chicken or 24 minutes for a 4-pound bird.

2 Release the pressure naturally and remove the lid, tilting the pot away from you to avoid the escaping steam. Carefully transfer the chicken to a cutting board, cover with aluminum foil, and allow to rest for 15 minutes before carving. Transfer the potatoes and carrots to a bowl.

3 Strain the sauce into a saucepan. Bring the sauce to a boil, and continue boiling for 5 minutes to reduce the sauce and concentrate its flavor. Stir together the butter and flour in a small bowl and whisk into the sauce, stirring constantly. Return to a boil, reduce the heat, and simmer, still whisking, until the sauce is thickened. Stir in the parsley and remove from the heat. Taste for seasoning and add more salt and pepper if necessary.

4 Carve the chicken into serving pieces and arrange on a serving platter, surrounded by the vegetables. Spoon some of the pan sauce over the chicken and vegetables, sprinkle with the reserved bacon, and pass the remaining sauce on the side.

CORNISH GAME HENS FOR TWO

These juicy hens, simmered in a garlicky wine sauce, are fall-apart tender when they emerge after less than half an hour in the pressure cooker. For a special dinner, stuff them with **FRUITED WILD RICE** (page 346) and cook the hens for an additional seven minutes.

SERVES **2**

....

2 TABLESPOONS EXTRA-VIRGIN OLIVE OIL

TWO 1- TO 1½-POUND CORNISH GAME HENS

1½ TEASPOONS SALT, PLUS MORE IF NEEDED

½ TEASPOON FRESHLY GROUND BLACK PEPPER, PLUS MORE IF NEEDED

8 GARLIC CLOVES, PEELED AND LEFT WHOLE

2 BAY LEAVES

2 TEASPOONS FINELY CHOPPED FRESH THYME

1 CUP DRY WHITE WINE, SUCH AS SAUVIGNON BLANC OR PINOT GRIGIO, OR DRY VERMOUTH

½ CUP CHICKEN STOCK (PAGE 19) OR STORE-BOUGHT CHICKEN BROTH

2 TABLESPOONS UNSALTED BUTTER, SOFTENED

2 TABLESPOONS ALL-PURPOSE FLOUR

¼ CUP FINELY CHOPPED FRESH FLAT-LEAF PARSLEY

1 Heat the oil in the pressure cooker over medium-high heat. Sprinkle the hens evenly inside and out with the salt and pepper. Brown the hens, one at a time, in the pressure cooker, removing them to a plate when they are done. Add the garlic, bay leaves, and thyme to the pot and cook until fragrant, about 1 minute. Pour in the wine and stock and arrange the hens in the pot. Lock the lid in place and cook at high pressure for 7 minutes.

2 Release the pressure naturally and remove the lid, tilting the pot away from you to avoid the escaping steam. Carefully remove the hens, transfer to a serving platter, and cover loosely with aluminum foil.

3 Strain the sauce into a saucepan, pushing down on the garlic to push it through the sieve. Discard any solids and bring the sauce to a boil. In a small bowl, stir the butter with the flour and whisk into the sauce. Return to a boil, reduce the heat, and simmer, whisking, until thickened. Stir in the parsley and remove from the heat. Taste the sauce for seasoning and add more salt and pepper if necessary. Spoon some of the sauce over the hens and pass the rest on the side.

BRAISED TURKEY BREAST WITH SAGE AND APPLE STUFFING

Turkey breast tends to dry out in the oven, but this turkey, filled with a savory stuffing, is moist, tender, and bursting with flavor.

SERVES **6**

SAGE AND APPLE STUFFING

2 TABLESPOONS UNSALTED BUTTER

2 MEDIUM SHALLOTS, FINELY CHOPPED

1 CUP FINELY CHOPPED DRIED APPLE

1 LARGE GRANNY SMITH APPLE, PEELED, CORED, AND FINELY CHOPPED

1 TEASPOON DRIED SAGE

½ TEASPOON DRIED THYME

½ TEASPOON SALT

4 DROPS OF TABASCO OR ANOTHER HOT SAUCE

2 CUPS FRESH BREAD CRUMBS (TOUGH CRUSTS REMOVED)

1 LARGE EGG, LIGHTLY BEATEN

TURKEY BREAST

ONE 3-POUND BONE-IN TURKEY BREAST, SKIN REMOVED

2 TEASPOONS SALT, PLUS MORE IF NEEDED

1 TEASPOON FRESHLY GROUND BLACK PEPPER, PLUS MORE IF NEEDED

2 TABLESPOONS EXTRA-VIRGIN OLIVE OIL

1 CUP CHICKEN STOCK (PAGE 19) OR STORE-BOUGHT CHICKEN BROTH

½ CUP RIESLING WINE

1 SPRIG FRESH THYME

1 BAY LEAF

2 TABLESPOONS UNSALTED BUTTER, SOFTENED

2 TABLESPOONS ALL-PURPOSE FLOUR

1 **To make the stuffing:** In a medium skillet, melt the butter over medium-high heat. Add the shallots, dried and fresh apples, sage, thyme, and salt and cook until the shallots begin to soften, about 2 minutes. Transfer to a mixing bowl, sprinkle with the Tabasco, and allow to cool. Add the bread crumbs and egg and stir together to blend.

2 **To make the turkey:** Sprinkle the turkey breast evenly with the salt and pepper. Pack the stuffing into the turkey cavity and tie the turkey with butcher's twine or secure with silicone bands to keep in the stuffing. Heat the oil in the pressure cooker over medium-high heat. Add the turkey and brown on all sides. Lay the turkey breast on its side in the pressure cooker. Add the stock, wine, thyme, and bay leaf. Lock the lid in place and cook the turkey at high pressure for 20 minutes.

3 Release the pressure naturally and remove the lid, tilting the pot away from you to avoid the escaping steam. Transfer the turkey to a cutting board. Remove the stuffing from the cavity, transfer to a serving bowl, and cover with aluminum foil to keep warm. Allow the turkey to rest for 15 minutes before carving.

4 Remove the thyme and bay leaf from the sauce and bring the sauce to a boil for 5 minutes to reduce and concentrate the sauce. In a small bowl, stir together the butter and flour and whisk into the sauce. Return to a boil, reduce the heat, and simmer, whisking, until thickened. Remove from the heat, taste the sauce for seasoning, and add more salt and pepper if necessary. Carve the turkey, transfer to a serving platter, and spoon some of the sauce over the turkey. Serve with the stuffing and additional sauce on the side.

TURKEY BRAISED WITH DRIED FRUITS AND SHERRY

The dried figs and sherry offer a nice counterpoint to the onions in the sweet and savory sauce, which permeates the turkey breast. Serve with wild rice and sautéed zucchini or **HONEYED CARROTS** (page 140).

SERVES 6

¼ CUP CANOLA OIL

ONE 1½-POUND BONELESS, SKINLESS TURKEY BREAST, TIED WITH BUTCHER'S TWINE

1 TEASPOON SALT

½ TEASPOON FRESHLY GROUND BLACK PEPPER

2 LARGE SWEET ONIONS, SUCH AS VIDALIA, COARSELY CHOPPED

12 LARGE DRIED FIGS, COARSELY CHOPPED

6 DRIED PLUMS, COARSELY CHOPPED

2 SPRIGS FRESH THYME

1 BAY LEAF

½ CUP SHERRY

1 CUP CHICKEN STOCK (PAGE 19) OR STORE-BOUGHT CHICKEN BROTH

2 TABLESPOONS CORNSTARCH MIXED WITH ¼ CUP WATER

¼ CUP FINELY CHOPPED FRESH FLAT-LEAF PARSLEY

1 Heat the oil in the pressure cooker over medium-high heat. Sprinkle the turkey evenly with the salt and pepper, add to the pressure cooker, brown on all sides, and transfer to a plate. Add the onions, figs, plums, thyme, and bay leaf to the pot. Cook for 2 minutes to begin to soften the onions and pour in the sherry and stock. Return the turkey to the pot. Lock the lid in place and cook at high pressure for 18 minutes.

2 Release the pressure naturally and remove the lid, tilting the pot away from you to avoid the escaping steam. Remove the turkey to a cutting board. Allow to rest for 15 minutes, loosely covered with aluminum foil, before carving.

3 Remove the bay leaf and thyme from the sauce and bring the sauce to a boil. Whisk in the cornstarch slurry and return to a boil, whisking until the sauce is thickened and glossy. Stir in the parsley. Slice the turkey breast and arrange on a platter. Spoon some of the sauce over the turkey and serve the rest on the side.

PORK

Pork cooks up juicy and delicious in the pressure cooker. The cooker transforms tougher cuts into fork-tender, succulent roasts, stews, ribs, and pulled pork. Braising the pork in the pressure cooker makes a great dinner happen in half the time it would take to cook conventionally. Precooking ribs in the pressure cooker before giving them a flip on the grill ensures tender, juicy meat every time. Pulled pork, which can take almost all day in a slow cooker or half a day in the oven, is ready in one hour, all set to be pulled and slathered with your favorite barbecue sauce, served as carnitas, or stirred into a pasta sauce. Pork loin, which can be dry and tasteless, absorbs flavors well in the pressure cooker and becomes moist and tender in about half an hour.

CUT OF PORK	COOKING TIME AT HIGH PRESSURE
Baby back rib racks	10 minutes
Country-style ribs	15 minutes
Pork chops (boneless, 1 inch thick)	7 minutes
Pork chops (bone in, 1 inch thick)	8 minutes
Pork loin (4 pounds)	25 minutes
Pork shoulder (bone in, 4 pounds)	55 minutes
Pork shoulder (boneless, 4 pounds)	45 minutes
Pork stew meat (1-inch pieces)	8 minutes
Pork meatballs	5 minutes
Ham loaf	15 minutes
Ham meatballs	5 minutes

These cooking times are based on a natural release of pressure. If your meat weighs less, subtract 10 minutes of cooking time per pound.

PULLED PORK SHOULDER WITH ALABAMA-STYLE BBQ SAUCE

Pulled pork barbecue is one of life's simple pleasures—fork-tender meat bathed in barbecue sauce and served on a soft roll with a side of slaw. The idea of making pulled pork instead of buying it at your local BBQ joint may not have occurred to you. But pulled pork is so simple to make in your pressure cooker and it takes only forty-five minutes. The beauty of making it at home is that you can serve several different barbecue sauces to complement the meat. We love it Alabama style.

SERVES **6** TO **8**

2 LARGE ONIONS, COARSELY CHOPPED

1½ CUPS CHICKEN OR BEEF STOCK (PAGE 19 OR 20) OR STORE-BOUGHT CHICKEN OR BEEF BROTH

2 TABLESPOONS CANOLA OIL

1 TABLESPOON GARLIC SALT

¼ CUP FIRMLY PACKED LIGHT BROWN SUGAR

2 TABLESPOONS SWEET PAPRIKA

1 TEASPOON CAYENNE PEPPER

1 TABLESPOON CELERY SEEDS

1 TEASPOON SALT

ONE 4-POUND BONELESS PORK SHOULDER ROAST

ALABAMA-STYLE BBQ SAUCE FOR SERVING (FACING PAGE)

SOFT ROLLS FOR SERVING

1 Scatter the onions in the bottom of the pressure cooker and pour in the stock. In a small bowl, combine the oil, garlic salt, sugar, paprika, cayenne, celery seeds, and salt. With the tip of a sharp knife, make 1-inch slits in the meat, about 2 inches apart. Rub the spice mixture into the meat, pushing it into the slits. Set the pork over the onions. Lock the lid in place and cook at high pressure for 45 minutes.

2 Release the pressure naturally and remove the lid, tilting the pot away from you to avoid the escaping steam. Transfer the meat to a cutting board, cover with aluminum foil to keep warm, and allow to rest for 15 minutes. Skim off any fat, strain the cooking liquid, and measure out ¼ cup for the barbecue sauce. (Discard the rest or save for another use.) Make the barbecue sauce.

3 Remove any large pieces of fat on the pork and pull it apart with two forks. Pile it onto a serving platter and serve with rolls and barbecue sauce on the side.

ALABAMA-STYLE BBQ SAUCE

My family and I are addicted to Big Bob Gibson's Championship Red barbecue sauce; it has the right balance of sweet and hot, and we think it would taste good served on anything! Big Bob's is located in Decatur, Alabama, and serves some of the most delectable BBQ you will ever taste. The sauce recipe presented here is pretty close to Big Bob's, but I think we need to sit in Big Bob's kitchen to find the secret ingredients!

MAKES ABOUT **3** CUPS

2 TABLESPOONS CANOLA OIL

1 LARGE SWEET ONION, SUCH AS VIDALIA, FINELY CHOPPED

2 GARLIC CLOVES, MINCED

½ TEASPOON CELERY SALT

⅛ TEASPOON CAYENNE PEPPER

1 TEASPOON SWEET PAPRIKA

1 TEASPOON DRY MUSTARD

2 CUPS KETCHUP

2 TABLESPOONS APPLE CIDER VINEGAR

½ CUP FIRMLY PACKED LIGHT BROWN SUGAR

¼ CUP MAPLE SYRUP

2 TABLESPOONS MOLASSES

3 TABLESPOONS WORCESTERSHIRE SAUCE

ONE 8-OUNCE CAN TOMATO SAUCE

1 TEASPOON LIQUID SMOKE

¼ CUP PORK COOKING LIQUID, FAT SKIMMED, OR BEEF BROTH

In a medium saucepan, heat the oil over medium-high heat. Add the onion, garlic, celery salt, cayenne, paprika, and dry mustard and sauté for 2 to 3 minutes to soften the onion. Add the remaining ingredients and simmer for 30 minutes, or until thickened. The sauce will keep in the refrigerator, covered, for up to 1 week.

PULLED PORK SHOULDER FOR CARNITAS

One of my favorite dishes at our local Mexican restaurants is carnitas tacos. The pork shoulder is cooked in lard until it is juicy on the inside, with a crisp crust on the outside. Traditional carnitas take at least four hours to cook, but in the pressure cooker the pork cooks in forty-five minutes. You can omit the lard and still get a succulent pork shoulder to pull apart for any south-of-the-border dish. Carnitas are traditionally served with refried beans, rice, and tortillas but serve them as soft tacos, with warm tortillas, guacamole, salsa, and chopped onion (see the Psst).

SERVES **6** TO **8**

2 TABLESPOONS CANOLA OIL

2 TEASPOONS SALT

1 TEASPOON ANCHO CHILE POWDER

1 TEASPOON GROUND CUMIN

½ TEASPOON DRIED OREGANO

4 GARLIC CLOVES, MINCED

ONE 4-POUND BONELESS PORK SHOULDER ROAST

2 LARGE ONIONS, COARSELY CHOPPED

1½ CUPS CHICKEN OR BEEF STOCK (PAGE 19 OR 20) OR STORE-BOUGHT CHICKEN OR BEEF BROTH

¼ CUP FINELY CHOPPED FRESH CILANTRO FOR GARNISH

1 In a small bowl, combine the oil, salt, chile powder, cumin, oregano, and garlic. With the tip of a sharp knife, cut 1-inch slits in the meat, about 2 inches apart. Spread the spice mixture over the pork and rub it into the slits. Scatter the onions in the pressure cooker and pour in the stock. Lay the pork on top of the onions. Lock the lid in place and cook at high pressure for 45 minutes.

2 Release the pressure naturally and remove the lid, tilting the pot away from you to avoid the escaping steam. Transfer the pork to a cutting board, cover with aluminum foil to keep warm, and allow to rest for 15 minutes before shredding. Skim off the fat from the cooking liquid, strain the liquid, and set aside.

3 Remove any large pieces of fat and pull apart the pork with two forks. Arrange the pork on a platter, moisten with some of the cooking liquid, and garnish with chopped cilantro. (If you have leftover pork, store it in the freezer for up to 3 months.)

PSST

I prefer to use boneless pork shoulder because you actually get more meat. When you buy it bone in, you are paying for that excess weight.

If you would like to use the carnitas in soft tacos, see the beef tacos recipe on page 277 for instructions on warming the tortillas and making guacamole.

PORK SHOULDER PASTA SAUCE

Cooking pork shoulder in tomato sauce will give you myriad choices for entrées. Use the sauce on stuffed shells or over spaghetti. Since pork is a sweet meat, it balances the acid in the tomatoes to give you a scrumptious sauce. It's also tasty spooned over polenta.

SERVES **6** TO **8**

4 TABLESPOONS EXTRA-VIRGIN OLIVE OIL

2 LARGE ONIONS, COARSELY CHOPPED

THREE 28-OUNCE CANS PLUM TOMATOES WITH THEIR JUICE

1 TEASPOON SALT, PLUS MORE IF NEEDED

PINCH OF RED PEPPER FLAKES

½ TEASPOON DRIED BASIL

½ TEASPOON DRIED OREGANO

3 GARLIC CLOVES, MINCED

ONE 4-POUND BONELESS PORK SHOULDER ROAST

¼ CUP PACKED FRESH BASIL LEAVES, THINLY SLICED

¼ CUP FINELY CHOPPED FRESH FLAT-LEAF PARSLEY

FRESHLY GROUND BLACK PEPPER (OPTIONAL)

1 Heat 2 tablespoons of the oil in the pressure cooker over medium-high heat. Add the onions and sauté for 2 minutes to soften them. Add the tomatoes and bring the mixture to a simmer.

2 In a small bowl, combine the remaining 2 tablespoons of oil with the salt, red pepper flakes, basil, oregano, and garlic. With a sharp knife, make 1-inch slits in the meat, about 2 inches apart, and rub the spice mixture into the pork, pushing the rub into the slits. Arrange the pork over the tomatoes in the pressure cooker. Lock the lid in place and cook at high pressure for 45 minutes.

3 Release the pressure naturally and remove the lid, tilting the pot away from you to avoid the escaping steam. Transfer the pork to a cutting board, cover with aluminum foil to keep warm, and allow to rest for 15 minutes before chopping.

4 Skim off the excess fat from the surface of the sauce and bring the sauce to a boil. Reduce the heat to maintain the sauce at a simmer and stir in the basil and parsley. Taste the sauce for seasoning and add more salt and some black pepper if necessary. Peel away any excess fat from the pork with your fingers and chop the meat into bite-size pieces. Add the pork to the sauce and simmer for another 10 minutes.

PORK SHOULDER, UMBRIAN STYLE

Porchetta is found all over Italy, but I like it best in the little cafés and bars of Umbria, where Mama is often in the back cooking. Filled with aromatic herbs and spices, the pork shoulder cooks for hours, until it almost falls apart. The pressure cooker makes a tender, juicy porchetta with delicious pan sauce in less than an hour.

SERVES 6 TO 8

ONE 4-POUND BONELESS PORK SHOULDER ROAST

2 TABLESPOONS EXTRA-VIRGIN OLIVE OIL

2 TEASPOONS SALT, PLUS MORE IF NEEDED

1 TEASPOON FRESHLY GROUND BLACK PEPPER, PLUS MORE IF NEEDED

2 TEASPOONS FINELY CHOPPED FRESH ROSEMARY

1 TEASPOON FENNEL SEEDS

2 MEDIUM SHALLOTS, FINELY CHOPPED

3 GARLIC CLOVES, MINCED

2 LARGE ONIONS, COARSELY CHOPPED

1 CUP DRY WHITE WINE, SUCH AS SAUVIGNON BLANC OR PINOT GRIGIO, OR DRY VERMOUTH

1 CUP CHICKEN STOCK (PAGE 19) OR STORE-BOUGHT CHICKEN BROTH

2 TABLESPOONS UNSALTED BUTTER, SOFTENED

2 TABLESPOONS ALL-PURPOSE FLOUR

1 Lay the pork shoulder on a cutting board, fat-side down. In a small bowl, combine the oil, salt, pepper, rosemary, fennel seeds, shallots, and garlic. Spread the mixture over the meat and roll it up, securing with butcher's twine or silicone bands. Scatter the onions in the bottom of the pressure cooker, pour in the wine and stock, and arrange the pork on top of the onions. Lock the lid in place and cook at high pressure for 45 minutes.

2 Release the pressure naturally and remove the lid, tilting the pot away from you to avoid the escaping steam. Transfer the pork to a cutting board and cover with aluminum foil to keep warm while it rests for 15 minutes.

3 Skim off any excess fat from the sauce. Bring to a boil and continue boiling for 5 minutes to concentrate the flavors. Meanwhile, in a small bowl, stir the butter and flour together to form a paste. Whisk into the sauce, return the sauce to a boil, reduce the heat, and simmer, whisking constantly, until thickened, about 5 to 10 minutes. Taste the sauce for seasoning and add more salt and pepper if necessary.

4 Remove the butcher's twine from the meat and slice ½ to ¾ inch thick. Arrange on a serving platter and spoon some of the pan sauce over the meat. Serve the remaining sauce on the side.

SHANGHAI RED-COOKED PORK SHOULDER

Red cooking is a Chinese technique for braising meat in a liquid containing a lot of soy sauce, which turns it a reddish brown. This sweet and spicy pork shoulder is a perfect entrée to serve with stir-fried veggies and sticky rice. And the best part is that the pork transforms into tender, juicy, and flavorful meat with just forty-five minutes of pressure cooking. Serve it simply with rice, or wrap it in warm flour tortillas with a dollop of hoisin sauce, some cucumber sticks, and green onion fans, just as you would serve Peking duck.

SERVES 6 TO 8

3 TABLESPOONS CANOLA OIL

2 LARGE ONIONS, COARSELY CHOPPED

1 CUP SOY SAUCE

½ CUP MIRIN (SWEET RICE WINE)

½ CUP HOISIN SAUCE

¼ CUP SUGAR

½ CUP CHICKEN STOCK (PAGE 19) OR STORE-BOUGHT CHICKEN BROTH

½ CUP KETCHUP

2 GARLIC CLOVES, MINCED

2 TEASPOONS GRATED FRESH GINGER

½ TEASPOON FIVE-SPICE POWDER

ONE 4-POUND BONELESS PORK SHOULDER ROAST

2 TABLESPOONS CORNSTARCH MIXED WITH ¼ CUP WATER

1 Heat 2 tablespoons of the oil in the pressure cooker over medium high-heat. Add the onions and sauté for 2 minutes to soften them. Reduce the heat to low and add the soy sauce, mirin, hoisin, sugar, stock, and ketchup, stirring to combine. Remove from the heat and set aside.

2 In a small bowl, combine the remaining tablespoon of oil, the garlic, ginger, and five-spice powder. With the tip of a sharp knife, make 1-inch slits in the pork, about 2 inches apart. Rub the spice mixture into the meat and push the rub into the slits. Put the pork in the pressure cooker, lock the lid in place, and cook at high pressure for 45 minutes.

3 Release the pressure naturally and remove the lid, tilting the pot away from you to avoid the escaping steam. Transfer the pork to a cutting board, cover with aluminum foil, and allow to rest for 15 minutes before cutting.

4 Skim off any excess fat from the sauce and bring the sauce to a boil. Whisk in the cornstarch slurry and return to a boil, whisking until the sauce is thickened and glossy. Reduce the heat to low and keep the sauce warm on the stove top.

5 Remove any excess fat from the outside of the meat and slice it ½ inch thick. Transfer the slices to a serving platter. Remove the sauce from the heat and spoon some over the meat. Serve the remaining sauce on the side.

JACK DANIEL'S AND COCA-COLA–GLAZED PORK SHOULDER

Drinks made with Jack Daniel's and Coca-Cola often appear at great Southern parties. This is my salute to the South, a pork shoulder glazed with Jack and Coke—falling-apart tender and moist, with a sticky glaze. Serve it with potato salad, slaw, baked beans, and corn bread for a great outdoor party. The pork marinates for at least eight hours, so plan accordingly.

SERVES **6** TO **8**

1 CUP JACK DANIEL'S

TWO 12-OUNCE CANS COCA-COLA (DON'T USE DIET)

1 CUP KETCHUP

1 TABLESPOON GARLIC SALT

ONE 4-POUND BONELESS PORK SHOULDER ROAST

2 LARGE ONIONS, COARSELY CHOPPED

2 CUPS CHICKEN STOCK (PAGE 19) OR STORE-BOUGHT CHICKEN BROTH

1 In a large zipper-top plastic bag, combine the Jack Daniel's, Coca-Cola, ketchup, and garlic salt. Add the pork to the bag, seal, and refrigerate for at least 8 hours or overnight.

2 Scatter the onions in the bottom of the pressure cooker and add the stock. Remove the pork from the marinade, reserving the marinade, and arrange the meat on top of the onions. Lock the lid in place and cook the pork at high pressure for 45 minutes. Meanwhile, pour the reserved marinade into a saucepan and bring to a boil. Reduce the heat and simmer the glaze while the pork is cooking.

3 When the pork is done, release the pressure naturally and remove the lid, tilting the pot away from you to avoid the escaping steam. Transfer the pork to a cutting board, cover loosely with aluminum foil, and allow to rest for 15 minutes before slicing.

4 Skim off any excess fat from the cooking liquid in the pot and add ½ cup of the liquid to the glaze in the saucepan. Remove any excess fat from the pork and brush it with some of the glaze. Slice the pork ½ inch thick and arrange on a serving platter. Spoon some of the remaining glaze over the slices and serve the rest on the side.

PORK LOIN BRAISED WITH APPLES AND CIDER

I was served a dish similar to this when my husband and I took a trip to Normandy. It is typical of the region: juicy slices of pork loin, covered with a creamy apple and onion sauce. The luxurious pan sauce is delicious over buttered noodles or mashed potatoes.

SERVES 6 TO 8

6 BACON STRIPS, CUT CROSSWISE INTO PIECES ½ INCH WIDE

2 LARGE SWEET ONIONS, SUCH AS VIDALIA, HALVED AND THINLY SLICED

4 GRANNY SMITH APPLES, PEELED, CORED, AND CUT INTO 8 WEDGES

1 TEASPOON DRIED THYME

1 BAY LEAF

1 CUP BEEF STOCK (PAGE 20) OR STORE-BOUGHT BEEF BROTH

1 CUP APPLE CIDER

ONE 4-POUND BONELESS PORK LOIN, ROLLED AND TIED (SEE PSST)

2 TABLESPOONS CORNSTARCH MIXED WITH ¼ CUP WATER

1 CUP HEAVY CREAM

¼ CUP FINELY CHOPPED FRESH FLAT-LEAF PARSLEY

SALT AND FRESHLY GROUND BLACK PEPPER (OPTIONAL)

1 In the pressure cooker, cook the bacon over medium heat until it is crisp, remove, and drain on paper towels. Remove all but 2 tablespoons of the fat from the pot. Add the onions, apples, thyme, and bay leaf and sauté for 2 minutes, or until the onions begin to soften. Add the stock, cider, and pork loin. Lock the lid in place and cook at high pressure for 25 minutes.

2 Release the pressure naturally and remove the lid, tilting the pot away from you to avoid the escaping steam. Carefully transfer the pork to a cutting board, cover loosely with aluminum foil, and allow to rest for 15 minutes before slicing.

3 Skim off any excess fat from the sauce, remove the bay leaf, and bring the sauce to a boil. Add the cornstarch slurry, return the sauce to a boil, and whisk until thickened and glossy. Add the cream and parsley and remove from the heat. Taste for seasoning and add salt and pepper if needed.

4 Slice the pork ½ inch thick and arrange on a serving platter. Spoon some of the sauce over the meat and scatter the reserved bacon over the top. Serve the remaining sauce on the side.

PSST

Pork loins are generally rolled and tied for you at the market. If yours wasn't, tie the roast at 1-inch intervals with butcher's twine or silicone bands.

ROSEMARY-AND-GARLIC-RUBBED PORK LOIN

This simple roast is rubbed with garlic and rosemary and pressure cooked in a garlicky broth for a Sunday supper that's sure to please—especially garlic lovers! And it's ready in less than half an hour. The leftover pork, if there is any, tastes delicious cold in a sandwich.

SERVES **6** TO **8**

12 GARLIC CLOVES, PEELED

¼ CUP EXTRA-VIRGIN OLIVE OIL

2 TABLESPOONS FINELY CHOPPED FRESH ROSEMARY

1 TEASPOON SALT, PLUS MORE IF NEEDED

½ TEASPOON FRESHLY GROUND BLACK PEPPER, PLUS MORE IF NEEDED

ONE 4-POUND BONELESS PORK LOIN ROAST

1 CUP CHICKEN STOCK (PAGE 19) OR STORE-BOUGHT CHICKEN BROTH

1 CUP BEEF STOCK (PAGE 20) OR STORE-BOUGHT BEEF BROTH

1 Mince 6 of the garlic cloves and slice the remaining 6 cloves. In a small mixing bowl, combine the oil, minced garlic, rosemary, salt, and pepper. With the tip of a sharp knife, make 1-inch slits in the pork about 2 inches apart. Rub the garlic and rosemary mixture on the pork, pushing it into the slits.

2 Heat the pressure cooker over medium-high heat. Add the pork and brown on all sides. Add the stocks and the sliced garlic. Lock the lid in place and cook at high pressure for 25 minutes.

3 Release the pressure naturally and remove the lid, tilting the pot away from you to avoid the escaping steam. Carefully transfer the meat to a cutting board, cover loosely with aluminum foil, and allow to rest for 15 minutes before carving.

4 Skim off any excess fat from the sauce and bring to a boil. Continue boiling for 10 minutes to reduce the sauce and concentrate the flavor. Discard the garlic and taste the sauce for seasoning, adding more salt and pepper if necessary.

5 Slice the pork ½ inch thick and spoon some of the sauce over the meat. Serve the rest of the sauce on the side.

PSST

If you would like to thicken the sauce, stir together 2 tablespoons of softened unsalted butter and 2 tablespoons of all-purpose flour to form a paste. Bring the sauce to a boil, whisk in the paste, and continue whisking until the sauce returns to a boil and thickens.

PORK LOIN STUFFED WITH APPLES

Dried apples, sweet onions, and walnuts flavor this delectable pork dish, cooked in a spicy red wine sauce that complements the tender pork and stuffing.

SERVES **6** TO **8**

....

STUFFING

2 TABLESPOONS UNSALTED BUTTER

1 CUP FINELY CHOPPED SWEET ONION, SUCH AS VIDALIA

1 TEASPOON DRIED THYME

1 CUP FINELY CHOPPED DRIED APPLES

⅔ CUP FINELY CHOPPED WALNUTS

PORK LOIN

ONE 4-POUND PORK LOIN ROAST, BUTTERFLIED (SEE PSST ON PAGE 215)

1 TEASPOON SALT, PLUS MORE IF NEEDED

½ TEASPOON FRESHLY GROUND BLACK PEPPER, PLUS MORE IF NEEDED

2 CUPS FULL-BODIED RED WINE, SUCH AS CHIANTI, ZINFANDEL, OR BAROLO

1 CUP BEEF STOCK (PAGE 20) OR STORE-BOUGHT BEEF BROTH

1 CINNAMON STICK

1 WHOLE CLOVE

2 TABLESPOONS UNSALTED BUTTER, SOFTENED

2 TABLESPOONS ALL-PURPOSE FLOUR

1 **To make the stuffing:** Melt the butter in a medium skillet over medium-high heat. Add the onion, thyme, and apples and sauté for 4 to 5 minutes, or until the onion is softened and the apples begin to turn golden. Remove from the heat and stir in the walnuts. Set aside and allow the stuffing to cool.

2 **To make the pork loin:** If the meat appears uneven, place a piece of plastic wrap over it and pound to an even thickness, about ½ inch. Sprinkle the meat with the salt and pepper and spread the apple and walnut stuffing evenly over the pork. Beginning on a long side, roll up the pork into a compact roll and tie with butcher's twine at 1-inch intervals or use silicone bands to secure the meat. Pour the wine and stock into the pressure cooker. Add the cinnamon stick and clove and set the pork in the liquid. Lock the lid in place and cook at high pressure for 25 minutes.

3 Release the pressure naturally and remove the lid, tilting the pot away from you to avoid the escaping steam. Carefully transfer the meat to a cutting board, cover loosely with aluminum foil, and allow to rest for 15 minutes before slicing.

4 Strain the cooking liquid and return it to the pressure cooker. Skim off any excess fat from the sauce and bring the sauce to a boil. Continue boiling for 10 minutes to reduce and concentrate the sauce. In a small bowl, stir together the butter and flour to form a paste. Whisk the paste into the sauce and return it to a boil. Reduce the heat and simmer, whisking constantly, until thickened. Taste the sauce for seasoning and add more salt and pepper if necessary.

5 Remove the butcher's twine or silicone bands from the meat, slice ½ inch thick, and arrange on a serving platter. Spoon some of the sauce over the pork and serve the remaining sauce on the side.

PORK LOIN STUFFED WITH SPINACH AND BACON

Smoky bacon and spinach team up here for a colorful and flavorful stuffing. The tender stuffed pork, simmered in a white wine sauce, is great with roasted corn or potatoes and a crisp green salad.

SERVES **6** TO **8**

STUFFING

6 BACON STRIPS, CUT CROSSWISE INTO PIECES ½ INCH WIDE

2 GARLIC CLOVES, MINCED

TWO 10-OUNCE BAGS BABY SPINACH, COARSELY CHOPPED, OR ONE 16-OUNCE PACKAGE FROZEN SPINACH, DEFROSTED

¼ TEASPOON FRESHLY GRATED NUTMEG

½ TEASPOON FRESHLY GROUND BLACK PEPPER

1 CUP FRESH BREAD CRUMBS

1 LARGE EGG, LIGHTLY BEATEN

PORK LOIN

ONE 4-POUND PORK LOIN ROAST, BUTTERFLIED (SEE PSST ON PAGE 215)

2 TEASPOONS SALT, PLUS MORE IF NEEDED

½ TEASPOON FRESHLY GROUND BLACK PEPPER, PLUS MORE IF NEEDED

1 LARGE ONION, COARSELY CHOPPED

3 MEDIUM CARROTS, COARSELY CHOPPED

3 CELERY STALKS, COARSELY CHOPPED

2 CUPS RIESLING WINE

1 CUP CHICKEN STOCK (PAGE 19) OR STORE-BOUGHT CHICKEN BROTH

1 BAY LEAF

1 TEASPOON DRIED THYME

2 TABLESPOONS UNSALTED BUTTER, SOFTENED

2 TABLESPOONS ALL-PURPOSE FLOUR

1 **To make the stuffing:** In a large skillet over medium-high heat, cook the bacon until crisp, remove, and drain on paper towels. Remove all but 2 tablespoons of fat from the skillet. Add the garlic and sauté for 1 minute, or until fragrant. Add the spinach, nutmeg, and pepper and sauté until the spinach is wilted. Transfer the mixture to a mixing bowl and allow to cool slightly. Add the bacon, bread crumbs, and egg and stir to combine. Set aside.

2 **To make the pork:** If the meat appears uneven, cover with plastic wrap and pound it to an even thickness, about ½ inch. Sprinkle the meat with the salt and pepper and spread the stuffing evenly over the meat. Beginning on a long side, roll the meat into a compact roll, tying it with butcher's twine at 1-inch intervals or securing it with silicone bands. Scatter the onion, carrots, and celery in the pressure cooker. Stir in the wine, stock, bay leaf, and thyme. Rest the meat on top of the vegetables. Lock the lid in place and cook at high pressure for 25 minutes.

3 Release the pressure naturally and remove the lid, tilting the pot away from you to avoid the escaping steam. Carefully transfer the meat to a cutting board, cover loosely with aluminum foil, and allow to rest for 15 minutes before carving.

4 Strain the sauce into a saucepan, discarding the solids. Skim off any excess fat from the sauce and bring to a boil. Continue boiling for 10 minutes to reduce and concentrate the sauce. Stir together the butter and flour in a small dish and whisk the paste into the sauce. Return the sauce to a boil. Reduce the heat and simmer, whisking constantly, until it thickens. Taste the sauce for seasoning and add more salt and pepper if necessary.

5 Remove the butcher's twine from the pork and slice the meat ½ to ¾ inch thick. Spoon some of the sauce over the meat and serve the remaining sauce on the side.

PORK LOIN STUFFED WITH DRIED APRICOTS AND PROSCIUTTO

I love dishes that are salty and sweet at the same time. This simple pork roast, layered with prosciutto, stuffed with dried apricots and herbs, and bathed in an apricot-flavored sauce, is a perfect example. It's great hot or cold.

SERVES **6** TO **8**

ONE 4-POUND PORK LOIN ROAST, BUTTERFLIED (SEE PSST ON PAGE 215)

6 THIN SLICES PROSCIUTTO DI PARMA

1½ CUPS DRIED APRICOTS

2 TEASPOONS FINELY CHOPPED FRESH THYME

2 MEDIUM SHALLOTS, FINELY CHOPPED

1 CUP DRY WHITE WINE, SUCH AS SAUVIGNON BLANC OR PINOT GRIGIO, OR DRY VERMOUTH

1 CUP CHICKEN STOCK (PAGE 19) OR STORE-BOUGHT CHICKEN BROTH

1 LARGE ONION, COARSELY CHOPPED

SALT AND FRESHLY GROUND BLACK PEPPER (OPTIONAL)

1 If the meat appears uneven, cover with plastic wrap and pound it to an even thickness, about ½ inch. Lay the slices of prosciutto over the meat to cover the surface. Chop 1 cup of the apricots and combine in a small bowl with the thyme and shallots. Spread the mixture evenly over the prosciutto. Roll up the meat into a compact roll, beginning on a long side. Tie with butcher's twine at 1-inch intervals or secure with silicone bands. Pour the wine and stock into the pressure cooker and stir in the onion and the remaining ½ cup of apricots. Lay the pork over the onion and apricots. Lock the lid in place and cook at high pressure for 25 minutes.

2 Release the pressure naturally and remove the lid, tilting the pot away from you to avoid the escaping steam. Carefully transfer the meat to a cutting board, loosely cover with aluminum foil, and allow to rest for 15 minutes before slicing.

3 Skim off any excess fat from the sauce and purée in the pressure cooker with an immersion blender. Taste for seasoning and add salt and pepper if necessary.

4 Remove the butcher's twine from the pork and slice ½ inch thick. Spoon some of the sauce over the pork and serve the remaining sauce on the side.

PORK LOIN STUFFED WITH CRANBERRIES AND WILD RICE

When you need an elegant dish to serve during the holidays, look no further. When sliced and arranged on a serving platter, this elegant pork loin reveals its colorful stuffing, which makes it a stunning main course to bring to the holiday table.

SERVES **6** TO **8**

2 TABLESPOONS UNSALTED BUTTER

2 MEDIUM SHALLOTS, FINELY CHOPPED

1 GARLIC CLOVE, MINCED

½ TEASPOON DRIED MARJORAM

1 TEASPOON DRIED THYME

2 CUPS BASIC WILD RICE (PAGE 345)

½ CUP DRIED APPLES, FINELY CHOPPED

1 CUP DRIED CRANBERRIES, COARSELY CHOPPED IF LARGE

1½ TEASPOONS FRESHLY GROUND BLACK PEPPER, PLUS MORE IF NEEDED

ONE 4-POUND PORK LOIN ROAST, BUTTERFLIED (SEE PSST ON PAGE 215)

2 TEASPOONS SALT, PLUS MORE IF NEEDED

1 LARGE SWEET ONION, SUCH AS VIDALIA, COARSELY CHOPPED

1 CUP CHICKEN STOCK (PAGE 19) OR STORE-BOUGHT CHICKEN BROTH

1 CUP RUBY PORT

1 BAY LEAF

2 TABLESPOONS UNSALTED BUTTER, SOFTENED

2 TABLESPOONS ALL-PURPOSE FLOUR

½ CUP FINELY CHOPPED FRESH FLAT-LEAF PARSLEY

1 Melt the butter in a medium skillet over medium-high heat. Add the shallots, garlic, marjoram, and thyme and sauté for 3 to 4 minutes, until the shallots are softened. Transfer the mixture to a bowl and allow to cool. Add the rice, apples, cranberries, and ½ teaspoon of the pepper and stir to blend.

2 If the meat appears uneven, cover with plastic wrap and pound it to an even thickness, about ½ inch. Sprinkle the meat with the salt and the remaining 1 teaspoon of pepper and spread the cranberry mixture evenly over the roast. Beginning on a long side, roll the pork into a compact roll and tie with butcher's twine or secure with silicone bands at 1-inch intervals. Scatter the onion in the pressure cooker and add the stock, port, and bay leaf. Set the pork on top of the onion. Lock the lid in place and cook at high pressure for 25 minutes.

3 Release the pressure naturally and remove the lid, tilting the pot away from you to avoid the escaping steam. Carefully transfer the meat to a cutting board, cover loosely with aluminum foil, and allow to rest for 15 minutes before carving.

4 Skim off any excess fat from the sauce, strain into a saucepan, and bring to a boil. In a small bowl, stir together the butter and flour and whisk into the sauce. Return to a boil, reduce the heat, and simmer, whisking constantly, until thickened. Stir in the parsley, taste for seasoning, and add more salt and pepper if necessary.

5 Remove the butcher's twine from the pork and slice the meat ½ to ¾ inch thick. Transfer to a serving platter and spoon some of the sauce over the pork. Serve the remaining sauce on the side.

PSST

This stuffing is also delicious in Cornish game hens and turkey.

PORK LOIN STUFFED WITH PLUMS IN PORT WINE SAUCE

Stuffed with plums, smoky ham, shallots, and herbs, this simple pork roast packs a lot of flavor. It's cooked in a delicious port wine sauce, which gives the tender meat a lovely ruby color.

SERVES **6** TO **8**

2 TABLESPOONS UNSALTED BUTTER

2 MEDIUM SHALLOTS, FINELY CHOPPED

1 CUP FINELY CHOPPED SMOKED HAM (ONE ½-INCH-THICK SLICE FROM THE DELI)

2 TEASPOONS FINELY CHOPPED FRESH THYME

4 TABLESPOONS FINELY CHOPPED FRESH FLAT-LEAF PARSLEY

1 CUP DRIED PLUMS, COARSELY CHOPPED

ONE 4-POUND PORK LOIN ROAST, BUTTERFLIED (SEE PSST ON PAGE 215)

2 TEASPOONS SALT, PLUS MORE IF NEEDED

1 TEASPOON FRESHLY GROUND BLACK PEPPER, PLUS MORE IF NEEDED

2 LARGE ONIONS, COARSELY CHOPPED

2 CUPS RUBY PORT

1 CUP BEEF STOCK (PAGE 20) OR STORE-BOUGHT BEEF BROTH

2 SPRIGS FRESH THYME

1 BAY LEAF

2 TABLESPOONS CORNSTARCH MIXED WITH ¼ CUP WATER

1 Melt the butter in a small skillet over medium-high heat. Add the shallots, ham, chopped thyme, and 2 tablespoons of the parsley and sauté for 3 to 4 minutes, or until the shallots are softened. Transfer the mixture to a small bowl, stir in the plums, and set aside.

2 If the meat appears uneven, cover with plastic wrap and pound it to an even thickness, about ½ inch. Sprinkle with the salt and pepper and spread the plum mixture evenly over the meat. Beginning on a long side, roll the pork into a compact roll, securing the meat with butcher's twine or silicone bands at 1-inch intervals. Scatter the onions in the pressure cooker and stir in the port, stock, thyme sprigs, and bay leaf. Set the pork on top of the onions. Lock the lid in place and cook at high pressure for 25 minutes.

3 Release the pressure naturally and remove the lid, tilting the pot away from you to avoid the escaping steam. Carefully transfer the meat to a cutting board, cover loosely with aluminum foil, and allow to rest for 15 minutes before slicing.

4 Remove any excess fat from the sauce, strain into a saucepan, and bring to a boil. Whisk in the cornstarch slurry and cook until the sauce is thick and glossy. Stir in the remaining 2 tablespoons of parsley and taste the sauce for seasoning, adding more salt and pepper if necessary.

5 Remove the butcher's twine from the pork and slice the meat ½ to ¾ inch thick. Transfer to a serving platter and spoon some of the sauce over the pork. Serve the remaining sauce on the side.

PORK LOIN WITH CRANBERRY-APRICOT STUFFING

Stuffed with corn bread, dried cranberries, and apricots and simmered in a white wine sauce, this pork loin is the perfect choice for a fall harvest dinner. Serve it with some mashed butternut squash and sautéed spinach.

SERVES 6

CORN BREAD STUFFING

2 TABLESPOONS UNSALTED BUTTER

2 MEDIUM SHALLOTS, FINELY CHOPPED

2 TEASPOONS FINELY CHOPPED
FRESH SAGE

1 TEASPOON FINELY CHOPPED
FRESH THYME

2 CUPS CRUMBLED CORN BREAD

½ CUP DRIED CRANBERRIES, CHOPPED

½ CUP DRIED APRICOTS, FINELY CHOPPED

1 TEASPOON SALT

3 DROPS OF TABASCO OR ANOTHER
HOT SAUCE

1 LARGE EGG, LIGHTLY BEATEN

1 To make the stuffing: Melt the butter in a small skillet over medium heat. Add the shallots, sage, and thyme and sauté for 3 to 4 minutes, or until the shallots are softened. Let the mixture cool and transfer to a mixing bowl. Add the remaining ingredients to the bowl and stir to combine. Set aside.

2 To make the pork loin: If the meat is uneven, cover with plastic wrap and pound it to an even thickness, about ½ inch. Sprinkle evenly with the salt and pepper. Spread the stuffing over the meat and roll the meat into a compact roll, beginning on a long side. Secure with butcher's twine or silicone bands at 1-inch intervals. Pour the stock and wine into the pressure cooker and add the meat and bay leaf. Lock the lid in place and cook at high pressure for 25 minutes.

3 Release the pressure naturally and remove the lid, tilting the pot away from you to avoid the escaping steam. Carefully remove the pork to a cutting board, cover loosely with aluminum foil, and allow to rest for 15 minutes before slicing.

4 Skim off any excess fat from the sauce, remove the bay leaf, and bring to a boil. In a small dish, stir together the butter and flour to form a paste. Add the cream and parsley to the sauce and whisk in the butter and flour paste. Return the sauce to a boil, reduce to a simmer, and cook, whisking constantly, until thickened. Taste the sauce for seasoning and add more salt and pepper if necessary.

PORK LOIN

ONE 4-POUND BONELESS PORK LOIN ROAST, BUTTERFLIED (SEE PSST)

2 TEASPOONS SALT, PLUS MORE IF NEEDED

1 TEASPOON FRESHLY GROUND BLACK PEPPER, PLUS MORE IF NEEDED

1 CUP BEEF STOCK (PAGE 20) OR STORE-BOUGHT BEEF BROTH

1 CUP RIESLING WINE

1 BAY LEAF

2 TABLESPOONS UNSALTED BUTTER, SOFTENED

2 TABLESPOONS ALL-PURPOSE FLOUR

½ CUP HEAVY CREAM

¼ CUP FINELY CHOPPED FRESH FLAT-LEAF PARSLEY

5 Remove the butcher's twine from the roast and slice the meat ½ to ¾ inch thick. Spoon some of the sauce over the meat and serve the remaining sauce on the side.

PSST

To butterfly the pork, lay the meat on a cutting board, fat-side up, with a short side facing you. Start at a long side, holding a long, sharp knife parallel to your cutting board. Cut the pork in half horizontally, leaving about 1 inch of the meat attached. As you cut the meat, roll the top layer away from the bottom, opening up the meat as you go, until you have one flat piece of meat.

PORK LOIN IN THE STYLE OF THE DORDOGNE

I have been privileged to teach at La Combe, a beautiful eighteenth-century country house in Périgord, in the Dordogne region of France. This recipe is always a favorite with my students, and it couldn't be simpler. The meat is cooked with dried plums in a bourbon-flavored broth, which sweetens the sauce and the falling-apart-tender meat. At La Combe, we serve this dish with potatoes sautéed in duck fat—the perfect accompaniment!

SERVES 6 TO 8

1 CUP BOURBON

2 CUPS BEEF STOCK (PAGE 20) OR STORE-BOUGHT BEEF BROTH

2 LARGE ONIONS, COARSELY CHOPPED

2 CUPS DRIED PLUMS

2 SPRIGS FRESH THYME

1 BAY LEAF

ONE 4-POUND PORK LOIN ROAST

2 TABLESPOONS CORNSTARCH MIXED WITH ¼ CUP WATER

¼ CUP FINELY CHOPPED FRESH FLAT-LEAF PARSLEY

SALT AND FRESHLY GROUND BLACK PEPPER (OPTIONAL)

1 In the pressure cooker, stir together the bourbon, stock, onions, plums, thyme, and bay leaf. Set the pork loin on the onions. Lock the lid in place and cook at high pressure for 25 minutes.

2 Release the pressure naturally and remove the lid, tilting the pot away from you to avoid the escaping steam. Carefully transfer the meat to a cutting board, cover loosely with aluminum foil, and allow to rest for 15 minutes before carving.

3 With a slotted spoon, remove the plums from the sauce and set aside. Skim off any excess fat from the sauce, strain the sauce into a saucepan, and bring to a boil. Whisk in the cornstarch slurry and boil until the sauce is glossy and thickened. Stir in the parsley and remove the sauce from the heat. Taste for seasoning and add salt and pepper if necessary.

4 Remove the butcher's twine from the roast and slice the meat ½ inch thick. Spoon some of the sauce over the pork and surround it with the reserved plums. Pass the remaining sauce on the side.

BREAKFAST SAUSAGE SOUFFLÉS

Flavored with Gruyère cheese, these soufflés make a lovely brunch entrée to serve with fruit or a green salad. With a pressure cooker, you don't need to worry about overcooked eggs; it gives you creamy and tender eggs every time. The soufflés can be prepared ahead and refrigerated for up to two days before cooking.

SERVES 6

½ POUND BULK PORK SAUSAGE

6 LARGE EGGS

1 CUP HEAVY CREAM

6 DROPS OF TABASCO OR ANOTHER HOT SAUCE

1 CUP FINELY SHREDDED IMPORTED SWISS CHEESE, PREFERABLY GRUYÈRE

2 CUPS TORN STALE WHITE CRUSTLESS BREAD CUBES

2 TABLESPOONS FINELY CHOPPED FRESH CHIVES, PLUS MORE (OPTIONAL) FOR GARNISH

1 TABLESPOON FINELY CHOPPED FRESH FLAT-LEAF PARSLEY, PLUS MORE (OPTIONAL) FOR GARNISH

2 CUPS WATER

1 Coat the insides of six 4-ounce ramekins with nonstick cooking spray. In a small skillet over medium-high heat, cook the sausage until it is no longer pink, breaking it up as it cooks. Set aside to cool.

2 In a large mixing bowl, whisk together the eggs, cream, and Tabasco. Add the cheese, bread cubes, cooled sausage, chives, and parsley, pressing down on the bread to make sure it absorbs the custard. Scoop about ⅓ cup of the mixture into each ramekin and cover tightly with aluminum foil.

3 Pour the water into the pressure cooker. Arrange the trivet and steamer basket in the bottom and stack the ramekins in the basket. Lock the lid in place and cook at high pressure for 7 minutes.

4 Release the pressure naturally and remove the lid, tilting the pot away from you to avoid the escaping steam. Remove the ramekins from the pot. Carefully remove the aluminum foil and blot any excess moisture on top of the soufflés. Tip each soufflé onto a plate and serve garnished with additional chives or parsley if desired.

GREEN EGGS AND HAM BREAD PUDDING

This soufflé-like breakfast treat is swirled with spinach pesto and studded with bits of smoked ham, and it oozes melted Gruyère cheese. It's a dish to serve for brunch or on any morning when you're not feeling rushed.

SERVES 6

SPINACH PESTO

1 CUP PACKED BABY SPINACH LEAVES

2 TABLESPOONS PINE NUTS

¼ CUP FRESHLY GRATED PARMIGIANO-REGGIANO CHEESE

1 GARLIC CLOVE

¼ CUP EXTRA-VIRGIN OLIVE OIL

SALT AND FRESHLY GROUND BLACK PEPPER

BREAD PUDDING

2 CUPS TORN STALE WHITE CRUSTLESS BREAD CUBES

1 CUP DICED SMOKED HAM (½-INCH DICE)

1 CUP DICED GRUYÈRE CHEESE (½-INCH DICE)

6 LARGE EGGS

1 CUP HEAVY CREAM

6 DROPS OF TABASCO OR ANOTHER HOT SAUCE

2 CUPS WATER

1 **To make the pesto:** In a food processor, process the spinach, pine nuts, cheese, and garlic until they are broken up. With the machine running, pour in the oil and process until the mixture forms a paste. Season the pesto with salt and pepper and set aside. (Any leftover pesto will keep covered in the refrigerator for up to 4 days or in the freezer for up to 3 months. It's delicious tossed with pasta.)

2 **To make the bread pudding:** In a large mixing bowl, combine the bread, ham, and cheese. In a small mixing bowl, whisk together the eggs, cream, and Tabasco. Pour the egg mixture over the bread mixture and press down to soak it.

3 Coat the insides of six 4-ounce ramekins with nonstick cooking spray. Scoop ¼ cup of the egg mixture into each ramekin, top with 1 tablespoon of the spinach pesto, and then with a few tablespoons more of the egg mixture, filling the ramekins to within ¼ inch of the rim. Cover each ramekin tightly with aluminum foil. Pour the water into the pressure cooker. Arrange the trivet and steamer basket in the bottom and stack the ramekins in the basket. Lock the lid in place and cook at high pressure for 7 minutes.

4 Release the pressure naturally and remove the lid, tilting the pot away from you to avoid the escaping steam. Carefully remove the ramekins from the pressure cooker. Remove the foil and blot any excess water on top of each bread pudding. Tip a ramekin out onto each plate and serve.

PORK RAGU WITH POLENTA

This is my family's favorite ragu, rich with pork and sweet Italian sausage and flavored with basil, parsley, and a touch of nutmeg. It is delicious over polenta, but you can serve it over pasta if you prefer. In less than ten minutes, the sauce emerges from the pressure cooker with a deep flavor, as if it had spent the day bubbling on the stove.

SERVES 6 TO 8

....

1 TABLESPOON EXTRA-VIRGIN OLIVE OIL

2 POUNDS LEAN GROUND PORK

1 POUND SWEET ITALIAN SAUSAGE

2 LARGE SWEET ONIONS, SUCH AS VIDALIA, FINELY CHOPPED

1 TEASPOON DRIED BASIL

⅛ TEASPOON FRESHLY GRATED NUTMEG

TWO 28-OUNCE CANS CRUSHED TOMATOES WITH THEIR JUICE

TWO 28-OUNCE CANS TOMATO PURÉE

¼ CUP PACKED FRESH BASIL LEAVES, FINELY CHOPPED

½ CUP FINELY CHOPPED FRESH FLAT-LEAF PARSLEY

SALT AND FRESHLY GROUND BLACK PEPPER (OPTIONAL)

1 RECIPE CHEESY POLENTA (PAGE 367)

1 Heat the oil in the pressure cooker over medium-high heat. Add the pork and sausage and sauté until no longer pink. Remove any excess fat or water from the bottom of the pot. Add the onions, basil, and nutmeg and cook for another 2 minutes to soften the onions. Pour in the crushed tomatoes and tomato purée. Lock the lid in place and cook at high pressure for 7 minutes.

2 Release the pressure naturally and remove the lid, tilting the pot away from you to avoid the escaping steam. Skim off any excess fat from the sauce and stir in the basil and parsley. Taste the sauce for seasoning and add salt and pepper if necessary. Serve over the polenta.

OLD-FASHIONED HAM AND BEANS

New England ham and bean suppers are a tradition that started at churches as a way to welcome newcomers into the community. Today, these suppers also entice visitors to picturesque New England towns. On almost any weekend, you can find ham and bean suppers happening all over New England. Ham and beans is basically a heartier version of Boston baked beans. The ham cooks along with the beans and their seasonings, emerging meltingly tender, juicy, and flavorful.

SERVES 6 to 8

1 LARGE SWEET ONION, SUCH AS VIDALIA, FINELY CHOPPED

2 GARLIC CLOVES, MINCED

1 TEASPOON DRIED THYME

1 BAY LEAF

1 WHOLE CLOVE

1 TEASPOON DRY MUSTARD

¼ TEASPOON GROUND GINGER

1½ CUPS SMALL WHITE BEANS, PRESOAKED (SEE PAGE 151) AND DRAINED

6 CUPS CHICKEN STOCK (PAGE 19) OR STORE-BOUGHT CHICKEN BROTH

¼ CUP MOLASSES

ONE 3-POUND BONELESS SMOKED HAM

SALT AND FRESHLY GROUND BLACK PEPPER (OPTIONAL)

1 Combine all the ingredients except the salt and pepper in the pressure cooker. Lock the lid in place and cook at high pressure for 30 minutes.

2 Release the pressure naturally and remove the lid, tilting the pot away from you to avoid the escaping steam. Carefully remove the ham to a cutting board, loosely tent with aluminum foil, and allow to rest for 15 minutes before slicing.

3 Skim off any excess fat from the beans. Remove the bay leaf and clove. Taste for seasoning, adding salt and pepper if necessary. Slice the ham ½ inch thick and serve with the beans on the side.

OLD-FASHIONED HAM LOAF WITH SWEET HOT MUSTARD SAUCE

Ham loaf is a great way to recycle leftover ham accumulating in your fridge. The sweet flavor of the ham makes it a perfect complement for the sweet and hot mustard sauce. Ham loaf is delicious warm, but it's equally good served cold in sandwiches. Or fry a few slices for breakfast on your griddle.

SERVES 6

SWEET HOT MUSTARD SAUCE

ONE 3½-OUNCE JAR COLMAN'S ENGLISH MUSTARD

½ CUP FIRMLY PACKED LIGHT BROWN SUGAR

2 TABLESPOONS WHITE VINEGAR

HAM LOAF

½ CUP FRESH BREAD CRUMBS

2 TABLESPOONS MILK

1½ POUNDS LEAN GROUND PORK

2 CUPS GROUND HAM (SEE PSST)

¼ CUP FINELY CHOPPED ONION

1 TEASPOON DRIED THYME

¼ CUP KETCHUP

1 TABLESPOON WORCESTERSHIRE SAUCE

1 LARGE EGG, LIGHTLY BEATEN

2 CUPS CHICKEN STOCK (PAGE 19) OR STORE-BOUGHT CHICKEN BROTH

1 **To make the sauce:** In a small bowl, combine all the ingredients, whisking until smooth. (Store any leftover sauce covered in the refrigerator for up to 2 weeks.)

2 **To make the ham loaf:** Put the bread crumbs in a large bowl and pour the milk over the crumbs. Stir to soak the bread in the milk and then add the pork, ham, onion, thyme, ketchup, Worcestershire, and egg. Shape the mixture into a loaf. Pour the stock into the pressure cooker and set the ham loaf in the cooker. Spread 3 tablespoons of the mustard sauce over the top of the loaf and set the remaining sauce aside. Lock the lid in place and cook at high pressure for 15 minutes.

3 Release the pressure naturally and remove the lid, tilting the pot away from you to avoid the escaping steam. With two long, wide spatulas, carefully remove the ham loaf to a cutting board, loosely tent with aluminum foil, and allow to rest for 10 minutes before slicing.

4 Skim off any excess fat from the cooking liquid in the pressure cooker and strain enough of it to measure ½ cup. (Discard the rest.) Gradually whisk the strained sauce into the mustard sauce. Slice the ham loaf ½ inch thick and serve the sauce on the side.

PSST

To grind the ham, cut into 1-inch pieces, put in the food processor, and pulse on and off until the ham is ground into tiny pieces.

BARBECUE MEATBALL SANDWICHES

Who can resist a sandwich packed with pork meatballs, bathed in a sweet and spicy barbecue sauce? The meatballs cook in just minutes. For a change of pace, serve the sandwiches for dinner with a fruit, vegetable, or pasta salad on the side.

SERVES 6

MEATBALLS

1 POUND LEAN GROUND PORK

¾ POUND BULK PORK SAUSAGE, SUCH AS JIMMY DEAN'S SAGE-FLAVORED SAUSAGE

¼ CUP KETCHUP

2 TEASPOONS WORCESTERSHIRE SAUCE

1 CUP FRESH BREAD CRUMBS

1 TEASPOON DRIED THYME

1 LARGE EGG, LIGHTLY BEATEN

BARBECUE SAUCE

2 TABLESPOONS CANOLA OIL

1 LARGE SWEET ONION, SUCH AS VIDALIA, FINELY CHOPPED

2 GARLIC CLOVES, MINCED

PINCH OF CAYENNE PEPPER

½ TEASPOON CELERY SALT

1 TEASPOON SWEET PAPRIKA

TWO 8-OUNCE CANS TOMATO SAUCE

1 CUP KETCHUP

2 TABLESPOONS WORCESTERSHIRE SAUCE

¼ CUP FIRMLY PACKED LIGHT BROWN SUGAR

6 CRUSTY TORPEDO ROLLS OR ANOTHER TYPE OF CRUSTY ROLL

1 **To make the meatballs:** In a large bowl, combine all the ingredients and mix until blended. Shape into 1-inch meatballs, using a cookie dough scoop to keep them uniform in size. Cover and set aside in the refrigerator while preparing the sauce.

2 **To make the sauce:** Heat the oil in the pressure cooker over medium-high heat. Add the onion, garlic, cayenne, celery salt, and paprika and sauté for 2 minutes, or until the onion begins to soften. Add the tomato sauce, ketchup, Worcestershire, and sugar, stirring to blend.

3 Carefully drop the meatballs into the sauce. Lock the lid in place and cook at high pressure for 5 minutes. Release the pressure naturally and remove the lid, tilting the pot away from you to avoid the escaping steam. Skim off any excess fat from the top of the sauce and stir the meatballs and sauce. Tuck the meatballs into the rolls and spoon some of the sauce inside each sandwich.

PSST

Make the meatballs bite-size and pressure cook them for 3 minutes. Then serve on 6-inch skewers at your next tailgate or grazing party.

Ribbing It

You can have succulent barbecued ribs with just ten minutes of precooking in the pressure cooker and twenty minutes on the grill. No more guesswork about whether the ribs will be tender when they come off the grill. The pressure cooker will ensure that they are delicious, and you will look like a genius! Other rib dishes are equally good, such as pork ribs with sauerkraut and apples (see page 225) and a French country pork rib cassoulet (see page 226).

There are three types of pork ribs: Baby back ribs are tender, meaty rib bones from the upper portion of the loin; they are pork chop bones that are removed in a slab. Baby backs are not the meatiest of the ribs, but they are leaner and more tender than the others. Spareribs are the thirteen ribs from the pork belly. Meaty, with a cap of fat, these ribs are some of the best on the pig. Country-style ribs are not technically ribs at all. They are pork blade chops that have been split. Inexpensive, meaty, and juicy, they stand up to long cooking and grilling times.

BARBECUE RIBS

All too often when barbecuing ribs, we sometimes end up with tough, chewy ribs, instead of the crisp, sauce-coated ribs that are the stuff of food magazine glamour photos. By pressure cooking the ribs before grilling, you ensure that the ribs will be tender and juicy and falling-off-the-bone delicious. The ribs steam in root beer, which gives them a great flavor.

SERVES 8

1 TABLESPOON GARLIC SALT

¼ CUP FIRMLY PACKED LIGHT BROWN SUGAR

2 TABLESPOONS SWEET PAPRIKA

1 TEASPOON CAYENNE PEPPER

1 TABLESPOON CELERY SEEDS

1 TEASPOON FRESHLY GROUND BLACK PEPPER

¼ TEASPOON GROUND CINNAMON

3 RACKS BABY BACK RIBS (3 TO 4 POUNDS TOTAL)

1½ CUPS ROOT BEER

2 CUPS BARBECUE SAUCE, HOMEMADE (PAGE 201) OR STORE-BOUGHT

1 In a small bowl, combine the garlic salt, sugar, paprika, cayenne, celery seeds, black pepper, and cinnamon, stirring to blend. Rub the spice mixture into the ribs.

2 Pour the root beer into the pressure cooker, arrange the trivet and steamer basket in the bottom, and arrange the ribs in the basket. I usually wind the ribs into a coil, but you may need to cut your ribs and lay them flat if you have a smaller cooker. Lock the lid in place and cook at high pressure for 10 minutes.

3 Release the pressure naturally and remove the lid, tilting the pot away from you to avoid the escaping steam. Carefully remove the ribs to a cutting board or platter.

4 Preheat a gas grill for 10 minutes on high or light a charcoal fire and spread out the coals when they're covered with a white ash. Place the ribs, bone-side up, on the grill, and cook until the ribs are sizzling and form a crust, about 10 minutes. Turn and brush with barbecue sauce. Grill the ribs for another 10 minutes, or until they are tender and cooked through (165 degrees F on an instant-read thermometer). Transfer the ribs to a cutting board and allow to rest for 5 minutes. Cut through the meat between the ribs to separate them. Serve with additional barbecue sauce on the side.

PSST

If it's too cold to grill, preheat your oven to 350 degrees F. Coat a rack with nonstick cooking spray and place in a baking pan. Brush the bone side of the ribs with barbecue sauce and lay the ribs on the rack, bone-side down. Brush the tops of the ribs with barbecue sauce and bake for 30 minutes, or until crusty, tender, and cooked through.

BABY BACKS WITH SAUERKRAUT AND APPLES

Tender baby back ribs braised with sauerkraut and apples makes a warm, comforting supper, especially when served with mashed potatoes. Apple cider sweetens the pork and balances the tangy sauerkraut. Look for sauerkraut in the fresh pickle section of your market; it's far superior to the canned versions.

SERVES 6

....

8 BACON STRIPS, CUT CROSSWISE INTO PIECES ½ INCH WIDE

2 LARGE ONIONS, COARSELY CHOPPED

4 MEDIUM GRANNY SMITH APPLES, PEELED, CORED, AND THINLY SLICED

4 CUPS FRESH SAUERKRAUT, DRAINED

2 RACKS BABY BACK RIBS (2 TO 3 POUNDS TOTAL), EACH RACK CUT INTO 4 SECTIONS, FOR A TOTAL OF 8

1 CUP APPLE CIDER

1 CUP BEEF STOCK (PAGE 20) OR STORE-BOUGHT BEEF BROTH

1 Cook the bacon in the pressure cooker over medium-high heat until crisp. Remove all but 2 tablespoons of the bacon fat from the pot. Add the onions and apples and sauté for 2 minutes, or until they begin to soften. Add the sauerkraut, stirring to combine. Arrange the ribs on top of the vegetables and pour in the cider and stock. Lock the lid in place and cook at high pressure for 10 minutes.

2 Release the pressure naturally and remove the lid, tilting the pot away from you to avoid the escaping steam. Carefully lift the ribs from the pot and put them on a clean surface. Remove the sauerkraut from the pressure cooker with a slotted spoon and transfer to a serving platter. Arrange the ribs on the sauerkraut and serve.

PORK RIB CASSOULET

A hearty combination of sausages, ribs, and rosemary-flavored white beans, cassoulet may seem like a daunting project for home cooks, but a pressure cooker makes it quick and easy. Ready in less than an hour, this warm and comforting dish from the Languedoc area of France is a real crowd-pleaser. And it can be made the day before and then reheated.

SERVES 6 TO 8

4 TABLESPOONS EXTRA-VIRGIN OLIVE OIL

1½ POUNDS SMOKED SAUSAGE, SUCH AS KIELBASA, CUT INTO 1-INCH ROUNDS

2 POUNDS COUNTRY-STYLE BONELESS SPARERIBS

2 CUPS FINELY CHOPPED SWEET ONIONS, SUCH AS VIDALIA

4 MEDIUM CARROTS, COARSELY CHOPPED

4 CELERY STALKS (INCLUDING THE LEAVES), COARSELY CHOPPED

½ CUP TOMATO PASTE

2 SPRIGS FRESH THYME

1 TEASPOON FINELY CHOPPED FRESH ROSEMARY

2 BAY LEAVES

2 CUPS SMALL WHITE BEANS, PRESOAKED (SEE PAGE 151) AND DRAINED

4 CUPS CHICKEN STOCK (PAGE 19) OR STORE-BOUGHT CHICKEN BROTH

2 CUPS BEEF STOCK (PAGE 20) OR STORE-BOUGHT BEEF BROTH

½ CUP FINELY CHOPPED FRESH FLAT-LEAF PARSLEY

SALT AND FRESHLY GROUND BLACK PEPPER (OPTIONAL)

1 Heat 2 tablespoons of the oil in the pressure cooker over medium-high heat. Add the sausage and ribs and brown, removing the meat to a plate when it's done. Add the onions, carrots, celery, and tomato paste to the pot and sauté for 2 minutes, or until the onions begin to soften. Return the meat to the pot and stir in the thyme, rosemary, bay leaves, beans, and stocks. Drizzle the remaining 2 tablespoons of oil over the stock. Lock the lid in place and cook at high pressure for 30 minutes.

2 Release the pressure naturally and remove the lid, tilting the pot away from you to avoid the escaping steam. Remove the bay leaves and thyme and skim off any excess fat from the sauce. Stir in the parsley, taste the beans for seasoning, and add salt and pepper if necessary. Transfer the cassoulet to a serving dish and serve warm.

A Few Links

Savory sausage blossoms in the pressure cooker, intensifying in flavor and emerging tender and succulent in no time! There are so many varieties of sausage available, including smoked sausages like kielbasa, beef and veal sausages like bratwurst, pork sausages like Italian sweet and hot, and an assortment of chicken and turkey sausages. If you love to grill, precooking raw sausages in the pressure cooker will shorten the grilling time.

ITALIAN SAUSAGE AND PEPPERS

Fragrant with oregano, red wine, and fennel-scented sausage, this is a great dish to serve any time you want to make a quick meal. I love it tucked into torpedo (Italian sub) rolls, but it's equally good over pasta or polenta.

SERVES 6

....

2 TABLESPOONS EXTRA-VIRGIN OLIVE OIL

2 LARGE SWEET ONIONS, SUCH AS VIDALIA, HALVED AND THINLY SLICED

2 GARLIC CLOVES, MINCED

2 MEDIUM RED BELL PEPPERS, SEEDED, DERIBBED, AND SLICED CROSSWISE

2 MEDIUM YELLOW BELL PEPPERS, SEEDED, DERIBBED, AND SLICED CROSSWISE

1 TEASPOON DRIED OREGANO

1 CUP CRUSHED TOMATOES WITH THEIR JUICE

1 CUP FULL-BODIED RED WINE, SUCH AS CHIANTI, ZINFANDEL, OR BAROLO

2 POUNDS SWEET ITALIAN SAUSAGE

¼ CUP FINELY CHOPPED FRESH FLAT-LEAF PARSLEY

6 FRESH BASIL LEAVES, THINLY SLICED

SALT AND FRESHLY GROUND BLACK PEPPER (OPTIONAL)

1 Heat the oil in the pressure cooker over medium-high heat. Add the onions, garlic, bell peppers, and oregano and cook for 5 minutes to soften the vegetables. Add the tomatoes and wine, stirring to blend. Prick the sausages with the tip of a sharp knife and add to the pot. Lock the lid in place and cook at high pressure for 10 minutes.

2 Release the pressure naturally and remove the lid, tilting the pot away from you to avoid the escaping steam. Skim off any excess fat from the sauce and stir in the parsley and basil. Taste for seasoning and add salt and pepper if necessary. Remove the sausages to a serving platter and top with the peppers and onions.

KIELBASA AND BEANS

The smoky sausage and creamy pink beans cook together for thirty minutes, producing a hearty entrée you can enjoy any night of the week. Serve this with black bread
and applesauce on a cold winter's night.

SERVES **6** TO **8**

2 POUNDS KIELBASA, CUT INTO 2-INCH
ROUNDS

2 MEDIUM ONIONS, FINELY CHOPPED

1 TEASPOON DRIED THYME

1 BAY LEAF

1 TEASPOON DRY MUSTARD

2 CUPS PINK BEANS, SMALL WHITE
BEANS, OR SMALL RED BEANS,
PRESOAKED (SEE PAGE 151) AND
DRAINED,

1 CUP KETCHUP

6 CUPS BEEF STOCK (PAGE 20) OR
STORE-BOUGHT BEEF BROTH

SALT AND FRESHLY GROUND BLACK
PEPPER (OPTIONAL)

1 Heat the pressure cooker over medium-high heat. Add the
sausage and sauté until it renders some of its fat. Add the onions,
thyme, bay leaf, and dry mustard and cook for 2 minutes to soften
the onions. Add the beans, ketchup, and stock, stirring to combine.
Lock the lid in place and cook at high pressure for 20 minutes.

2 Release the pressure naturally and remove the lid, tilting
the pot away from you to avoid the escaping steam. Skim off any
excess fat from the surface of the beans and remove the bay leaf.
Taste the beans and season with salt and pepper if necessary.
Transfer the beans and sausage to a serving bowl and serve hot.

LAMB

Lean and flavorful, lamb is cooked in many home kitchens around the world. If you have not experienced the pleasures of Mediterranean, Indian, or North African cuisine, this is the time to play with your food! The pressure cooker will help you to put succulent lamb stews, tagines, and more on the table in less than an hour.

The cuts of lamb that do well in the pressure cooker are mostly the less expensive, tougher cuts, such as shoulder, stew pieces (which are sometimes cut-up shoulder), blade chops, and shanks. One exception to this rule is rolled leg of lamb, which is neither cheap nor tough, but it does well in the pressure cooker.

The cooking liquid and spices add flavor and depth to this lean meat. I've suggested a combination of chicken broth and beef broth in the recipes that follow, but if you can get lamb broth, that would be even better.

CUT OF LAMB	COOKING TIME AT HIGH PRESSURE
Ground lamb (meat loaf)	15 minutes
Ground lamb (meatballs)	5 minutes
Lamb shanks (1 pound)	30 minutes
Lamb shoulder stew meat	14 minutes
Leg of lamb (boneless, 3 to 4 pounds)	35 to 45 minutes

These cooking times are based on a natural release of pressure. If your meat weighs less than the amount specified in the chart, subtract 10 minutes of cooking time per pound.

CABERNET-BRAISED LEG OF LAMB

A boneless leg of lamb, tied and ready to cook, can be an elegant meal waiting to happen. This dish would be excellent for a festive dinner, whether it's to celebrate a holiday or a significant event. Marinate the lamb for at least twelve hours so that the wine will flavor and tenderize the meat. The beauty of this recipe is that it can be made the day before in the pressure cooker and then reheated on the stove top before serving.

SERVES 6 TO 8

MARINADE

2½ CUPS CABERNET SAUVIGNON OR BURGUNDY WINE

4 GARLIC CLOVES, MINCED

1½ TABLESPOONS FINELY CHOPPED FRESH ROSEMARY

⅔ CUP EXTRA-VIRGIN OLIVE OIL

6 DROPS OF TABASCO OR ANOTHER HOT SAUCE

1 CUP FINELY CHOPPED SWEET ONION, SUCH AS VIDALIA

½ CUP HONEY

ONE 3- TO 4-POUND BONELESS LEG OF LAMB, TIED WITH BUTCHER'S TWINE (SEE PSST)

1 CUP CHICKEN STOCK (PAGE 19) OR STORE-BOUGHT CHICKEN BROTH

1 CUP BEEF STOCK (PAGE 20) OR STORE-BOUGHT BEEF BROTH

1 **To make the marinade:** In a large mixing bowl, whisk together all the ingredients. Put the lamb in a 1-gallon zipper-top plastic bag and pour half the marinade over the meat. Seal the bag and refrigerate for at least 12 hours or up to 24 hours. Add the stocks to the remaining marinade and refrigerate.

2 Remove the meat from the marinade and discard the marinade in the plastic bag. Pour the marinade and stock mixture into the pressure cooker and arrange the meat in the cooker. Lock the lid in place and cook on high pressure for 35 minutes.

3 Release the pressure naturally and remove the lid, tilting the pot away from you to avoid the escaping steam. Transfer the leg of lamb to a cutting board and allow to rest for 15 minutes, loosely covered with aluminum foil.

4 Skim off any excess fat from the surface of the sauce, strain the sauce into a saucepan, and bring to a boil. Continue boiling for 10 minutes to reduce the sauce and concentrate its flavors. Remove the twine from the roast, slice the meat, and serve with the sauce on the side.

PSST

Leg of lamb usually comes already tied. If yours wasn't, tie it at 1-inch intervals with butcher's twine or silicone bands.

ROSEMARY-DIJON ROLLED LEG OF LAMB

The bright flavors of southern France make this dish sparkle. It's just the thing for a fancy dinner party, and you can make it in less than one hour. I like to serve it with goat cheese–mashed potatoes and haricots verts (tiny French green beans), tossed in walnut oil and garnished with toasted walnuts.

SERVES **6** TO **8**

3 TABLESPOONS EXTRA-VIRGIN OLIVE OIL

2 TEASPOONS SALT

½ TEASPOON FRESHLY GROUND BLACK PEPPER

3 GARLIC CLOVES, MINCED

1 TEASPOON FINELY CHOPPED FRESH ROSEMARY

ONE 3- TO 4-POUND BONELESS LEG OF LAMB, TIED WITH BUTCHER'S TWINE

1½ CUPS CHICKEN STOCK (PAGE 19) OR STORE-BOUGHT CHICKEN BROTH

1 CUP BEEF STOCK (PAGE 20) OR STORE-BOUGHT BEEF BROTH

½ CUP DRY WHITE WINE, SUCH AS SAUVIGNON BLANC OR PINOT GRIGIO, OR DRY VERMOUTH

½ CUP DIJON MUSTARD

1 In a small bowl, combine 1 tablespoon of the oil with the salt, pepper, garlic, and rosemary. With the point of a sharp knife, make cross-shaped slits in the meat, about 1 inch apart, and rub the meat with the herb mixture, pushing the rub into the slits.

2 Heat the remaining 2 tablespoons of oil in the pressure cooker over medium-high heat. Add the meat and brown on all sides. Add both stocks, wine, and mustard. Lock the lid in place and cook at high pressure for 35 minutes.

3 Release the pressure naturally and remove the lid, tilting the pot away from you to avoid the escaping steam. Remove the meat to a cutting board, cover loosely with aluminum foil, and allow to rest for 15 minutes.

4 Skim off any excess fat from the top of the sauce, bring to a boil, and continue boiling for 5 to 10 minutes to concentrate the flavors. Remove the twine from the roast and cut into thin slices. Serve the meat with the sauce spooned over it and any additional sauce on the side.

WHITE BEAN AND LAMB CASSOULET

Cassoulet is a big production in many places in France, requiring duck and pork and sausages and assorted other meats in addition to beans. This cassoulet pairs creamy white beans with rich lamb shanks in a delicious wine-and-thyme flavored sauce. The result is sublime. I like to include veal demi-glace because it deepens the flavor considerably (see the Psst).

SERVES 6

4 TABLESPOONS EXTRA-VIRGIN OLIVE OIL

6 THICK-CUT SMOKED BACON STRIPS, CUT INTO 1-INCH DICE

FOUR ½-POUND LAMB SHANKS

2 GARLIC CLOVES, MINCED

1 TEASPOON DRIED THYME

1 BAY LEAF

2 LARGE ONIONS, FINELY CHOPPED

4 CELERY STALKS, FINELY CHOPPED

ONE 14½-OUNCE CAN CRUSHED TOMATOES WITH THEIR JUICE

½ CUP DRY WHITE WINE, SUCH AS SAUVIGNON BLANC OR PINOT GRIGIO, OR DRY VERMOUTH

4 CUPS VEAL DEMI-GLACE (SEE PSST) OR CHICKEN STOCK (PAGE 19) OR STORE-BOUGHT CHICKEN BROTH

1½ CUPS GREAT NORTHERN OR CANNELLINI BEANS, PRESOAKED (SEE PAGE 151) AND DRAINED

SALT AND FRESHLY GROUND BLACK PEPPER (OPTIONAL)

½ CUP FINELY CHOPPED FRESH FLAT-LEAF PARSLEY FOR GARNISH

1 Heat 2 tablespoons of the oil in the pressure cooker over medium-high heat. Add the bacon and cook until it has rendered its fat and begins to crisp. Remove the bacon, drain on paper towels, and remove all but 3 tablespoons of the fat from the pot. Add the lamb shanks, brown on all sides, and transfer to a plate. Return the bacon to the pot. Add the garlic, thyme, bay leaf, onions, and celery and sauté for 4 to 6 minutes, or until the onions begin to soften. Add the tomatoes and wine and bring to a boil. Add the demi-glace, beans, and lamb shanks and drizzle with the remaining 2 tablespoons of oil. Lock the lid in place and cook at high pressure for 30 minutes.

2 Release the pressure naturally and remove the lid, tilting the pot away from you to avoid the escaping steam. Remove the bay leaf, transfer the lamb shanks to a tureen or large serving bowl, and cover loosely with aluminum foil. Remove any beans that aren't cooked (they are usually floating on the top) and skim off any excess fat from the liquid. Taste the stock for seasoning and add salt and pepper if needed. Transfer the contents of the pot to the serving bowl and garnish with the parsley before serving.

PSST

Demi-glace is a classic preparation of veal stock and *sauce espagnole* (a rich sauce), which is reduced until it is syrupy. Sold as a base that is reconstituted with water, demi-glace is great to have on hand to give soups and sauces a deeper flavor. A reliable brand is More Than Gourmet, which is available at fine cookware stores.

LAMB STEW WITH VEGETABLES

Try this comforting stew for a change of pace. It will make a great weeknight meal for your family, and when the weather is cold, it will warm their tummies.

SERVES **6**

2 TABLESPOONS EXTRA-VIRGIN OLIVE OIL

3 POUNDS LEG OF LAMB, CUT INTO 1-INCH PIECES

2 TEASPOONS SALT

1 TEASPOON FRESHLY GROUND BLACK PEPPER

2 GARLIC CLOVES, MINCED

1 LARGE ONION, FINELY CHOPPED

1½ TEASPOONS DRIED THYME

1½ CUPS CHICKEN STOCK (PAGE 19) OR STORE-BOUGHT CHICKEN BROTH

1½ CUPS BEEF STOCK (PAGE 20) OR STORE-BOUGHT BEEF BROTH

12 SMALL RED-SKINNED OR YUKON GOLD POTATOES, SCRUBBED AND HALVED

4 MEDIUM CARROTS, PEELED AND CUT INTO 2-INCH LENGTHS

12 PEARL ONIONS, PEELED

2 CUPS FROZEN PETITE PEAS, DEFROSTED

1 Heat the oil in the pressure cooker over medium-high heat. Sprinkle the lamb evenly with salt and pepper, add the meat to the pot, a few pieces at a time, being careful not to crowd the pot, and brown, transferring the browned meat to a plate. Add the garlic, onion, and thyme to the pot and sauté for 2 minutes, or until the onion begins to soften. Add the stocks, scraping up any browned bits on the bottom. Return the lamb to the pot and add the potatoes, carrots, and pearl onions. Lock the lid in place and cook at high pressure for 14 minutes.

2 Release the pressure naturally and remove the lid, tilting the pot away from you to avoid the escaping steam. Carefully remove the meat and vegetables to a serving bowl. Remove any excess fat from the surface of the sauce and stir in the peas. Cook for 1 minute over medium-high heat to warm the peas. Pour the sauce over the meat and vegetables and serve immediately.

DUBLINER STEW WITH CHIVE MASHED POTATOES

It wouldn't be an Irish stew without the Guinness to give it a sweet note. The gloriously flavored chive mashed potatoes make this a delicious meal to serve to family or company.

SERVES 6

DUBLINER STEW

2 TABLESPOONS EXTRA-VIRGIN OLIVE OIL

2 POUNDS LEG OF LAMB, CUT INTO 1-INCH PIECES

1½ TEASPOONS SALT, PLUS MORE IF NEEDED

½ TEASPOON FRESHLY GROUND BLACK PEPPER, PLUS MORE IF NEEDED

2 MEDIUM ONIONS, FINELY CHOPPED

1 TEASPOON DRIED THYME

ONE 15-OUNCE CAN GUINNESS STOUT

1½ CUPS BEEF STOCK (PAGE 20) OR STORE-BOUGHT BEEF BROTH

4 MEDIUM CARROTS, PEELED AND CUT INTO 2-INCH LENGTHS

2 MEDIUM PARSNIPS, CUT INTO 2-INCH LENGTHS

2 TEASPOONS CORNSTARCH MIXED WITH 1 TABLESPOON WATER

1 CUP FROZEN PETITE SIZE PEAS, DEFROSTED

CHIVE MASHED POTATOES

6 MEDIUM RUSSET POTATOES, PEELED AND CUT INTO 1-INCH PIECES

4 TABLESPOONS UNSALTED BUTTER

⅓ CUP HEAVY CREAM

1½ TEASPOONS SALT

½ TEASPOON FRESHLY GROUND BLACK PEPPER

2 TABLESPOONS FINELY CHOPPED FRESH CHIVES

1 **To make the stew:** Heat the oil in the pressure cooker over medium-high heat. Sprinkle the lamb evenly with the salt and pepper, add a few pieces at a time to the pot, being careful not to crowd the pot, and brown, transferring the browned meat to a plate. Add the onions and thyme to the pot and sauté for 2 minutes, or until the onions begin to soften. Add the Guinness and stock and stir up any browned bits on the bottom of the pot. Return the lamb to the pot and add the carrots and parsnips. Lock the lid in place and cook at high pressure for 14 minutes.

2 Release the pressure naturally and remove the lid, tilting the pot away from you to avoid the escaping steam. Skim off any fat from the top of the sauce. Taste for seasoning, adding more salt and pepper if needed. Bring the sauce to a boil, add the cornstarch slurry, and return to a boil until thickened. Stir in the peas and remove from the heat. Allow the stew to rest for 3 to 5 minutes.

3 **To make the potatoes:** While the stew is in the pressure cooker, put the potatoes in a 4-quart saucepan with water to cover, bring to a boil, and continue boiling for 15 to 20 minutes, or until the potatoes are tender. In a small saucepan, melt the butter with the cream and keep warm. Drain the potatoes and return to the pan over medium heat for a minute or two to dry out the potatoes. Add half the butter and cream mixture and mash it into the potatoes until smooth. Add the salt and pepper and mash in the remaining cream mixture if the potatoes seem too dry. Stir in the chives. Transfer the potatoes to a serving bowl and, if the stew is not ready, cover with aluminum foil to keep warm. Serve with the stew.

SAFFRON LAMB STEW

This aromatic stew is a one-pot meal that can be on your table in less than thirty minutes. The lamb and orzo cook in a saffron-and-tomato-flavored sauce, which is thickened by the starch of the pasta. If you decide to leave out the pasta, the stew will be thinner.

SERVES 6

2½ CUPS CHICKEN STOCK (PAGE 19) OR STORE-BOUGHT CHICKEN BROTH

1 TEASPOON SAFFRON THREADS, CRUSHED IN THE PALM OF YOUR HAND

3 TABLESPOONS EXTRA-VIRGIN OLIVE OIL

1 TEASPOON SWEET PAPRIKA

½ TEASPOON GROUND TURMERIC

2 POUNDS LEG OF LAMB, CUT INTO 1-INCH PIECES

1 CUP FINELY CHOPPED SWEET ONION, SUCH AS VIDALIA

4 MEDIUM CARROTS, CUT INTO 2-INCH LENGTHS

ONE 14½-OUNCE CAN CHOPPED TOMATOES, DRAINED

1 CUP ORZO

GRATED ZEST OF 1 ORANGE

½ CUP FINELY CHOPPED FRESH FLAT-LEAF PARSLEY

1 Pour the stock into a large measuring cup and sprinkle with the saffron. Allow the saffron to bloom while preparing the stew. In a small bowl, make a paste with 1 tablespoon of the oil, the paprika, and the turmeric and rub it into the lamb.

2 Heat the remaining 2 tablespoons of oil in the pressure cooker over medium-high heat. Add a few pieces of the lamb at a time, being careful not to crowd the pot, and brown, transferring the browned meat to a plate. Add the onion and sauté for 2 minutes, until it begins to soften. Add the carrots, tomatoes, and saffron stock and return the lamb to the pot, stirring up any browned bits on the bottom of the pot. Add the orzo, pushing it under the liquid. Lock the lid in place and cook at high pressure for 14 minutes.

3 Release the pressure naturally and remove the lid, tilting the pot away from you to avoid the escaping steam. Stir in the orange zest and parsley and allow to rest for 3 to 5 minutes before serving.

LAMB PROVENÇAL

This simple lamb and artichoke stew from the South of France is perfumed with tarragon, garlic, and plenty of Dijon mustard. It's delicious over rice or pasta, or serve it with a salad and lots of crusty bread to soak up the sauce.

SERVES **6**

2 TABLESPOONS EXTRA-VIRGIN OLIVE OIL

2 POUNDS LAMB SHOULDER, CUT INTO 2-INCH PIECES

1½ TEASPOONS SALT

½ TEASPOON FRESHLY GROUND BLACK PEPPER

3 GARLIC CLOVES, SLICED

½ CUP BEEF STOCK (PAGE 20) OR STORE-BOUGHT BEEF BROTH

1 CUP CHICKEN STOCK (PAGE 19) OR STORE-BOUGHT CHICKEN BROTH

1 TEASPOON DRIED TARRAGON

¼ CUP DIJON MUSTARD

ONE 10-OUNCE PACKAGE FROZEN ARTICHOKE HEARTS, DEFROSTED AND PATTED DRY

1 Heat the oil in the pressure cooker over medium-high heat. Sprinkle the lamb evenly with the salt and pepper, add to the pot in small batches, being careful not to crowd the pot, and brown, transferring the lamb to a plate when it's done. Return the browned meat to the pot and add the garlic, stocks, tarragon, and mustard. Lock the lid in place and cook at high pressure for 14 minutes.

2 Release the pressure naturally and remove the lid, tilting the pot away from you to avoid the escaping steam. Remove the meat from the pot and skim off any excess fat from the top. Return the meat to the pot and add the artichokes. Simmer for 5 to 10 minutes to concentrate the flavors. Serve immediately.

FRUITED LAMB TAGINE

A tagine is a type of stew, which is named for the vessel in which it's cooked. It's popular in Morocco, where it is often served with couscous. The vessel has a conical top with a vent, which perfumes the kitchen with the aromas of prunes, oranges, and saffron while the stew bubbles away for hours. The pressure cooker makes quick work of this colorful dish; you can have it on the table in less than one hour.

SERVES **6**

2 CUPS CHICKEN STOCK (PAGE 19) OR STORE-BOUGHT CHICKEN BROTH

1 CUP ORANGE JUICE

1 TEASPOON SAFFRON THREADS, CRUSHED IN THE PALM OF YOUR HAND

½ TEASPOON GROUND CORIANDER

¼ TEASPOON GROUND CINNAMON

½ TEASPOON SWEET PAPRIKA

½ TEASPOON GROUND TURMERIC

1½ TEASPOONS SALT, PLUS MORE IF NEEDED

½ TEASPOON FRESHLY GROUND BLACK PEPPER, PLUS MORE IF NEEDED

2 POUNDS LEG OF LAMB OR LAMB SHOULDER, CUT INTO 2-INCH PIECES

2 TABLESPOONS EXTRA-VIRGIN OLIVE OIL

1 CUP FINELY CHOPPED SWEET ONION, SUCH AS VIDALIA

1 CUP LARGE PITTED PRUNES, HALVED

3 NAVEL ORANGES, PEELED, PITH REMOVED, AND SLICED CROSSWISE, FOR GARNISH

½ CUP FINELY CHOPPED FRESH CILANTRO FOR GARNISH

COOKED COUSCOUS FOR SERVING

1 Pour the stock and orange juice into a large measuring cup and sprinkle the saffron over the top. In a small bowl, combine the coriander, cinnamon, paprika, turmeric, salt, and pepper. Sprinkle over the lamb and rub into the meat.

2 Heat the oil in the pressure cooker over medium-high heat. Add the lamb, a few pieces at a time, and brown, being careful not to burn the spices, transferring the browned meat to a plate. Add the onion to the pot and sauté for 2 minutes, until it begins to soften. Add the stock mixture and the prunes and return the meat to the pot. Lock the lid in place and cook at high pressure for 14 minutes.

3 Release the pressure naturally and remove the lid, tilting the pot away from you to avoid the escaping steam. Transfer the meat to a serving bowl and remove any excess fat from the top of the sauce. Taste the sauce for seasoning and add more salt and pepper if necessary. Pour the sauce over the meat and garnish with the orange slices and cilantro. Serve the tagine with couscous.

INDIAN BRAISED LAMB WITH TOMATOES AND YOGURT

This delicious dish will take you on a trip to India. Its spicy flavor and cooling yogurt sauce pair perfectly with basmati rice or naan, an Indian flatbread.

SERVES 6

3 TABLESPOONS CANOLA OIL

1 TEASPOON GROUND CORIANDER

½ TEASPOON GROUND CUMIN

½ TEASPOON GROUND TURMERIC

½ TEASPOON GARAM MASALA

2 POUNDS LEG OF LAMB, CUT INTO 1-INCH PIECES

1 LARGE ONION, FINELY CHOPPED

2 TEASPOONS GRATED FRESH GINGER

1 GARLIC CLOVE, MINCED

1 TEASPOON SALT, PLUS MORE IF NEEDED

1 CUP CHOPPED TOMATOES

1 CUP CHICKEN STOCK (PAGE 19) OR STORE-BOUGHT CHICKEN BROTH

2 TEASPOONS CORNSTARCH

1½ CUPS PLAIN NONFAT YOGURT, AT ROOM TEMPERATURE

FRESHLY GROUND BLACK PEPPER (OPTIONAL)

COOKED LONG-GRAIN RICE, SUCH AS BASMATI, FOR SERVING

¼ CUP FINELY CHOPPED FRESH CILANTRO FOR GARNISH

1 In a small bowl, stir 1 tablespoon of the oil, the coriander, cumin, turmeric, and garam masala into a paste. Rub the mixture into the lamb.

2 Heat the remaining 2 tablespoons of oil in the pressure cooker over medium-high heat. Add the lamb, a few pieces at a time, being careful not to crowd the pot, and brown, removing the browned meat to a plate. Add the onion, ginger, and garlic to the pot and cook for 2 minutes, or until the onion is softened and fragrant. Add the salt, tomatoes, and stock and bring to a boil. Return the lamb to the pot, lock the lid in place, and cook at high pressure for 15 minutes.

3 Release the pressure naturally and remove the lid, tilting the pot away from you to avoid the escaping steam. Remove the lamb from the pot and cover loosely with aluminum foil. Stir the cornstarch into the yogurt and whisk the mixture into the sauce. Warm the sauce over medium heat, taste for seasoning, and add more salt and some pepper if needed. Return the lamb to the pot and serve the stew over the rice, garnished with cilantro.

SPICY LAMB MEATBALLS IN RED WINE SAUCE

A potful of spicy meatballs in a luscious red wine sauce screams for a bed of orzo or smashed potatoes with feta cheese. This is a great weeknight dinner, but you can also make the meatballs smaller and serve them as appetizers at your next soirée. Either way, they are sure to become a favorite in your home.

SERVES 6

RED WINE SAUCE

3 TABLESPOONS UNSALTED BUTTER

½ CUP FINELY CHOPPED ONION

3 TABLESPOONS ALL-PURPOSE FLOUR

1½ CUPS DRY RED WINE, SUCH AS CHIANTI, ZINFANDEL, OR BAROLO

⅔ CUP BEEF STOCK (PAGE 20) OR STORE-BOUGHT BEEF BROTH

ONE 15½-OUNCE CAN CHOPPED TOMATOES WITH THEIR JUICE

1 TEASPOON SALT

½ TEASPOON FRESHLY GROUND BLACK PEPPER

MEATBALLS

½ POUND GROUND BEEF (85% LEAN)

1 POUND GROUND LAMB

½ CUP FINELY CHOPPED ONION

1 CUP FRESH BREAD CRUMBS

1 LARGE EGG, WELL BEATEN

1 GARLIC CLOVE, MINCED

1 TABLESPOON CHOPPED FRESH OREGANO OR 1 TEASPOON DRIED

1½ TEASPOONS SALT

½ TEASPOON FRESHLY GROUND BLACK PEPPER

1 TABLESPOON CHOPPED FRESH FLAT-LEAF PARSLEY, PLUS A FEW SPRIGS FOR GARNISH

1 TABLESPOON CHOPPED FRESH MINT, PLUS A FEW SPRIGS FOR GARNISH

1 **To make the sauce:** In the pressure cooker, melt the butter over medium heat. Add the onion and cook, stirring, until softened, about 3 minutes. Whisk in the flour and cook until white bubbles form. Cook for an additional 2 minutes, then whisk in the wine, stock, and tomatoes. Bring to a boil, stirring, and continue boiling, stirring constantly, until the sauce thickens. Stir in the salt and pepper, lower the heat, and maintain the sauce at a simmer while you make the meatballs.

2 **To make the meatballs:** In a large mixing bowl, blend all the ingredients together. Form into golf ball–size meatballs and drop into the sauce in the pressure cooker. Lock the lid in place and cook at high pressure for 5 minutes.

3 Release the pressure naturally and remove the lid, tilting the pot away from you to avoid the escaping steam. With a slotted spoon, transfer the meatballs to a serving platter. Spoon some of the sauce over the meatballs, garnish with the parsley and mint sprigs, and serve.

GYROS-STYLE MEAT LOAF FOR PITA SANDWICHES

The gyro is a Middle Eastern and Greek snack food consisting of a spicy ground-meat mixture that is formed into a large loaf and cooked on a spit. When the outer layer is cooked and crispy, it is sliced off and served in pita bread with tzatziki sauce and salad ingredients. It is sold from stands in many urban areas of the United States. Lamb, beef, and chicken versions are all popular. Our meat loaf, made with a combination of ground lamb and ground pork, isn't cooked on a spit. But it is delicious and emerges from the pressure cooker in less than half an hour. Serve it with pita and the tzatziki sauce on the side. A large salad with red wine vinaigrette completes the meal. This is great hot, at room temperature, or even cold. Note that the tzatziki sauce should be made at least two hours in advance. The key ingredient is Greek-style yogurt, which is available in well-stocked supermarkets.

SERVES 6

TZATZIKI SAUCE

1 ENGLISH CUCUMBER

2 CUPS GREEK-STYLE YOGURT

2 GARLIC CLOVES, MINCED

2 TABLESPOONS RED WINE

1 TABLESPOON FINELY CHOPPED FRESH DILL

1½ TEASPOONS SALT

½ TEASPOON FRESHLY GROUND BLACK PEPPER

1 **To make the sauce:** Peel the cucumber and grate it. Drain it in a colander for 30 minutes. Transfer the cucumber to a glass bowl and whisk in the remaining ingredients. Cover and refrigerate for at least 2 hours or up to 36 hours before serving.

2 **To make the meat loaf:** In a mixing bowl, combine the lamb, pork, onion, garlic, salt, pepper, oregano, marjoram, and lemon zest. Using your hands, shape the mixture into a loaf about 5 inches long.

3 Pour the stocks and wine into the pressure cooker and stir to combine. Set the loaf in the middle of the cooker. Lock the lid in place and cook at high pressure for 15 minutes.

MEAT LOAF

1½ POUNDS GROUND LAMB

½ POUND LEAN GROUND PORK

½ CUP FINELY CHOPPED ONION

3 GARLIC CLOVES, MINCED

1½ TEASPOONS SALT

½ TEASPOON FRESHLY GROUND BLACK PEPPER

1 TEASPOON DRIED OREGANO

½ TEASPOON DRIED MARJORAM

1 TEASPOON GRATED LEMON ZEST

1 CUP CHICKEN STOCK (PAGE 19) OR STORE-BOUGHT CHICKEN BROTH

1 CUP BEEF STOCK (PAGE 20) OR STORE-BOUGHT BEEF BROTH

½ CUP DRY RED WINE, SUCH AS CHIANTI, BAROLO, OR ZINFANDEL

PITA BREAD, HALVED, FOR SERVING

4 Release the pressure naturally and remove the lid, tilting the pot away from you to avoid the escaping steam. Using two long spatulas, carefully remove the meat loaf to a cutting board and allow to rest for about 15 minutes, covered loosely with aluminum foil to keep warm. To serve, cut the meat loaf into thin slices and tuck into the pita bread. Spoon the tzatziki sauce into the pocket.

PSST

Tzatziki can also be used as a dip for vegetables or pita chips.

Or, instead of making sandwiches, you can serve the meat with thickened pot juices. First, bring the pot juices to a boil and cook for about 10 minutes to reduce and concentrate the flavors.

VEAL & BEEF

Juicy, tender, and flavorful, beef is my idea of the perfect main course, especially when it's a pot roast or stew. The pressure cooker produces full-flavored pot roasts and stews in record time, sometimes within half an hour. Inexpensive and relatively tough cuts of meat, such as chuck, short ribs, and round, emerge from the pressure cooker rich with flavor and are melt-in-your-mouth delicious.

Veal tastes mild in comparison to beef, has little fat on it, and can be dry or chewy when cooked conventionally. The pressure cooker turns veal into richly flavored, falling-apart tender meat, and makes quick work of it. VEAL OSSO BUCCO (page 251), which is normally a three-hour production on the stove top or in the oven, takes about half an hour with a pressure cooker! If you prefer not to eat veal, you can substitute pork for the recipes.

CUT OF VEAL	COOKING TIME AT HIGH PRESSURE
Veal shanks	20 minutes
Veal stew meat (1-inch chunks)	10 minutes
Veal chops (1½ inches thick, stuffed)	20 minutes

CUT OF BEEF OR PREPARATION

Beef stew meat (1-inch pieces)	15 minutes
Brisket (4 pounds)	55 minutes
Chuck roast (5 pounds)	60 minutes
Corned beef (4 pounds)	50 minutes
Flank steak (1 pound)	25 minutes
Meatballs	5 minutes
Meat loaf	15 minutes
Round or rump roast (4 pounds)	55 minutes
Short ribs	25 minutes
Sirloin roast (3 pounds)	40 minutes
Sirloin tips	20 minutes

These cooking times are based on a natural release of pressure. If your meat weighs less than the amount specified in the chart, subtract 10 minutes of cooking time per pound.

VEAL CACCIATORE

This simple entrée is terrific with polenta or risotto on the side. *Cacciatore* literally means "hunters' style," and most cacciatore in Italy is made with ingredients a hunter would carry with him—usually a bit of lardo, oil, vinegar, and foraged herbs. (The addition of tomato seems to be an American variation.) This recipe relies on the woodsy flavors of rosemary and cremini mushrooms. Serve it over polenta, mashed potatoes, pasta, or risotto.

SERVES **6** TO **8**

3 TABLESPOONS EXTRA-VIRGIN OLIVE OIL

1½ TEASPOONS SALT

½ TEASPOON FRESHLY GROUND BLACK PEPPER

2 GARLIC CLOVES, MINCED

1½ TEASPOONS FINELY CHOPPED FRESH ROSEMARY

3 POUNDS VEAL SHOULDER, CUT INTO 1-INCH PIECES

3 PANCETTA SLICES, CUT INTO ½-INCH DICE

1 POUND CREMINI MUSHROOMS, QUARTERED

1½ CUPS WHITE WINE, SUCH AS ORVIETO, OR DRY VERMOUTH

2 TABLESPOONS UNSALTED BUTTER, CUT INTO SMALL BITS

1 In a small bowl, combine 1 tablespoon of the oil with the salt, pepper, garlic, and rosemary and rub the mixture into the veal.

2 Heat the remaining 2 tablespoons of oil in the pressure cooker over medium-high heat. Add the pancetta and cook until it renders its fat. Brown the veal, a few pieces at a time, removing them to a plate when they are browned. Add the mushrooms to the pot and sauté for about 3 minutes. Add the wine and bring to a boil, stirring up any browned bits sticking to the bottom. Return the veal to the pressure cooker. Lock the lid in place and cook at high pressure for 10 minutes.

3 Release the pressure naturally and remove the lid, tilting the pot away from you to avoid the escaping steam. Remove the veal and mushrooms from the pressure cooker, arrange on a plate, and cover with aluminum foil to keep warm. Reduce the sauce in the pressure cooker over high heat for 5 minutes, and then whisk in the butter, a bit at a time, until the sauce is emulsified. Return the veal and mushrooms to the pan and serve immediately.

CORN BREAD–STUFFED VEAL CHOPS IN WHITE WINE SAUCE

These thick-cut veal chops, stuffed with corn bread and sage, simmer in a white wine sauce in the pressure cooker. The meat becomes succulent and almost falls off the bone, all in the span of twenty-five minutes! This is great for a company dinner and it pairs well with roasted asparagus or broccoli.

SERVES 6

STUFFING

2 TABLESPOONS UNSALTED BUTTER

4 THIN SLICES PROSCIUTTO DI PARMA, FINELY CHOPPED

2 MEDIUM SHALLOTS, FINELY CHOPPED

4 FRESH SAGE LEAVES, FINELY CHOPPED

2 CUPS CRUMBLED CORN BREAD (ABOUT HALF OF A 9-INCH SQUARE CORN BREAD)

½ CUP CHICKEN STOCK (PAGE 19) OR STORE-BOUGHT CHICKEN BROTH

VEAL CHOPS

6 VEAL CHOPS, 1½ INCHES THICK

2 TEASPOONS SALT, PLUS MORE IF NEEDED

1 TEASPOON FRESHLY GROUND BLACK PEPPER, PLUS MORE IF NEEDED

2 TABLESPOONS EXTRA-VIRGIN OLIVE OIL

3 MEDIUM LEEKS (WHITE AND TENDER GREEN PARTS), FINELY CHOPPED,

1 CUP DRY WHITE WINE, SUCH AS SAUVIGNON BLANC OR PINOT GRIGIO, OR DRY VERMOUTH

1½ CUPS CHICKEN STOCK (PAGE 19) OR STORE-BOUGHT CHICKEN BROTH

2 TABLESPOONS UNSALTED BUTTER, SOFTENED

2 TABLESPOONS ALL-PURPOSE FLOUR

1 **To make the stuffing:** Melt the butter in a small sauté pan over medium-high heat. Add the prosciutto and cook until crisp. Add the shallots and sage and cook until the shallots are softened, about 3 minutes. Transfer the mixture to a mixing bowl, add the corn bread, and stir to combine. Sprinkle the stock over the mixture, a few tablespoons at a time, tossing to combine. Stop adding stock when the stuffing begins to hold together. Set aside while preparing the chops.

2 **To make the veal chops:** With the bone away from you, cut a 2-inch lengthwise slit into the side of a chop for the filling. Using your paring knife, open up the pocket so that it reaches within ¾ inch of the bone. Sprinkle the veal inside and out with the salt and pepper. Stuff the pocket with 2 to 3 tablespoons of the corn bread stuffing, secure the pocket with a toothpick if necessary, and set aside. Repeat with the remaining chops.

3 Heat the oil in the pressure cooker over medium-high heat. Add the chops a few at a time and brown in the oil (if you have a tall cooker, you may have to brown them one at a time). Remove the chops to a plate as they are browned. Add the leeks to the pot and pour in the wine and stock. Stack the chops in the pressure cooker. Lock the lid in place and cook at high pressure for 20 minutes.

4 Release the pressure naturally and remove the lid, tilting the pot away from you to avoid the escaping steam. Carefully remove the chops to a plate and cover loosely with aluminum foil to keep warm. Mix the butter with the flour in a small bowl to form a paste. Skim off any excess fat from the sauce in the pot, bring to a boil, and whisk in the flour and butter. Return the sauce to a boil and remove from the heat. Taste the sauce for seasoning and add more salt and pepper if needed. Remove the toothpicks from the chops and serve napped with some of the sauce.

VEAL STEW WITH FORTY CLOVES OF GARLIC

Not to worry; you won't have to count the garlic cloves that go into this stew. But you will love the mellow flavor that the garlic develops when cooked under pressure along with sage, white wine, and tomatoes. This dish is a takeoff on a French dish introduced to Americans by James Beard—chicken with forty cloves of garlic. That was back in the days when polite society didn't eat much garlic, and Beard's readers were shocked. Serve the stew over mashed potatoes, pappardelle (flat, long pasta noodles), or polenta. And don't forget to provide plenty of crusty bread to dip into the sauce.

SERVES 6

2 TABLESPOONS EXTRA-VIRGIN OLIVE OIL

2 POUNDS VEAL STEW MEAT, OR 3 POUNDS VEAL SHOULDER CHOPS, CUT INTO 1-INCH PIECES

2 TEASPOONS SALT, PLUS MORE IF NEEDED

1 TEASPOON FRESHLY GROUND BLACK PEPPER, PLUS MORE IF NEEDED

3 GARLIC BULBS, SEPARATED INTO CLOVES AND PEELED

4 MEDIUM CARROTS, COARSELY CHOPPED

½ TEASPOON DRIED SAGE

½ CUP DRY WHITE WINE, SUCH AS SAUVIGNON BLANC OR PINOT GRIGIO, OR DRY VERMOUTH

ONE 15-OUNCE CAN CHOPPED TOMATOES WITH THEIR JUICE

1 CUP BEEF STOCK (PAGE 20) OR STORE-BOUGHT BEEF BROTH

6 FRESH SAGE LEAVES, FINELY CHOPPED

1 Heat the oil in the pressure cooker over medium-high heat. Sprinkle the meat evenly with the salt and pepper, add to the pressure cooker and brown, in batches if necessary. Return the browned meat to the pan and add the garlic, carrots, dried sage, wine, tomatoes, and stock. Lock the lid in place and cook at high pressure for 10 minutes.

2 Release the pressure naturally and remove the lid, tilting the pot away from you to avoid the escaping steam. Stir in the fresh sage, taste the sauce for seasoning, and add more salt and pepper if needed. Serve immediately.

VEAL OSSO BUCCO

A classic dish from Milan, this simple braise is elegant and comforting. Meaty veal shanks cook in an aromatic sauce until they are meltingly tender and almost fall off the bones. A garlicky garnish of gremolata finishes off the dish, which is traditionally served with risotto.

SERVES **4** TO **6**

2 TABLESPOONS EXTRA-VIRGIN OLIVE OIL

6 MEATY VEAL SHANKS (ABOUT ¾ POUND EACH), TIED WITH BUTCHER'S TWINE OR SILICONE BANDS

2 TEASPOONS SALT, PLUS MORE IF NEEDED

1 TEASPOON FRESHLY GROUND BLACK PEPPER, PLUS MORE IF NEEDED

2 TABLESPOONS UNSALTED BUTTER

2 LARGE ONIONS, FINELY CHOPPED

4 MEDIUM CARROTS, FINELY CHOPPED

3 CELERY STALKS (INCLUDING THE LEAVES), CHOPPED

1 TEASPOON FINELY CHOPPED FRESH THYME

1 CUP DRY WHITE WINE, SUCH AS SAUVIGNON BLANC OR PINOT GRIGIO, OR DRY VERMOUTH

1 CUP CHICKEN STOCK (PAGE 19) OR STORE-BOUGHT CHICKEN BROTH

ONE 15-OUNCE CAN CHOPPED TOMATOES WITH THEIR JUICE

½ CUP FINELY CHOPPED FRESH FLAT-LEAF PARSLEY

¼ CUP PACKED FRESH BASIL LEAVES, FINELY CHOPPED

GRATED ZEST OF 1 ORANGE

GRATED ZEST OF 1 LEMON

3 GARLIC CLOVES, MINCED

1 Heat the oil in the pressure cooker over medium-high heat. Sprinkle the shanks evenly with the salt and pepper, add to the pressure cooker a few at a time, and brown, removing them to a plate when they are browned. Add the butter to the pot and sauté the onions, carrots, celery, and thyme for 2 minutes to soften the onions. Add the wine, stock, and tomatoes and return the veal shanks to the pot. Lock the lid in place and cook at high pressure for 20 minutes.

2 Release the pressure naturally and remove the lid, tilting the pot away from you to avoid the escaping steam. Carefully remove the veal shanks from the pot and set aside. Skim off any excess fat from the sauce, taste for seasoning, and add more salt and pepper if needed. In a small bowl, make the gremolata by tossing together the parsley, basil, orange and lemon zests, and garlic. Stir into the sauce. Serve each veal shank covered with some of the sauce.

PSST

Generally, the gremolata garnish is served sprinkled over the top of each serving, but I love the fresh finish it gives to the sauce, so I stir it in at the last minute.

VEAL-STUFFED FLANK STEAK IN TOMATO CREAM SAUCE

The spicy veal stuffing marries well with the beefy flavor of the flank steak. It's cooked in a delicious tomato sauce finished with cream to round out its luscious flavor. This meal is awesome served with pasta, a vegetable risotto, or polenta.

SERVES **6**

STUFFING

1 POUND GROUND VEAL

2 GARLIC CLOVES, MINCED

¼ CUP FINELY CHOPPED FRESH FLAT-LEAF PARSLEY

¼ CUP FINELY CHOPPED SUN-DRIED TOMATOES PACKED IN OIL

¼ CUP FRESHLY GRATED PARMIGIANO-REGGIANO CHEESE

⅛ TEASPOON FRESHLY GRATED NUTMEG

½ CUP FRESH BREAD CRUMBS

1 LARGE EGG LIGHTLY, BEATEN

STEAK AND SAUCE

ONE 1-POUND FLANK STEAK, BUTTERFLIED (SEE PSST ON FACING PAGE)

1½ TEASPOONS SALT, PLUS MORE IF NEEDED

½ TEASPOON FRESHLY GROUND BLACK PEPPER, PLUS MORE IF NEEDED

2 TABLESPOONS EXTRA-VIRGIN OLIVE OIL

2 LARGE SWEET ONIONS, SUCH AS VIDALIA, CHOPPED

3 MEDIUM CARROTS, COARSELY CHOPPED

4 CELERY STALKS (INCLUDING THE LEAVES), COARSELY CHOPPED

1½ TEASPOONS DRIED SAGE

1 BAY LEAF

1 CUP BEEF STOCK (PAGE 20) OR STORE-BOUGHT BEEF BROTH

ONE 28-OUNCE CAN CRUSHED TOMATOES WITH THEIR JUICE

1 CUP HEAVY CREAM

6 FRESH SAGE LEAVES, FINELY CHOPPED

1 **To make the stuffing:** In a large mixing bowl, combine all the ingredients until blended.

2 **To make the steak and sauce:** Sprinkle the meat evenly with the salt and pepper and spread the stuffing evenly over the flank steak. Beginning with a long side, roll up the meat into a compact roll. Tie with butcher's twine or use silicone bands to secure the roll. Heat the oil in the pressure cooker over medium-high heat. Add the onions, carrots, celery, and dried sage and sauté for 2 minutes to soften the onions. Add the bay leaf, stock, and tomatoes and put the flank steak in the pressure cooker. Lock the lid in place and cook at high pressure for 25 minutes.

3 Release the pressure naturally and remove the lid, tilting the pot away from you to avoid the escaping steam. Carefully remove the steak to a cutting board and cover loosely with aluminum foil to keep warm. Skim off any excess fat from the top of the sauce, remove and discard the bay leaf, and add the cream and fresh sage. Taste the sauce for seasoning and add more salt and pepper if necessary. Warm the sauce. Remove the butcher's twine from the flank steak and cut crosswise into 1-inch slices. Serve each slice in a pool of sauce.

MEDITERRANEAN STUFFED FLANK STEAK WITH RED WINE SAUCE

Any time you serve this gorgeous flank steak stuffed with cheese, salami, and artichokes, your family will think it's a special occasion. The delicious oregano-infused sauce is great over pasta, and the beef melts in your mouth. All this in just twenty-five minutes of cooking time. *Mama mia!*

SERVES 6

ONE 1-POUND FLANK STEAK, BUTTERFLIED (SEE PSST)

1½ TEASPOONS SALT, PLUS MORE IF NEEDED

½ TEASPOON FRESHLY GROUND BLACK PEPPER, PLUS MORE IF NEEDED

8 SLICES SOPRESSATA OR GENOA SALAMI, FINELY CHOPPED

½ CUP GRATED PECORINO ROMANO CHEESE

ONE 6-OUNCE JAR MARINATED ARTICHOKE HEARTS, DRAINED AND COARSELY CHOPPED

1 CUP FRESH BREAD CRUMBS

1 LARGE EGG, LIGHTLY BEATEN

2 TABLESPOONS EXTRA-VIRGIN OLIVE OIL

1 LARGE ONION, FINELY CHOPPED

1 TEASPOON DRIED OREGANO

2 CUPS FULL-BODIED RED WINE, SUCH AS CHIANTI, ZINFANDEL, OR SANGIOVESE

1 CUP BEEF STOCK (PAGE 20) OR STORE-BOUGHT BEEF BROTH

½ CUP FINELY CHOPPED FRESH FLAT-LEAF PARSLEY

1 Sprinkle the meat evenly with the salt and pepper and set aside while making the filling.

2 In a mixing bowl, combine the sopressata, cheese, artichokes, bread crumbs, and egg, stirring until the mixture comes together. Spread the mixture evenly over the steak. Beginning with a long side, roll up the steak into a compact roll. Tie the roll with butcher's twine or use silicone bands to secure.

3 Heat the oil in the pressure cooker over medium-high heat. Add the onion and oregano and sauté for 2 minutes, or until the onion begins to soften. Add the wine and stock, stirring to blend. Set the stuffed flank steak in the stock. Lock the lid in place and cook at high pressure for 25 minutes.

4 Release the pressure naturally and remove the lid, tilting the pot away from you to avoid the escaping steam. Carefully transfer the flank steak to a cutting board and loosely cover with aluminum foil to keep warm. Stir the parsley into the sauce and taste for seasoning, adding more salt and pepper if necessary. Cut the butcher's twine from the flank steak and cut the steak crosswise into 1-inch slices. Serve each slice in a pool of the red wine sauce.

PSST

To butterfly the flank steak, start at the long side, holding a long, sharp knife parallel to your cutting board. Cut the steak in half horizontally, leaving the meat attached on one side so that it opens like a book. The steak should now be twice its original size.

MOM'S POT ROAST

This is a classic beef pot roast, the kind you would find on many American tables in the 1950s—a mahogany brown roast, cooked to melting perfection, surrounded by potatoes and carrots and bathed in a delicious pan gravy. Pot roast normally takes at least three hours to slow cook, but the pressure cooker brings you that slow-cooked goodness in less than an hour.

SERVES 6 TO 8

2 TABLESPOONS CANOLA OIL

ONE 3-POUND BONELESS RUMP ROAST, TIED AT 1-INCH INTERVALS

2 TEASPOONS SALT, PLUS MORE IF NEEDED

1 TEASPOON FRESHLY GROUND BLACK PEPPER, PLUS MORE IF NEEDED

2 LARGE SWEET ONIONS, SUCH AS VIDALIA, FINELY CHOPPED

4 CELERY STALKS, FINELY CHOPPED

1 TEASPOON DRIED THYME

1 BAY LEAF

¼ CUP SOY SAUCE

2½ CUPS BEEF STOCK (PAGE 20) OR STORE-BOUGHT BEEF BROTH

12 SMALL YUKON GOLD POTATOES, SCRUBBED

4 MEDIUM CARROTS, CUT INTO 2-INCH LENGTHS, OR 2 CUPS BABY CARROTS

2 TABLESPOONS FLOUR MIXED WITH ¼ CUP WATER

1 Heat the oil in the pressure cooker over medium-high heat. Sprinkle the roast evenly with the salt and pepper, add it to the pressure cooker, and sear on all sides, until it is evenly browned. Remove the roast from the pan. Add the onions, celery, thyme, and bay leaf and sauté for 2 minutes, or until the onions begin to soften. Add the soy sauce and stock and return the beef to the pan. Arrange the potatoes and carrots on top of the roast. Lock the lid in place and cook at high pressure for 50 minutes.

2 Release the pressure naturally and remove the lid, tilting the pot away from you to avoid the escaping steam. Remove the meat and vegetables to a serving platter and cover loosely with aluminum foil. Skim off any excess fat from the liquid, remove the bay leaf, and bring the liquid in the pot to a boil. Stir in the flour and water slurry and return the liquid to a boil. Taste for seasoning and add more salt and pepper if necessary. Remove the strings from the meat and carve into slices. Pour some of the gravy over the meat and pass the rest separately.

POT ROAST ITALIANO

It's hard to believe: a meltingly tender pot roast in an hour. The pressure cooker builds slow-cooked taste into this quickie dish. This roast gets its flavor from red wine, garlic, and rosemary. An orange zest gremolata stirred in at the end gives it a little pizzazz. *Buon appetito!*

SERVES 6

....

2 TABLESPOONS EXTRA-VIRGIN OLIVE OIL

2 CUPS COARSELY CHOPPED SWEET ONIONS, SUCH AS VIDALIA

3 CARROTS, COARSELY CHOPPED

1 TABLESPOON FINELY CHOPPED FRESH ROSEMARY

ONE 3½- TO 4-POUND BONELESS CHUCK ROAST, TIED WITH BUTCHER'S TWINE AT 1-INCH INTERVALS

2 TEASPOONS SALT, PLUS MORE IF NEEDED

1 TEASPOON FRESHLY GROUND BLACK PEPPER, PLUS MORE IF NEEDED

1 CUP FULL-BODIED RED WINE, SUCH AS CHIANTI, ZINFANDEL, OR BAROLO

½ CUP BEEF STOCK (PAGE 20) OR STORE-BOUGHT BEEF BROTH

2 TEASPOONS CORNSTARCH

GRATED ZEST OF 1 ORANGE

2 GARLIC CLOVES, MINCED

2 TABLESPOONS FINELY CHOPPED FRESH FLAT-LEAF PARSLEY

1 Heat the oil in the pressure cooker over medium-high heat. Add the onions, carrots, and rosemary and sauté for 2 minutes, or until the onions begin to soften. Sprinkle the roast with the salt and pepper and add it to the pot. Pour in the wine and stock. Lock the lid in place and cook at high pressure for 45 to 55 minutes, depending on the weight of the roast.

2 Release the pressure naturally and remove the lid, tilting the pot away from you to avoid the escaping steam. Remove the beef from the pan and cover loosely with aluminum foil. Skim off any excess fat from the sauce and taste for seasoning, adding more salt and pepper as necessary.

3 Bring the sauce to a boil. Mix the cornstarch with ¼ cup of the sauce and stir it into the pot. Bring the liquid to a boil, whisking until glossy and thickened. In a small bowl, mix together the orange zest, garlic, and parsley and stir into the sauce. Slice the meat, return it to the sauce, and serve.

GUINNESS POT ROAST

Although wine seems to be the standard liquid for braising a pot roast, beer, ale, and stout all add significant flavor and help to tenderize pot roasts and stews. This pot roast takes on the delicious flavor of Guinness, an Irish dark beer.

SERVES 6

2 TABLESPOONS CANOLA OIL

ONE 3-POUND RUMP ROAST, TIED AT 1-INCH INTERVALS

2 TEASPOONS SALT, PLUS MORE IF NEEDED

1 TEASPOON FRESHLY GROUND BLACK PEPPER, PLUS MORE IF NEEDED

2 MEDIUM SWEET ONIONS, SUCH AS VIDALIA, COARSELY CHOPPED

TWO 12-OUNCE CANS GUINNESS STOUT

1 CUP BEEF STOCK (PAGE 20) OR STORE-BOUGHT BEEF BROTH

1 SPRIG FRESH THYME

1 BAY LEAF

6 MEDIUM YUKON GOLD OR RED-SKINNED POTATOES, SCRUBBED AND QUARTERED

4 LARGE CARROTS, CUT INTO 2-INCH LENGTHS

2 TABLESPOONS UNSALTED BUTTER, SOFTENED

2 TABLESPOONS ALL-PURPOSE FLOUR

1 Heat the oil in the pressure cooker over medium-high heat. Sprinkle the meat evenly with the salt and pepper, add to the pressure cooker, and brown on all sides. Remove the meat to a plate. Add the onions, Guinness, stock, thyme, and bay leaf to the pot. Put the roast in the stock and scatter the potatoes and carrots over the roast. Lock the lid in place and cook at high pressure for 50 minutes.

2 Release the pressure naturally and remove the lid, tilting the pot away from you to avoid the escaping steam. Remove the meat to a cutting board and allow to rest for 10 minutes before slicing. Transfer the vegetables to a serving bowl and cover with aluminum foil. Skim off any fat from the surface of the sauce, remove the thyme sprig and bay leaf, and bring the sauce to a boil. In a small bowl, stir together the butter and flour to form a paste, whisk it into the sauce, and bring to a boil. Remove from the heat and taste the sauce for seasoning, adding salt and pepper if necessary. Slice the meat and serve with the vegetables and sauce.

BRISKET WITH POTATOES AND ROOT VEGETABLES

This is a great pot roast recipe if you love brisket; the vegetables absorb the beefy flavor of the cooking liquid and make a beautiful garnish for the finished dish. Although brisket is a tough cut of meat, it becomes tender and juicy when braised in the pressure cooker.

SERVES **6** TO **8**

2 CUPS BEEF STOCK (PAGE 20) OR STORE-BOUGHT BEEF BROTH

½ CUP SOY SAUCE

2 GARLIC CLOVES, SLICED

ONE 3- TO 4-POUND BRISKET, FAT TRIMMED (SEE PSST)

4 MEDIUM YUKON GOLD OR RED-SKINNED POTATOES, SCRUBBED AND HALVED

6 MEDIUM CARROTS, CUT INTO 2-INCH LENGTHS

4 MEDIUM SWEET ONIONS, SUCH AS VIDALIA, HALVED

2 TABLESPOONS CORNSTARCH MIXED WITH ¼ CUP WATER

¼ CUP FINELY CHOPPED FRESH FLAT-LEAF PARSLEY

SALT AND FRESHLY GROUND BLACK PEPPER (OPTIONAL)

1 In the pressure cooker, combine the stock, soy sauce, and garlic. Put the brisket in the liquid and stack the potatoes, carrots, and onions on top. Lock the lid in place and cook at high pressure for 45 to 55 minutes.

2 Release the pressure naturally and remove the lid, tilting the pot away from you to avoid the escaping steam. Carefully transfer the vegetables to a serving bowl. Transfer the brisket to a cutting board and allow to rest for 15 minutes before slicing.

3 Skim the fat from the top of the sauce, bring the sauce to a boil, and add the cornstarch slurry. Return the sauce to a boil, whisking until glossy and thickened. Stir in the parsley and remove from the heat. Taste the sauce for seasoning and add salt and pepper if necessary. Slice the brisket against the grain and arrange on a serving platter, napped with some of the sauce. Serve the remaining sauce and the vegetables on the side.

PSST

Brisket gives off a lot of water; that is why there is only a small amount of liquid in this recipe.

If the brisket is too large to lay flat, cut it in half and stack the halves in the pressure cooker.

BRAISED BRISKET WITH PLUM AND GOLDEN RAISIN SAUCE

The fruity sauce is a great complement to the beefy brisket, which absorbs flavors well. Serve this over buttered noodles for a delicious Sunday supper.

SERVES 6 TO 8

2 TABLESPOONS CANOLA OIL

2 MEDIUM SWEET ONIONS, SUCH AS VIDALIA, FINELY CHOPPED

2 SPRIGS FRESH THYME

1 BAY LEAF

¼ CUP FIRMLY PACKED LIGHT BROWN SUGAR

¼ CUP DIJON MUSTARD

½ CUP APPLE JUICE

2 CUPS BEEF STOCK (PAGE 20) OR STORE-BOUGHT BEEF BROTH

1 CUP GOLDEN RAISINS

1 CUP DRIED PLUMS

ONE 3- TO 4-POUND BRISKET, FAT TRIMMED

2 TABLESPOONS CORNSTARCH MIXED WITH ¼ CUP WATER

¼ CUP FINELY CHOPPED FRESH FLAT-LEAF PARSLEY

SALT AND FRESHLY GROUND BLACK PEPPER (OPTIONAL)

1 Heat the oil in the pressure cooker over medium-high heat. Add the onions, thyme, and bay leaf and sauté for 2 minutes to soften the onions. Add the sugar and mustard and stir to dissolve the sugar. Add the apple juice, stock, raisins, and dried plums. Arrange the brisket in the pressure cooker. Lock the lid in place and cook at high pressure for 45 to 55 minutes.

2 Release the pressure naturally and remove the lid, tilting the pot away from you to avoid the escaping steam. Transfer the brisket to a cutting board to rest for 15 minutes. Remove the thyme and bay leaf and skim any excess fat from the surface of the sauce.

3 Bring the sauce to a boil and whisk in the cornstarch slurry. Return to a boil, whisking until the sauce is thickened and glossy. Add the parsley and remove from the heat. Taste the sauce for seasoning and add salt and pepper if necessary. Slice the brisket across the grain and serve napped with the sauce.

BARBECUED BRISKET

This has to be the easiest recipe for barbecued beef that I know. It was inspired by an old recipe made with dried onion soup mix, bottled chili sauce, and beer. I've jazzed it up a bit, and the result is scrumptious. Serve it on rolls with potato salad and lots of cold beer.

SERVES **6** TO **8**

ONE 12-OUNCE CAN BEER (PALE LAGER, RATHER THAN ALE)

2 CUPS KETCHUP

2 TABLESPOONS WORCESTERSHIRE SAUCE

2 LARGE SWEET ONIONS, SUCH AS VIDALIA, FINELY CHOPPED

2 BEEF BOUILLON CUBES, OR 2 TEASPOONS BEEF SOUP BASE

ONE 3- TO 4-POUND BRISKET, FAT TRIMMED

SALT AND FRESHLY GROUND BLACK PEPPER (OPTIONAL)

1 In the pressure cooker, combine the beer, ketchup, Worcestershire, onions, and bouillon cubes. Put the brisket in the sauce. Lock the lid in place and cook at high pressure for 45 to 55 minutes.

2 Release the pressure naturally and remove the lid, tilting the pot away from you to avoid the escaping steam. Transfer the brisket to a cutting board and let rest for 15 minutes. Skim off the excess fat from the sauce and taste for seasoning, adding salt and pepper if needed. Purée the sauce with an immersion blender. Cut the beef across the grain into thin slices and return to the sauce.

CORNED BEEF, POTATOES, AND ROOT VEGGIES IN STOUT

My Irish roots come out on St. Patty's Day, and I love to celebrate with homemade corned beef. Instead of water, I use Guinness to flavor the corned beef and vegetables. The salty corned beef benefits from the sweetness of the stout broth, and the vegetables cook along with the beef in the pressure cooker in less than an hour. Serve the corned beef with Colman's English mustard or your favorite condiment.

SERVES **8**

TWO 12-OUNCE CANS GUINNESS STOUT

1 LARGE SWEET ONION, SUCH AS VIDALIA, COARSELY CHOPPED

1 BAY LEAF

ONE 4-POUND CORNED BEEF BRISKET, DRAINED

4 MEDIUM YUKON GOLD POTATOES, SCRUBBED AND QUARTERED

6 MEDIUM CARROTS, CUT INTO 2-INCH LENGTHS

4 MEDIUM PARSNIPS, PEELED AND CUT INTO 2-INCH LENGTHS

2 MEDIUM SWEET POTATOES, PEELED AND CUT INTO 2-INCH CHUNKS

4 TABLESPOONS UNSALTED BUTTER, MELTED

SALT AND FRESHLY GROUND BLACK PEPPER

1 Pour the stout into the pressure cooker, spread out the onions in the bottom of the cooker, and add the bay leaf. Place the corned beef on top of the onions and pile the potatoes, carrots, parsnips, and sweet potatoes on top of the corned beef. Lock the lid in place and cook at high pressure for 55 minutes.

2 Release the pressure naturally and remove the lid, tilting the pot away from you to avoid the escaping steam. Remove the vegetables to a serving platter, pour the butter over them, and sprinkle with salt and pepper to taste. Cover with aluminum foil to keep warm.

3 Transfer the corned beef to a cutting board and allow to rest for 15 minutes. Cut across the grain into thin slices. Arrange the slices on a serving platter, spoon some of the cooking liquid over the meat, and serve with the vegetables.

PSST

If you have leftover corned beef, use it to make Reuben sandwiches or corned beef hash.

CORNED BEEF AND CABBAGE

Although corned beef and cabbage is traditionally served on St. Patrick's Day here in the States, I don't remember my Irish granny ever making the dish. She certainly wouldn't recognize this version, made with wine and herbs. The sweet Riesling balances the salty taste of the corned beef and tones down the flavor of the cabbage, making this a lovely dish to serve any day of the week.

SERVES 6 TO 8

2 CUPS RIESLING WINE (SEE PSST)

ONE 4-POUND CORNED BEEF, DRAINED

1 BAY LEAF

2 SPRIGS FRESH THYME

6 MEDIUM RED-SKINNED POTATOES, SCRUBBED AND QUARTERED

3 MEDIUM SWEET ONIONS, SUCH AS VIDALIA, QUARTERED

4 TABLESPOONS UNSALTED BUTTER, MELTED

SALT AND FRESHLY GROUND BLACK PEPPER

1 LARGE HEAD GREEN CABBAGE, CUT INTO 6 OR 8 WEDGES

1 Pour the wine into the pressure cooker. Add the corned beef, bay leaf, and thyme. Pile the potatoes and onions on top of the corned beef. Lock the lid in place and cook at high pressure for 55 minutes.

2 Release the pressure naturally and remove the lid, tilting the pot away from you to avoid the escaping steam. Transfer the potatoes and onions to a serving bowl, drizzle with the butter, and season with salt and pepper. Cover the vegetables with aluminum foil to keep them warm. Remove the corned beef to a cutting board and allow to rest for 15 minutes. Add the cabbage to the cooking liquid and bring to a boil. Lower the heat and simmer for 5 minutes, or until tender.

3 Drain the cabbage and transfer to a serving platter (discard the bay leaf and thyme sprigs). Cut the corned beef across the grain into thin slices and lay the slices over the cabbage. Serve with the potatoes and onions.

PSST

If you want to make a nonalcoholic version, chicken broth makes a good substitute for the Riesling.

SWEET-AND-SOUR STUFFED CABBAGE

Although my mom was Italian, this Eastern European dish was a staple in our house during the cold winter months in Boston, and it was always accompanied by mashed potatoes and applesauce. I later learned that a Polish neighbor had shared the recipe, and I'm so glad that she did. It's still just what I want when the mercury drops. The rich meat filling absorbs the delicious tomato sauce, resulting in a hearty, spicy dish with a bit of sweetness. And the cabbage rolls are out of the pressure cooker in five minutes!

SERVES 6 TO 8

8 QUARTS WATER

1 LARGE HEAD GREEN CABBAGE

1½ POUNDS LEAN GROUND BEEF (92% LEAN)

½ CUP FINELY CHOPPED SWEET ONION, SUCH AS VIDALIA

2 TEASPOONS SALT, PLUS MORE IF NEEDED

1 TEASPOON FRESHLY GROUND BLACK PEPPER, PLUS MORE IF NEEDED

1 CUP COOKED LONG-GRAIN RICE, SUCH AS UNCLE BEN'S

1 LARGE EGG, LIGHTLY BEATEN

2 TABLESPOONS CANOLA OIL

1 LARGE RED ONION, COARSELY CHOPPED

2 CUPS FRESH SAUERKRAUT, RINSED AND DRAINED

ONE 28-OUNCE CAN CRUSHED TOMATOES WITH THEIR JUICE OR TOMATO PURÉE

½ CUP CHICKEN STOCK (PAGE 19) OR STORE-BOUGHT CHICKEN BROTH

2 TABLESPOONS BALSAMIC VINEGAR, PLUS MORE IF NEEDED

3 TABLESPOONS SUGAR, PLUS MORE IF NEEDED

1 Bring the water to a simmer in a large pot. Cut off 6 to 8 of the largest cabbage leaves, trying to keep them intact. Dip each leaf into the simmering water to soften it and drain thoroughly. Core and coarsely chop the remaining cabbage and set aside.

2 In a large mixing bowl, mix together the beef, onion, salt, pepper, rice, and egg until well combined. Shape into 6 to 8 ovals, about 2 inches wide. Place an oval in the center of a cabbage leaf. Beginning at the bottom (core end) of the leaf, roll it up, folding in the sides to make a neat package. Place the cabbage roll on a plate, seam side down, and stuff and roll up the remaining cabbage leaves.

3 Heat the oil in the pressure cooker over medium-high heat. Add the onion and the reserved chopped cabbage and sauté for 2 minutes to soften them. Add the sauerkraut, tomatoes, stock, vinegar, and sugar and stir together. Arrange the cabbage rolls in the sauce. Lock the lid in place and cook at high pressure for 5 minutes.

4 Release the pressure naturally and remove the lid, tilting the pot away from you to avoid the escaping steam. Taste the sauce and add more salt, pepper, vinegar, or sugar if needed. Serve the cabbage rolls napped with some of the sauce.

SHORT RIBS PROVENÇAL

This is a Provençal variation of *boeuf en daube*, a traditional French braised dish. Here, the short ribs are cooked in a wine sauce, which contains tomatoes and thyme and rosemary, two herbs that grow throughout the region. French stews are great examples of how one region will adjust a dish in order to use the ingredients that are available locally. Serve this with plenty of crusty bread to soak up the sauce.

SERVES 6

4 TABLESPOONS EXTRA-VIRGIN OLIVE OIL

3 POUNDS BONELESS SHORT RIBS, OR 5 POUNDS BONE-IN SHORT RIBS

2 TEASPOONS SALT, PLUS MORE IF NEEDED

1 TEASPOON FRESHLY GROUND BLACK PEPPER, PLUS MORE IF NEEDED

2 LARGE ONIONS, THINLY SLICED

3 GARLIC CLOVES, MINCED

1 TEASPOON FINELY CHOPPED FRESH THYME

1 TEASPOON FINELY CHOPPED FRESH ROSEMARY

ONE 14-OUNCE CAN CHOPPED TOMATOES, DRAINED

1 CUP FULL-BODIED RED WINE, SUCH AS A RHÔNE

1 CUP BEEF STOCK (PAGE 20) OR STORE-BOUGHT BEEF BROTH

½ CUP FINELY CHOPPED FRESH FLAT-LEAF PARSLEY

1 CUP PITTED BRINED PICHOLINE GREEN OLIVES (SEE PSST ON PAGE 85)

1 Heat 2 tablespoons of the oil in the pressure cooker over medium-high heat. Sprinkle the meat evenly with the salt and pepper, add to the pressure cooker in small batches, and brown, removing it to a plate when it's done. Add the remaining 2 tablespoons of oil to the pan, add the onion, garlic, thyme, and rosemary, and sauté for 2 minutes to soften the onions. Add the tomatoes, wine, and stock and return the beef to the pan. Lock the lid in place and cook at high pressure for 25 minutes.

2 Release the pressure naturally and remove the lid, tilting the pot away from you to avoid the escaping steam. Skim off any excess fat from the sauce and stir in the parsley and olives. Taste for seasoning and add more salt and pepper if necessary. Serve immediately.

ASIAN SHORT RIBS

One of my favorite weeknight dinners during the winter is this fragrant beef dish, with its mahogany-colored sauce redolent with garlic, ginger, hoisin, and soy. It only needs twenty-five minutes in the pressure cooker, which is just enough time for me to steam some sticky rice and put together an Asian slaw to serve alongside.

SERVES 6

4 TABLESPOONS CANOLA OIL

3 POUNDS BONELESS SHORT RIBS, OR 5 POUNDS BONE-IN SHORT RIBS

2 TEASPOONS SALT

1 TEASPOON FRESHLY GROUND BLACK PEPPER

4 GARLIC CLOVES, MINCED

2 TEASPOONS FRESHLY GRATED GINGER

¼ CUP SOY SAUCE

¼ CUP HOISIN SAUCE

¼ CUP KETCHUP

1½ CUPS BEEF STOCK (PAGE 20) OR STORE-BOUGHT BEEF BROTH

2 TABLESPOONS CORNSTARCH

¼ CUP WATER OR BROTH

4 GREEN ONIONS (GREEN AND WHITE PARTS), FINELY CHOPPED, FOR GARNISH

2 TABLESPOONS TOASTED SESAME SEEDS FOR GARNISH

1 Heat 2 tablespoons of the oil in the pressure cooker over medium-high heat. Sprinkle the ribs evenly with the salt and pepper, add to the pressure cooker, and brown, transferring them to a plate as they're done. Heat the remaining 2 tablespoons of oil and add the garlic, ginger, soy sauce, hoisin, ketchup, and stock to the pot, stirring to blend. Return the browned beef to the pot. Lock the lid in place and cook at high pressure for 25 minutes.

2 Release the pressure naturally and remove the lid, tilting the pot away from you to avoid the escaping steam. Skim off any excess fat from the top of the sauce and bring the sauce to a boil. Mix the cornstarch with the water and stir into the sauce. Return the sauce to a boil, stirring until thickened. Serve the beef garnished with the green onions and sesame seeds.

SOUTH-OF-THE-BORDER SHORT RIBS

Flavored with smoky chipotle chiles and cumin, this beef dish is perfect served over rice with black beans on the side or fajita style, with tortillas and condiments. Or shred the meat and use it as a filling for burritos or tacos.

SERVES 6

4 TABLESPOONS CANOLA OIL

3 POUNDS BONELESS SHORT RIBS, OR 5 POUNDS BONE-IN SHORT RIBS

2 TEASPOONS SALT

1 TEASPOON FRESHLY GROUND BLACK PEPPER

1 LARGE RED ONION, FINELY CHOPPED

2 CHIPOTLE CHILES IN ADOBO SAUCE, DRAINED AND FINELY CHOPPED

1 TEASPOON GROUND CUMIN

½ TEASPOON DRIED OREGANO

1 MEDIUM GREEN BELL PEPPER, SEEDED, DERIBBED, AND COARSELY CHOPPED

ONE 14-OUNCE CAN CHOPPED TOMATOES WITH THEIR JUICE

3 CUPS BEEF STOCK (PAGE 20) OR STORE-BOUGHT BEEF BROTH

¼ CUP ORANGE JUICE

¼ CUP FINELY CHOPPED FRESH CILANTRO

1 Heat 2 tablespoons of the oil in the pressure cooker over medium-high heat. Sprinkle the meat evenly with the salt and pepper, add to the pressure cooker a few pieces at a time, and brown, removing the meat to a plate when done. Add the remaining 2 tablespoons of oil to the pan, add the onion, chipotle chiles, cumin, and oregano, and sauté for 2 minutes, or until the onion begins to soften. Add the pepper, tomatoes, stock, and orange juice and return the beef to the pan. Lock the lid in place and cook at high pressure for 25 minutes.

2 Release the pressure naturally and remove the lid, tilting the pot away from you to avoid the escaping steam. Skim off any excess fat from the top of the sauce and stir in the cilantro. Serve the beef napped with the sauce.

BRAISED SHORT RIBS ITALIANO

Short ribs are among my favorite things to cook in the pressure cooker. The succulent meat absorbs whatever flavors are in the pot and is compatible with a variety of cuisines. This satisfying dish is super easy to make and suitable for company or a family meal. Serve it over pasta, polenta, mashed potatoes, or rice to soak up the tomato sauce. I find that boneless short ribs have more meat and you don't have to deal with the bones falling off after cooking. But you can use bone-in ribs if you like. Or, even better, see the Psst for another alternative.

SERVES **6**

4 TABLESPOONS EXTRA-VIRGIN OLIVE OIL

3 POUNDS BONELESS SHORT RIBS, OR 5 POUNDS BONE-IN SHORT RIBS (SEE PSST)

2 TEASPOONS SALT, PLUS MORE IF NEEDED

1 TEASPOON FRESHLY GROUND BLACK PEPPER, PLUS MORE IF NEEDED

2 MEDIUM SWEET ONIONS, SUCH AS VIDALIA, COARSELY CHOPPED

2 GARLIC CLOVES, MINCED

1 TEASPOON DRIED OREGANO

1 CUP FULL-BODIED RED WINE, SUCH AS CHIANTI, ZINFANDEL, OR BAROLO

1 CUP BEEF STOCK (PAGE 20) OR STORE-BOUGHT BEEF BROTH

ONE 28-OUNCE CAN CRUSHED TOMATOES WITH THEIR JUICE

½ CUP FINELY CHOPPED FRESH FLAT-LEAF PARSLEY

1 Heat 2 tablespoons of the oil in the pressure cooker over medium-high heat. Sprinkle the ribs with the salt and pepper, add them to the pressure cooker in small batches, and brown, removing them to a plate when they're done. Add the remaining 2 tablespoons of oil to the pot, add the onions, garlic, and oregano, and sauté for 2 minutes, or until the onions begin to soften. Add the wine, stock, and tomatoes, stirring to blend. Return the browned ribs to the pot. Lock the lid in place and cook at high pressure for 25 minutes.

2 Release the pressure naturally and remove the lid, tilting the pot away from you to avoid the escaping steam. Skim off any excess fat from the sauce and stir in the parsley. Taste the sauce for seasoning and add more salt and pepper if necessary. Serve immediately.

PSST

If you can't find boneless ribs, I recommend cutting up a beef shoulder chuck roast or sirloin tips (a bit pricey but worth the splurge) into 1- to 2-inch pieces. Then proceed with the recipe.

BRAISED SHORT RIBS WITH PAPPARDELLE

Serve these tender short ribs and sauce with pappardelle, a wide pasta strand. The dish will transport you and your guests to Italy for the night. Or serve it to your tired family after a long day.

SERVES 6

2½ TO 3 POUNDS BONELESS SHORT RIBS, OR 4½ TO 5 POUNDS BONE-IN SHORT RIBS

1½ TEASPOONS SALT

½ TEASPOON FRESHLY GROUND BLACK PEPPER

½ CUP ALL-PURPOSE FLOUR

¼ CUP EXTRA-VIRGIN OLIVE OIL

2 LARGE SWEET ONIONS, SUCH AS VIDALIA, FINELY CHOPPED

2 GARLIC CLOVES, MINCED

8 FRESH SAGE LEAVES, THINLY SLICED

2 CUPS FULL-BODIED RED WINE, SUCH AS CHIANTI, ZINFANDEL, OR BAROLO

2 TABLESPOONS TOMATO PASTE

1 CUP CHICKEN STOCK (PAGE 19) OR STORE-BOUGHT CHICKEN BROTH

1 CUP BEEF STOCK (PAGE 20) OR STORE-BOUGHT BEEF BROTH

1 POUND PAPPARDELLE PASTA

1 Sprinkle the beef with the salt and pepper, turning the pieces so that they are seasoned evenly. Put the flour in a shallow dish and dredge the beef in the flour, shaking off any excess. Heat the oil in the pressure cooker over medium-high heat. Add the beef a few pieces at a time and brown on all sides, transferring them to a plate when done. Add the onions, garlic, and sage to the pot and sauté until the onions begin to soften, about 3 minutes. Return the beef to the pot and stir in the wine, tomato paste, and stocks. Lock the lid in place and cook at high pressure for 25 minutes.

2 Meanwhile, bring 8 quarts of salted water to a boil for the pasta. When the beef is almost done, cook the pappardelle for 8 to 10 minutes, until al dente. (It's a good idea to check the timing on the package directions.) Drain the pasta and arrange on a serving platter.

3 Quick release the pressure of the cooker and remove the lid, being careful to tilt the pot away from you to avoid the escaping steam. Remove the short ribs to a cutting board and cover with aluminum foil to keep warm. Remove any excess fat from the sauce, bring the sauce to a boil, and boil gently to reduce the sauce until it thickens slightly, 5 to 8 minutes. Serve the short ribs over the pappardelle and spoon the sauce over the meat.

TRADITIONAL BEEF STEW

When you lift off the lid to serve this mouthwatering stew, warm and welcoming aromas will emanate from your pressure cooker, enticing your family to the dinner table. They won't be disappointed when they taste the tender chunks of meat in a savory sauce. And the best news is that the stew cooks in less than twenty minutes.

SERVES 6

2 TABLESPOONS EXTRA-VIRGIN OLIVE OIL

2 POUNDS BEEF STEW MEAT, CUT INTO 1-INCH PIECES

2 TEASPOONS SALT, PLUS MORE IF NEEDED

1 TEASPOON FRESHLY GROUND BLACK PEPPER, PLUS MORE IF NEEDED

3 GARLIC CLOVES, MINCED

1 LARGE SWEET ONION, SUCH AS VIDALIA, FINELY CHOPPED

1 TEASPOON FINELY CHOPPED FRESH THYME

3 CUPS BEEF STOCK (PAGE 20) OR STORE-BOUGHT BEEF BROTH

4 MEDIUM RED-SKINNED POTATOES, SCRUBBED AND QUARTERED

4 MEDIUM CARROTS, CUT INTO 2-INCH LENGTHS, OR 2 CUPS BABY CARROTS

2 CUPS CORN KERNELS, FRESHLY CUT FROM THE COB, OR FROZEN CORN, DEFROSTED

1½ CUPS FROZEN PETITE GREEN PEAS

2 TABLESPOONS UNSALTED BUTTER, SOFTENED

2 TABLESPOONS ALL-PURPOSE FLOUR

1 Heat the oil in the pressure cooker over medium-high heat. Sprinkle the meat evenly with salt and pepper, add to the pressure cooker a few pieces at a time, and brown on all sides, removing the meat to a plate when done. Add the garlic, onion, and thyme and sauté for 2 minutes, or until the onion begins to soften. Return the meat to the pot and add the stock. Pile the potatoes and carrots on top of the meat. Lock the lid in place and cook at high pressure for 15 minutes.

2 Release the pressure naturally and remove the lid, tilting the pot away from you to avoid the escaping steam. Skim off any excess fat from the sauce and add the corn and peas to the pot. Bring the stew to a boil. In a small dish, stir together the butter and flour to form a paste and add it to the pot. Return the stew to a boil, reduce the heat, and simmer for 2 minutes. Taste the sauce for seasoning and add more salt and pepper if necessary. Serve the stew in shallow bowls or hollowed-out-bread bowls.

SOUTHWESTERN-STYLE BEEF STEW

Combine tender beef, vegetables, and pinto beans in a chili-flavored sauce, and you have a great one-pot meal to serve on a cold night. I like to serve this over rice, accompanied by a fruit salad to balance the spicy stew.

SERVES 6

4 TABLESPOONS CANOLA OIL

2½ POUNDS BEEF STEW MEAT, CUT INTO 1-INCH PIECES

2 TEASPOONS SALT

1 TEASPOON FRESHLY GROUND BLACK PEPPER

2 MEDIUM SWEET ONIONS, SUCH AS VIDALIA, FINELY CHOPPED

2 GARLIC CLOVES, MINCED

1 TEASPOON GROUND CUMIN

1 ANAHEIM CHILE PEPPER, SEEDED, DERIBBED, AND COARSELY CHOPPED

1 MEDIUM RED BELL PEPPER, SEEDED, DERIBBED, AND COARSELY CHOPPED

1 MEDIUM YELLOW OR ORANGE BELL PEPPER, SEEDED, DERIBBED, AND COARSELY CHOPPED

ONE 14-OUNCE CAN CRUSHED TOMATOES WITH THEIR JUICE

2 CUPS PINTO BEANS, PRESOAKED (PAGE 151) AND DRAINED

6 CUPS BEEF STOCK (PAGE 20) OR STORE-BOUGHT BEEF BROTH

2 CUPS CORN KERNELS, FRESHLY CUT FROM THE COB, OR FROZEN CORN, DEFROSTED

¼ CUP FINELY CHOPPED FRESH CILANTRO

1 Heat 2 tablespoons of the oil in the pressure cooker over medium-high heat. Sprinkle the meat evenly with the salt and pepper, add to the pressure cooker a few pieces at a time, and brown, removing them to a plate when done. Add 2 tablespoons of the oil to the pot. Add the onions, garlic, cumin, and Anaheim pepper and sauté for 2 minutes to soften the onions. Add the bell peppers, tomatoes, beans, and stock and return the beef to the pot. Lock the lid in place and cook at high pressure for 15 minutes.

2 Release the pressure naturally and remove the lid, tilting the pot away from you to avoid the escaping steam. Skim any excess fat from the surface of the sauce and stir in the corn and cilantro. Warm the stew over medium-high heat and serve.

BRACIOLE

A traditional dish in Southern Italy, braciole are beefy rolls filled with a savory stuffing and served in a hearty wine and tomato sauce. My version includes a bread stuffing filled with bits of spicy capocollo and sharp provolone cheese, which melts into the stuffing for a delicious contrast with the robust sauce. Round steak, which is very lean, is the perfect cut of meat for this dish. Look for thinly sliced round steaks, which are sometimes called "minute steaks" because they cook quickly.

SERVES **8**

STUFFING

2 CUPS FRESH BREAD CRUMBS

6 THIN SLICES CAPOCOLLO, FINELY CHOPPED (SEE PSST)

3 OUNCES SHARP PROVOLONE CHEESE OR ASIAGO, CUT INTO ½-INCH DICE

6 FRESH SAGE LEAVES, FINELY CHOPPED

¼ CUP FINELY CHOPPED FRESH FLAT-LEAF PARSLEY

1 LARGE EGG, LIGHTLY BEATEN

STEAKS AND SAUCE

8 ROUND STEAKS, ABOUT ½ INCH THICK AND 6 INCHES ACROSS (BETWEEN 1½ AND 2 POUNDS TOTAL)

2 TEASPOONS SALT, PLUS MORE IF NEEDED

1 TEASPOON FRESHLY GROUND BLACK PEPPER, PLUS MORE IF NEEDED

2 TABLESPOONS EXTRA-VIRGIN OLIVE OIL

2 LARGE SWEET ONIONS, SUCH AS VIDALIA, FINELY CHOPPED

2 GARLIC CLOVES, SLICED

1 TEASPOON DRIED OREGANO

1 CUP FULL-BODIED RED WINE, SUCH AS CHIANTI, ZINFANDEL, OR BAROLO

ONE 28-OUNCE CAN CRUSHED TOMATOES WITH THEIR JUICE

2 TABLESPOONS BALSAMIC VINEGAR

1 **To make the stuffing:** In a large mixing bowl, combine all the ingredients and stir until well combined.

2 **To make the steaks and sauce:** Lay the steaks on a cutting board and sprinkle evenly with the salt and pepper. Spread 1 to 2 tablespoons of the stuffing over a steak. Beginning with a long side, roll up the steak, folding in the sides to form a compact package. Secure with silicone bands or toothpicks. Repeat with the remaining steaks and stuffing.

3 Heat the oil in the pressure cooker over medium-high heat. Add the onions, garlic, and oregano and sauté for 2 minutes, or until the onions begin to soften. Add the wine and bring to a boil. Pour in the tomatoes and arrange the rolls in the sauce. Lock the lid in place and cook at high pressure for 25 minutes.

4 Release the pressure naturally and remove the lid, tilting the pot away from you to avoid the escaping steam. Carefully remove the rolls and transfer to a cutting board. Skim off any excess fat from the sauce, add the vinegar, and bring to a boil. Taste the sauce for seasoning and add more salt and pepper if necessary. Remove from the heat. Remove the toothpicks or silicone bands from the rolls and cut each in half to expose the filling. Arrange 2 halves in a pool of sauce on each plate.

PSST

Capocollo is a spicy Italian ham. It is sold in most full-service delis in large supermarkets and at Italian grocery stores. For a less spicy filling, try prosciutto or your favorite baked ham.

KOREAN BARBECUE SIRLOIN

When my family lived in Japan, South Korea was a favorite destination. We all enjoyed the people, culture, and food, even my picky-eater son Ryan! He loves Korean barbecue, which is flavored with soy, garlic, sweet rice wine, sesame oil, and green onion. It pairs perfectly with sticky rice, sautéed spinach with garlic, and kimchee—a traditional hot cabbage dish.

SERVES 6

....

½ CUP SOY SAUCE

1 CUP MIRIN (SWEET RICE WINE)

¼ CUP CANOLA OIL

5 GARLIC CLOVES, MINCED

¼ CUP SUGAR

1 TABLESPOON TOASTED SESAME OIL

4 GREEN ONIONS (WHITE AND GREEN PARTS), FINELY CHOPPED, PLUS MORE FOR GARNISH

2 POUNDS BEEF SIRLOIN TIPS

2 CUPS BEEF STOCK (PAGE 20) OR STORE-BOUGHT BEEF BROTH

2 TABLESPOONS CORNSTARCH

2 TABLESPOONS TOASTED SESAME SEEDS FOR GARNISH

1 In a large bowl, combine the soy sauce, mirin, canola oil, garlic, sugar, sesame oil, and green onions, whisking to combine. Put the meat in a 1-gallon zipper-top plastic bag. Pour the marinade over the beef, seal the bag, and marinate in the refrigerator for at least 2 hours and up to 8 hours.

2 Remove the beef from the marinade, reserving the marinade, and put the beef in the pressure cooker. Add the stock. Lock the lid in place and cook at high pressure for 20 minutes. Meanwhile, bring the marinade to a boil in a medium saucepan, lower the heat, and maintain at a simmer.

3 Release the pressure naturally and remove the lid, tilting the pot away from you to avoid the escaping steam. Transfer the beef to a cutting board. In a small bowl, mix ¼ cup of the cooking liquid with the cornstarch. Add 1 cup of the cooking liquid to the marinade in the saucepan. Bring the marinade and cooking liquid in the saucepan to a boil, add the cornstarch mixture, and return to a boil, whisking until the sauce is thickened and glossy. Slice the beef, arrange on a serving platter, and pour the sauce over the beef. Serve garnished with chopped green onions and sesame seeds.

SIRLOIN RAGOUT

This robust and comforting dish features beef sirloin, rosemary, and white wine. It's terrific over orzo pasta or cheesy mashed potatoes.

SERVES 6

¼ CUP EXTRA-VIRGIN OLIVE OIL

2 POUNDS BONELESS BEEF SIRLOIN, FAT TRIMMED, AND CUT INTO 1-INCH PIECES

1½ TEASPOONS SALT, PLUS MORE IF NEEDED

½ TEASPOON FRESHLY GROUND BLACK PEPPER, PLUS MORE IF NEEDED

3 GARLIC CLOVES, SLICED

1½ TABLESPOONS FINELY CHOPPED FRESH ROSEMARY

1 CUP DRY WHITE WINE

1 CUP BEEF STOCK (PAGE 20) OR STORE-BOUGHT BEEF BROTH

2 TABLESPOONS UNSALTED BUTTER, SOFTENED

2 TABLESPOONS ALL-PURPOSE FLOUR

1 Heat the oil in the pressure cooker, over medium-high heat. Sprinkle the meat evenly with the salt and pepper, add to the pressure cooker in small batches, and brown, removing the meat to a plate when done. Add the garlic and rosemary to the pot and sauté for 1 minute. Return the meat to the pan and pour in the wine and stock, stirring up any browned bits on the bottom of the pot. Lock the lid in place and cook at high pressure for 15 minutes.

2 Quick release the pressure and remove the lid, tilting the pot away from you to avoid the escaping steam. Taste the sauce for seasoning and add more salt and pepper if necessary. In a small bowl, stir together the butter and flour to form a paste. Return the pot to the stove and bring the sauce to a boil. Whisk in the butter and flour paste. Return the sauce to a boil, reduce the heat, and simmer for 2 minutes. Serve the ragout immediately.

BEEF RANCHERO

This south-of-the-border dish makes a terrific weeknight meal. In less than half an hour, you can enjoy tender, melt-in-your-mouth morsels of beef surrounded by a savory cumin-scented tomato sauce. I like to make quesadillas for this dish and serve the beef over the melted cheese and tortillas. The beef is also delicious served in a soft taco or fajita style. Or, for a change of pace, serve it over rice with a side of pinto beans.

SERVES **8**

2 TABLESPOONS CANOLA OIL

2 POUNDS BEEF SIRLOIN, CUT INTO 1-INCH PIECES

2 TEASPOONS SALT, PLUS MORE IF NEEDED

1 TEASPOON FRESHLY GROUND BLACK PEPPER, PLUS MORE IF NEEDED

2 LARGE SWEET ONIONS, SUCH AS VIDALIA, COARSELY CHOPPED

2 GARLIC CLOVES, MINCED

1 MEDIUM RED BELL PEPPER, SEEDED, DERIBBED, AND COARSELY CHOPPED

1 MEDIUM YELLOW OR ORANGE BELL PEPPER, SEEDED, DERIBBED, AND COARSELY CHOPPED

1 TEASPOON GROUND CUMIN

½ TEASPOON DRIED OREGANO

PINCH OF CHILI POWDER

¼ CUP TEQUILA

½ CUP BEEF STOCK (PAGE 20) OR STORE-BOUGHT BEEF BROTH

ONE 28-OUNCE CAN TOMATO PURÉE

½ CUP FINELY CHOPPED FRESH CILANTRO

1 Heat the oil in the pressure cooker over medium-high heat. Sprinkle the meat evenly with the salt and pepper, add to the pressure cooker a few pieces at a time, and brown, removing the pieces to a plate when done. Add the onions, garlic, bell peppers, cumin, oregano, and chili powder to the pan and sauté for 2 minutes, or until the onions begin to soften. Add the tequila, stock, and tomato purée and return the beef to the pot. Lock the lid in place and cook at high pressure for 15 minutes.

2 Release the pressure naturally and remove the lid, tilting the pot away from you to avoid the escaping steam. Skim off any excess fat from the sauce and add the cilantro. Taste for seasoning, adding more salt and pepper if necessary, and serve.

BEEF AU POIVRE

Steak au poivre, the classic French dish served in bistros and elegant restaurants, goes for a steam bath in the pressure cooker and emerges as moist, tender chunks of beef steeped in a peppery sauce. Serve this over mashed or oven-fried potatoes, along with a crisp green salad and a nice Burgundy wine.

SERVES 6

2 TABLESPOONS EXTRA-VIRGIN OLIVE OIL

2 POUNDS BEEF SIRLOIN, CUT INTO 1-INCH PIECES

2 TEASPOONS SALT

2 TEASPOONS FRESHLY GROUND BLACK PEPPER

2 GARLIC CLOVES, MINCED

¼ CUP BRANDY

2 CUPS BEEF STOCK (PAGE 20) OR STORE-BOUGHT BEEF BROTH

2 TABLESPOONS UNSALTED BUTTER, SOFTENED

2 TABLESPOONS ALL-PURPOSE FLOUR

¼ CUP FINELY CHOPPED FRESH FLAT-LEAF PARSLEY

1 Heat the oil in the pressure cooker over medium-high heat. Sprinkle the beef evenly with the salt and pepper, add to the pressure cooker in batches, and brown, removing the pieces to a plate when done. Return the browned meat to the pot, add the garlic and brandy, and bring to a boil. Pour in the stock. Lock the lid in place and cook at high pressure for 15 minutes.

2 Release the pressure naturally and remove the lid, tilting the pot away from you to avoid the escaping steam. Bring the sauce to a boil. In a small bowl, stir together the butter and flour to form a paste and whisk into the sauce. Return the sauce to a boil, reduce the heat, and simmer for 2 minutes. Stir in the parsley and serve immediately.

BOEUF BOURGUIGNONNE

Succulent morsels of beef bubble in a smoky, wine-flavored sauce, finished with meaty cremini mushrooms and caramelized pearl onions. This dish was once described by Julia Child as the best beef stew known to man, and I would agree with her. I think the quick cooking time would have made her smile! Serve the stew over buttered noodles, mashed potatoes, or rice.

SERVES 6

4 THICK-CUT BACON STRIPS, CUT CROSSWISE INTO PIECES ½ INCH WIDE

3 POUNDS BEEF SIRLOIN, CUT INTO 1-INCH PIECES

2 SPRIGS FRESH THYME, PLUS 1 FINELY CHOPPED TEASPOON

1 BAY LEAF

2 GARLIC CLOVES, SLICED

3 CUPS BURGUNDY WINE

1 CUP BEEF STOCK (PAGE 20) OR STORE-BOUGHT BEEF BROTH

6 TABLESPOONS UNSALTED BUTTER, SOFTENED

1 POUND SMALL CREMINI MUSHROOMS, QUARTERED

¼ POUND PEARL ONIONS, PEELED (SEE PSST)

2 TABLESPOONS ALL-PURPOSE FLOUR

½ CUP FINELY CHOPPED FRESH FLAT-LEAF PARSLEY

SALT AND FRESHLY GROUND BLACK PEPPER (OPTIONAL)

1 Cook the bacon in the pressure cooker over medium heat until crisp, remove from the pan, and drain on paper towels. Leave 2 tablespoons of the bacon drippings in the pan. Add the beef in batches and brown, removing them to a plate when done. Return the meat to the pot and add the thyme sprigs, bay leaf, garlic, wine, and stock. Lock the lid in place and cook at high pressure for 15 minutes.

2 While the stew is cooking, melt 4 tablespoons of the butter in a large skillet over medium-high heat. Add the mushrooms and cook until they begin to turn golden around the edges. Add the onions and chopped thyme and continue cooking until the onions begin to caramelize and turn golden brown. Set aside.

3 When the stew has cooked for 15 minutes, release the pressure naturally and remove the lid, tilting the pot away from you to avoid the escaping steam. Remove the thyme sprigs and bay leaf from the sauce, skim off any excess fat from the top, and bring to a boil. Stir together the remaining 2 tablespoons of butter and the flour to make a paste and whisk into the sauce. Return to a boil, reduce the heat, and simmer for 2 minutes to thicken. Stir in the onions and mushrooms, reserved bacon, and the parsley. Taste the stew for seasoning and add salt and pepper if necessary.

PSST

Peeling pearl onions is simple. Bring a pot of water to a boil. Pop the onions into the water for 3 minutes and drain. When the onions are cool enough to handle, cut off the stem end; the skin should slip right off. If you are short of time, you can use frozen pearls (but never canned, which will disintegrate into an ugly mess). Defrost the frozen onions and then drain them thoroughly before sautéing.

SHREDDED BEEF FOR TACOS, ENCHILADAS, AND NACHOS

Cooking doesn't get any simpler than this: There are only six ingredients, and they take only a few minutes of prep time. Then just forty-five minutes in the pressure cooker and you have savory shredded meat flavored with tomato, cumin, and smoky chipotle for making enchiladas, tacos, or nachos.

MAKES ENOUGH TO FILL
12 SIX-INCH TORTILLAS

....

2 TABLESPOONS EXTRA-VIRGIN OLIVE OIL

1 LARGE WHITE ONION, COARSELY CHOPPED

1 TEASPOON GROUND CUMIN

2 CHIPOTLE CHILES IN ADOBO SAUCE, DRAINED AND FINELY CHOPPED

3 CUPS STORE-BOUGHT MEDIUM SALSA (SEE PSST ON FACING PAGE)

TWO 1-POUND FLANK STEAKS

1 Heat the oil in the pressure cooker over medium-high heat. Add the onion, cumin, chipotle chiles, and salsa, and cook for 2 minutes. Roll the flank steaks, beginning at a short side, into compact rolls. Set them in the pressure cooker and spoon some of the sauce over them. Lock the lid in place and cook at high pressure for 45 minutes.

2 Release the pressure and remove the lid, tilting the pot away from you to avoid the escaping steam. Carefully lift out the rolled flank steaks and place on a cutting board. Remove any excess fat from the sauce. Shred the meat by pulling it apart with two forks; the meat should offer no resistance. Pile the meat on a serving platter and serve some of the sauce on the side or return the meat to the sauce and serve it in the sauce.

SAN DIEGO BEEF TACOS

I like to serve this dish as a taco bar and let everyone fill their own tacos. You can also assemble the tacos yourself, but it's a lot of fun to let your family and friends play with their food.

SERVES 6

GUACAMOLE

2 LARGE HASS AVOCADOS, PEELED AND PITTED

2 TABLESPOONS FRESH LIME JUICE

1 GARLIC CLOVE, MINCED

2 GREEN ONIONS (WHITE AND TENDER GREEN PARTS), FINELY CHOPPED

2 TABLESPOONS SALSA (SEE PSST)

SALT AND FRESHLY GROUND BLACK PEPPER (OPTIONAL)

½ CUP SOUR CREAM

TWELVE 6-INCH CORN TORTILLAS

1 RECIPE SHREDDED BEEF FOR TACOS, ENCHILADAS, AND NACHOS, INCLUDING 1 TO 2 CUPS OF THE SAUCE (FACING PAGE)

2 TO 3 CUPS FINELY SHREDDED MILD CHEDDAR CHEESE

1 TO 2 CUPS THINLY SLICED LETTUCE

½ CUP PICKLED JALAPEÑOS

1 **To make the guacamole:** In a mixing bowl, mash the avocados with a fork and stir in the lime juice, garlic, onions, and salsa. Taste for seasoning and add salt and pepper if necessary. Cover the guacamole with the sour cream all the way to the edges of the bowl. Cover with plastic wrap and refrigerate for at least 1 hour or up to 8 hours When ready to serve, stir the sour cream into the guacamole.

2 Preheat the oven to 350 degrees F. Wrap the tortillas in aluminum foil and heat for 10 minutes. Turn the tortillas over and heat for another 10 minutes. Remove from the oven and remove the foil. If you are assembling the tacos yourself, cover the tortillas with a kitchen towel to keep warm. Lay a tortilla on a cutting board and fill with some of the beef, cheese, lettuce, the sauce from the beef, jalapeños, and guacamole. Fold the tortilla in half and repeat with the remaining tortillas and filling.

PSST

Frontera brand's tomatillo salsa is delicious, and La Victoria's salsa ranchera is a nice spicy one.

BARBECUE BEEF SANDWICHES

Braised beef in a hearty barbecue sauce served on a roll makes a great dinner any night of the week. The beef cooks up tender and juicy in less than an hour, giving you time to prepare slaw or potato salad to go with it—or to relax with a cup of coffee.

SERVES 6

4 TABLESPOONS CANOLA OIL

3 POUNDS TRI-TIP SIRLOIN (SEE PSST)

2 TEASPOONS SALT

1 TEASPOON FRESHLY GROUND BLACK PEPPER

2 CUPS BEEF STOCK (PAGE 20) OR STORE-BOUGHT BEEF BROTH

1 LARGE SWEET ONION, SUCH AS VIDALIA, FINELY CHOPPED

3 GARLIC CLOVES, MINCED

¼ CUP FIRMLY PACKED LIGHT BROWN SUGAR

ONE 28-OUNCE CAN TOMATO PURÉE

1 CUP KETCHUP

2 TABLESPOONS WORCESTERSHIRE SAUCE

1 TEASPOON DRY MUSTARD

6 DROPS OF TABASCO OR ANOTHER HOT SAUCE

6 KAISER ROLLS

1 Heat 2 tablespoons of the oil in the pressure cooker over medium-high heat. Sprinkle the meat with the salt and pepper, add to the pressure cooker in batches, and brown, removing it to a plate as it's done. Return all the meat to the pot and pour in the stock. Lock the lid in place and cook at high pressure for 40 minutes.

2 Release the pressure naturally and remove the lid, tilting the pot away from you to avoid the escaping steam. Transfer the beef to a cutting board and allow to rest for 15 minutes while you make the sauce.

3 Strain the cooking liquid and measure out 1¼ cups. Set aside. (Save the rest of the liquid for another use.) In the pressure cooker, heat the remaining 2 tablespoons of oil over medium-high heat. Add the onion and garlic and sauté for 2 minutes to soften them. Add the sugar and cook, stirring, until the sugar dissolves into the onion. Add the tomato purée, ketchup, reserved cooking liquid, Worcestershire, dry mustard, and hot sauce. Bring to a boil, reduce the heat, and simmer for 10 minutes.

4 Slice the beef thinly and add it to the hot barbecue sauce. Serve warm on the rolls.

PSST

Tri-tip is a sirloin cut that can be difficult to find east of the Rio Grande. If you can't find it, top sirloin or sirloin tips will work just as well.

MEAT LOAF

Meat loaf has experienced a revival lately. Although it can be deadly dull, a good one is the stuff of nostalgic dreams. It should have just the right amount of spices, some onion, maybe some ketchup, Worcestershire, and a bit of smoky flavor. My version combines all of the above and cooks with a delicious barbecue sauce. After about half an hour in the pressure cooker, the meat loaf emerges tender and moist. It's what every home cook could wish for in a weeknight dish.

SERVES 6

SAUCE

2 TABLESPOONS CANOLA OIL

2 SWEET ONIONS, SUCH AS VIDALIA, FINELY CHOPPED

2 TEASPOONS GARLIC POWDER

¼ TEASPOON CAYENNE PEPPER

¼ TEASPOON CELERY SEEDS

1½ CUPS KETCHUP

½ CUP LIGHT BROWN SUGAR

ONE 8-OUNCE CAN TOMATO SAUCE

½ CUP BEEF STOCK (PAGE 20) OR STORE-BOUGHT BEEF BROTH

2 TABLESPOONS WORCESTERSHIRE SAUCE

½ TEASPOON LIQUID SMOKE

MEAT LOAF

¼ CUP MILK

½ CUP FRESH BREAD CRUMBS

1½ POUNDS LEAN GROUND BEEF (92% LEAN)

⅔ POUND BULK PORK SAUSAGE

¼ CUP FINELY CHOPPED RED ONION

1 TABLESPOON WORCESTERSHIRE SAUCE

1 TEASPOON DRY MUSTARD

½ TEASPOON DRIED THYME

⅓ CUP KETCHUP

1 LARGE EGG, LIGHTLY BEATEN

1 **To make the sauce:** Heat the oil in the pressure cooker over medium-high heat. Add the onions, garlic powder, cayenne, and celery seeds and cook for 2 minutes to soften the onions. Add the remaining ingredients, bring to a simmer, and maintain at a simmer until the meat loaf is done.

2 **To make the meat loaf:** In a large mixing bowl, pour the milk over the bread crumbs and let the bread crumbs soak for 2 minutes. Add the remaining ingredients and stir to combine. Shape the mixture into a loaf and carefully lower the loaf into the sauce. Lock the lid in place and cook at high pressure for 15 minutes.

3 Release the pressure naturally and remove the lid, tilting the pot away from you to avoid the escaping steam. Carefully remove the meat loaf from the sauce with a long, wide spatula and transfer to a cutting board. Allow the meat loaf to rest for 10 minutes, then slice. Skim off any excess fat from the top of the sauce and serve the meat loaf with the sauce.

NONA'S SUNDAY SAUCE WITH MEATBALLS

In many households in Italy, Sunday is enjoyed with the extended family. One tradition in parts of Southern Italy is to make a pot of tomato sauce with a variety of meats for dinner. The sauce bubbles on the stove for hours, the inviting aromas enticing everyone into the kitchen to snatch a taste before it's done. But this Sunday sauce takes so little time, you will be able to sit back and relax for the rest of the day without all the stirring and tending that is normally required. Our Sunday sauce has meatballs, which are spicy, tender, and melt-in-your-mouth delicious after only five minutes of cooking time. Traditionally, the leftover sauce is reheated and served once or twice during the week, but you don't have to do that; it freezes well. Serve the meatballs over pasta, mashed potatoes, or polenta or tucked into bread for the ultimate meatball sandwich.

SERVES **8**

....

SAUCE

2 TABLESPOONS EXTRA-VIRGIN OLIVE OIL

2 LARGE SWEET ONIONS, SUCH AS VIDALIA, FINELY CHOPPED

2 TEASPOONS DRIED BASIL

½ CUP FULL-BODIED RED WINE, SUCH AS CHIANTI, ZINFANDEL, OR BAROLO (OPTIONAL, BUT OH SO GOOD!)

TWO 28-OUNCE CANS CRUSHED TOMATOES WITH THEIR JUICE

MEATBALLS

¼ CUP MILK

1 CUP FRESH BREAD CRUMBS

1½ POUNDS LEAN GROUND BEEF (92% LEAN)

¾ POUND BULK ITALIAN SWEET SAUSAGE

½ CUP FINELY CHOPPED SWEET ONION, SUCH AS VIDALIA

½ CUP FINELY CHOPPED FRESH FLAT-LEAF PARSLEY

½ CUP GRATED PECORINO ROMANO CHEESE

¼ CUP FINELY CHOPPED OIL-PACKED SUN-DRIED TOMATOES

1 LARGE EGG, LIGHTLY BEATEN

SALT AND FRESHLY GROUND BLACK PEPPER (OPTIONAL)

1 **To make the sauce:** Heat the oil in the pressure cooker over medium-high heat. Add the onions and basil and sauté for 2 minutes to soften the onions. Add the wine (if using) and tomatoes and bring to a boil. Reduce the heat and simmer while you make the meatballs.

2 **To make the meatballs:** In a large mixing bowl, combine the milk and bread crumbs and allow to soak for 5 minutes. Stir in the beef, sausage, onion, ¼ cup of the parsley, the cheese, tomatoes, and egg. Form the mixture into 2-inch balls (a cookie dough scoop helps to keep them uniform in size) and drop the meatballs into the simmering sauce. Lock the lid in place and cook at high pressure for 5 minutes.

3 Release the pressure naturally and remove the lid, tilting the pot away from you to avoid the escaping steam. Skim any excess fat from the top of the sauce and add the remaining ¼ cup of parsley. Taste for seasoning and add salt and pepper if necessary. Serve the meatballs with the sauce.

MOROCCAN MEATBALLS WITH SPICY EGGPLANT AND TOMATO SAUCE

Seasoned with traditional Moroccan spices like cumin and cinnamon, the meatballs soak up the gingery, smoky sauce. It's a luscious combination for a weeknight dinner or an easy meal on the weekend. If you like, you can even make the meatballs a day or two in advance. The sauce is delicious by itself served with couscous or orzo or tucked into pita bread.

SERVES **4** TO **6**

....

MEATBALLS

1 SLICE ITALIAN WHITE BREAD WITH A SOFT CRUST, TORN INTO ½-INCH PIECES

2 TABLESPOONS MILK

¾ POUND GROUND VEAL

½ POUND GROUND PORK

1 GARLIC CLOVE, MINCED

1 TEASPOON GRATED LEMON ZEST

1 TABLESPOON FINELY CHOPPED FRESH CILANTRO

½ TEASPOON GROUND CUMIN

¼ TEASPOON GROUND CINNAMON

1 LARGE EGG, LIGHTLY BEATEN

SPICY EGGPLANT AND TOMATO SAUCE

2 TABLESPOONS EXTRA-VIRGIN OLIVE OIL

1 LARGE SWEET ONION, SUCH AS VIDALIA, FINELY CHOPPED

1 LARGE PURPLE EGGPLANT, TRIMMED AND CUT INTO ½-INCH DICE

1 TEASPOON SMOKED SPANISH PAPRIKA

½ TEASPOON GROUND GINGER

½ TEASPOON GROUND CUMIN

⅛ TEASPOON CAYENNE PEPPER

2 TEASPOONS GRATED ORANGE ZEST

1 TEASPOON SALT, PLUS MORE IF NEEDED

TWO 14½-OUNCE CANS CHOPPED TOMATOES WITH THEIR JUICE

½ CUP CHICKEN STOCK (PAGE 19) OR STORE-BOUGHT CHICKEN BROTH

FRESHLY GROUND BLACK PEPPER (OPTIONAL)

1 **To make the meatballs:** In a large bowl, mix the ingredients until well combined. Shape into 1-inch balls or use a large cookie dough scoop to shape the meatballs. Set them aside while you prepare the sauce. (At this point, the meatballs can be covered and refrigerated for up to 2 days.)

2 **To make the sauce:** Heat the oil in the pressure cooker over medium-high heat. Add the onion, eggplant, paprika, ginger, cumin, cayenne, orange zest, and salt and sauté for 3 to 5 minutes, or until the onion begins to soften and the spices become fragrant. Add the tomatoes and stock, stirring to blend. Carefully drop the meatballs into the sauce, piling them on top of each other. Lock the lid in place and cook at high pressure for 5 minutes.

3 Release the pressure naturally and remove the lid, tilting the pot away from you to avoid the escaping steam. Stir the meatballs and sauce together and allow to rest for about 5 minutes. Taste for seasoning and add more salt and some black pepper if needed. Transfer the meatballs to a serving platter, spoon the sauce over the meatballs, and serve.

SEAFOOD

I have to admit that I was skeptical when I began testing seafood recipes in the pressure cooker. Fish cooks relatively quickly with conventional methods, and I wasn't sure how high pressure would affect seafood. What kept me going were the delicious meals we were having, and in almost no time! The full-flavored **PAELLA** (page 288), **SPICY CRAB BOIL** (page 286), **SWORDFISH SICILIANA** (page 299), and **MISO COD PACKETS** (page 292) were all awesome. Many people shy away from preparing seafood at home, but I'm convinced the pressure cooker is a terrific way to cook it. Pressure cooking keeps all the flavors in the pot and produces moist and tender seafood every time.

SEAFOOD	COOKING TIME AT HIGH PRESSURE
Clams (littlenecks)	4 minutes
Cod (1 inch thick)	5 minutes
Halibut (1 inch thick)	5 minutes
Mussels	4 minutes
Salmon (1 inch thick)	6 minutes
Sea bass (1 inch thick)	7 minutes
Shrimp (large)	3 minutes
Swordfish (1 inch thick)	6 minutes
Tuna steaks (1 inch thick)	10 minutes

These cooking times are based on a quick release of pressure.

GARLIC CLAMS

I love this recipe because it's amazingly simple and produces terrific results. The clams are steamed in white wine with lots of garlic, some spices, and lemon, and they emerge from the pressure cooker tender and delicious.

SERVES **4**

....

2 TABLESPOONS EXTRA-VIRGIN OLIVE OIL

10 GARLIC CLOVES, MINCED

1 TABLESPOON OLD BAY SEASONING OR SEAFOOD SEASONING, SUCH AS PENZEYS

3 CUPS DRY WHITE WINE, SUCH AS SAUVIGNON BLANC OR PINOT GRIGIO, OR DRY VERMOUTH

1 LARGE LEMON, SLICED CROSSWISE ½ INCH THICK, PLUS LEMON WEDGES FOR GARNISH

3 TO 4 POUNDS LITTLENECK CLAMS, SCRUBBED

1 Heat the oil in the pressure cooker over medium-high heat. Add the garlic and Old Bay and sauté for 2 minutes, or until fragrant. Add the wine and lemon slices and stir to blend. Arrange the trivet and steamer basket in the bottom of the pressure cooker and pile the clams in the basket. Lock the lid in place and cook at high pressure for 4 minutes.

2 Quick release the pressure and remove the lid, tilting the pot away from you to avoid the escaping steam. Discard any unopened clams. Strain the stock through cheesecloth to catch any sand. Transfer the clams to a serving bowl and serve with lemon wedges and the strained clam stock. (Freeze any leftover stock to make your favorite fish stew or chowder.)

MUSSELS MARINARA

Bathed in a vibrant, garlicky red sauce, these mussels are messy and delicious—perfect for a casual dinner with friends. The mussels steam for a quick four minutes under pressure and emerge perfectly cooked. Serve them with linguine or spaghetti, or a crusty bread and a salad.

SERVES 4

2 TABLESPOONS EXTRA-VIRGIN OLIVE OIL

4 GARLIC CLOVES, MINCED

1 TEASPOON DRIED BASIL

PINCH OF RED PEPPER FLAKES

1 CUP DRY WHITE WINE, SUCH AS SAUVIGNON BLANC OR PINOT GRIGIO, OR DRY VERMOUTH

TWO 28-OUNCE CANS CRUSHED TOMATOES WITH THEIR JUICE

3 POUNDS MUSSELS, SCRUBBED

½ CUP FINELY CHOPPED FRESH FLAT-LEAF PARSLEY

¼ CUP PACKED FRESH BASIL LEAVES, FINELY CHOPPED

SALT AND FRESHLY GROUND BLACK PEPPER (OPTIONAL)

1 Heat the oil in the pressure cooker over medium-high heat. Add the garlic, basil, and pepper flakes and cook for 1 minute, or until fragrant. Pour in the wine and stir to blend. Add the tomatoes and mussels and turn the mussels in the sauce. Lock the lid in place and cook at high pressure for 4 minutes.

2 Quick release the pressure and remove the lid, tilting the pot away from you to avoid the escaping steam. Discard any mussels that haven't opened. Stir in the parsley and basil and taste the sauce for seasoning, adding salt and pepper if necessary. Transfer the mussels and sauce to a serving bowl and serve 6 to 8 mussels per person.

SPICY CRAB BOIL

Because it is delicate, most crab is cooked either on the boats after it's caught or at the dock when it's brought in. Here, the cooked crab is steamed in beer and seasonings, which gives it an irresistible spicy coating. Be sure to crack the crabs so they are easier to eat.

SERVES 4

....

TWO 12-OUNCE CANS BEER

¼ CUP OLD BAY SEASONING OR SEAFOOD SEASONING, SUCH AS PENZEYS

2 LEMONS, QUARTERED

3 POUNDS COOKED KING CRAB LEGS AND CLAWS, CUT TO FIT THE POT AND SLIT WITH KITCHEN SCISSORS

1 CUP (2 STICKS) UNSALTED BUTTER, MELTED, FOR DIPPING

1 Pour the beer into the pressure cooker and stir in the Old Bay. Squeeze the lemon quarters over the pot and toss them in. Stack the crab in the pot, spooning some of the beer mixture over it. Lock the lid in place and cook at high pressure for 3 minutes.

2 Quick release the pressure and remove the lid, tilting the pot away from you to avoid the escaping steam. Transfer the crab to a large serving bowl and serve with the melted butter for dipping.

SPICY SHRIMP BOIL

Peel and eat these shrimp outdoors with your favorite pals. It's a great way to serve dinner—on butcher paper, with lots of melted butter or cocktail sauce. Or this can be your new way to make shrimp for salads and shrimp cocktail. Feel free to use store-bought cocktail sauce, or serve the shrimp with just the melted butter.

SERVES 6

COCKTAIL SAUCE

1 CUP KETCHUP

2 TABLESPOONS WORCESTERSHIRE SAUCE

2 TEASPOONS HORSERADISH

2 TEASPOONS FRESH LEMON JUICE

PINCH OF SUGAR

6 DROPS OF TABASCO OR ANOTHER HOT SAUCE

2 CUPS WATER

¼ CUP OLD BAY SEASONING OR SEAFOOD SEASONING, SUCH AS PENZEYS

3 LEMONS, QUARTERED

3 POUNDS LARGE OR JUMBO SHRIMP

1 CUP (2 STICKS) UNSALTED BUTTER, MELTED, FOR SERVING (OPTIONAL)

1 **To make the cocktail sauce:** In a small bowl, stir together the ingredients until combined. Cover and refrigerate for at least 2 hours or up to 4 days.

2 Pour the water into the pressure cooker and add the Old Bay. Squeeze the lemons over the pot and drop them into the water. Add the shrimp and turn the shrimp in the liquid to coat. Lock the lid in place and cook at high pressure for 3 minutes.

3 Quick release the pressure and remove the lid, tilting the pot away from you to avoid the escaping steam. Drain the shrimp, transfer to a large serving bowl, and serve with the cocktail sauce and melted butter, if using.

PAELLA

Paella is served all over Spain, but it originated in the eastern coastal regions, where rice and seafood are plentiful. Regional differences abound when it comes to cooking paella, but it almost always contains rice, olive oil, and saffron. The remaining ingredients are up to the cook to decide and usually depend on what is fresh in the local markets. Cooking paella in the pressure cooker is quick and simple. When it's ready, toss the whole potful into a large round serving bowl and serve family-style.

SERVES 6

4 TABLESPOONS EXTRA-VIRGIN OLIVE OIL

¼ POUND SPANISH CHORIZO (SEE PSST ON PAGE 54) OR ITALIAN SOPRESSATA, FINELY DICED

2 BONELESS, SKINLESS CHICKEN BREASTS, CUT INTO BITE-SIZE PIECES

1 LARGE SWEET ONION, SUCH AS VIDALIA, FINELY CHOPPED

2 GARLIC CLOVES, MINCED

1 TEASPOON SAFFRON THREADS, CRUSHED IN THE PALM OF YOUR HAND

1 MEDIUM RED BELL PEPPER, SEEDED, DERIBBED, AND COARSELY CHOPPED

1 MEDIUM YELLOW BELL PEPPER, SEEDED, DERIBBED, AND COARSELY CHOPPED

1½ CUPS ARBORIO RICE

3 CUPS CHICKEN STOCK (PAGE 19) OR STORE-BOUGHT CHICKEN BROTH

ONE 14-OUNCE CAN CHOPPED TOMATOES, DRAINED

1 POUND MEDIUM SHRIMP, PEELED AND DEVEINED

12 LITTLENECK CLAMS, SCRUBBED

1 CUP FROZEN PETITE PEAS, DEFROSTED

SALT AND FRESHLY GROUND BLACK PEPPER (OPTIONAL)

¼ CUP FINELY CHOPPED FRESH FLAT-LEAF PARSLEY FOR GARNISH

2 LEMONS, CUT INTO WEDGES, FOR SERVING

1 Heat 2 tablespoons of the oil in the pressure cooker over medium-high heat. Add the chorizo and sauté until it renders some of its fat. Transfer to a plate and set aside. Add the chicken to the pot and sauté until lightly browned all over. Transfer to a plate.

2 Heat the remaining 2 tablespoons of oil in the pressure cooker over medium-high heat. Add the onion, garlic, saffron, and bell peppers and sauté for 3 minutes, or until the onion begins to soften. Add the rice and stir to coat the rice with the oil. Stir in the chicken, chorizo, stock, tomatoes, shrimp, and clams. Lock the lid in place and cook at high pressure for 3 minutes.

3 Release the pressure naturally and remove the lid, tilting the pot away from you to avoid the escaping steam. Discard any clams that haven't opened. Stir in the peas and re-cover the pot. Allow the paella to steam off the heat for 2 minutes more. Taste for seasoning and add salt and pepper if necessary. Transfer the paella to a large serving platter, sprinkle with the parsley, and arrange the lemon wedges along the edge of the serving platter.

JAMBALAYA

A Cajun classic from the Gulf Coast region of Louisiana, jambalaya always includes the Creole trinity of onion, celery, and bell pepper, as well as long-grain rice. After that, you are on your own. Like paella, it's an adaptable dish. This recipe is made with shrimp, chicken, and spicy andouille sausage, a Cajun specialty.

SERVES 6

2 TABLESPOONS CANOLA OIL

1 POUND ANDOUILLE SAUSAGE, CUT INTO ½-INCH ROUNDS

2 BONELESS, SKINLESS CHICKEN BREAST HALVES, CUT INTO ½-INCH PIECES

1 LARGE SWEET ONION, SUCH AS VIDALIA, FINELY CHOPPED

2 GARLIC CLOVES, MINCED

1 MEDIUM GREEN BELL PEPPER, SEEDED, DERIBBED, AND COARSELY CHOPPED

4 CELERY STALKS, COARSELY CHOPPED

½ TEASPOON DRIED THYME

½ TEASPOON DRIED OREGANO

½ TEASPOON DRIED BASIL

½ TEASPOON SWEET PAPRIKA

⅛ TEASPOON CAYENNE PEPPER

1½ CUPS LONG-GRAIN RICE, SUCH AS UNCLE BEN'S

ONE 14-OUNCE CAN CHOPPED TOMATOES WITH THEIR JUICE

2 CUPS CHICKEN STOCK (PAGE 19) OR STORE-BOUGHT CHICKEN BROTH

1 BAY LEAF

1½ POUNDS LARGE SHRIMP, PEELED AND DEVEINED (SEE PSST)

¼ CUP FINELY CHOPPED FRESH FLAT-LEAF PARSLEY FOR GARNISH

4 SCALLIONS (WHITE AND TENDER GREEN PARTS), FINELY CHOPPED, FOR GARNISH

ASSORTED HOT SAUCES FOR SERVING, SUCH AS FRANK'S REDHOT AND TABASCO

1 Heat the oil in the pressure cooker over medium-high heat. Add the sausage and cook until it renders some of its fat. Transfer it to a plate. Add the chicken, a few pieces at a time, and brown, removing the browned chicken to the plate with the sausage. Add the onion, garlic, bell pepper, celery, thyme, oregano, basil, paprika, and cayenne to the pot and sauté for 3 minutes, until the onion begins to soften. Add the rice and stir to coat. Add the tomatoes, stock, and bay leaf and return the chicken and sausage to the pot. Lock the lid in place and cook at high pressure for 5 minutes.

2 Release the pressure naturally and remove the lid, tilting the pot away from you to avoid the escaping steam. Remove the bay leaf, stir the shrimp into the pot, and re-cover the pot. Allow the shrimp to steam off the heat for 10 minutes. Transfer the jambalaya to a large serving platter. Sprinkle with the parsley and scallions and serve with the hot sauces.

PSST

If you would like to vary the seafood, substitute lump crabmeat or crawfish for the shrimp or use a combination of shellfish.

BOUILLABAISSE

A saffron-scented fish stew from Marseilles, bouillabaisse is traditionally made with fish, a bit of tomato, garlic, and herbes de Provence. It's served with toasted bread, spread with a garlicky red pepper mayonnaise called a rouille. I prefer a simpler sauce, which has all of the kick of a rouille but none of the labor-intensive preparation.

SERVES 6

ROASTED CROUTONS
12 SLICES CRUSTY BREAD, ½ INCH THICK
¼ CUP EXTRA-VIRGIN OLIVE OIL

RED PEPPER–GARLIC SAUCE
ONE 6-OUNCE JAR ROASTED RED PEPPERS, DRAINED
4 GARLIC CLOVES, MINCED
1 TEASPOON SALT
½ TEASPOON FRESHLY GROUND BLACK PEPPER
¼ CUP EXTRA-VIRGIN OLIVE OIL

BOUILLABAISSE
2 TABLESPOONS EXTRA-VIRGIN OLIVE OIL
4 GARLIC CLOVES, MINCED
2 MEDIUM LEEKS (WHITE AND TENDER GREEN PARTS), COARSELY CHOPPED
2 TEASPOONS SAFFRON THREADS, CRUSHED IN THE PALM OF YOUR HAND
1 TEASPOON DRIED THYME
ONE 14-OUNCE CAN CHOPPED TOMATOES WITH THEIR JUICE
1 BAY LEAF
2 CUPS SEAFOOD STOCK (PAGE 22) OR STORE-BOUGHT SEAFOOD BROTH, OR 1 CUP CHICKEN STOCK (PAGE 19) OR STORE-BOUGHT CHICKEN BROTH MIXED WITH 1 CUP BOTTLED CLAM JUICE
1 POUND HALIBUT OR SEA BASS, CUT INTO 1-INCH PIECES
½ POUND MEDIUM SHRIMP, PEELED AND DEVEINED
2 LOBSTER TAILS, CUT INTO 1-INCH PIECES
12 MUSSELS, SCRUBBED
¼ CUP FINELY CHOPPED FRESH FLAT-LEAF PARSLEY
SALT AND FRESHLY GROUND BLACK PEPPER (OPTIONAL)

1 **To make the croutons:** Preheat the oven to 400 degrees F. Line a baking sheet with parchment paper, aluminum foil, or a silicone baking liner. Brush the bread with the oil and bake for 5 minutes, or until hard. Let the croutons cool before using.

2 **To make the sauce:** In a food processor or blender, process the peppers, garlic, salt, and black pepper until smooth. With the machine running, pour in the oil and process until smooth and emulsified. (Store any leftovers in the refrigerator for up to 4 days.)

3 **To make the bouillabaisse:** Heat the oil in the pressure cooker over medium heat. Add the garlic, leeks, saffron, and thyme and sauté for 2 to 3 minutes, or until the leeks soften. Add the tomatoes, bay leaf, and stock. Bring to a boil and continue boiling the sauce for 3 minutes. Add the halibut, shrimp, lobster, and mussels. Lock the lid in place and cook at high pressure for 4 minutes.

4 Release the pressure naturally and remove the lid, tilting the pot away from you to avoid the escaping steam. Discard any unopened mussels and the bay leaf. Stir in the parsley and taste the stock for seasoning, adding salt and pepper if necessary.

5 Spread the croutons with the red pepper–garlic sauce. Serve the bouillabaisse in large soup bowls and float 2 croutons in each serving.

SEAFOOD TAGINE

Seafood tagines are hearty dishes full of firm-fleshed fish, flavored with saffron, tomatoes, cumin, and fresh ginger. This dish is a great one to serve to dinner guests. Accompany it with a fruit salad to cool down some of the spice in the tagine. Cod, halibut, or sea bass works well here.

SERVES 6

¼ CUP EXTRA-VIRGIN OLIVE OIL

2 GARLIC CLOVES, MINCED

1 TEASPOON GRATED FRESH GINGER

1 TEASPOON SWEET PAPRIKA

1 TEASPOON GROUND CUMIN

2 TEASPOONS SAFFRON THREADS, CRUSHED IN THE PALM OF YOUR HAND

1 LARGE RED ONION, COARSELY CHOPPED

3 MEDIUM CARROTS, COARSELY CHOPPED

ONE 14-OUNCE CAN CHOPPED TOMATOES WITH THEIR JUICE

¼ CUP CHICKEN STOCK (PAGE 19) OR STORE-BOUGHT CHICKEN BROTH

2 POUNDS COD, SEA BASS, OR HALIBUT FILLETS

1 CUP OIL-CURED BLACK OR GREEN OLIVES, PITTED AND CHOPPED

SALT AND FRESHLY GROUND BLACK PEPPER (OPTIONAL)

1 LEMON, THINLY SLICED CROSSWISE, FOR GARNISH

¼ CUP FINELY CHOPPED FRESH CILANTRO FOR GARNISH

1 Heat the oil in the pressure cooker over medium-high heat. Add the garlic, ginger, paprika, cumin, saffron, and onion and sauté for 2 minutes, or until the onion begins to soften. Add the carrots, tomatoes, and stock, stirring to blend. Add the fillets to the sauce and spoon some of the sauce over the fillets. Lock the lid in place and cook at high pressure for 5 minutes, or 7 minutes if you're using sea bass.

2 Quick release the pressure and remove the lid, tilting the pot away from you to avoid the escaping steam. Carefully remove the fish to a serving platter and cover with aluminum foil to keep warm. Bring the sauce to a boil, add the olives, and remove from the heat. Taste the sauce for seasoning and add salt and pepper if necessary. Spoon some of the sauce over the fish and garnish with the lemon slices and cilantro.

MISO COD PACKETS

Sealing cod in packets along with vegetables and seasonings is a terrific way to cook this fish in the pressure cooker, resulting in moist, flaky fillets. Miso and cod are a match made in culinary heaven; the mild fish absorbs the miso's salty flavor. Scallions and ginger add complexity to the dish.

SERVES 4

MISO GLAZE

½ CUP WHITE MISO

⅓ CUP MIRIN (SWEET RICE WINE)

2 TABLESPOONS SOY SAUCE

1 TEASPOON SESAME OIL

3 TABLESPOONS SUGAR

1 TEASPOON FINELY GRATED FRESH GINGER

COD FILLETS

4 COD FILLETS (ABOUT 6 OUNCES EACH)

1 SMALL HEAD NAPA CABBAGE, CORED AND THINLY SLICED

2 MEDIUM CARROTS, JULIENNED

3 SCALLIONS (WHITE AND TENDER GREEN PARTS), THINLY SLICED ON THE DIAGONAL

2 CUPS WATER

2 TABLESPOONS BLACK SESAME SEEDS (SEE PSST)

1 **To make the glaze:** In a small saucepan, bring the ingredients to a boil. Reduce the heat, simmer for 5 minutes, and let the glaze cool completely.

2 **To make the cod:** Cut four 12-inch squares of parchment paper or aluminum foil. Arrange a cod fillet in the center of each square. Brush each fillet with some of the cooled glaze and top with a quarter of the cabbage, carrots, and scallions. Drizzle with 1 tablespoon of the miso glaze. Bring two opposite sides of the parchment or foil together and fold over several times, leaving some room for the steam, which will accumulate in the packet. Fold over each of the remaining sides a few times to seal the package. Set aside the remaining miso glaze.

3 Pour the water into the pressure cooker. Arrange the trivet and steamer basket in the bottom and stack the cod packets, folded-side up, in the basket. Lock the lid in place and cook at high pressure for 5 minutes.

4 Quick release the pressure and remove the lid, tilting the pot away from you to avoid the escaping steam. Carefully lift out each fish packet and transfer to a cutting board. Bring the remaining miso glaze to a boil and remove from the heat. Cut open the top of each packet and transfer to a dinner plate. Drizzle the fish with a bit of the warm glaze and sprinkle with the sesame seeds before serving.

PSST

Black sesame seeds can be found in some supermarkets in the Asian section, in Asian markets, and at Penzeys Spices (www.penzeys.com).

COCONUT AND CILANTRO FISH PACKETS

This is a great way to serve fish with a pan-Asian flavor. The sauce is made with coconut milk and cilantro, and the fish is topped with finely chopped mango. The result is a fish entrée with a complex flavor and moist texture.

SERVES **4**

COCONUT MILK SAUCE

1 CUP COCONUT MILK

¼ CUP FINELY CHOPPED FRESH CILANTRO

GRATED ZEST OF 1 LEMON

2 SCALLIONS (WHITE AND TENDER GREEN PARTS), FINELY CHOPPED

HALIBUT

FOUR 6-OUNCE HALIBUT FILLETS

1 TEASPOON SWEET PAPRIKA

2 SCALLIONS (WHITE AND TENDER GREEN PARTS), FINELY CHOPPED

1 RIPE MANGO, PITTED, PEELED, AND FINELY CHOPPED (SEE PSST, PAGE 309)

2 CUPS WATER

¼ CUP FINELY CHOPPED FRESH CILANTRO

1 **To make the sauce:** In a small saucepan, combine the ingredients and bring to a boil. Reduce the heat and simmer for 5 minutes, stirring occasionally. Remove from the heat.

2 **To make the halibut:** Cut four 12-inch squares of parchment paper or aluminum foil and put a fillet in the center of each square. Sprinkle each fillet with ¼ teaspoon of the paprika and a quarter of the scallions and top with 2 tablespoons of the mango. Spoon 1 tablespoon of the sauce over the fillet. Bring two opposite sides of the parchment or foil together and fold over a few times, leaving some room for the steam that will accumulate in the packet. Fold in each of the remaining two sides a few times to seal the packet.

3 Pour the water into the pressure cooker. Arrange the trivet and steamer basket in the bottom and stack the fish packets into the basket, folded-side up. Lock the lid in place and cook at high pressure for 5 minutes.

4 Quick release the pressure and remove the lid, tilting the pot away from you to avoid the escaping steam. Carefully lift out each fish packet and transfer to a cutting board. Bring the remaining coconut milk sauce to a boil, reduce the heat, and simmer for 10 minutes to reduce and concentrate the flavors. Cut open the top of each fish packet and transfer to a dinner plate. Drizzle the fish with a bit of the warm sauce and sprinkle with the cilantro.

GARLIC BUTTER–GLAZED HALIBUT

If you have picky eaters in your house, halibut is the fish for you, because it really does taste like chicken! It's also a no-brainer to cook in the pressure cooker, so give this delicious dish a try. The halibut cooks in a garlic, lemon, and butter sauce, which makes the fish succulent and juicy. It's terrific served with potatoes au gratin (topped with cheese and bread crumbs) and roasted asparagus.

SERVES 6

¾ CUP (1½ STICKS) UNSALTED BUTTER

3 GARLIC CLOVES, MINCED

1 TABLESPOON OLD BAY SEASONING OR SEAFOOD SEASONING, SUCH AS PENZEYS

2 TABLESPOONS FRESH LEMON JUICE

⅓ CUP CHICKEN STOCK (PAGE 19) OR STORE-BOUGHT CHICKEN BROTH

2 POUNDS HALIBUT FILLETS

¼ CUP FINELY CHOPPED FRESH CHIVES

1 Melt the butter in the pressure cooker over medium-high heat. Add the garlic and Old Bay and cook for 2 minutes, or until the garlic is fragrant. Add the lemon juice and stock and stir to combine. Arrange the halibut in the pressure cooker, stacking the fillets if necessary. Lock the lid in place and cook at high pressure for 5 minutes.

2 Quick release the pressure and remove the lid, tilting the pot away from you to avoid the escaping steam. Carefully remove the fish from the pot and transfer to a serving platter. Cover with aluminum foil to keep warm.

3 Bring the buttery stock to a boil and continue boiling for 5 minutes to concentrate the flavor. Stir in the chives, pour the butter mixture over the halibut, and serve.

SEA BASS VERACRUZ

Sea bass is a great fish for novice cooks to try. It's almost impossible to overcook it, even if you ignore the ten-minutes-per-inch rule, which applies to cooking most fish. In this savory dish, the fish is sauced with onions, Anaheim chiles, tomatoes, and cumin. It makes a delicious main course to serve with steamed rice and your choice of vegetable. The sea bass is also great tucked into soft corn tortillas for fish tacos.

SERVES 6

2 TABLESPOONS EXTRA-VIRGIN OLIVE OIL

1 LARGE SWEET ONION, SUCH AS VIDALIA, FINELY CHOPPED

1 ANAHEIM CHILE PEPPER, SEEDED, DERIBBED, AND FINELY CHOPPED

1 TEASPOON GROUND CUMIN

ONE 14-OUNCE CAN CRUSHED TOMATOES WITH THEIR JUICE

½ CUP CHICKEN STOCK (PAGE 19) OR STORE-BOUGHT CHICKEN BROTH

2 POUNDS SEA BASS FILLET

¼ CUP FINELY CHOPPED FRESH CILANTRO

SALT AND FRESHLY GROUND BLACK PEPPER (OPTIONAL)

1 CUP FINELY SHREDDED MONTEREY JACK CHEESE

1 Heat the oil in the pressure cooker over medium-high heat. Add the onion, chile, and cumin and cook for 2 minutes to soften the onion. Add the tomatoes and stock, stirring to combine. Set the sea bass in the sauce, spooning some of the sauce over the fish. Lock the lid in place and cook at high pressure for 7 minutes.

2 Quick release the pressure and remove the lid, tilting the pot away from you to avoid the escaping steam. Carefully remove the sea bass from the pot and transfer to a serving platter. Stir the cilantro into the sauce and taste for seasoning, adding salt and black pepper if necessary. Spoon the sauce over the fish and sprinkle with the cheese.

BRAISED SALMON IN RED WINE

The fruity Pinot Noir braises the salmon to a deep red, giving it a sweet flavor and making a delicious pan sauce. Serve the fish with risotto or rice pilaf to soak up the savory juices.

SERVES **6**

2 TABLESPOONS EXTRA-VIRGIN OLIVE OIL

2 LEEKS (WHITE AND TENDER GREEN PARTS), CLEANED AND FINELY CHOPPED

1½ CUPS PINOT NOIR

3 BLACK PEPPERCORNS

2 POUNDS SALMON FILLETS

2 TABLESPOONS UNSALTED BUTTER, SOFTENED

2 TABLESPOONS ALL-PURPOSE FLOUR

¼ CUP FINELY CHOPPED FRESH CHIVES

1 Heat the oil in the pressure cooker over medium-high heat. Add the leeks and sauté for 2 minutes, or until they are softened. Next, add the wine and peppercorns, stirring to blend. Add the salmon and spoon some of the sauce over the fillets. Lock the lid in place and cook at high pressure for 6 minutes.

2 Quick release the pressure and remove the lid, tilting the pot away from you to avoid the escaping steam. Carefully transfer the salmon to a serving platter and cover with aluminum foil to keep warm.

3 Remove the peppercorns from the sauce and bring the sauce to a boil. In a small dish, stir together the butter and flour and whisk into the sauce. Return to a boil, reduce the heat, and simmer, whisking constantly, until the sauce is thickened. Spoon a bit of the sauce over the salmon on the platter, sprinkle with the chives, and serve with the remaining sauce on the side.

SALMON TERIYAKI

Salmon braised in sweet and salty teriyaki sauce is moist and full of flavor. And the best news is that it's ready in six minutes. Serve the salmon with stir-fried veggies and sticky rice for a weeknight change of pace.

SERVES 6

½ CUP SOY SAUCE

¼ CUP MIRIN (SWEET RICE WINE)

½ CUP CHICKEN STOCK (PAGE 19) OR STORE-BOUGHT CHICKEN BROTH

1 TEASPOON TOASTED SESAME OIL

2 GARLIC CLOVES, MINCED

2 TEASPOONS GRATED FRESH GINGER

2 POUNDS SALMON FILLETS

1 TEASPOON CORNSTARCH MIXED WITH 2 TABLESPOONS WATER

4 SCALLIONS (WHITE AND TENDER GREEN PARTS), FINELY CHOPPED

2 TABLESPOONS TOASTED SESAME SEEDS

1 In the pressure cooker, combine the soy sauce, mirin, stock, sesame oil, garlic, and ginger. Add the salmon and turn it in the sauce. Lock the lid in place and cook at high pressure for 6 minutes.

2 Quick release the pressure and remove the lid, tilting the pot away from you to avoid the escaping steam. Carefully remove the salmon from the pot, transfer to a serving platter, and cover with aluminum foil to keep warm.

3 Bring the sauce to a boil and whisk in the cornstarch slurry. Return to a boil and cook until the sauce thickens and turns glossy. Spoon some of the sauce over the salmon and sprinkle with the scallions and sesame seeds. Pass the remaining sauce on the side.

TUNA PROVENÇAL

Cooked with plenty of olive oil, as well as garlic, red pepper, and tomato, the tuna acquires a deep flavor and melt-in-your-mouth tender texture. The recipe was inspired by the technique of poaching food in olive oil, which produces rich results similar to this dish. Serve it over pasta for a great weeknight meal.

SERVES **6**

½ CUP EXTRA-VIRGIN OLIVE OIL

4 GARLIC CLOVES, MINCED

PINCH OF RED PEPPER FLAKES

1 LARGE ONION, FINELY CHOPPED

ONE 28-OUNCE CAN CRUSHED TOMATOES WITH THEIR JUICE

2 SPRIGS FRESH THYME

1 BAY LEAF

¼ CUP BRINE-CURED CAPERS, DRAINED AND FINELY CHOPPED IF LARGE

2 POUNDS TUNA STEAKS, 1 INCH THICK

¼ CUP FINELY CHOPPED FRESH FLAT-LEAF PARSLEY

SALT AND FRESHLY GROUND BLACK PEPPER (OPTIONAL)

1 Heat the oil in the pressure cooker over medium-high heat. Add the garlic, pepper flakes, and onion and sauté for 2 minutes to soften the onion. Add the tomatoes, thyme, bay leaf, and capers. Lower the tuna into the sauce. Lock the lid in place and cook at high pressure for 3 minutes.

2 Release the pressure naturally. Once the pressure is released, leave the lid on for another 10 minutes while the fish steeps in the oil. Remove the lid, tilting the pot away from you to avoid the escaping steam. Lift the tuna out of the pot and transfer to a serving platter.

3 Skim off any excess fat from the sauce and remove the thyme sprigs and bay leaf. Add the parsley to the sauce, taste for seasoning, and add salt and pepper if necessary. Spoon the sauce over the tuna and serve any remaining sauce on the side.

SWORDFISH SICILIANA

Sunny Sicily is famous for its food, history, and wine. And since it is the largest island in the Mediterranean, it is no surprise that seafood is a big part of Sicilians' diet. This braised swordfish is a typical dish, which can be found in trattorias near Messina and Taormina on the southeastern coast. The sauce is fragrant with garlic, capers, and olives. A sprinkling of fresh parsley and lemon zest add bright, fresh flavors. This dish is sure to please even the most avowed carnivore.

SERVES 6

2 TABLESPOONS EXTRA-VIRGIN OLIVE OIL

3 GARLIC CLOVES, MINCED

2 MEDIUM SHALLOTS, FINELY CHOPPED

½ TEASPOON DRIED OREGANO

ONE 14-OUNCE CAN CRUSHED TOMATOES WITH THEIR JUICE

2 TABLESPOONS BRINE-CURED CAPERS, DRAINED AND CHOPPED IF LARGE

½ CUP OIL-CURED BLACK OLIVES, PITTED

2 TABLESPOONS BALSAMIC VINEGAR

2 POUNDS SWORDFISH FILLETS

¼ CUP FINELY CHOPPED FRESH FLAT-LEAF PARSLEY

GRATED ZEST OF 1 LEMON

1 Heat the oil in the pressure cooker over medium-high heat. Add the garlic, shallots, and oregano and cook for 2 minutes to soften the shallots. Add the tomatoes, capers, olives, and vinegar, stirring to combine. Arrange the fish in the pressure cooker, stacking the fillets if necessary. Spoon some of the sauce over the fish. Lock the lid in place and cook at high pressure for 6 minutes.

2 Quick release the pressure and remove the lid, tilting the pot away from you to avoid the escaping steam. Carefully remove the swordfish from the pot and transfer to a serving platter. Spoon the sauce over the fish and sprinkle with the parsley and lemon zest.

PASTA & RICE

Pasta The pressure cooker can be invaluable when you want to make a one-pot meal with pasta. Choose pasta that is short and compact like farfalle, elbows, shells, orecchiette, or penne, rather than long ribbons like spaghetti or linguine. Long pastas cook unevenly in the pressure cooker. For every cup of dried pasta, you will need one cup of liquid to ensure the pasta will cook evenly and completely under pressure. The beauty of this technique is that the other flavors in the pot saturate the pasta under pressure, giving you a full-flavored and delicious meal.

Always use pasta made from durum wheat. I prefer imported Italian pastas, which hold their shapes well and cook up beautifully every time.

Rice Brown rice is the entire grain of rice after the husk has been removed. It includes the bran, which is the coating that surrounds the rice. The bran gives the rice a chewy texture, making it a great choice for side dishes and salads, or to add to casseroles. Brown rice is rich in fiber and B vitamins.

White rice is what's left after the husk and bran have been removed during processing. This process removes some of the grain's fiber and vitamins, too. White rice is a staple around the world. It makes an easy, satisfying side dish to accompany almost any main course. Adding rice to salads, soups, and casseroles helps to stretch your food dollar and enrich your dishes.

Long-grain white rice is fluffy. The grains remain separate at the end of the cooking time, rather than sticking together. Basmati rice is a long-grain rice from Asia with a buttery, aromatic quality.

Short- and medium-grain white rice contain higher levels of starch than long-grain, and the grains stick together when cooked. Arborio is a short-grain Italian rice that can be used in risotto or rice pudding. Carnaroli and Vialone Nano are types of Italian medium-grain starchy rice with a core that retains its firmness when cooked. These are preferred for risotto. The rice releases starch into the dish, imparting a luxuriously creamy texture.

The grains of short-grain Asian rice have a tendency to stick together when cooked, making it a good choice for Asian stir-fries and curry because the rice soaks up the sauces. It is also a good choice for rice puddings, and it's essential for sushi.

Wild rice is not technically rice, but rather an aquatic grass grown in the far northern regions of the United States and Canada. It has a chewy texture, which adds a lovely contrast to pilafs, stuffings for poultry, and salads. Once cooked, wild rice can be frozen in one-cup packages for up to four months.

DILLY ZUCCHINI, CORN, TOMATOES, AND PASTA

This is a great one-pot meat to make when your garden is overrun with zucchini and tomatoes. Or serve it cold for a terrific pasta salad (see below).

SERVES **6**

4 TABLESPOONS UNSALTED BUTTER

2 GARLIC CLOVES, MINCED

1 TEASPOON DRIED DILL WEED

4 MEDIUM ZUCCHINI, DICED

2 CUPS CORN KERNELS, FRESHLY CUT FROM THE COB, OR FROZEN CORN, DEFROSTED

2 CUPS MEDIUM SHELL PASTA

2 CUPS CHICKEN OR VEGETABLE STOCK (PAGE 19 OR 21) OR STORE-BOUGHT CHICKEN OR VEGETABLE BROTH

2 CUPS CHERRY TOMATOES, HALVED

½ CUP FINELY CHOPPED FRESH CHIVES

1 Melt 2 tablespoons of the butter in the pressure cooker over medium-high heat. Add the garlic and dill and sauté for 2 minutes, or until fragrant. Add the zucchini and corn and stir to coat the vegetables with the butter mixture. Add the pasta and stock, pushing the pasta under the liquid. Lock the lid in place and cook at high pressure for 6 minutes.

2 Quick release the pressure and remove the lid, tilting the pot away from you to avoid the escaping steam. Stir in the tomatoes. Place the pressure cooker over medium-high heat and add the remaining 2 tablespoons of butter and the chives, stirring to melt the butter and incorporate the chives. Serve immediately.

PASTA SALAD

Omit the last 2 tablespoons of butter and allow the pasta to cool. Use your favorite dressing or whisk together ½ cup of extra-virgin olive oil, 3 tablespoons of rice vinegar, and salt and freshly ground black pepper and toss with the pasta. Add the tomatoes and chives, toss, and serve. This is terrific served with grilled steak or fish.

BUTTERNUT SQUASH AND RADICCHIO WITH FARFALLE

Sweet and savory, this pasta dish is perfect for dinner in the fall when local butternut squash is at its peak flavor. The slightly bitter radicchio makes a nice counterpoint to the sweetness of the squash.

SERVES 6

4 TABLESPOONS UNSALTED BUTTER

2 TABLESPOONS EXTRA-VIRGIN OLIVE OIL

1 MEDIUM GRANNY SMITH APPLE, PEELED, CORED, AND COARSELY CHOPPED

2 CUPS CHOPPED BUTTERNUT SQUASH (½-INCH CUBES)

2 CUPS FARFALLE PASTA

3½ CUPS CHICKEN OR VEGETABLE STOCK (PAGE 19 OR 21) OR STORE-BOUGHT CHICKEN OR VEGETABLE BROTH

2 SMALL HEADS RADICCHIO, CORED AND THINLY SLICED

½ CUP FRESHLY GRATED PARMIGIANO-REGGIANO CHEESE

¼ CUP TOASTED PINE NUTS FOR GARNISH

1 Melt 2 tablespoons of the butter with the oil in the pressure cooker over medium-high heat. Add the apple and squash and sauté for about 5 minutes, or until the squash begins to turn golden. Add the farfalle and stock. Lock the lid in place and cook at high pressure for 7 minutes.

2 Quick release the pressure and remove the lid, tilting the pot away from you to avoid the escaping steam. Stir the radicchio into the pot and add the remaining 2 tablespoons of butter and the cheese. Serve immediately, garnishing each serving with some of the pine nuts.

BROCCOLI RABE, SAUSAGE, AND ORECCHIETTE

This stick-to-your-ribs classic made with bitter greens and sweet sausage is my idea of a great spur-of-the-moment dinner for friends and family. And since everything cooks in the pressure cooker, there is only one pot to clean up!

SERVES **6**

2 TABLESPOONS EXTRA-VIRGIN OLIVE OIL

1 GARLIC CLOVE, SLICED

PINCH OF RED PEPPER FLAKES

1 POUND SWEET ITALIAN SAUSAGE, CASINGS REMOVED

1 POUND BROCCOLI RABE, STEMS TRIMMED, AND CUT INTO 1-INCH PIECES

3 CUPS CHICKEN OR VEGETABLE STOCK (PAGE 19 OR 21) OR STORE-BOUGHT CHICKEN OR VEGETABLE BROTH

2 CUPS ORECCHIETTE PASTA

SALT AND FRESHLY GROUND BLACK PEPPER (OPTIONAL)

½ CUP FRESHLY GRATED PARMIGIANO-REGGIANO CHEESE FOR GARNISH

1 Heat the oil in the pressure cooker over medium-high heat. Add the garlic and pepper flakes and cook for 10 seconds. Add the sausage and cook, breaking up any large pieces, until the sausage loses its pink color. Add the broccoli rabe and cook for 3 minutes, or until it begins to wilt. Add the stock and pasta, pushing the pasta down under the liquid. Lock the lid in place and cook at high pressure for 6 minutes.

2 Quick release the pressure and remove the lid, tilting the pot away from you to avoid the escaping steam. Stir the pasta and taste for seasoning, adding salt and black pepper if necessary. Garnish each serving with Parmigiano-Reggiano cheese.

RIGATONI ALLA NORMA

Named after an opera written by the Sicilian composer Vincenzo Bellini, this pasta dish has become standard in many Italian American red sauce restaurants. The eggplant pairs beautifully with the tomatoes, basil, ricotta salata, and hot pepper.

SERVES 6

3 TABLESPOONS EXTRA-VIRGIN OLIVE OIL

1 CUP FINELY CHOPPED SWEET ONION, SUCH AS VIDALIA

4 GARLIC CLOVES, MINCED

PINCH OF RED PEPPER FLAKES

4 CUPS CHOPPED JAPANESE EGGPLANT (¾-INCH CHUNKS)

ONE 28-OUNCE CAN CRUSHED TOMATOES WITH THEIR JUICE

2 CUPS CHICKEN OR VEGETABLE STOCK (PAGE 19 OR 21) OR STORE-BOUGHT CHICKEN OR VEGETABLE BROTH

2 CUPS RIGATONI

10 FRESH BASIL LEAVES, FINELY CHOPPED

¼ CUP FINELY CHOPPED FRESH FLAT-LEAF PARSLEY

1 CUP GRATED RICOTTA SALATA (SEE PSST)

1 Heat the oil in the pressure cooker over medium-high heat. Add the onion, garlic, and pepper flakes and sauté for 2 minutes to soften the onion. Add the eggplant and sauté for 3 to 4 minutes, to coat with the garlic and oil. Add the tomatoes, stock, and rigatoni. Lock the lid in place and cook at high pressure for 7 minutes.

2 Quick release the pressure and remove the lid, tilting the pot away from you to avoid the escaping steam. Add the basil, parsley, and ½ to ¾ cup of the cheese, stirring to melt the cheese. Serve the pasta immediately, garnished with the remaining cheese.

PSST

If you can't find ricotta salata, which is aged ricotta cheese, substitute an imported Pecorino Romano.

BASIC BROWN RICE

Basic brown rice is a great platform. It makes a significant contribution to soups, salads, and casseroles. You can cook brown rice in minutes in a pressure cooker. Use it right away or let cool and store it to use later. I like to dress brown rice with olive oil, salt, and pepper and serve it as a side dish.

MAKES **4** CUPS

....

2 TABLESPOONS UNSALTED BUTTER

2 CUPS BROWN RICE, RINSED AND DRAINED

4 CUPS WATER

SALT AND FRESHLY GROUND BLACK PEPPER

1 Melt the butter in the pressure cooker over medium-high heat. Add the rice and stir to coat. Stir in the water. Lock the lid in place and cook at high pressure for 18 minutes.

2 Release the pressure naturally and remove the lid, tilting the pot away from you to avoid the escaping steam. Fluff the rice, season with salt and pepper, and serve. Or let cool and store in airtight containers in the refrigerator for up to 3 days or freeze for up to 3 months.

BROWN RICE SALAD WITH MANGO AND CURRY VINAIGRETTE

Slightly sweet, with the flavor of curry, this salad is filled with chewy brown rice, nuggets of mango, and vegetables. It's a lovely dish to take along to a picnic or to serve at home alongside grilled entrées in the summertime.

SERVES 6

1 RECIPE BASIC BROWN RICE (FACING PAGE), COOLED

¼ CUP FINELY CHOPPED RED ONION

1 LARGE RIPE MANGO, PITTED, PEELED, AND FINELY CHOPPED (SEE PSST)

3 CELERY STALKS, FINELY CHOPPED

2 MEDIUM CARROTS, FINELY CHOPPED

½ CUP CANOLA OIL

¼ CUP RICE VINEGAR

1 TEASPOON MADRAS CURRY POWDER

2 TABLESPOONS SUGAR

1 GARLIC CLOVE, MINCED

1 TEASPOON WORCESTERSHIRE SAUCE

1 CUP TOASTED SLICED ALMONDS FOR GARNISH (SEE PSST ON PAGE 114)

In a large serving bowl, combine the cooked rice, onion, mango, celery, and carrots. In a small mixing bowl, whisk together the oil, vinegar, curry powder, sugar, garlic, and Worcestershire. Pour the dressing over the salad and toss to coat the ingredients. Garnish with the toasted almonds and serve.

PSST

Pitting the mango after you have peeled it, instead of before, is like trying to wrestle with a greased pig. The flesh is slippery, and you can cut yourself easily. With the skin on, cut off the bottom of the mango and set it on a cutting board with the bottom down. Cut down the sides of the mango, following the shape of the ovoid pit and separating it from the flesh. Peel each mango half. Or get hold of a mango pitter, a terrific tool sold in gourmet and kitchenware stores.

BROWN RICE PILAF

For a pilaf, the rice is first sautéed in oil and then cooked with broth and maybe some herbs and vegetables. Pilafs are enjoyed in the Middle East and in India, sometimes as a festive dish to replace steamed or boiled rice. This is a basic pilaf. You can add more vegetables and flavorings if you like, but I love the simplicity this dish brings to the dinner table.

SERVES **6**

2 TABLESPOONS EXTRA-VIRGIN OLIVE OIL

2 CUPS BROWN RICE, RINSED AND DRAINED

½ CUP FINELY CHOPPED RED ONION

3 MEDIUM CARROTS, FINELY CHOPPED

2 CELERY STALKS, FINELY CHOPPED

4 CUPS CHICKEN STOCK (PAGE 19) OR STORE-BOUGHT CHICKEN BROTH

SALT AND FRESHLY GROUND BLACK PEPPER (OPTIONAL)

1 Heat the oil in the pressure cooker over medium-high heat. Add the rice and toast the grains for 2 minutes. Add the onion, carrots, and celery and cook for about 2 minutes to soften the onion. Pour in the stock. Lock the lid in place and cook at high pressure for 18 minutes.

2 Release the pressure naturally and remove the lid, tilting the pot away from you to avoid the escaping steam. Fluff the rice and taste for seasoning, adding salt and pepper if necessary. Serve immediately.

CRANBERRY BROWN RICE PILAF

Studded with dried cranberries and bits of apricot, this rice pilaf is great to serve with a weeknight dinner. But it can also be a showstopper for the holidays, especially when served as a stuffing for turkey, Cornish game hens, chicken, or a crown roast of pork.

SERVES **6**

2 TABLESPOONS UNSALTED BUTTER

1 TABLESPOON CANOLA OIL

2 CUPS BROWN RICE, RINSED AND DRAINED

½ CUP FINELY DICED SWEET ONION, SUCH AS VIDALIA

1 TEASPOON DRIED THYME

½ TEASPOON CELERY SEEDS

½ CUP DRIED CRANBERRIES

½ CUP FINELY CHOPPED DRIED APRICOTS (SEE PSST)

4 CUPS CHICKEN STOCK (PAGE 19) OR STORE-BOUGHT CHICKEN BROTH

SALT AND FRESHLY GROUND BLACK PEPPER (OPTIONAL)

1 Melt the butter with the oil in the pressure cooker over medium-high heat. Add the rice and cook for 2 minutes to toast the grains. Add the onion, thyme, and celery seeds and cook for another 2 minutes to soften the onion. Add the cranberries, apricots, and stock. Lock the lid in place and cook at high pressure for 18 minutes.

2 Release the pressure naturally and remove the lid, tilting the pot away from you to avoid the escaping steam. Fluff the rice and taste for seasoning, adding salt and pepper if necessary. Serve immediately.

PSST

When cutting dried fruits, spray your knife with nonstick cooking spray or rub with a bit of canola oil to make the job a lot easier!

BASIC LONG-GRAIN WHITE RICE

Cooking long-grain rice in a pressure cooker is super-simple and gives you great results. Each grain is fluffy and separate. You may decide to store that old rice cooker in the garage to free up valuable space on your countertop. Serve the rice right from the pot or store it to serve later.

MAKES **4** CUPS

....

2 TABLESPOONS UNSALTED BUTTER

1½ CUPS LONG-GRAIN WHITE RICE, SUCH AS BASMATI

2⅓ CUPS WATER

SALT AND FRESHLY GROUND BLACK PEPPER

1 Melt the butter in the pressure cooker over medium-high heat. Add the rice, tossing to coat with the butter. Stir in the water. Lock the lid in place and cook at high pressure for 4 minutes.

2 Reduce the pressure naturally for 5 minutes, then quick release the pressure. Remove the lid, tilting the pot away from you to avoid the escaping steam. Stir the rice and season with salt and pepper. Serve immediately. Or let cool and refrigerate in airtight containers for up to 3 days or freeze for up to 3 months.

TRADITIONAL RICE PILAF

Simple yet elegant, rice pilaf made with long-grain white rice is like a little black dress—it never goes out of style. I like to make this with chicken broth, but feel free to substitute beef or vegetable broth if you would like.

SERVES **6**

....

2 TABLESPOONS UNSALTED BUTTER

1 TABLESPOON CANOLA OIL

½ CUP FINELY CHOPPED SWEET ONION, SUCH AS VIDALIA

1½ CUPS LONG-GRAIN WHITE RICE

2¼ CUPS CHICKEN STOCK (PAGE 19) OR STORE-BOUGHT CHICKEN BROTH

SALT AND FRESHLY GROUND BLACK PEPPER (OPTIONAL)

¼ CUP FINELY CHOPPED FRESH FLAT-LEAF PARSLEY FOR GARNISH

1 Melt the butter with the oil in the pressure cooker over medium-high heat. Add the onion and rice and cook for 2 to 3 minutes to soften the onion. Pour in the stock. Lock the lid in place and cook at high pressure for 4 minutes.

2 Release the pressure naturally and remove the lid, tilting the pot away from you to avoid the escaping steam. Fluff the rice, taste for seasoning, and add salt and pepper if necessary. Serve the rice hot, garnished with the chopped parsley.

FRUITED RICE PILAF

Dried fruit transforms into a pleasingly soft surprise in this pilaf. Although the recipe calls for dried apple and cranberries, feel free to substitute your favorites, such as apricots, golden raisins, pineapple, or mango.

SERVES **6**

2 TABLESPOONS UNSALTED BUTTER

1 TABLESPOON CANOLA OIL

½ CUP FINELY CHOPPED SWEET ONION, SUCH AS VIDALIA

1½ CUPS LONG-GRAIN WHITE RICE

½ CUP CHOPPED DRIED APPLE

½ CUP DRIED CRANBERRIES

2¼ CUPS CHICKEN STOCK (PAGE 19) OR STORE-BOUGHT CHICKEN BROTH

SALT AND FRESHLY GROUND BLACK PEPPER (OPTIONAL)

1 Melt the butter with the oil in the pressure cooker over medium-high heat. Add the onion and rice and cook for 2 to 3 minutes to soften the onion. Add the apple, cranberries, and stock. Lock the lid in place and cook at high pressure for 4 minutes.

2 Release the pressure naturally and remove the lid, tilting the pot away from you to avoid the escaping steam. Fluff the rice, taste for seasoning, and add salt and pepper if necessary. Serve the rice hot.

SAFFRON RICE

Simple to make but with a complex flavor, this saffron-scented rice is a crowd-pleaser. Serve it alongside grilled chicken or seafood or as a bed for steak with chimichurri sauce. Be forewarned that saffron, the dried stigma of the crocus plant, is expensive, but well worth the price.

SERVES 6

2 TABLESPOONS UNSALTED BUTTER

1 TABLESPOON CANOLA OIL

½ CUP FINELY CHOPPED SHALLOTS

2 TEASPOONS SAFFRON THREADS, CRUSHED IN THE PALM OF YOUR HAND

1½ CUPS LONG-GRAIN WHITE RICE

2¼ CUPS CHICKEN STOCK (PAGE 19) OR STORE-BOUGHT CHICKEN BROTH

SALT AND FRESHLY GROUND BLACK PEPPER (OPTIONAL)

1 Melt the butter with the oil in the pressure cooker over medium-high heat. Add the shallots and saffron and cook for 2 minutes to soften the shallots. Add the rice and stir to coat with the butter mixture. Pour in the chicken stock. Lock the lid in place and cook at high pressure for 4 minutes.

2 Release the pressure naturally and remove the lid, tilting the pot away from you to avoid the escaping steam. Fluff the rice and taste for seasoning, adding salt and pepper if necessary. Serve the rice hot.

SPANISH RICE

Fragrant with garlic, tomato, and Spanish paprika, this richly colored rice is beautiful on the plate and delicious on the tongue. Often confused with its stepbrother, Mexican rice (see facing page), this dish is rich and smoky, with bits of bacon and bell pepper throughout.

SERVES **6**

2 TABLESPOONS EXTRA-VIRGIN OLIVE OIL

4 BACON STRIPS, CUT CROSSWISE INTO PIECES ½ INCH WIDE

½ CUP FINELY CHOPPED SWEET ONION, SUCH AS VIDALIA

1 MEDIUM GREEN BELL PEPPER, SEEDED, DERIBBED, AND FINELY CHOPPED

2 TEASPOONS SPANISH SMOKED PAPRIKA

2 CUPS LONG-GRAIN WHITE RICE

ONE 14½-OUNCE CAN CHOPPED TOMATOES WITH THEIR JUICE

1½ CUPS CHICKEN STOCK (PAGE 19) OR STORE-BOUGHT CHICKEN BROTH

SALT AND FRESHLY GROUND BLACK PEPPER (OPTIONAL)

¼ CUP FINELY CHOPPED FRESH FLAT-LEAF PARSLEY FOR GARNISH

1 Heat the oil in the pressure cooker over medium-high heat. Add the bacon and sauté until crisp. Add the onion, bell pepper, and paprika and cook for 3 minutes, or until the onion is softened. Add the rice and stir to coat the grains. Add the tomatoes and stock. Lock the lid in place and cook at high pressure for 4 minutes.

2 Release the pressure naturally and remove the lid, tilting the pot away from you to avoid the escaping steam. Fluff the rice, taste for seasoning, and add salt and pepper if necessary. Transfer to a serving bowl and garnish with the parsley before serving.

SOUTH-OF-THE-BORDER RICE

There are as many versions of this dish as there are cooks in Mexico! I love this one—filled with chiles and tomatoes and flavored with cumin and cilantro—because it makes a big statement on the plate. Serve it with fajitas or other grilled entrées for your next fiesta.

SERVES 6

2 TABLESPOONS CANOLA OIL

½ CUP FINELY CHOPPED SWEET ONION, SUCH AS VIDALIA

2 ANAHEIM CHILE PEPPERS, SEEDED, DERIBBED, AND FINELY CHOPPED

1 TEASPOON GROUND CUMIN

1 TEASPOON DRIED OREGANO

2 CUPS LONG-GRAIN WHITE RICE

ONE 14½-OUNCE CAN FIRE-ROASTED CHOPPED TOMATOES WITH THEIR JUICES, SUCH AS MUIR GLEN OR TRADER JOE'S BRANDS

1½ CUPS CHICKEN STOCK (PAGE 19) OR STORE-BOUGHT CHICKEN BROTH

SALT AND FRESHLY GROUND BLACK PEPPER (OPTIONAL)

¼ CUP FINELY CHOPPED FRESH CILANTRO FOR GARNISH

1 Heat the oil in the pressure cooker over medium-high heat. Add the onion, chiles, cumin, oregano, and rice, stirring to coat the rice. Cook for 2 minutes, or until the onion begins to soften. Add the tomatoes and stock and stir to combine. Lock the lid in place and cook at high pressure for 4 minutes.

2 Release the pressure naturally and remove the lid, tilting the pot away from you to avoid the escaping steam. Fluff the rice, taste for seasoning, and add salt and black pepper if necessary. Transfer to a serving bowl and garnish with cilantro.

CAJUN RICE

This highly seasoned rice gets a kick from tiny pieces of andouille sausage, a bit of Creole seasoning, and the trinity of Creole cuisine: onion, celery, and bell pepper. If you wish to tone this down a bit, I'd suggest mild smoked sausage, like kielbasa.

SERVES 6

2 TABLESPOONS CANOLA OIL

½ POUND ANDOUILLE SAUSAGE, FINELY CHOPPED

½ CUP FINELY CHOPPED SWEET ONION, SUCH AS VIDALIA

½ CUP FINELY CHOPPED CELERY

½ CUP FINELY CHOPPED GREEN BELL PEPPER

1 GARLIC CLOVE, MINCED

2 TEASPOONS CREOLE OR CAJUN SEASONING (SEE PSST)

2 CUPS LONG-GRAIN WHITE RICE

ONE 14½-OUNCE CAN CHOPPED TOMATOES WITH THEIR JUICE

1½ CUPS CHICKEN STOCK (PAGE 19) OR STORE-BOUGHT CHICKEN BROTH

SALT AND FRESHLY GROUND BLACK PEPPER (OPTIONAL)

¼ CUP FINELY CHOPPED FRESH FLAT-LEAF PARSLEY FOR GARNISH

1 Heat the oil in the pressure cooker over medium-high heat. Add the sausage, onion, celery, bell pepper, garlic, and Creole seasoning. Cook for 3 minutes, stirring constantly to avoid burning the spices. Add the rice and stir to coat the grains. Add the tomatoes and stock. Lock the lid in place and cook at high pressure for 4 minutes.

2 Release the pressure naturally and remove the lid, tilting the pot away from you to avoid the escaping steam. Fluff the rice and taste for seasoning, adding salt and pepper if necessary. Transfer to a serving bowl and garnish with the chopped parsley.

PSST

There are many brands of Creole and Cajun seasoning on the market. I recommend Penzeys.

EAT-YOUR-VEGGIES RICE

This dish makes a great way to sneak a few vitamins and minerals into a weeknight meal. The rice is riddled with colorful and tasty vegetables, which cook along with the rice. Feel free to vary the vegetables, but be sure to cut them all the same size so that they will cook evenly.

SERVES 6

2 TABLESPOONS UNSALTED BUTTER

¼ CUP FINELY CHOPPED SWEET ONION, SUCH AS VIDALIA

2 MEDIUM CARROTS, FINELY CHOPPED

2 CUPS LONG-GRAIN RICE

1 CUP FROZEN PETITE PEAS, DEFROSTED

1 CUP FROZEN CORN KERNELS, DEFROSTED

1 CUP SUGAR SNAP PEAS, TRIMMED AND TOUGH STRINGS REMOVED

2¼ CUPS CHICKEN OR VEGETABLE STOCK (PAGE 19 OR 21) OR STORE-BOUGHT CHICKEN OR VEGETABLE BROTH

SALT AND FRESHLY GROUND BLACK PEPPER (OPTIONAL)

1 Melt the butter in the pressure cooker over medium-high heat. Add the onion and carrots and sauté for 2 minutes, or until the onion begins to soften. Add the rice and stir to coat the grains. Add the peas, corn, snap peas, and stock. Lock the lid in place and cook at high pressure for 4 minutes.

2 Release the pressure naturally and remove the lid, tilting the pot away from you to avoid the escaping steam. Fluff the rice, taste for seasoning, and add salt and pepper if necessary. Serve immediately.

BEEFY MUSHROOM RICE

Sometimes a change from the usual mashed or baked potatoes is just the thing to perk up a roasted or grilled meat. This beefy rice, filled with dried porcini and sautéed cremini mushrooms, is a terrific side dish to serve any night of the week and it dresses up nicely for special occasions, too.

SERVES **6**

2 OUNCES DRIED PORCINI MUSHROOMS

2¼ CUPS BEEF STOCK (PAGE 20) OR STORE-BOUGHT BEEF BROTH

3 TABLESPOONS UNSALTED BUTTER

2 TABLESPOONS EXTRA-VIRGIN OLIVE OIL

½ CUP FINELY CHOPPED SHALLOTS

1 TEASPOON DRIED THYME

2 CUPS LONG-GRAIN WHITE RICE

1 POUND CREMINI MUSHROOMS, THINLY SLICED

SALT AND FRESHLY GROUND BLACK PEPPER

¼ CUP FINELY CHOPPED FRESH FLAT-LEAF PARSLEY FOR GARNISH

1 In a medium bowl, crumble the porcini into the stock and allow to rehydrate while you prepare the rice.

2 Melt 1 tablespoon of the butter with the oil in the pressure cooker over medium-high heat. Add the shallots and thyme and sauté until the shallots are softened, about 2 minutes. Add the rice and stir to coat the grains. Pour in the porcini and stock. Lock the lid in place and cook at high pressure for 4 minutes.

3 While the rice is cooking, melt the remaining 2 tablespoons of butter in a large skillet over medium-high heat. Add the cremini mushrooms and sauté until they begin to turn golden around the edges. Season with salt and pepper and set aside.

4 When the rice has cooked, quick release the pressure and remove the lid, tilting the pot away from you to avoid the escaping steam. Stir in the cremini mushrooms and transfer the rice to a serving bowl. Garnish with the parsley and serve.

SPINACH PILAF

Referred to as "green rice" at the Phillips house, this rice has a lot going for it, including its attractive green and white coloring. Cooked in chicken broth and flavored with nutmeg and garlic, the rice also has a more complex taste than everyday rice.

SERVES **6**

3 TABLESPOONS UNSALTED BUTTER

1 TABLESPOON EXTRA-VIRGIN OLIVE OIL

½ CUP FINELY CHOPPED SWEET ONION, SUCH AS VIDALIA

2 GARLIC CLOVES, MINCED

TWO 10-OUNCE BAGS BABY SPINACH, COARSELY CHOPPED; OR ONE 1-POUND PACKAGE FROZEN CHOPPED SPINACH, DEFROSTED

2 TEASPOONS SALT

½ TEASPOON FRESHLY GRATED NUTMEG

½ TEASPOON FRESHLY GROUND BLACK PEPPER

2 CUPS LONG-GRAIN WHITE RICE

2¼ CUPS CHICKEN STOCK (PAGE 19) OR STORE-BOUGHT CHICKEN BROTH

1 Melt the butter with the olive oil in the pressure cooker over medium-high heat. Add the onion and garlic and sauté for 2 minutes, or until the onion begins to soften. Add the spinach, salt, nutmeg, and pepper and sauté until the spinach looks dry and there is no more liquid in the pot. Add the rice and stock. Lock the lid in place and cook at high pressure for 4 minutes.

2 Quick release the pressure and remove the lid, tilting the pot away from you to avoid the escaping steam. Stir the rice, transfer to a serving bowl, and serve immediately.

PSST

Try substituting your favorite vegetables in this dish; broccoli and artichoke hearts work very well here.

CONGEE BREAKFAST RICE WITH CONDIMENTS

This simple rice dish is known in China and Korea as *jook*. The rice is a combination of short-grain and long-grain, cooked in the broth until is almost like porridge. Congee is traditionally served with all manner of salty and pickled Asian condiments, as well as stir-fried foods. In China, congee is often eaten for breakfast, which is how I treat it here. Cook the rice in milk and broth and serve it with the suggested condiments, which are either in your pantry or at the local market.

SERVES **4**

CONGEE

1 CUP MILK

3 CUPS CHICKEN OR VEGETABLE STOCK (PAGE 19 OR 21) OR STORE-BOUGHT CHICKEN OR VEGETABLE BROTH

1 CUP SHORT-GRAIN RICE, SUCH AS SUSHI RICE

1 CUP LONG-GRAIN RICE

1 TEASPOON SALT

2 TABLESPOONS UNSALTED BUTTER

CONDIMENTS

GRANOLA

DRIED FRUITS (CRANBERRIES, BLUEBERRIES, CHOPPED APRICOTS, GOLDEN RAISINS)

TOASTED NUTS (WALNUTS, PECANS, ALMONDS, MACADAMIA NUTS; SEE PSST ON PAGE 114)

FRESH BERRIES

SLICED BANANAS, PEACHES, OR NECTARINES

RHUBARB COMPOTE (PAGE 425)

STEWED APPLES

STEAMED MILK

BROWN SUGAR

MAPLE SYRUP

ORANGE BLOSSOM HONEY

1 **To make the congee:** Combine all the ingredients in the pressure cooker. Lock the lid in place and cook at high pressure for 15 minutes.

2 Quick release the pressure and remove the lid, tilting the pot away from you to avoid the escaping steam. Stir the congee; it should be soupy and the rice should be well cooked. If the rice is still a bit firm, lock the lid in place and allow the rice to steam for another 5 minutes off the heat. Serve the congee in bowls, with the condiments on the side.

FRUITED BASMATI RICE

The sweet mango and crunchy peanuts give this simple dish an appealing sweet and salty quality. Basmati is a long-grain aromatic rice that is a staple of Indian cuisine.

SERVES **6**

2 TABLESPOONS UNSALTED BUTTER

2 CUPS BASMATI RICE

2¼ CUPS WATER

2 TEASPOONS SALT

1 MEDIUM MANGO, PITTED, PEELED, AND FINELY CHOPPED (SEE PSST ON PAGE 309)

½ CUP CHOPPED ROASTED PEANUTS

4 GREEN ONIONS (WHITE AND TENDER GREEN PARTS), FINELY CHOPPED

1 Melt the butter in the pressure cooker over medium-high heat. Add the rice and stir to coat the grains with the butter. Add the water and salt. Lock the lid in place and cook at high pressure for 4 minutes.

2 Quick release the pressure and remove the lid, tilting the pot away from you to avoid the escaping steam. Stir in the mango, peanuts, and green onions. Transfer to a serving bowl and serve immediately.

CREAMY CURRIED BASMATI RICE

This curried rice is sublime—creamy with coconut milk and fragrant with curry spices.

SERVES 6

....

2 TABLESPOONS CANOLA OIL

2 CUPS BASMATI RICE

2 TEASPOONS MADRAS CURRY POWDER

1 CUP COCONUT MILK

1¼ CUPS CHICKEN OR VEGETABLE STOCK (PAGE 19 OR 21) OR STORE-BOUGHT CHICKEN OR VEGETABLE BROTH

SALT AND FRESHLY GROUND BLACK PEPPER (OPTIONAL)

1 Heat the oil in the pressure cooker over medium-high heat. Add the rice and curry powder and sauté for 1 minute to coat the grains. Add the coconut milk and stock. Lock the lid in place and cook at high pressure for 4 minutes.

2 Quick release the pressure and remove the lid, tilting the pot away from you to avoid the escaping steam. Fluff the rice, taste for seasoning, add salt and pepper if necessary, and transfer to a serving bowl.

TROUBLESHOOTING RISOTTO IN THE PRESSURE COOKER

I tell students that risotto is an absolute no-brainer in the pressure cooker. That being said, each stove and pressure cooker is a little different. Here are a few hints that will help you toward risotto nirvana.

1 If you're making substitutions, such as adding more broth instead of using wine, make sure the total amount of liquid remains the same.

2 Dry vermouth makes an adequate substitute for white wine in risotto.

3 Beef broth is usually too strong for a risotto, but chicken and vegetable broths can be used interchangeably in recipes.

4 Use only medium-grain rice in these recipes, such as Carnaroli and Vialone Nano. You can use them interchangeably. Arborio is a shorter grain and will give you a stickier risotto than the other two. Don't substitute another type of rice, such as long-grain; the result will not be the same.

5 When you remove the lid from the pressure cooker, taste the rice. If it is not quite al dente, return the pot to the stove top and cook for an additional 1 or 2 minutes without pressure. Sometimes the ambient heat from the pot itself will continue to cook the rice to al dente.

6 When adding cheese, take the pot off the heat first; otherwise, the cheese may separate and get stringy.

7 Taste for seasoning after cooking. Because broth already has salt and pepper in it, you may not need additional salt or pepper when the risotto is done. Cheese will also add salt to the finished dish.

WHITE RISOTTO WITH ACETO BALSAMICO

I had this risotto in Modena, the home of traditionally made balsamic vinegar (and also of Luciano Pavarotti). At the end of a long day of touring, we were shown to a private dining room. This was the first course, which was served with a drizzle of twenty-five-year-old balsamic vinegar—*delizioso*!

SERVES **4** TO **6**

4 TABLESPOONS UNSALTED BUTTER

1 TABLESPOON EXTRA-VIRGIN OLIVE OIL

1 SHALLOT, FINELY CHOPPED

1½ CUPS CARNAROLI OR VIALONE NANO RICE

½ CUP DRY WHITE WINE, SUCH AS SAUVIGNON BLANC OR PINOT GRIGIO, OR DRY VERMOUTH

3½ CUPS CHICKEN STOCK (PAGE 19) OR STORE-BOUGHT CHICKEN BROTH

½ CUP FRESHLY GRATED PARMIGIANO-REGGIANO CHEESE

SALT AND FRESHLY GROUND BLACK PEPPER (OPTIONAL)

¼ CUP AGED BALSAMIC VINEGAR

1 Melt 2 tablespoons of the butter with the oil in the pressure cooker over medium-high heat. Add the shallot and sauté for 1 minute, or until fragrant. Add the rice and toss to coat. Pour in the wine and stock. Lock the lid in place and cook at high pressure for 8 minutes.

2 Quick release the pressure and remove the lid, tilting the pot away from you to allow the steam to escape. Stir in the remaining 2 tablespoons of butter and the cheese. Taste the rice for seasoning, adding salt and pepper if necessary. Allow the rice to stand for 2 minutes and stir again. If the risotto is not quite cooked, give it another minute over medium heat. Serve in shallow bowls and drizzle with some of the balsamic vinegar.

PSST

Recipes that call for grated cheese usually tell you what fraction of a cup you need. But you may have no idea how much to buy in the store, so here is a general guide.

For 1 cup of grated cheese, you'll need:

- 3 ounces of a hard-grating cheese, such as Parmigiano-Reggiano or Pecorino Romano
- ¼ pound of grating cheese, such as cheddar or Swiss
- ¼ pound of crumbled blue or goat cheese

RISOTTO ALLA MILANESE

A classic dish from the region of Emilia-Romagna, Risotto Alla Milanese is sophisti-cated and luxurious, just like the city of Milan. It makes a terrific first course, or it can be served on the side with grilled meats, poultry, or seafood.

SERVES **4** TO **6**

½ CUP DRY WHITE WINE, SUCH AS SAUVIGNON BLANC OR PINOT GRIGIO, OR DRY VERMOUTH

½ TEASPOON SAFFRON THREADS, CRUSHED IN THE PALM OF YOUR HAND

3 TABLESPOONS UNSALTED BUTTER

1 TABLESPOON EXTRA-VIRGIN OLIVE OIL

1 MEDIUM SHALLOT, FINELY CHOPPED

1 CUP CARNAROLI OR VIALONE NANO RICE

2 CUPS CHICKEN STOCK (PAGE 19) OR STORE-BOUGHT CHICKEN BROTH

¼ CUP FRESHLY GRATED PARMIGIANO-REGGIANO CHEESE, PLUS MORE (OPTIONAL) FOR GARNISH

SALT AND FRESHLY GROUND BLACK PEPPER (OPTIONAL)

1 Pour the wine over the saffron threads in a small measuring cup and set aside. Melt 1 tablespoon of the butter with the oil in the pressure cooker over medium-high heat. Add the shallot and sauté until it is translucent, about 3 minutes. Add the rice and stir to coat with the butter and oil. Stir in the wine and saffron and bring to a boil. Stir in the stock. Lock the lid in place and cook at high pressure for 7 minutes.

2 Quick release the pressure and remove the lid, tilting the pot away from you to allow the steam to escape. Stir in the cheese and the remaining 2 tablespoons of butter. Taste for seasoning and add salt and pepper if necessary. Serve immediately, sprinkled with additional cheese if desired.

RISOTTO AL TARTUFO

Tartufo, or truffles, are luxurious, spectacular additions to a variety of dishes. Unfortunately, truffles are very expensive, but you can incorporate their flavor into your cooking by using a high-quality truffle oil (see the Psst). This dish makes a terrific first course to serve to special friends and family.

SERVES 4 TO 6

4 TABLESPOONS WHITE TRUFFLE OIL, PLUS ADDITIONAL FOR DRIZZLING

1 MEDIUM SHALLOT, FINELY CHOPPED

1½ CUPS CARNAROLI OR VIALONE NANO RICE

½ CUP DRY WHITE WINE, SUCH AS SAUVIGNON BLANC OR PINOT GRIGIO, OR DRY VERMOUTH

3½ CUPS CHICKEN STOCK (PAGE 19) OR STORE-BOUGHT CHICKEN BROTH

ONE 1-OUNCE FRESH TRUFFLE (OPTIONAL)

1 Heat 2 tablespoons of the oil in the pressure cooker over medium-high heat. Add the shallot and cook for 1 to 2 minutes, or until the shallot is softened. Add the rice and stir to coat all the grains with the oil. Add the wine and bring to a boil. Add the stock, lock the lid in place, and cook at high pressure for 7 minutes.

2 Quick release the pressure and remove the lid, tilting the pot away from you to avoid the escaping steam. Stir in the remaining 2 tablespoons of truffle oil and serve immediately. If you've splurged on a fresh truffle, shave some over each portion.

PSST

The best truffle oils come from Italy and France and are infused with a piece of truffle. D'Artagnan, an American company that imports fine foods, has a line of truffle products, including oil, which you can order online (www.dartagnan.com).

SAFFRON RISOTTO WITH SAUSAGE AND SWEET PEAS

Sweet and spicy, this risotto is almost a meal. The saffron gives the rice a golden color and infuses the dish with its exotic flavor.

SERVES **4** TO **6**

½ POUND BULK SWEET ITALIAN SAUSAGE

½ CUP FINELY CHOPPED SHALLOT

1 TEASPOON SAFFRON THREADS, CRUSHED IN THE PALM OF YOUR HAND

1½ CUPS CARNAROLI OR VIALONE NANO RICE

½ CUP DRY WHITE WINE, SUCH AS SAUVIGNON BLANC OR PINOT GRIGIO, OR DRY VERMOUTH

3½ CUPS CHICKEN STOCK (PAGE 19) OR STORE-BOUGHT CHICKEN BROTH

2 TABLESPOONS UNSALTED BUTTER, SOFTENED

1½ CUPS FROZEN PETITE PEAS, DEFROSTED

SALT AND FRESHLY GROUND BLACK PEPPER (OPTIONAL)

1 Sauté the sausage in the pressure cooker over medium-high heat, breaking up any large pieces. When the sausage has lost its pink color, add the shallot and saffron and sauté for 2 minutes, or until the shallot has softened. Add the rice and toss to coat the grains. Add the wine and stir up any browned bits that have stuck to the bottom of the pot. Pour in the stock and stir the risotto. Lock the lid in place and cook at high pressure for 7 minutes.

2 Quick release the pressure and remove the lid, tilting the pot away from you to avoid the escaping steam. Add the butter and peas, stirring to coat the rice with butter and blend the peas into the risotto. Taste for seasoning, add salt and pepper if necessary, and serve immediately.

BUTTERNUT SQUASH AND SAGE RISOTTO

There is something so comforting about butternut squash. It's sweet and becomes almost smooth in the pressure cooker. The addition of fried sage at the end provides a crunchy finale for this beautiful dish.

SERVES 4 TO 6

4 TABLESPOONS UNSALTED BUTTER

½ CUP FINELY CHOPPED SWEET ONION, SUCH AS VIDALIA

2 CUPS CHOPPED BUTTERNUT SQUASH (½-INCH PIECES)

1½ CUPS CARNAROLI OR VIALONE NANO RICE

½ CUP DRY WHITE WINE, SUCH AS SAUVIGNON BLANC OR PINOT GRIGIO, OR DRY VERMOUTH

3½ CUPS CHICKEN STOCK (PAGE 19) OR STORE-BOUGHT CHICKEN BROTH

2 TABLESPOONS EXTRA-VIRGIN OLIVE OIL

¼ CUP PACKED FRESH SAGE LEAVES, THINLY SLICED

¼ CUP FRESHLY GRATED PARMIGIANO-REGGIANO CHEESE

SALT AND FRESHLY GROUND BLACK PEPPER (OPTIONAL)

1 Melt 2 tablespoons of the butter in the pressure cooker over medium-high heat. Add the onion and squash and sauté for 2 to 3 minutes, until the onion begins to soften. Add the rice and stir to coat the grains. Add the wine and bring to a boil. Pour in the stock and stir to combine. Lock the lid in place and cook at high pressure for 7 minutes.

2 While the risotto is cooking, heat the oil in a small skillet over medium-high heat. Fry the sage until crispy, about 5 minutes. Remove the sage from the oil and drain on paper towels.

3 When the risotto is cooked, quick release the pressure and remove the lid, tilting the pot away from you to avoid the escaping steam. Stir in the remaining 2 tablespoons of butter and the cheese and taste for seasoning, adding salt and pepper if needed. Spoon the risotto onto plates and sprinkle with the fried sage leaves.

ZUCCHINI RISOTTO

This creamy zucchini risotto is flavored with leeks and a hint of garlic, along with the final swirl of Parmigiano at the end of the cooking time. Serve it as an elegant first course or a side dish with grilled chicken or lamb.

SERVES 4 TO 6

4 TABLESPOONS UNSALTED BUTTER

1 LEEK (WHITE AND TENDER GREEN PARTS), CLEANED AND THINLY SLICED

3 MEDIUM ZUCCHINI, COARSELY GRATED

1 GARLIC CLOVE, MINCED

1½ CUPS CARNAROLI OR VIALONE NANO RICE

½ CUP DRY WHITE WINE, SUCH AS SAUVIGNON BLANC OR PINOT GRIGIO, OR DRY VERMOUTH

3½ CUPS CHICKEN STOCK (PAGE 19) OR STORE-BOUGHT CHICKEN BROTH

¼ CUP FRESHLY GRATED PARMIGIANO-REGGIANO CHEESE

SALT AND FRESHLY GROUND BLACK PEPPER (OPTIONAL)

1 Melt 2 tablespoons of the butter in the pressure cooker over medium-high heat. Add the leek, zucchini, and garlic and sauté for 2 minutes, or until the leek becomes softened. Add the rice and stir to coat the grains with butter. Add the wine and bring to a boil. Pour in the stock. Lock the lid in place and cook at high pressure for 7 minutes.

2 Quick release the pressure and remove the lid, tilting the pot away from you to avoid the escaping steam. Stir in the remaining 2 tablespoons of butter and the cheese. Taste for seasoning, adding salt and pepper if necessary, and serve immediately.

PECORINO RISOTTO

The sharp flavor of this risotto comes from the Pecorino Romano, a sheep's milk cheese from Umbria, which replaces the usual Parmigiano-Reggiano. If you can find Pecorino with peppercorns, it will enhance the flavor of this simple dish. Serve as a side dish with grilled steak or seafood, or as a first course before a roasted game hen or lemon chicken entrée. It's bound to become a family favorite.

SERVES 4 TO 6

2 TABLESPOONS EXTRA-VIRGIN OLIVE OIL

1½ CUPS CARNAROLI OR VIALONE NANO RICE

½ CUP DRY WHITE WINE, SUCH AS SAUVIGNON BLANC OR PINOT GRIGIO, OR DRY VERMOUTH

3 CUPS CHICKEN STOCK (PAGE 19) OR STORE-BOUGHT CHICKEN BROTH

2 TABLESPOONS UNSALTED BUTTER

⅓ CUP FRESHLY GRATED PECORINO ROMANO, PLUS MORE (OPTIONAL) FOR GARNISH

SALT AND FRESHLY GROUND BLACK PEPPER (OPTIONAL)

1 Heat the oil in the pressure cooker over medium-high heat. Add the rice, stirring to coat the grains with the oil. Add the wine, bring to a boil, and pour in the stock. Lock the lid in place and cook on high pressure for 7 minutes.

2 Quick release the pressure and remove the lid, tilting the pot away from you to avoid the escaping steam. Add the butter and cheese, stirring to melt the cheese. Taste the risotto for seasoning and add salt and pepper if needed. Serve immediately, garnished with additional cheese if desired.

SUN-DRIED TOMATO AND WILD MUSHROOM RISOTTO

Flecked with flavorful sun-dried tomatoes and mushrooms, this risotto makes a delicious first course before a rustic grilled entrée, such as steak, whole fish, pork, or leg of lamb. Use sun-dried tomatoes packed in oil. In addition to the tomatoes, you get the benefit of the oil, which you can use to sauté the vegetables, giving the rice a rich flavor.

SERVES **4** TO **6**

2 TABLESPOONS OIL FROM THE SUN-DRIED TOMATOES OR EXTRA-VIRGIN OLIVE OIL

½ CUP FINELY CHOPPED SWEET ONION, SUCH AS VIDALIA

1 POUND ASSORTED WILD OR CULTIVATED MUSHROOMS (CREMINI, CHANTERELLE, OYSTER, MOREL, SHIITAKE, OR TRUMPET), TOUGH STEMS REMOVED, AND COARSELY CHOPPED

¼ CUP SUN-DRIED TOMATOES PACKED IN OIL, DRAINED AND FINELY CHOPPED

1½ CUPS CARNAROLI OR VIALONE NANO RICE

½ CUP DRY WHITE WINE, SUCH AS SAUVIGNON BLANC OR PINOT GRIGIO

3½ CUPS CHICKEN STOCK (PAGE 19) OR STORE-BOUGHT CHICKEN BROTH

2 TABLESPOONS UNSALTED BUTTER, SOFTENED

¼ CUP FRESHLY GRATED PARMIGIANO-REGGIANO CHEESE

SALT AND FRESHLY GROUND BLACK PEPPER (OPTIONAL)

¼ CUP PACKED FRESH BASIL LEAVES, THINLY SLICED, FOR GARNISH

1 Heat the oil in the pressure cooker over medium-high heat. Add the onion and mushrooms and sauté for 3 minutes, or until the mushrooms begin to soften. Add the tomatoes and stir to combine. Add the rice, stirring to coat the grains with the oil. Pour in the wine, bring to a boil, and add the stock. Lock the lid in place and cook at high pressure for 7 minutes.

2 Quick release the pressure and remove the lid, tilting the pot away from you to avoid the escaping steam. Add the butter and cheese, stirring to melt the cheese. Taste the risotto for seasoning and add salt and pepper if necessary. Serve immediately, garnished with the basil leaves.

PESTO RISOTTO WITH SCAMPI

Garlicky pesto and shrimp are a match made in culinary heaven. The creamy rice absorbs all their scrumptious flavors, which explode in your mouth. I love to serve this with a fruity white wine like Riesling or Chenin Blanc to balance the spicy flavor of the pesto.

SERVES 4

3 TABLESPOONS UNSALTED BUTTER

2 TABLESPOONS EXTRA-VIRGIN OLIVE OIL

2 GARLIC CLOVES, MINCED

1½ CUPS CARNAROLI OR VIALONE NANO RICE

½ CUP DRY WHITE WINE, SUCH AS SAUVIGNON BLANC OR PINOT GRIGIO

3½ CUPS VEGETABLE STOCK (PAGE 21) OR STORE-BOUGHT VEGETABLE BROTH

1 POUND MEDIUM SHRIMP, PEELED AND DEVEINED

½ CUP BASIL PESTO (FACING PAGE)

SALT AND FRESHLY GROUND BLACK PEPPER (OPTIONAL)

1 Melt 1 tablespoon of the butter with the oil in the pressure cooker over medium-high heat. Add the garlic and cook for 30 seconds. Add the rice, stirring to coat the grains with the butter and oil. Add the wine, bring to a boil, and pour in the stock. Lock the lid in place and cook at high pressure for 5 minutes.

2 Quick release the pressure and remove the lid, tilting the pot away from you to avoid the escaping steam. Return the pot to medium heat, stir in the shrimp, and cook until the shrimp turn pink, about 2 minutes. Stir in the pesto and taste for seasoning, adding salt and pepper if necessary. Serve immediately.

BASIL PESTO

MAKES ABOUT 1½ CUPS

1 CUP PACKED FRESH BASIL LEAVES

½ CUP FRESHLY GRATED PARMIGIANO-REGGIANO CHEESE

2 TABLESPOONS PINE NUTS

2 GARLIC CLOVES

¼ CUP EXTRA-VIRGIN OLIVE OIL

1 In the bowl of a food processor or blender, pulse together the basil, cheese, pine nuts, and garlic to break up the ingredients. With the machine running, add the oil, a few drops at a time, until the pesto begins to come together; this pesto will be a thin sauce.

2 Transfer any leftover pesto to a storage container and float a little olive oil on the top. Refrigerate for up to 2 weeks or freeze for up to 4 months. Stir the oil into the pesto when ready to use and bring to room temperature before using.

PSST

In the summer, when fresh basil is plentiful, make extra pesto and freeze it in small containers so you can use it throughout the year.

SHRIMP AND ARTICHOKE RISOTTO

It's a pleasure to bring this dish to the table. The golden saffron, light green artichoke hearts, and delicate pink shrimp make it a real showstopper. The risotto is a delightful first course for any occasion.

SERVES **4** TO **6**

....

1 TEASPOON SAFFRON THREADS, CRUSHED IN THE PALM OF YOUR HAND

½ CUP DRY WHITE WINE, SUCH AS SAUVIGNON BLANC OR PINOT GRIGIO, OR DRY VERMOUTH

4 TABLESPOONS UNSALTED BUTTER

½ CUP FINELY CHOPPED SWEET ONION, SUCH AS VIDALIA

ONE 10-OUNCE PACKAGE FROZEN ARTICHOKE HEARTS, DEFROSTED AND HALVED

1½ CUPS CARNAROLI OR VIALONE NANO RICE

3½ CUPS SEAFOOD STOCK (PAGE 22), LOBSTER STOCK (SEE PSST PAGE 338), OR STORE-BOUGHT SEAFOOD BROTH, OR 2 CUPS CHICKEN STOCK (PAGE 19) OR STORE-BOUGHT CHICKEN BROTH MIXED WITH 1½ CUPS BOTTLED CLAM JUICE

1 POUND MEDIUM SHRIMP, PEELED AND DEVEINED

SALT AND FRESHLY GROUND BLACK PEPPER (OPTIONAL)

1 Sprinkle the saffron over the white wine in a measuring cup and set aside to let the saffron bloom.

2 Melt 2 tablespoons of the butter in the pressure cooker over medium-high heat. Add the onion and artichokes and sauté for 3 minutes, or until they begin to soften. Add the rice and stir to coat the grains with the butter. Pour in the wine and saffron, bring to a boil, and add the stock. Lock the lid in place and cook at high pressure for 5 minutes.

3 Quick release the pressure and remove the lid, tilting the pot away from you to avoid the escaping steam. Return the pot to medium heat, add the shrimp, and cook for 3 to 4 minutes, or until the shrimp have turned pink and the risotto is cooked. Taste for seasoning, add salt and pepper if necessary, and serve immediately.

LUMP CRAB AND CORN RISOTTO

This risotto almost got a standing ovation from my husband. The sweet corn and luscious crabmeat make it a special-occasion dish. I like to use white corn because it is sweet, but yellow corn or a combination of white and yellow corn is fine.

SERVES 6

....

4 TABLESPOONS UNSALTED BUTTER

1 MEDIUM SHALLOT, FINELY CHOPPED

1 TEASPOON OLD BAY SEASONING OR SEAFOOD SEASONING, SUCH AS PENZEYS

1½ CUPS CARNAROLI OR VIALONE NANO RICE

½ CUP DRY WHITE WINE, SUCH AS SAUVIGNON BLANC OR PINOT GRIGIO, OR DRY VERMOUTH

3½ CUPS SEAFOOD STOCK (PAGE 22) OR STORE-BOUGHT SEAFOOD BROTH, OR 2 CUPS CHICKEN STOCK (PAGE 19) OR STORE-BOUGHT CHICKEN BROTH MIXED WITH 1½ CUPS BOTTLED CLAM JUICE

2 CUPS WHITE CORN KERNELS, FRESHLY CUT FROM THE COB, OR FROZEN WHITE CORN, DEFROSTED

½ POUND LUMP CRABMEAT

SALT AND FRESHLY GROUND BLACK PEPPER (OPTIONAL)

¼ CUP FINELY CHOPPED FRESH CHIVES FOR GARNISH

1 Melt 2 tablespoons of the butter in the pressure cooker over medium-high heat. Add the shallot and Old Bay and sauté until the shallot is softened, about 2 minutes. Add the rice, stirring to coat with the butter mixture. Pour in the wine, bring to a boil, and add the stock. Lock the lid in place and cook at high pressure for 5 minutes.

2 Quick release the pressure and remove the lid, tilting the pot away from you to avoid the escaping steam. Return the pot to the stove top and stir in the corn, crab, and remaining 2 tablespoons of butter, stirring until the corn and crab are warm and the rice is creamy, about 3 minutes. Taste for seasoning, add salt and pepper if necessary, and serve immediately, garnishing each serving with some of the chives.

LOBSTER RISOTTO

There is something so decadent about lobster—its rich, sweet flavor balanced by its luxurious texture. Add it to risotto with a bit of brandy, and you have a dish that is truly fit for a king. Use a good-quality lobster stock to flavor this risotto, and make sure to cut the lobster into bite-size pieces so that everyone can enjoy some in each bite.

SERVES 6

4 TABLESPOONS UNSALTED BUTTER

½ CUP FINELY CHOPPED SWEET ONION, SUCH AS VIDALIA

1½ CUPS CARNAROLI OR VIALONE NANO RICE

½ CUP BRANDY

3½ CUPS LOBSTER STOCK (SEE PSST)

2 CUPS COOKED LOBSTER MEAT, CUT INTO BITE-SIZE PIECES

SALT AND FRESHLY GROUND BLACK PEPPER (OPTIONAL)

1 Melt 2 tablespoons of the butter in the pressure cooker over medium-high heat. Add the onion and sauté for 2 minutes, or until the onion begins to soften. Add the rice and stir to coat the grains with the butter. Add the brandy, bring to a boil, and add the stock. Lock the lid in place and cook at high pressure for 6 minutes.

2 Quick release the pressure and remove the lid, tilting the pot away from you to avoid the escaping steam. Stir in the remaining 2 tablespoons of butter and the lobster meat and return the pot to medium heat. Cook for another minute, or until the lobster is warm and the rice is creamy. Taste for seasoning, adding salt and pepper if needed. Serve immediately.

PSST

You can buy lobster stock at gourmet markets or your local fish market. Better Than Bouillon makes a lobster stock base that I love as a backup. Cooked lobster meat is available at local fish markets, too. You may have to buy a whole lobster and have the fishmonger steam it for you so you can remove the meat.

LEMON RISOTTO

This zesty risotto, finished with lemon rind and juice, makes a fine bed for grilled seafood or a first course before a seafood dinner. Since most supermarket lemons are treated with wax, be sure to remove the wax with a plastic scrubber. Otherwise, the wax from the rind will melt into your risotto.

SERVES 6

3 TABLESPOONS UNSALTED BUTTER

1 TABLESPOON EXTRA-VIRGIN OLIVE OIL

½ CUP FINELY CHOPPED SWEET ONION, SUCH AS VIDALIA

1½ CUPS CARNAROLI OR VIALONE NANO RICE

½ CUP DRY WHITE WINE, SUCH AS SAUVIGNON BLANC OR PINOT GRIGIO, OR DRY VERMOUTH

3 CUPS CHICKEN OR VEGETABLE STOCK (PAGE 19 OR 21) OR STORE-BOUGHT CHICKEN OR VEGETABLE BROTH

2 TABLESPOONS FRESH LEMON JUICE

1 TABLESPOON GRATED LEMON ZEST

½ CUP FRESHLY GRATED PARMIGIANO-REGGIANO CHEESE

SALT AND FRESHLY GROUND BLACK PEPPER (OPTIONAL)

¼ CUP FINELY CHOPPED FRESH FLAT-LEAF PARSLEY FOR GARNISH

1 Melt 2 tablespoons of the butter with the oil in the pressure cooker over medium-high heat. Add the onion and sauté for 2 minutes, or until the onion begins to soften. Add the rice and stir to coat the grains. Add the wine, bring to a boil, and pour in the stock. Lock the lid in place and cook at high pressure for 6 minutes.

2 Quick release the pressure and remove the lid, tilting the pot away from you to avoid the escaping steam. Return the pot to medium heat, stir in the juice and lemon zest, and cook stirring for another minute, or until the rice is al dente. Remove from the heat and stir in the cheese. Taste for seasoning and add salt and pepper if needed. Serve immediately, garnishing each serving with a sprinkling of parsley.

WILD MUSHROOM RISOTTO

This makes a terrific starter, which pairs well with a full-bodied red wine, such as Chianti, Zinfandel, or Barolo. Choose an assortment of mushrooms for the dish.

SERVES 6

3 TABLESPOONS UNSALTED BUTTER

1 TABLESPOON EXTRA-VIRGIN OLIVE OIL

1 MEDIUM SHALLOT, FINELY CHOPPED

1 POUND ASSORTED WILD OR CULTIVATED MUSHROOMS (CREMINI, CHANTERELLE, OYSTER, MOREL, SHIITAKE, OR TRUMPET), TOUGH STEMS REMOVED, AND FINELY CHOPPED

2 TEASPOONS FINELY CHOPPED FRESH SAGE

1½ CUPS CARNAROLI OR VIALONE NANO RICE

½ CUP DRY WHITE WINE, SUCH AS SAUVIGNON BLANC OR PINOT GRIGIO, OR DRY VERMOUTH

2 CUPS CHICKEN STOCK (PAGE 19) OR STORE-BOUGHT CHICKEN BROTH

1½ CUPS BEEF STOCK (PAGE 20) OR STORE-BOUGHT BEEF BROTH

½ CUP FRESHLY GRATED PARMIGIANO-REGGIANO CHEESE

SALT AND FRESHLY GROUND BLACK PEPPER (OPTIONAL)

¼ CUP FINELY CHOPPED CHIVES

1 Melt 2 tablespoons of the butter with the oil in the pressure cooker over medium-high heat. Add the shallot and cook for 2 minutes, or until the shallot is softened. Add the mushrooms and sage to the pot and cook for 10 to 12 minutes, or until the liquid from the mushrooms has evaporated. Add the rice and wine, bring to a boil, and add the stocks. Lock the lid in place and cook at high pressure for 7 minutes.

2 Quick release the pressure and remove the lid, tilting the pot away from you to avoid the escaping steam. Stir in the remaining tablespoon of butter and the cheese. Taste for seasoning and add salt and pepper if needed. Garnish with the chives and serve immediately.

PSST

This risotto is delicious with peas. At the end of the cooking time, add 1 cup of defrosted frozen petite peas and stir to combine.

ZUCCHINI AND LEEK RISOTTO

A lovely taste of spring, this beautifully colored, subtly flavored risotto is just the dish to brighten up dinnertime.

SERVES 6

4 TABLESPOONS UNSALTED BUTTER

2 MEDIUM LEEKS (WHITE AND TENDER GREEN PARTS), CLEANED AND FINELY CHOPPED

2 MEDIUM ZUCCHINI, SHREDDED

1½ CUPS CARNAROLI OR VIALONE NANO RICE

½ CUP DRY WHITE WINE, SUCH AS SAUVIGNON BLANC OR PINOT GRIGIO, OR DRY VERMOUTH

3½ CUPS CHICKEN OR VEGETABLE STOCK (PAGE 19 OR 21) OR STORE-BOUGHT CHICKEN OR VEGETABLE BROTH

1 CUP FRESHLY GRATED PARMIGIANO-REGGIANO CHEESE

SALT AND FRESHLY GROUND BLACK PEPPER (OPTIONAL)

¼ CUP FINELY CHOPPED FRESH CHIVES FOR GARNISH

1 Melt 2 tablespoons of the butter in the pressure cooker over medium-high heat. Add the leeks and zucchini and sauté for 2 to 3 minutes, until the leeks begin to soften. Add the rice, stirring to coat the grains. Add the wine and bring to a boil. Add the stock, lock the lid in place, and cook at high pressure for 7 minutes.

2 Quick release the pressure and remove the lid, tilting the pot away from you to avoid the escaping steam. Stir in the remaining butter and the Parmigiano. Taste for seasoning and add salt and pepper if needed. Serve immediately, garnished with the chives.

ARTICHOKE RISOTTO

I have the pleasure of teaching at La Combe in Périgord, in the Dordogne region of France. One year, I was there when artichokes were in season, and we had them at every meal. This risotto was served one night as the first course, a very special one, before our dinner of roast baby lamb. You can also serve it as a side dish with grilled or roasted entrées.

SERVES **6** TO **8**

5 TABLESPOONS UNSALTED BUTTER

1 MEDIUM ONION, FINELY CHOPPED

1 GARLIC CLOVE, MINCED

TWO 10-OUNCE PACKAGES FROZEN ARTICHOKE HEARTS, DEFROSTED

1½ CUPS CARNAROLI OR VIALONE NANO RICE

½ CUP DRY WHITE WINE, SUCH AS SAUVIGNON BLANC OR PINOT GRIGIO, OR DRY VERMOUTH

3½ CUPS CHICKEN OR VEGETABLE STOCK (PAGE 19 OR 21) OR STORE-BOUGHT CHICKEN OR VEGETABLE BROTH

1 CUP FRESHLY GRATED PARMIGIANO-REGGIANO CHEESE

SALT AND FRESHLY GROUND BLACK PEPPER (OPTIONAL)

1 Melt 3 tablespoons of the butter in the pressure cooker over medium-high heat. Add the onion and garlic and cook for 2 minutes to soften the onion. Add the artichoke hearts and sauté for another 5 to 6 minutes, or until they begin to turn golden. Add the rice and stir to coat the grains of rice with the butter. Add the wine, bring to a boil, and pour in the stock. Lock the lid in place and cook at high pressure for 7 minutes.

2 Quick release the pressure and remove the lid, tilting the pot way from you to avoid the escaping steam. Add the remaining 2 tablespoons of butter and ½ cup of the cheese, stirring until the butter and cheese are melted. Taste for seasoning, adding salt and pepper if necessary. Serve immediately, garnished with the remaining ½ cup of cheese.

RISOTTO WITH GORGONZOLA AND RADICCHIO

I call this risotto "red, white, and blue" because it's garnished with thinly sliced radicchio and includes a cupful of Gorgonzola cheese. Serve this when roast or grilled beef is on the menu. Begin the meal with a wallop of flavor or serve the risotto as a side dish.

SERVES 6

3 TABLESPOONS UNSALTED BUTTER

2 MEDIUM SHALLOTS, FINELY CHOPPED

1½ CUPS CARNAROLI OR VIALONE NANO RICE

½ CUP DRY WHITE WINE, SUCH AS SAUVIGNON BLANC OR PINOT GRIGIO, OR DRY VERMOUTH

3½ CUPS CHICKEN STOCK (PAGE 19) OR STORE-BOUGHT CHICKEN BROTH

¼ POUND GORGONZOLA, CRUMBLED (ABOUT 1 CUP)

SALT AND FRESHLY GROUND BLACK PEPPER (OPTIONAL)

1 HEAD RADICCHIO, THINLY SLICED (ABOUT 1 CUP) FOR GARNISH

1 Melt 2 tablespoons of the butter in the pressure cooker over medium-high heat. Add the shallots and cook for 3 minutes, or until the shallots are softened. Add the rice and stir to coat the grains of rice. Add the wine, bring to a boil, and stir in the stock. Lock the lid in place and cook at high pressure for 7 minutes.

2 Quick release the pressure and remove the lid, tilting the pot away from you to avoid the escaping steam. Stir in the remaining tablespoon of butter and the cheese. Taste for seasoning, adding salt and pepper if needed. Garnish each serving with some of the radicchio.

SWEET PEA, CORN, AND PANCETTA RISOTTO

Sweet and smoky, this colorful risotto is almost a meal in itself. Serve it with grilled or roasted chicken, salmon, or shrimp.

SERVES 6

4 TABLESPOONS UNSALTED BUTTER

2 PANCETTA SLICES, FINELY CHOPPED

½ CUP FINELY CHOPPED SWEET ONION, SUCH AS VIDALIA

1½ CUPS CARNAROLI OR VIALONE NANO RICE

½ CUP DRY WHITE WINE, SUCH AS SAUVIGNON BLANC OR PINOT GRIGIO, OR DRY VERMOUTH

3½ CUPS CHICKEN OR VEGETABLE STOCK (PAGE 19 OR 21) OR STORE-BOUGHT CHICKEN OR VEGETABLE BROTH

1 CUP CORN KERNELS, FRESHLY CUT FROM THE COB, OR FROZEN CORN, DEFROSTED

1 CUP FROZEN PETITE PEAS, DEFROSTED

½ CUP FRESHLY GRATED PARMIGIANO-REGGIANO CHEESE

SALT AND FRESHLY GROUND BLACK PEPPER (OPTIONAL)

¼ CUP FINELY CHOPPED FRESH CHIVES FOR GARNISH

1 Melt 2 tablespoons of the butter in the pressure cooker over medium-high heat. Add the pancetta and sauté for 3 to 4 minutes, until the fat from the pancetta is rendered. Add the onion and sauté for 2 minutes, or until it begins to soften. Add the rice, stirring to coat the grains with the fat. Add the wine, bring to a boil, and stir in the stock. Lock the lid in place and cook at high pressure for 6 minutes.

2 Quick release the pressure and remove the lid, tilting the pot away from you to avoid the escaping steam. Return the pot to medium heat and add the corn and peas. Cook, stirring, for an additional minute. Stir in the remaining 2 tablespoons of butter and the cheese. Taste for seasoning, adding salt and pepper if necessary. Serve immediately, garnished with the chives.

BASIC WILD RICE

Nutty, chewy wild rice can turn an ordinary dinner into an occasion because it's a little out of the ordinary. It cooks beautifully in the pressure cooker and can be refrigerated or frozen to use later in casseroles, salads, soups, and pilafs.

MAKES **4** CUPS

1 CUP WILD RICE

4 CUPS CHICKEN OR VEGETABLE STOCK (PAGE 19 OR 21) OR STORE-BOUGHT CHICKEN OR VEGETABLE BROTH

1 TABLESPOON CANOLA OIL

SALT AND FRESHLY GROUND BLACK PEPPER (OPTIONAL)

1 Combine the rice and stock in the pressure cooker and drizzle the oil over the stock. Lock the lid in place and cook at high pressure for 20 minutes.

2 Quick release the pressure and remove the lid, tilting the pot away from you to avoid the escaping steam. Taste for seasoning and add salt and pepper if needed. The rice will not have absorbed all the liquid. Use a slotted spoon to transfer the rice to a serving bowl or let cool and transfer to airtight storage containers and refrigerate for up to 3 days or freeze for up to 3 months.

FRUITED WILD RICE

With its crunchy texture, wild rice pairs well with dried fruit and a snappy Granny Smith apple. This is terrific for stuffing Cornish game hens or to serve as a side dish with roast turkey, chicken, or pork. Feel free to vary the fruit to suit your family members' tastes.

SERVES **6**

1 CUP WILD RICE

1 CUP DRIED CRANBERRIES

1 TEASPOON DRIED THYME

4 CUPS CHICKEN OR VEGETABLE STOCK (PAGE 19 OR 21) OR STORE-BOUGHT CHICKEN OR VEGETABLE BROTH

1 TABLESPOON CANOLA OIL

4 TABLESPOONS UNSALTED BUTTER

½ CUP FINELY CHOPPED SHALLOTS

1 GRANNY SMITH APPLE, CORED AND CUT INTO ½-INCH PIECES

SALT AND FRESHLY GROUND BLACK PEPPER (OPTIONAL)

1 Combine the rice, cranberries, thyme, and stock in the pressure cooker. Drizzle the oil over the stock. Lock the lid in place and cook at high pressure for 20 minutes.

2 While the rice is cooking, melt the butter in a large skillet over medium-high heat. Add the shallots and apple and cook for 4 minutes, or until the shallots are softened.

3 When the rice has cooked, quick release the pressure and remove the lid, tilting the pot away from you to avoid the escaping steam. There will still be liquid in the pot, so use a slotted spoon to transfer the rice and cranberry mixture to the skillet. Toss to combine with the shallots and apple. Taste for seasoning and add salt and pepper if necessary.

4 Transfer the rice to a serving bowl and serve immediately. Or, if you would like to use the rice for a stuffing, let it cool to room temperature before using.

CREMINI WILD RICE WITH TOASTED ALMONDS

Meaty cremini mushrooms are actually midget portobellos. With that connection established, you won't be surprised to learn that this dish has a hearty, stick-to-your-ribs quality that complements roast prime rib, grilled pork chops, or steak. The garnish of toasted almonds gives the dish extra crunch.

SERVES 6

1 CUP WILD RICE

4 CUPS CHICKEN OR BEEF STOCK (PAGE 19 OR 20) OR STORE-BOUGHT CHICKEN OR BEEF BROTH

1 TABLESPOON CANOLA OIL

4 TABLESPOONS UNSALTED BUTTER

½ CUP FINELY CHOPPED SWEET ONION, SUCH AS VIDALIA

1 POUND CREMINI MUSHROOMS, SLICED

2 TEASPOONS FINELY CHOPPED FRESH SAGE

2 TABLESPOONS DRY SHERRY

SALT AND FRESHLY GROUND BLACK PEPPER

1 CUP TOASTED SLICED ALMONDS (SEE PSST ON PAGE 114) FOR GARNISH

1 Combine the rice and stock in the pressure cooker and drizzle the oil over the stock. Lock the lid in place and cook at high pressure for 20 minutes.

2 While the rice is cooking, melt the butter in a large skillet over medium-high heat. Add the onion, mushrooms, and sage and sauté until the mushrooms begin to turn golden. Add the sherry, bring it to a boil, and season with salt and pepper. Set aside.

3 After the rice has cooked, quick release the pressure and remove the lid, tilting the pot away from you to avoid the escaping steam. There will still be liquid in the pot, so use a slotted spoon to transfer the rice to the skillet. Stir the rice with the onion and mushrooms to combine. Taste for seasoning and add more salt and pepper if needed. Transfer to a serving bowl and garnish with the toasted almonds.

WHOLE GRAINS

The benefits of whole grains in the diet have been touted for years, but many of us shy away from cooking with them, either from a lack of knowledge or because they can take extra time to prepare. Cooking whole grains isn't difficult, though, and with a pressure cooker, you can cook them in the same time it would take to make a batch of rice on the stove top. Whole grains are delicious in one-pot meals, soups, and salads. Although there are many different grains to choose from in health food and natural grocery stores, I've stuck with the ones that are simple to prepare and family friendly, including farro, bulgur, quinoa, and barley.

Farro is an ancient grain that was eaten by the Romans for centuries. In more recent times, other grains gained favor with the public, and farro all but disappeared. Then some wily French chefs started serving it in soups and casseroles. Italians, not to be outdone, began to harvest the few remaining fields of farro. Now it can be found on many menus in Umbria and Tuscany. Farro has a chewy texture, which lends itself to soups, salads, and casseroles. It is sometimes confused with two other grains: spelt and emmer wheat. Farro cooks differently from these grains, and they should not be substituted in recipes calling for farro. Farro is high in protein like other grains and has the added benefits of vitamins A, C, and E, and the B vitamins.

Bulgur wheat is made from wheat kernels that have been steamed, dried, and crushed. It is rich in fiber and B vitamins, as well as minerals. Bulgur has a chewy texture similar to brown rice and can be added to salads, pilaf, and soups.

Quinoa (pronounced KEEN-wah) is another ancient grain. It's packed with protein and contains a lot of iron and lysine, which is an amino acid. These small grains are good in salads and in hot dishes containing vegetables.

Protein-rich barley is high in minerals, as well as folic acid. It has a chewy texture and can be used in place of potatoes or rice at the dinner table, but I think it shines in soups, stews, and salads. Barley can also be cooked as a breakfast cereal with steamed milk and honey, for a great send-off in the morning.

GRAIN	COOKING TIME AT HIGH PRESSURE
Barley	18 minutes
Bulgur	6 minutes
Farro	12 minutes
Oatmeal (steel-cut)	5 minutes
Polenta	9 minutes
Quinoa	5 minutes

These cooking times are based on a quick release of pressure.

BASIC FARRO

Simple to prepare, cooked farro is especially good in soups and salads. But you can also eat it as is, with a drizzle of good olive oil over the top.

MAKES **4** TO **5** CUPS

2 TABLESPOONS EXTRA-VIRGIN OLIVE OIL

2 CUPS FARRO, RINSED AND DRAINED

6 CUPS CHICKEN OR VEGETABLE STOCK (PAGE 19 OR 21) OR STORE-BOUGHT CHICKEN OR VEGETABLE BROTH OR WATER

1½ TEASPOONS SALT

½ TEASPOON FRESHLY GROUND BLACK PEPPER

1 Combine all the ingredients in the pressure cooker, lock the lid in place, and cook at high pressure for 12 minutes.

2 Quick release the pressure and remove the lid, tilting the pot away from you to avoid the escaping steam. Fluff the farro and serve, or let cool and store in airtight containers in the refrigerator for up to 3 days or in the freezer for up to 3 months.

FARRO RISOTTO

Farro becomes creamy like Italian rice in risotto, and like all risottos, this one can be served as a first course or as a side. Feel free to add your favorite vegetables; artichoke hearts, zucchini, carrots, and spinach are all great add-ins.

SERVES 4

4 TABLESPOONS UNSALTED BUTTER

1 MEDIUM SHALLOT, FINELY CHOPPED

½ TEASPOON SAFFRON THREADS, CRUSHED IN THE PALM OF YOUR HAND

1 CUP FARRO, RINSED AND DRAINED

½ CUP DRY WHITE WINE, SUCH AS SAUVIGNON BLANC OR PINOT GRIGIO, OR DRY VERMOUTH

2½ CUPS CHICKEN STOCK (PAGE 19) OR STORE-BOUGHT CHICKEN BROTH

¼ CUP FINELY GRATED PARMIGIANO-REGGIANO CHEESE

SALT AND FRESHLY GROUND BLACK PEPPER (OPTIONAL)

1 Melt 2 tablespoons of the butter in the pressure cooker over medium-high heat. Add the shallot and saffron and sauté for 2 minutes, or until the shallot is softened. Add the farro and toss in the butter mixture to coat. Add the wine and cook until the wine has almost completely evaporated and a thin film remains on the bottom of the pot. Pour in the stock. Lock the lid in place and cook at high pressure for 12 minutes.

2 Quick release the pressure and remove the lid, tilting the pot away from you to avoid the escaping steam. Stir in the remaining 2 tablespoons of butter and the cheese and taste for seasoning, adding salt and pepper if needed. Serve immediately.

KALE AND FARRO RISOTTO

My daughter, Carrie, and her family love farro's chewy texture and nutritional goodness. They developed this risotto recipe for the pressure cooker, and we all loved the results and the rich flavor of the kale. If you aren't fond of kale, however, Swiss chard leaves make a nice substitute.

MAKES **4** TO **5** CUPS

4 TABLESPOONS UNSALTED BUTTER

1 MEDIUM SHALLOT, FINELY CHOPPED

2 GARLIC CLOVES, MINCED

2 CUPS THINLY SLICED KALE

1 TEASPOON SALT

½ TEASPOON FRESHLY GROUND BLACK PEPPER

1 CUP FARRO, RINSED AND DRAINED

½ CUP DRY WHITE WINE, SUCH AS SAUVIGNON BLANC OR PINOT GRIGIO, OR DRY VERMOUTH

2½ CUPS CHICKEN STOCK (PAGE 19) OR STORE-BOUGHT CHICKEN BROTH

¼ CUP FINELY GRATED PARMIGIANO-REGGIANO CHEESE

1 Melt 2 tablespoons of the butter in the pressure cooker over medium-high heat, add the shallot and garlic and sauté for 2 minutes, or until the shallot softens. Add the kale and sauté for 1 minute to coat with the butter and garlic mixture. Season the kale with the salt and pepper and add the farro and wine. Cook until the wine has almost completely evaporated and there is only a thin film on the bottom of the pot. Pour in the stock. Lock the lid in place and cook at high pressure for 12 minutes.

2 Quick release the pressure and remove the lid, tilting the pot away from you to avoid the escaping steam. Taste the farro. If it is still not tender, lock the lid in place and let the farro steam for 5 minutes. Remove the lid and stir in the remaining 2 tablespoons of butter and the cheese. Serve immediately.

FARRO AND CHICKPEA SALAD

Farro is terrific in salads because it absorbs the dressing without getting soggy. This salad is a riot of color, and the green zucchini, red tomatoes, and basil add flavor and texture, in addition to brightening up the dish.

SERVES 6

4 CUPS BASIC FARRO (PAGE 351), COOLED

½ CUP FINELY CHOPPED RED ONION

ONE 15½-OUNCE CAN CHICKPEAS, RINSED AND DRAINED

2 MEDIUM ZUCCHINI, FINELY CHOPPED

1 CUP CHERRY TOMATOES, QUARTERED

½ CUP PACKED FRESH BASIL LEAVES, FINELY CHOPPED

½ CUP EXTRA-VIRGIN OLIVE OIL

¼ CUP RICE VINEGAR

1 TEASPOON SALT, PLUS MORE IF NEEDED

½ TEASPOON FRESHLY GROUND BLACK PEPPER, PLUS MORE IF NEEDED

TOASTED PINE NUTS FOR GARNISH

1 In a large serving bowl, combine the farro, onion, chickpeas, zucchini, tomatoes, and basil. In a small bowl, whisk together the oil, vinegar, salt, and pepper. Taste the dressing for seasoning and add more salt and pepper if needed.

2 Pour the dressing over the salad and toss to combine. Serve the salad at room temperature, garnished with the toasted pine nuts.

PSST

If you would like to make the salad in advance, make the dressing, along with the salad, and refrigerate them separately. Take the salad out of the refrigerator 30 minutes before serving and toss with the dressing just before serving.

FARRO AND ARTICHOKE SALAD

Artichoke hearts, kalamata olives, red bell pepper, chunks of Pecorino Romano cheese, and a tasty sun-dried tomato vinaigrette come together for a scrumptious summer salad. Serve it as a main course. It's a great way to use cooked farro and leftover cooked chicken.

SERVES 6

4 CUPS BASIC FARRO (PAGE 351)

2 CUPS FINELY CHOPPED COOKED CHICKEN

ONE 10-OUNCE PACKAGE FROZEN ARTICHOKE HEARTS, DEFROSTED AND QUARTERED

1 CUP KALAMATA OLIVES, PITTED AND COARSELY CHOPPED

1 MEDIUM RED BELL PEPPER, SEEDED, DERIBBED, AND FINELY CHOPPED

1 CUP CHOPPED PECORINO ROMANO (½-INCH PIECES), PREFERABLY WITH BLACK PEPPERCORNS

½ CUP EXTRA-VIRGIN OLIVE OIL

3 TABLESPOONS RED WINE VINEGAR

½ CUP SUN-DRIED TOMATOES PACKED IN OIL, DRAINED

1 TABLESPOON FINELY CHOPPED FRESH OREGANO

GRATED ZEST OF 1 LEMON

1 TEASPOON SALT, PLUS MORE IF NEEDED

½ TEASPOON FRESHLY GROUND BLACK PEPPER, PLUS MORE IF NEEDED

In a large bowl, combine the farro, chicken, artichoke hearts, olives, bell pepper, and cheese. In the food processor or blender, process the oil, vinegar, sun-dried tomatoes, oregano, zest, salt, and pepper. Taste the dressing for seasoning and add more salt and pepper if needed. Pour the dressing over the salad, toss to coat the ingredients, and serve immediately.

BREAKFAST FARRO

It is an Umbrian tradition to serve farro to women who have just given birth. Its many nutritional benefits help with the recovery process and are said to aid in milk production. Even if you're not a new mother, this is a terrific way to start the day. I recommend that you find a lovely lavender, sage, or orange blossom honey to serve with this dish. It is a riff on one served at Le Pain Quotidien in Beverly Hills.

SERVES 4

4 CUPS MILK

¼ TEASPOON ALMOND EXTRACT

½ TEASPOON VANILLA BEAN PASTE (SEE PSST)

¼ CUP FIRMLY PACKED LIGHT BROWN SUGAR

½ TEASPOON SALT

1 CUP FARRO, RINSED AND DRAINED

½ CUP DRIED CRANBERRIES (SEE PSST)

½ CUP TOASTED PECANS (SEE PSST ON PAGE 114) FOR GARNISH

½ CUP TOASTED WALNUTS (SEE PSST ON PAGE 114) FOR GARNISH

¼ CUP ORANGE BLOSSOM, SAGE, OR LAVENDER HONEY FOR DRIZZLING

1 Coat the inside of the pressure cooker with nonstick cooking spray. Add 3 cups of the milk, the almond extract, vanilla bean paste, and sugar to the pot, whisking to blend. Add the salt, farro, and cranberries. Lock the lid in place and cook at high pressure for 12 minutes. While the farro is cooking, heat the remaining 1 cup of milk and pour into a small pitcher.

2 Quick release the pressure and remove the lid, tilting the pot away from you to avoid the escaping steam. Stir the mixture and spoon 1-cup servings into bowls. Pour a bit of hot milk over each portion and garnish with the nuts and a drizzle of honey.

PSST

Vanilla bean paste is chopped vanilla beans in an emulsion. I prefer the paste over vanilla extract for cooked dishes like this one. Vanilla extract contains so much alcohol that it burns off during cooking. The manufacturer recommends making a 1:1 substitution—meaning if a recipe calls for 1 teaspoon of extract, substitute 1 teaspoon of paste. I hope you will try it; I know you will be sold!

You can substitute dried blueberries, cherries, or finely chopped apricots for the cranberries.

BASIC BULGUR

Simple to prepare, bulgur is super to add to salads, soups, and casseroles. This basic recipe can be the jumping-off point for many delicious dishes made with this stellar grain.

MAKES ABOUT **5** CUPS

2 CUPS BULGUR, RINSED AND DRAINED (SEE PSST)

4 CUPS CHICKEN OR VEGETABLE STOCK (PAGE 19 OR 21) OR STORE-BOUGHT CHICKEN OR VEGETABLE BROTH OR WATER

2 TEASPOONS SALT, PLUS MORE IF NEEDED

FRESHLY GROUND BLACK PEPPER

EXTRA-VIRGIN OLIVE OIL FOR DRIZZLING

1 In the pressure cooker, combine the bulgur, stock, and salt. Lock the lid in place and cook at high pressure for 6 minutes.

2 Quick release the pressure and remove the lid, tilting the pot away from you to avoid the escaping steam. Fluff the bulgur, season with pepper and additional salt if necessary, and serve drizzled with the olive oil. Or let cool and store in airtight containers in the refrigerator for up to 4 days or in the freezer for up to 3 months.

PSST

Bob's Red Mill bulgur is toasted and has a wonderful nutty flavor. If your supermarket doesn't carry it, try your local organic or health food market.

MEDITERRANEAN BULGUR SALAD

Bulgur is mostly found in that ubiquitous salad, tabbouleh, which often languishes at local deli counters, with no takers. Tabbouleh is a Lebanese dish with lots of chopped parsley, cooked bulgur, and a dressing. The deli version can be pretty lackluster, but this salad takes the flavors of the Mediterranean and transforms that sad deli salad into a sunny, lemon-flavored one. It's a terrific side dish for a barbecue or picnic. The salad should be served at room temperature. If you need to make it ahead of time, dress it right before serving.

SERVES 6

1 RECIPE BASIC BULGUR (PAGE 357)

4 SCALLIONS (WHITE AND TENDER GREEN PARTS), FINELY CHOPPED

3 CELERY STALKS, FINELY CHOPPED

½ CUP KALAMATA OLIVES, PITTED AND FINELY CHOPPED

1 CUP CHERRY TOMATOES, QUARTERED

1½ CUPS CRUMBLED FETA CHEESE

¼ CUP FINELY CHOPPED FRESH FLAT-LEAF PARSLEY

1 TABLESPOON FINELY CHOPPED FRESH MINT

⅔ CUP EXTRA-VIRGIN OLIVE OIL

¼ CUP FRESH LEMON JUICE

GRATED ZEST OF 1 LEMON

1 TEASPOON SALT

½ TEASPOON FRESHLY GROUND BLACK PEPPER

2 GARLIC CLOVES, MINCED

In a large salad bowl, combine the bulgur, scallions, celery, olives, tomatoes, feta, parsley, and mint. In a small bowl, whisk together the oil, lemon juice and zest, salt, pepper, and garlic until blended. Pour the dressing over the salad and toss to coat the ingredients. Serve the salad at room temperature.

BULGUR AND BEET SALAD

Colorful and good for you, this salad offers a different flavor and texture in every bite. If you can find varicolored beets, they will provide a gorgeous contrast with the cooked bulgur and make a statement on the dinner table.

SERVES **6**

....

1 CUP WATER

4 MEDIUM BEETS

3 CUPS BASIC BULGUR (PAGE 357)

¼ CUP FINELY CHOPPED SHALLOT

ONE 10-OUNCE BAG BABY SPINACH, FINELY CHOPPED

⅔ CUP CANOLA OIL

⅓ CUP RICE VINEGAR

2 TABLESPOONS SUGAR

¼ CUP PACKED FRESH BASIL LEAVES, FINELY CHOPPED

1 TEASPOON SALT

½ TEASPOON FRESHLY GROUND BLACK PEPPER

1 CUP CRUMBLED FRESH GOAT CHEESE

1 Pour the water into the pressure cooker. Arrange the trivet and steamer in the bottom and put the beets in the basket. Lock the lid in place and cook at high pressure for 15 minutes.

2 Quick release the pressure and remove the lid, tilting the pot away from you to avoid the escaping steam. Insert the sharp tip of a knife into the center of a beet to make sure it is tender. Allow the beets to cool and then peel and cut into ½-inch dice.

3 In a large serving bowl, combine the beets with the bulgur, shallot, and spinach. In a small mixing bowl, whisk together the oil, vinegar, sugar, basil, salt, and pepper until blended. Pour over the salad and toss to coat the ingredients. Add the goat cheese and toss again. Serve the salad at room temperature.

BASIC BARLEY

Here's another whole grain that can help to stretch your food dollar when it's included in soups and salads. Use broth if you want to flavor the barley, or water if you plan to use it in salads and you want the barley to absorb the flavors of the dressing. Barley has a tendency to foam when cooked under pressure, and a drizzle of oil helps to keep it down. If you're not using the barley right away, store it in the refrigerator or freezer.

MAKES ABOUT **4** CUPS

....

1¾ CUPS PEARL BARLEY

6 CUPS WATER OR CHICKEN OR VEGETABLE STOCK (PAGE 19 OR 21) OR STORE-BOUGHT CHICKEN OR VEGETABLE BROTH

2 TEASPOONS SALT (OPTIONAL)

1 TABLESPOON CANOLA OIL

1 Combine the barley, water, and salt (if using water) in the pressure cooker. Drizzle the oil over the water. Lock the lid in place and cook at high pressure for 18 minutes.

2 Quick release the pressure and remove the lid, tilting the pot away from you to avoid the escaping steam. Fluff the barley and transfer it to a serving bowl with a slotted spoon. Serve immediately or refrigerate for up to 3 days or freeze for up to 2 months in airtight containers.

BARLEY SALAD WITH CORN, BACON, AND SNAP PEAS

Smoky and sweet, this salad is a great change of pace from pasta salads and travels well in case you want to take it along to a potluck or tailgate party. Feel free to customize the salad with your favorite vegetables or the overflow from your garden. Chopped tomatoes and zucchini make good additions.

SERVES **6**

3 CUPS BASIC BARLEY (FACING PAGE)

4 THICK-CUT BACON STRIPS, CUT CROSSWISE INTO PIECES ½ INCH WIDE

½ CUP FINELY CHOPPED RED ONION

2 CUPS CORN KERNELS, FRESHLY CUT FROM THE COB, OR FROZEN CORN, DEFROSTED

1 CUP SUGAR SNAP PEAS, TRIMMED AND TOUGH STRINGS REMOVED

2 TABLESPOONS CANOLA OIL

2 TABLESPOONS LIGHT BROWN SUGAR

2 TABLESPOONS RED WINE VINEGAR

1 TEASPOON DIJON MUSTARD

SALT AND FRESHLY GROUND BLACK PEPPER (OPTIONAL)

1 Put the barley in a large serving bowl. In a large skillet over medium-high heat, cook the bacon until crisp, remove from the pot, and drain on paper towels. Add the onion, corn, and snap peas to the pan and sauté for 3 to 4 minutes, or until the onion is softened. Transfer the vegetables to the serving bowl with the barley.

2 Combine the oil, sugar, vinegar, and mustard in the same skillet over medium-high heat and bring to a boil. Remove the dressing from the heat and pour over the barley and vegetables, mixing to coat the salad ingredients with the dressing. Taste for seasoning and add salt and pepper if needed. Garnish the salad with the crisp bacon and serve.

CRANBERRY BARLEY

A terrific substitute for rice or potatoes on the dinner table, this thyme-scented barley has lovely tender cranberries throughout. The toasted almond garnish adds a nice crunch. This dish would also make a terrific stuffing for a crown roast of pork or a bed for serving roast turkey or game hens.

SERVES 6

2 TABLESPOONS UNSALTED BUTTER

½ CUP FINELY CHOPPED SWEET ONION, SUCH AS VIDALIA

3 CELERY STALKS, FINELY CHOPPED

1 TEASPOON DRIED THYME

1¼ CUPS PEARL BARLEY

1 CUP DRIED CRANBERRIES

5 CUPS CHICKEN STOCK (PAGE 19) OR STORE-BOUGHT CHICKEN BROTH

1 TABLESPOON CANOLA OIL

SALT AND FRESHLY GROUND BLACK PEPPER

½ CUP TOASTED SLICED ALMONDS (SEE PSST ON PAGE 114) FOR GARNISH

1 Melt the butter in the pressure cooker over medium-high heat. Add the onion, celery, and thyme and sauté for 2 minutes, or until the onion begins to soften. Add the barley and cranberries, stirring to coat them with the butter. Pour in the stock and stir to combine. Drizzle the stock with the oil. Lock the lid in place and cook at high pressure for 18 minutes.

2 Quick release the pressure and remove the lid, tilting the pot away from you to avoid the escaping steam. Fluff the barley, season with salt and pepper, and transfer to a serving bowl. Sprinkle the salad with the almonds and serve immediately.

BASIC QUINOA

Quinoa is actually a seed. It has a somewhat crunchy texture and a nutty flavor when cooked. Lovely to use in salads, it's also good in soups and casseroles. It cooks in only five minutes in the pressure cooker, and like other grains, it stores well in the refrigerator or freezer.

MAKES **4** CUPS

1½ CUPS QUINOA
2½ CUPS WATER
3 TO 4 TABLESPOONS CANOLA OIL
SALT AND FRESHLY GROUND BLACK PEPPER

1 Combine the quinoa with the water in the pressure cooker, and drizzle the water with 1 tablespoon of the oil. Lock the lid in place and cook at high pressure for 5 minutes.

2 Quick release the pressure and remove the lid, tilting the pot away from you to avoid the escaping steam. Stir the quinoa. If there is still some water in the bottom of the pot, use a slotted spoon to transfer the quinoa to a serving bowl. Season with salt and pepper. If you're serving immediately, drizzle with the additional 2 to 3 tablespoons of oil. Or let cool and store in airtight containers in the refrigerator for up to 2 days or in the freezer for up to 1 month.

QUINOA SALAD WITH ZUCCHINI, PEAS, AND SMOKED TURKEY

Meal-in-a-bowl salads are favorites in our house. The combination of starch, protein, and veggies seems to give us a different taste in each bite. Quinoa salads are delicious, and this one is dressed with a lovely lemon and dill vinaigrette.

SERVES 6

3 CUPS BASIC QUINOA (PAGE 363)

¼ CUP FINELY CHOPPED FRESH CHIVES

2 MEDIUM ZUCCHINI, CUT INTO
½-INCH DICE

2 CUPS FROZEN PETITE PEAS, DEFROSTED

2 MEDIUM CARROTS, CUT INTO
½-INCH DICE

2 CUPS FINELY DICED SMOKED TURKEY
(ABOUT ⅓ POUND)

⅓ CUP EXTRA-VIRGIN OLIVE OIL

¼ CUP CANOLA OIL

2 TABLESPOONS WHITE WINE VINEGAR

2 TABLESPOONS FINELY CHOPPED
FRESH DILL

1½ TEASPOONS SALT

½ TEASPOON FRESHLY GROUND BLACK
PEPPER

1 In a large salad bowl, combine the quinoa, chives, zucchini, peas, carrots, and turkey.

2 In a small mixing bowl, whisk together the oils, vinegar, dill, salt, and pepper until blended. Pour the dressing over the salad and toss to coat the ingredients. Serve the salad cool or at room temperature.

QUINOA SALAD WITH BLACK BEANS, CORN, AND SALSA DRESSING

I love this colorful salad and its spicy salsa dressing. Quinoa is perfect here because it soaks up all the delicious dressing and gives the salad a great texture. And it's good for you!

SERVES 6

3 CUPS BASIC QUINOA (PAGE 363)

4 SCALLIONS (WHITE AND TENDER GREEN PARTS), FINELY CHOPPED

2 CUPS COOKED BLACK BEANS (SEE PAGE 151)

1 CUP FROZEN CORN, DEFROSTED

1 MEDIUM HASS AVOCADO, PITTED, PEELED, AND FINELY CHOPPED

½ CUP CANOLA OIL

¼ CUP FRESH LIME JUICE

¼ CUP FINELY CHOPPED RED ONION

1 GARLIC CLOVE

1 TABLESPOON FINELY CHOPPED JALAPEÑO PEPPER

1 CUP CANNED FIRE-ROASTED TOMATOES, SUCH AS MUIR GLEN OR TRADER JOE'S BRANDS, DRAINED

1 TEASPOON GROUND CUMIN

¼ CUP FINELY CHOPPED FRESH CILANTRO FOR GARNISH

1 In a large mixing bowl, combine the quinoa, scallions, beans, corn, and avocado. In a food processor or blender, combine the oil, lime juice, onion, garlic, jalapeño, tomatoes, and cumin and process until smooth.

2 Pour ½ to ¾ cup of the dressing over the salad and toss to combine. Add more dressing if necessary. Garnish the salad with the chopped cilantro. (Cover and refrigerate the leftover dressing to use as a salsa with chips or as a dressing for romaine lettuce.)

BASIC POLENTA

Polenta is a coarse cornmeal. It cooks well in the pressure cooker without much trouble, but I do like to coat the inside of the cooker with nonstick cooking spray, which makes for an easy cleanup. Although cooked polenta is really just cornmeal mush, it became a rock star on the culinary scene after it began showing up on menus at fancy Mediterranean restaurants. Polenta dresses up well with greens, cheese, or prosciutto for a fancy presentation. It's also terrific as a substitute for pasta. Try it with shrimp sautéed in a garlicky wine sauce or as a bed for a rustic beef stew.

SERVES **6**

4½ CUPS CHICKEN OR VEGETABLE STOCK (PAGE 19 OR 21) OR STORE-BOUGHT CHICKEN OR VEGETABLE BROTH

1½ CUPS POLENTA

1 TEASPOON SALT

2 TABLESPOONS UNSALTED BUTTER, MELTED

1 Coat the inside of the pressure cooker with nonstick cooking spray. Pour in the stock and bring to a boil. Add the polenta and salt and stir. Drizzle with the butter. Lock the lid in place and cook at high pressure for 9 minutes.

2 Quick release the pressure and remove the lid, tilting the pot away from you to avoid the escaping steam. Stir the polenta and transfer to a serving dish. Store leftover polenta in an airtight container in the refrigerator for up to 3 days. It will solidify when cold.

PSST

You can make patties out of it and sauté the patties in butter to serve as a side dish for dinner or as a breakfast dish with warm maple or fruit syrup.

CHEESY POLENTA

Creamy polenta riddled with Parmigiano and garnished with crispy prosciutto is everything I love about Italian food—it's simple and scrumptious. **PORK RAGU WITH POLENTA** (page 219) is one very tasty way to use this dish.

SERVES **6**

2 TABLESPOONS EXTRA-VIRGIN OLIVE OIL

6 THIN PROSCIUTTO DI PARMA SLICES, FINELY CHOPPED

4½ CUPS CHICKEN OR VEGETABLE STOCK (PAGE 19 OR 21) OR STORE-BOUGHT CHICKEN OR VEGETABLE BROTH

1½ CUPS POLENTA

1 TEASPOON SALT

4 TABLESPOONS UNSALTED BUTTER, MELTED

⅓ CUP FRESHLY GRATED PARMIGIANO-REGGIANO CHEESE

1 Heat the oil in a skillet over medium-high heat. Add the prosciutto and sauté until crispy. Remove from the pan, drain on paper towels, and set aside while making the polenta.

2 Coat the inside of the pressure cooker with nonstick cooking spray. Pour in the stock and bring to a boil. Add the polenta and salt and stir. Drizzle 2 tablespoons of the butter over the stock. Lock the lid in place and cook at high pressure for 9 minutes.

3 Quick release the pressure and remove the lid, tilting the pot away from you to avoid the escaping steam. Stir the remaining 2 tablespoons of butter and the cheese into the polenta and transfer it to a serving dish. Garnish with the crispy prosciutto.

BASIC OATMEAL

Steel-cut oats are not only delicious; they also pack a wallop in nutritional value. They're a good source of protein and have properties that help lower cholesterol—not bad for a lowly oat. The problem with steel-cut oats, also known as Irish oatmeal, is that they take forever to cook. So if you are hankering for a bowl of Irish oatmeal and you don't have a lot of time, the pressure cooker will become your new best friend. In five minutes, the steel-cut oats emerge creamy and perfectly cooked, ready for a dollop of butter or some hot milk and maybe some coarse brown sugar. Then just dig in.

SERVES 4

1 CUP STEEL-CUT OATS, SUCH AS MCCANN'S

3½ CUPS WATER

1 TEASPOON SALT

4 TABLESPOONS UNSALTED BUTTER, MELTED

1 In the pressure cooker, combine the oats, water, and salt and drizzle 2 tablespoons of the butter over the water. Lock the lid in place and cook at high pressure for 5 minutes.

2 Quick release the pressure and remove the lid, tilting the pot away from you to avoid the escaping steam. Stir the oatmeal and serve in individual bowls, drizzled with the remaining butter.

LOADED OATMEAL

Zinc Cafe and Market here in San Diego serves oatmeal that gets people lining up around the block every morning. Zinc serves the oatmeal three different ways: One version is topped with steamed milk, homemade fruit-filled granola, and toasted nuts. The fresh "load" is topped with steamed milk, brown sugar, and fresh berries of the season. And the super load is a combination of the first two, for oatmeal nirvana. After eating this version of the super load, you may be good to go until dinnertime!

SERVES 4

1 CUP STEEL-CUT OATS, SUCH AS MCCANN'S

3½ CUPS WATER

1 TEASPOON SALT

2 TABLESPOONS UNSALTED BUTTER, MELTED

1 CUP STEAMED MILK

¼ CUP LIGHT BROWN SUGAR OR RAW SUGAR

1 CUP FRUITED GRANOLA (SEE PSST)

1 CUP MIXED FRESH BERRIES, SUCH AS BLUEBERRIES AND RED RASPBERRIES

½ CUP TOASTED PECANS, WALNUTS, OR SLICED ALMONDS (SEE PSST ON PAGE 114)

1 In the pressure cooker, combine the oats, water, and salt and drizzle the butter over the water. Lock the lid in place and cook at high pressure for 5 minutes.

2 Quick release the pressure and remove the lid, tilting the pot away from you to avoid the escaping steam. Stir the oatmeal and divide among four bowls. Top each serving with a quarter of the steamed milk, brown sugar, granola, fresh berries, and toasted nuts.

PSST

Bear Naked Brand makes good fruited granola and so does Trader Joe's.

DESSERTS

When I first started testing recipes for desserts in the pressure cooker, I was stunned by the results I was getting: perfectly creamy crème brûlée, creamy rice pudding, and smooth-topped cheesecake in twenty minutes or less. Bread puddings took a bit longer, but they were scrumptious. Fruit desserts like poached pears, apples, and peaches were all richly flavored in wine or fruit sauces, demonstrating the myriad choices for cooking up a great dessert in this awesome piece of kitchen equipment.

CLASSIC CRÈME BRÛLÉE

A classic crème brûlée is a perfect dessert; it emerges from the pressure cooker silky smooth, creamy, and fragrant with vanilla. If you're not familiar with vanilla bean paste, it's worth giving it a try. See the Psst on page 356.

SERVES 6

2 CUPS HEAVY CREAM

½ CUP GRANULATED SUGAR

5 LARGE EGG YOLKS

2 TEASPOONS VANILLA BEAN PASTE OR VANILLA EXTRACT

2 CUPS WATER

¼ CUP DEMERARA OR COARSE SUGAR

1 In a small saucepan, heat the cream and granulated sugar over medium-high heat until the sugar dissolves. Set aside to cool slightly. In a mixing bowl, whisk together the egg yolks and vanilla. In a slow stream, pour the cream mixture into the eggs, whisking until blended. Strain the mixture into a large measuring cup and pour into six 4-ounce ramekins. Cover the ramekins tightly with aluminum foil.

2 Pour the water into the pressure cooker, arrange the trivet and steamer basket in the bottom, and stack the ramekins in the basket. Lock the lid in place and cook at high pressure for 10 minutes.

3 Release the pressure naturally and remove the lid, tilting the pot away from you to avoid the escaping steam. Let the custards cool for about 10 minutes in the pressure cooker. Remove them from the pressure cooker and remove the aluminum foil. Blot any accumulated moisture from the top of the custards and cool completely. Refrigerate for at least 4 hours or up to 24 hours.

4 When ready to serve, sprinkle each custard with some of the Demerara sugar. Holding a kitchen torch 10 inches from the custards, melt and caramelize the sugar, about 3 minutes. (Or, preheat the broiler, arrange the custards on a baking sheet, and broil 4 inches from the heat until the sugar begins to caramelize, about 3 minutes.) Serve the crèmes brûlées immediately.

CHOCOLATE CRÈME BRÛLÉE

Dense, smooth, and outrageously rich, this version of crème brûlée has to be one of my favorites. I love serving it to surprised guests, who think that vanilla is the only flavor that crème brûlée comes in! Be sure to use a good-quality chocolate, such as Guittard, Ghirardelli, Lindt, Scharffen Berger, or Valrhona.

SERVES **6**

2 CUPS HEAVY CREAM

⅓ CUP GRANULATED SUGAR

6 OUNCES BITTERSWEET CHOCOLATE, CHOPPED

5 LARGE EGG YOLKS

2 TEASPOONS VANILLA BEAN PASTE OR VANILLA EXTRACT

2 CUPS WATER

¼ CUP DEMERARA OR COARSE SUGAR

1 In a small saucepan, heat the cream and granulated sugar over medium-high heat until the sugar dissolves. Remove from the heat and add the chocolate, stirring until the chocolate is melted. Set aside to cool slightly. In a mixing bowl, whisk together the egg yolks and vanilla. In a slow stream, pour the chocolate cream into the eggs, whisking until blended. Strain the mixture into a large measuring cup and pour into six 4-ounce ramekins. Cover the ramekins tightly with aluminum foil.

2 Pour the water into the pressure cooker, arrange the trivet and steamer basket in the bottom, and stack the ramekins in the basket. Lock the lid in place and cook at high pressure for 8 minutes.

3 Release the pressure naturally and remove the lid, tilting the pot away from you to avoid the escaping steam. Let the custards cool for about 10 minutes in the pressure cooker. Remove them from the pressure cooker and take off the aluminum foil. Blot any accumulated moisture from the top of the custards and cool completely. Refrigerate for at least 4 hours or up to 24 hours.

4 When ready to serve, sprinkle each custard with some of the Demerara sugar. Holding a kitchen torch 10 inches from the custards, melt and caramelize the sugar, about 3 minutes. (Or, preheat the broiler and arrange the custards on a baking sheet. Broil 4 inches away from the heat until the sugar begins to caramelize, about 3 minutes.) Serve the crèmes brûlées immediately.

GINGER CRÈME BRÛLÉE

Crystallized ginger lends an exotic flavor to these creamy packages, for a perfect ending to an elegant meal. Serve the crèmes brûlées with lavender or poppy seed shortbread cookies.

SERVES 6

2 CUPS HEAVY CREAM

½ CUP GRANULATED SUGAR

2 TABLESPOONS CRYSTALLIZED GINGER, FINELY CHOPPED

5 LARGE EGG YOLKS

2 CUPS WATER

¼ CUP DEMERARA OR COARSE SUGAR

1 In a small saucepan, heat the cream and granulated sugar over medium-high heat until the sugar dissolves. Add the ginger and allow the mixture to steep until cooled. In a mixing bowl, whisk the egg yolks and pour in the cream mixture, whisking until blended. Strain the mixture into a large measuring cup and pour into six 4-ounce ramekins. Cover the ramekins tightly with aluminum foil.

2 Pour the water into the pressure cooker, arrange the trivet and steamer basket in the bottom, and stack the ramekins in the basket. Lock the lid in place and cook at high pressure for 10 minutes.

3 Release the pressure naturally and remove the lid, tilting the pot away from you to avoid the escaping steam. Let the custards cool for about 10 minutes in the pressure cooker. Remove them from the pressure cooker and take off the aluminum foil. Blot any accumulated moisture from the top of the custards and cool completely. Refrigerate for at least 4 hours or up to 24 hours.

4 When ready to serve, sprinkle each custard with some of the Demerara sugar. Holding a kitchen torch 10 inches from the custards, melt and caramelize the sugar, about 3 minutes. (Or, preheat the broiler, arrange the custards on a baking sheet, and broil 4 inches away from the heat until the sugar begins to caramelize, about 3 minutes.) Serve the crèmes brûlées immediately.

CARAMEL PUMPKIN CRÈME BRÛLÉE

Dark brown sugar gives this pumpkin crème brûlée a rich caramel flavor. Think about making this for dessert at the holidays for a change of pace.

SERVES 6

2 CUPS HEAVY CREAM

½ CUP FIRMLY PACKED DARK BROWN SUGAR

5 LARGE EGG YOLKS

1 CUP CANNED PUMPKIN PURÉE

½ TEASPOON GROUND CINNAMON

¼ TEASPOON GROUND GINGER

⅛ TEASPOON GROUND CLOVES

2 CUPS WATER

¼ CUP DEMERARA OR COARSE SUGAR

1 In a small saucepan, heat the cream and brown sugar over medium-high heat until the sugar dissolves. Set aside to cool slightly. In a large mixing bowl, whisk together the egg yolks, pumpkin, cinnamon, ginger, and cloves. In a slow stream, pour the cream mixture into the egg yolks mixture, whisking until blended. Strain the mixture into a large measuring cup and pour into six 4-ounce ramekins. Cover the ramekins tightly with aluminum foil.

2 Pour the water into the pressure cooker, arrange the trivet and steamer basket in the bottom, and stack the ramekins in the basket. Lock the lid in place and cook at high pressure for 10 minutes.

3 Release the pressure naturally and remove the lid, tilting the pot away from you to avoid the escaping steam. Let the custards cool for about 10 minutes in the pressure cooker. Remove them from the pressure cooker and take off the aluminum foil. Blot any accumulated moisture from the top of the custards and cool completely. Refrigerate for at least 4 hours or up to 24 hours.

4 When ready to serve, sprinkle each custard with some of the Demerara sugar. Holding a kitchen torch 10 inches from the custards, melt and caramelize the sugar, about 3 minutes. (Or, preheat the broiler, arrange the custards on a baking sheet, and broil 4 inches away from the heat until the sugar begins to caramelize, about 3 minutes.) Serve the crèmes brûlées immediately.

COCONUT CUSTARD BRÛLÉE

I'm a coconut girl from way back. As a child, my favorite birthday cakes were tall coconut layer cakes with creamy frosting. I love a good coconut custard pie, and I'm so addicted, I eat toasted coconut from the baking sheet. This creamy brûlée is just about perfect, with its silken custard and coconut topping.

SERVES 6

2 CUPS HEAVY CREAM

½ CUP GRANULATED SUGAR

5 EGG YOLKS

2 TEASPOONS VANILLA BEAN PASTE OR VANILLA EXTRACT

1½ CUPS SWEETENED SHREDDED COCONUT

2 CUPS WATER

¼ CUP DEMERARA OR COARSE SUGAR

1 In a small saucepan, heat the cream and granulated sugar over medium-high heat until the sugar dissolves. Set aside to cool slightly. In a mixing bowl, whisk together the egg yolks and vanilla. In a slow stream, pour the cream mixture into the egg yolks, whisking until blended. Put 3 tablespoons of coconut in the bottom of each of six 4-ounce ramekins. Strain the egg and cream mixture into a large measuring cup and pour into the ramekins. Cover the ramekins tightly with aluminum foil.

2 Pour the water into the pressure cooker, arrange the trivet and steamer basket in the bottom, and stack the ramekins in the basket. Lock the lid in place and cook at high pressure for 10 minutes.

3 Release the pressure naturally and remove the lid, tilting the pot away from you to avoid the escaping steam. Let the custards cool for about 10 minutes. Remove them from the pressure cooker and take off the aluminum foil. Blot any accumulated moisture from the top of the custards and cool completely. Refrigerate for at least 4 hours or up to 24 hours.

4 When ready to serve, sprinkle each custard with some of the Demerara sugar. Holding a kitchen torch 10 inches from the custards, melt and caramelize the sugar, about 3 minutes. (Or, preheat the broiler, arrange the custards on a baking sheet, and broil 4 inches away from the heat until the sugar begins to cara-melize, about 3 minutes.) Serve the crèmes brûlées immediately.

LEMON POT DE CRÈME

Pot de crème is an old-fashioned French dessert made with a combination of half-and-half and heavy cream. Luxuriously smooth and intensely flavored, pots de crème are a terrific dessert any time. Since we have a lemon tree in our tiny yard, I made good use of its fruit in this dessert.

SERVES **6**

1½ CUPS HALF-AND-HALF

¼ CUP HEAVY CREAM

GRATED ZEST OF 1 LEMON

½ CUP SUGAR

1 LARGE EGG PLUS 3 LARGE EGG YOLKS

2 TEASPOONS LEMON EXTRACT

2 CUPS WATER

WHIPPED CREAM FOR SERVING

SHAVED WHITE CHOCOLATE FOR GARNISH

1 In a small saucepan, heat the half-and-half, cream, lemon zest, and sugar over medium-high heat, stirring to dissolve the sugar. Set aside for 5 minutes to cool. In a large mixing bowl, whisk together the egg and egg yolks with the lemon extract and slowly pour the half-and-half mixture into the eggs, whisking until smooth. Strain the mixture into a large measuring cup and pour into six 4-ounce ramekins. Cover tightly with aluminum foil.

2 Pour the water into the pressure cooker, arrange the trivet and steamer basket in the bottom, and stack the ramekins in the basket. Lock the lid in place and cook at high pressure for 10 minutes.

3 Release the pressure naturally and remove the lid, tilting the pot away from you to avoid the escaping steam. Remove the ramekins from the pressure cooker, discard the aluminum foil, and blot any accumulated moisture from the tops of the ramekins. Cool completely and cover each one with plastic wrap. Refrigerate for at least 4 hours or up to 2 days. Serve each pot de crème with a dollop of whipped cream and shaved white chocolate.

EGGNOG POT DE CRÈME

Redolent of nutmeg and a bit of brandy, these pots de crème are a terrific way to use up eggnog during the holidays.

SERVES 6

1 CUP HALF-AND-HALF

1 CUP HEAVY CREAM

½ CUP SUGAR

¼ TEASPOON FRESHLY GRATED NUTMEG

⅛ TEASPOON GROUND CINNAMON

4 LARGE EGG YOLKS

2 TABLESPOONS BRANDY OR RUM

2 CUPS WATER

1 In a small saucepan, heat the half-and-half, cream, sugar, nutmeg, and cinnamon over medium-high heat, stirring until the sugar dissolves. Cool slightly. In a large mixing bowl, whisk together the egg yolks and brandy and then, in a slow stream, whisk in the cream mixture until smooth. Strain the mixture into a large measuring cup and pour into six 4-ounce ramekins. Cover tightly with aluminum foil.

2 Pour the water into the pressure cooker, arrange the trivet and steamer basket in the bottom, and stack the ramekins in the basket. Lock the lid in place and cook at high pressure for 10 minutes.

3 Release the pressure naturally and remove the lid, tilting the pot away from you to avoid the escaping steam. Carefully remove the ramekins from the pressure cooker and discard the aluminum foil. Blot any accumulated moisture from the tops of the ramekins and cool completely. Cover with plastic wrap and refrigerate for at least 4 hours or up to 2 days before serving.

CAPPUCCINO POT DE CRÈME

I love the foamy top on a hot cup of cappuccino, especially if there are biscotti to be dipped! When you eat one of these pots de crème, you will feel transported to a small bar in Italy, where the barista has just set the perfect cappuccino before you— *molto buono!*

SERVES **6**

1 CUP HEAVY CREAM

1 CUP HALF-AND-HALF

1 TABLESPOON INSTANT ESPRESSO POWDER

½ CUP SUGAR

¼ TEASPOON GROUND CINNAMON

4 LARGE EGG YOLKS

2 CUPS WATER

1 In a small saucepan, heat the cream, half-and-half, espresso, sugar, and cinnamon over medium heat, stirring until the sugar dissolves. Cool the mixture slightly. In a large mixing bowl, whisk the egg yolks and, in a slow stream, pour in the cream mixture, whisking until smooth. Strain the mixture into a large measuring cup and pour into six 4-ounce ramekins. Cover tightly with aluminum foil.

2 Pour the water into the pressure cooker, arrange the trivet and steamer basket in the bottom, and stack the ramekins in the basket. Lock the lid in place and cook at high pressure for 10 minutes.

3 Release the pressure naturally and remove the lid, tilting the pot away from you to avoid the escaping steam. Carefully remove the ramekins from the pressure cooker and discard the aluminum foil. Blot any accumulated moisture from the tops of the ramekins and cool completely. Cover with plastic wrap and refrigerate for at least 4 hours or up to 2 days before serving.

CHAI POT DE CRÈME

Spicy chai tea makes a lovely ending to an Asian-inspired meal. Smooth, creamy, and rich in chai flavor, these pots de crème will make a unique dessert to serve to your guests.

SERVES 6

¾ CUP HALF-AND-HALF

1 CUP HEAVY CREAM

½ CUP SUGAR

¼ CUP CHAI TEA CONCENTRATE (SEE PSST)

4 LARGE EGG YOLKS

2 CUPS WATER

1 In a small saucepan, heat the half-and-half, cream, sugar, and chai concentrate over medium-high heat, stirring until the sugar is dissolved. Set aside to cool slightly. In a large bowl, whisk the egg yolks and slowly pour in the cream mixture, whisking until smooth. Strain the mixture into a large measuring cup and pour into six 4-ounce ramekins. Cover each one tightly with aluminum foil.

2 Pour the water into the pressure cooker, arrange the trivet and steamer basket in the bottom, and stack the ramekins in the basket. Lock the lid in place and cook at high pressure for 10 minutes.

3 Release the pressure naturally and remove the lid, tilting the pot away from you to avoid the escaping steam. Carefully remove the ramekins from the pressure cooker, discard the aluminum foil, and blot any accumulated moisture from the tops of the ramekins. Cool completely. Cover each ramekin with plastic wrap and refrigerate for at least 4 hours or up to 2 days before serving.

PSST

Tazo brand chai tea concentrate can be found in the tea aisle in gourmet markets.

VANILLA BEAN POT DE CRÈME

Smooth, creamy, and bursting with vanilla flavor, these pots de crème are perfect to serve with a berry purée. Or, scatter fresh berries over the pots de crème.

SERVES 6

1 CUP HEAVY CREAM

1 CUP HALF-AND-HALF

½ CUP SUGAR

1 TABLESPOON VANILLA BEAN PASTE, OR 1 VANILLA BEAN, SPLIT

4 LARGE EGG YOLKS

2 CUPS WATER

1 In a small saucepan, heat the cream, half-and-half, sugar, and vanilla bean paste over medium-high heat, stirring until the sugar dissolves. Cool slightly. If using the vanilla bean, scrape the tiny seeds into the cream and discard the vanilla bean pod.

2 In a large mixing bowl, whisk the egg yolks and slowly pour in the cream mixture, whisking until smooth. Strain the mixture into a large measuring cup and pour into six 4-ounce ramekins. Cover each one tightly with aluminum foil.

3 Pour the water into the pressure cooker, arrange the trivet and steamer basket in the bottom, and stack the ramekins in the basket. Lock the lid in place and cook at high pressure for 10 minutes.

4 Release the pressure naturally and remove the lid, tilting the pot away from you to avoid the escaping steam. Carefully remove the ramekins from the pressure cooker, remove the aluminum foil, and blot any accumulated moisture from the tops of the ramekins. Cool completely. Cover the pots de crème with plastic wrap and refrigerate for at least 4 hours or up to 2 days before serving.

CLASSIC BITTERSWEET CHOCOLATE POT DE CRÈME

Chocolate pots de crème are a luscious dessert—rich, dark, and velvety. Your only dilemma will be whether to make several batches to satisfy your cravings for this divine creation. Use a high-quality bittersweet chocolate; the results will be well worth the extra price.

SERVES 6

1 CUP HEAVY CREAM

1 CUP HALF-AND-HALF

½ CUP SUGAR

3 OUNCES BITTERSWEET CHOCOLATE, FINELY CHOPPED

4 LARGE EGG YOLKS

2 CUPS WATER

1 In a small saucepan, heat the cream, half-and-half, and sugar over medium-high heat, stirring to dissolve the sugar. Remove from the heat and add the chocolate, whisking to melt it. In a large mixing bowl, whisk the egg yolks and slowly pour in the cream mixture, whisking until smooth. Strain the mixture into a large measuring cup and pour into six 4-ounce ramekins. Cover each one tightly with aluminum foil.

2 Pour the water into the pressure cooker, arrange the trivet and steamer basket in the bottom, and stack the ramekins in the basket. Lock the lid in place and cook at high pressure for 10 minutes.

3 Release the pressure naturally and remove the lid, tilting the pot away from you to avoid the escaping steam. Carefully remove the ramekins from the pressure cooker, remove the aluminum foil, and blot any accumulated moisture from the tops of the ramekins. Cool completely. Cover the pots de crème with plastic wrap and refrigerate for at least 4 hours or up to 2 days before serving.

WICKED CHOCOLATE POT DE CRÈME

Master chocolatier Jacques Torres sells a wicked hot chocolate at his New York City and Brooklyn chocolate shops. He adds a pinch of cayenne pepper to perk up the drink's flavor, which inspired these hot little desserts.

SERVES 6

1 CUP HEAVY CREAM

1 CUP HALF-AND-HALF

⅛ TEASPOON CAYENNE PEPPER

½ CUP SUGAR

3 OUNCES BITTERSWEET CHOCOLATE, FINELY CHOPPED

4 LARGE EGG YOLKS

2 CUPS WATER

1 In a small saucepan, heat the cream, half-and-half, cayenne, and sugar over medium-high heat, stirring to dissolve the sugar. Remove from the heat and add the chocolate, whisking to melt it. In a large bowl, whisk the egg yolks and slowly pour in the cream mixture, whisking until smooth. Strain the mixture into a large measuring cup and pour into six 4-ounce ramekins. Cover each ramekin tightly with aluminum foil.

2 Pour the water into the pressure cooker, arrange the trivet and steamer basket in the bottom, and stack the ramekins in the basket. Lock the lid in place and cook at high pressure for 10 minutes.

3 Release the pressure naturally and remove the lid, tilting the pot away from you to avoid the escaping steam. Carefully remove the ramekins from the pressure cooker, remove the aluminum foil, and blot any accumulated moisture from the tops of the ramekins. Cool completely. Cover the pots de crème with plastic wrap and refrigerate for at least 4 hours or up to 2 days before serving.

BUTTERSCOTCH POT DE CRÈME

The rich taste of butterscotch permeates these pots de crème. They're delicious served with almond tuiles, a thin, curled cookie. Like pots de crème, tuiles are a classic French sweet.

SERVES **6**

4 TABLESPOONS UNSALTED BUTTER

⅔ CUP FIRMLY PACKED DARK BROWN SUGAR

2 CUPS HEAVY CREAM

4 LARGE EGG YOLKS

2 TABLESPOONS SCOTCH WHISKY

2 CUPS WATER

1 In a small saucepan, melt the butter over medium-high heat and add the sugar, stirring until the sugar dissolves. Continue cooking, without stirring, for 3 to 4 minutes, until the mixture has thickened and turned dark golden brown. Slowly add the cream and stir until the mixture is well blended. In a large mixing bowl, whisk together the egg yolks and Scotch until blended. Slowly add the cream mixture, whisking until smooth. Strain the mixture into a large measuring cup and pour into six 4-ounce ramekins. Cover the ramekins tightly with aluminum foil.

2 Pour the water into the pressure cooker, arrange the trivet and steamer basket in the bottom, and stack the ramekins in the basket. Lock the lid in place and cook at high pressure for 10 minutes.

3 Release the pressure naturally and remove the lid, tilting the pot away from you to avoid the escaping steam. Carefully remove the ramekins from the pressure cooker, remove the aluminum foil, and blot any accumulated moisture from the tops of the ramekins. Cool completely. Cover the pots de crème with plastic wrap and refrigerate for at least 4 hours or up to 2 days before serving.

OLD-FASHIONED RICE PUDDING

Old-fashioned comforting desserts like this one are making a comeback, not only in home kitchens but also in restaurants. Studded with plump short-grain rice and flavored with vanilla and cinnamon, this pudding will be out of your pressure cooker after fifteen minutes at low pressure.

SERVES **6** TO **8**

1½ CUPS ARBORIO OR ANOTHER SHORT-GRAIN RICE

2 CUPS WHOLE MILK

2 CUPS HALF-AND-HALF

1 CUP SUGAR

1 TABLESPOON VANILLA BEAN PASTE OR VANILLA EXTRACT

½ TEASPOON GROUND CINNAMON

⅛ TEASPOON GROUND NUTMEG

1 Coat the inside of the pressure cooker with nonstick cooking spray. Combine all the ingredients in the cooker, stirring to blend. Lock the lid in place and cook at low pressure for 15 minutes.

2 Quick release the pressure and remove the lid, tilting the pot away from you to avoid the escaping steam. Transfer the pudding to a serving bowl and serve warm. Or, cool completely, refrigerate, and serve cold.

PSST

This pudding cooks at low pressure to prevent it from scorching.

CRANBERRY ALMOND RICE PUDDING

Dried cranberries emerge plump and flavorful in this orange-and-almond-scented rice pudding. It's great for breakfast or dessert. The leftovers never seem to last too long in our fridge.

SERVES **6** TO **8**

....

1½ CUPS ARBORIO OR ANOTHER SHORT-GRAIN RICE

2 CUPS WHOLE MILK

1½ CUPS HALF-AND-HALF

½ CUP ORANGE JUICE

1 CUP SUGAR

1 CUP DRIED CRANBERRIES

GRATED ZEST OF 1 ORANGE

½ TEASPOON ALMOND EXTRACT

1 CUP TOASTED SLICED ALMONDS (SEE PSST ON PAGE 114) FOR GARNISH

1 Coat the inside of the pressure cooker with nonstick cooking spray. Combine the rice, milk, half-and-half, orange juice, sugar, cranberries, orange zest, and almond extract in the pressure cooker, stirring to blend. Lock the lid in place and cook at low pressure for 15 minutes.

2 Quick release the pressure and remove the lid, tilting the pot away from you to avoid the escaping steam. Transfer the pudding to a serving bowl and serve warm, garnished with the toasted almonds. Or, cool completely, refrigerate, and serve cold, sprinkled with the nuts.

CHAI BASMATI RICE PUDDING

Fragrant chai tea teams up with aromatic basmati rice in this pudding, which is delicious garnished with chopped kiwi and pineapple.

SERVES **6** TO **8**

1½ CUPS BASMATI RICE

2 CUPS WHOLE MILK

1½ CUPS HALF-AND-HALF

½ CUP CHAI TEA CONCENTRATE
(SEE PSST ON PAGE 380)

1 CUP SUGAR

1 Coat the inside of the pressure cooker with nonstick cooking spray. Combine all the ingredients in the cooker, stirring to blend. Lock the lid in place and cook at low pressure for 15 minutes.

2 Quick release the pressure and remove the lid, tilting the pot away from you to avoid the escaping steam. Transfer the pudding to a serving bowl and serve warm. Or, cool completely, refrigerate, and serve cold.

TOASTED COCONUT RICE PUDDING

The combination of toasted coconut, creamy coconut milk, and a touch of ground nutmeg may fool you into thinking that you're eating a coconut custard pie. I love this pudding topped with chopped fresh pineapple or mango and garnished with more toasted coconut.

SERVES 6 TO 8

1½ CUPS ARBORIO OR ANOTHER SHORT-GRAIN RICE

1½ CUPS WHOLE MILK

1 CUP HALF-AND-HALF

ONE 14-OUNCE CAN COCONUT MILK

1 CUP SUGAR

2 CUPS TOASTED SWEETENED SHREDDED COCONUT (SEE PSST ON PAGE 188)

¼ TEASPOON FRESHLY GRATED NUTMEG

1 Coat the inside of the pressure cooker with nonstick cooking spray. Combine the rice, milk, half-and-half, coconut milk, sugar, 1 cup of the toasted coconut, and the nutmeg in the pressure cooker, stirring to blend. Lock the lid in place and cook at low pressure for 15 minutes.

2 Quick release the pressure and remove the lid, tilting the pot away from you to avoid the escaping steam. Transfer the pudding to a serving bowl and serve warm, garnished with the remaining cup of toasted coconut. Or, cool completely, refrigerate, and serve cold, sprinkled with the toasted coconut.

LOADED RICE PUDDING

I call this "the kitchen sink" rice pudding because I add whatever ingredients I have on hand that will jazz up the pudding. You can toss in up to two cups of dried fruits and nuts without any problems. This pudding is flavored with vanilla and cinnamon, but feel free to flavor yours with citrus zest or other aromatics.

SERVES **6** TO **8**

1½ CUPS ARBORIO OR ANOTHER SHORT-GRAIN RICE

2 CUPS WHOLE MILK

2 CUPS HALF-AND-HALF

1 CUP SUGAR

½ CUP GOLDEN RAISINS

½ CUP CHOPPED DRIED APRICOTS

½ CUP CHOPPED DRIED PINEAPPLE

1 TABLESPOON VANILLA BEAN PASTE OR VANILLA EXTRACT

½ TEASPOON GROUND CINNAMON

1 CUP GRANOLA FOR GARNISH

2 CUPS MIXED FRESH BERRIES, SUCH AS SLICED STRAWBERRIES, BLUEBERRIES, BLACKBERRIES, AND RASPBERRIES FOR GARNISH

1 Coat the inside of the pressure cooker with nonstick cooking spray. Combine the rice, milk, half-and-half, sugar, dried fruit, vanilla, and cinnamon in the pressure cooker, stirring to blend. Lock the lid in place and cook at low pressure for 15 minutes.

2 Quick release the pressure and remove the lid, tilting the pot away from you to avoid the escaping steam. Transfer the pudding to a serving bowl and serve warm, garnished with granola and berries. Or, cool completely, refrigerate, and serve cold with the garnishes.

PSST

You can use any short-grain rice here, but I prefer the creaminess of Arborio.

OLD-FASHIONED BREAD AND BUTTER PUDDING WITH WHISKEY SAUCE

Sweet custard-soaked bread, flavored with cinnamon and nutmeg, bakes in your pressure cooker for twenty-five minutes. It emerges moist and flavorful, ready to be served warm, with a lovely whiskey sauce. The bread pudding was inspired by the bread pudding soufflé served at Commander's Palace, an elegant restaurant in the Garden District of New Orleans. The whiskey sauce they served over it, re-created here, was lick-off-the-spoon delicious. Try it over cake or ice cream, swirled through pudding, over pots de crème, or layered in trifle. For the bread pudding, you will need a 2-quart ceramic or metal soufflé dish that fits into your pressure cooker. You will also need to make an aluminum foil sling that you can use to lower the soufflé dish into the pressure cooker (see the Psst).

SERVES 6

BREAD AND BUTTER PUDDING

6 LARGE EGGS

1½ CUPS HEAVY CREAM

1 CUP WHOLE MILK

1 TEASPOON GROUND CINNAMON

⅛ TEASPOON FRESHLY GRATED NUTMEG

½ CUP SUGAR

1 TABLESPOON VANILLA BEAN PASTE OR VANILLA EXTRACT

6 CUPS TORN EGG BREAD
(1-INCH CUBES; SEE PSST)

2 TABLESPOONS UNSALTED BUTTER, MELTED

2 CUPS WATER

1 Coat the inside of a 2-quart soufflé dish with nonstick cooking spray. Make a sling for the soufflé dish (see Psst) and place the dish in the center of the sling.

2 **To make the pudding:** In a large mixing bowl, whisk together the eggs, cream, milk, cinnamon, nutmeg, sugar, and vanilla. Add the bread cubes, press the cubes into the custard, and stir until the liquid is absorbed. Transfer the mixture to the prepared soufflé dish and drizzle with the melted butter.

3 Pour the water into the pressure cooker and arrange the trivet in the pot. Using the sling, lower the soufflé dish into the pressure cooker and fold the ends over the bread pudding to keep them inside the pressure cooker. Lock the lid in place and cook at high pressure for 25 minutes.

4 Release the pressure naturally and remove the lid, tilting the pot away from you to avoid the escaping steam. Using the sling, lift the soufflé dish out of the pot and transfer to a cooling rack. Let rest for 15 minutes.

WHISKEY SAUCE

4 TABLESPOONS UNSALTED BUTTER

1 CUP FIRMLY PACKED LIGHT
BROWN SUGAR

1 CUP HEAVY CREAM

¼ CUP WHISKEY, SUCH AS JACK DANIEL'S,
MAKER'S MARK, OR YOUR FAVORITE; OR
¼ CUP RUM

UNSWEETENED WHIPPED CREAM
FOR SERVING

5 **To make the sauce:** In a small saucepan, melt the butter over medium-high heat. Add the brown sugar and stir to dissolve. Continue cooking, without stirring, for 4 minutes, or until the sugar begins to caramelize and turn golden brown. Add the cream and bring to a boil. Add the whiskey and simmer for 5 minutes, or until the sauce is thickened. (Store any leftover sauce covered in the refrigerator for up to 1 week. Reheat over low heat on the stove top.)

6 Serve the pudding warm with the whisky sauce and a dollop of unsweetened whipped cream.

PSST

I like to use challah or Hawaiian sweet egg bread for this, but you can also use a white bread with some structure, like a home-style white.

To make a sling for the soufflé dish, cut a piece of heavy-duty aluminum foil 24 inches long. Fold it in half lengthwise, and then in half again two more times, to create a 3-by-24-inch strip.

CHOCOLATE CROISSANT BREAD PUDDING WITH VANILLA CUSTARD SAUCE

Studded with melting chunks of chocolate, this airy croissant bread pudding makes a delicious finale to any meal. The vanilla custard sauce is a thin sauce, which you can also spoon over slices of cake or fresh fruit.

SERVES **6**

BREAD PUDDING

6 LARGE EGGS

1½ CUPS HEAVY CREAM

1 CUP WHOLE MILK

½ CUP SUGAR

1 TABLESPOON VANILLA BEAN PASTE OR VANILLA EXTRACT

6 CUPS TORN EGG BREAD (1-INCH CUBES)

1½ CUPS BITTERSWEET CHOCOLATE CHUNKS

2 TABLESPOONS UNSALTED BUTTER, MELTED

2 CUPS WATER

VANILLA CUSTARD SAUCE

⅓ CUP SUGAR

1 TABLESPOON CORNSTARCH

3 CUPS WHOLE MILK

6 LARGE EGG YOLKS

2 TEASPOONS VANILLA BEAN PASTE OR VANILLA EXTRACT

1 Coat the inside of a 2-quart soufflé dish with nonstick cooking spray. (Make sure the dish will fit inside your cooker.) Make a sling for the soufflé dish (see Psst on page 391) and place the soufflé dish in the center of the sling.

2 **To make the pudding:** In a large mixing bowl, whisk together the eggs, cream, milk, sugar, and vanilla. Add the bread cubes and chocolate, pressing the cubes into the custard, and stir until the liquid is absorbed by the bread. Transfer the mixture to the prepared dish and drizzle with the melted butter.

3 Pour the water into the pressure cooker and place the trivet in the pot. Using the sling, lower the soufflé dish into the pressure cooker and fold the ends over the pudding to keep them inside the pressure cooker. Lock the lid in place and cook at high pressure for 25 minutes.

4 Release the pressure naturally and remove the lid, tilting the pot away from you to avoid the escaping steam. Using the sling, lift the soufflé dish out of the pot and transfer to a cooling rack. Let rest for 15 minutes.

5 **To make the sauce:** In a 2-quart saucepan, stir together all the ingredients and cook over medium heat, whisking occasionally, until the mixture thickens and comes to a boil. Strain into a heat-proof bowl and cool completely. (Store any leftover sauce in airtight containers in the refrigerator for up to 1 week or in the freezer for up to 2 months.)

6 Serve the bread pudding warm with the custard sauce.

COFFEE TOFFEE BREAD PUDDING WITH CARAMEL SAUCE

The espresso-flavored custard, tender bread, and toffee nuggets are a luscious combination. A quickly made caramel sauce is the perfect topping for this simple dessert. Although not a true caramel sauce, it is buttery with the flavor of caramel.

SERVES 6

BREAD PUDDING

6 LARGE EGGS

1½ CUPS HEAVY CREAM

1 CUP WHOLE MILK

1 TABLESPOON INSTANT ESPRESSO POWDER

½ CUP GRANULATED SUGAR

1 TABLESPOON VANILLA BEAN PASTE OR VANILLA EXTRACT

6 CUPS TORN EGG BREAD (1-INCH CUBES)

1 CUP COARSELY CHOPPED ALMOND ROCA

2 TABLESPOONS UNSALTED BUTTER, MELTED

2 CUPS WATER

CARAMEL SAUCE

½ CUP (1 STICK) UNSALTED BUTTER

1 CUP FIRMLY PACKED DARK BROWN SUGAR

1¼ CUPS HEAVY CREAM

UNSWEETENED WHIPPED CREAM FOR SERVING

1 Coat the inside of a 2-quart soufflé dish with nonstick cooking spray. (Make sure the dish will fit inside your cooker.) Make a sling for the soufflé dish (see Psst on page 391) and place the soufflé dish in the center of the sling.

2 **To make the pudding:** In a large mixing bowl, whisk together the eggs, cream, milk, espresso powder, granulated sugar, and vanilla. Add the bread cubes and toffee bits, press the cubes into the custard, and stir until the liquid is absorbed by the bread. Transfer the mixture to the prepared dish and drizzle with the melted butter.

3 Pour the water into the pressure cooker and place the trivet in the pot. Using the sling, lower the soufflé dish into the pressure cooker and fold the ends over the pudding to keep them inside the pressure cooker. Lock the lid in place and cook at high pressure for 25 minutes.

4 Release the pressure naturally and remove the lid, tilting the pot away from you to avoid the escaping steam. Using the sling, lift the soufflé dish out of the pot and transfer to a cooling rack to rest for 15 minutes.

5 **To make the sauce:** In a 2-quart saucepan, melt the butter over medium-high heat. Add the brown sugar and cook, stirring, for 4 minutes, to melt the sugar and brown the butter. Add the cream, bring to a boil, stirring, and cook until the sauce is clear. Remove from the heat and serve warm. (Refrigerate any leftover sauce in airtight containers for up to 1 week. Reheat over low heat before serving.)

6 Serve the bread pudding warm with the caramel sauce and a dollop of the whipped cream.

ELVIS HAS LEFT THE BUILDING PEANUT BUTTER BREAD PUDDING WITH BANANAS FOSTER SAUCE

The King was famous for his late-night cravings for peanut butter and banana sandwiches. Legend has it that he would call down to the kitchen at all hours of the day and night to have his cook Pauline make him a sandwich, grilled just the way he liked it. I think he would have enjoyed this dessert: egg bread swirled with peanut butter custard and topped with rum-soaked bananas Foster sauce. In New Orleans, the sauce is served flambéed over ice cream.

SERVES **6**

BREAD PUDDING

6 LARGE EGGS

1½ CUPS HEAVY CREAM

1 CUP WHOLE MILK

½ CUP GRANULATED SUGAR

1 TEASPOON VANILLA BEAN PASTE OR VANILLA EXTRACT

1 CUP CREAMY PEANUT BUTTER

6 CUPS TORN EGG BREAD (1-INCH CUBES)

2 TABLESPOONS UNSALTED BUTTER, MELTED

2 CUPS WATER

BANANAS FOSTER SAUCE

½ CUP (1 STICK) UNSALTED BUTTER

1 CUP FIRMLY PACKED DARK BROWN SUGAR

¼ TEASPOON GROUND CINNAMON

4 MEDIUM RIPE BANANAS, PEELED AND SLICED ½ INCH THICK

¼ CUP DARK RUM

UNSWEETENED WHIPPED CREAM FOR SERVING

1 Coat the inside of a 2-quart soufflé dish with nonstick cooking spray. (Make sure the dish will fit inside your cooker.) Make a sling for the soufflé dish (see Psst on page 391) and place the soufflé dish in the center of the sling.

2 **To make the pudding:** In a large mixing bowl, combine the eggs, cream, milk, granualted sugar, vanilla, and peanut butter, whisking until almost smooth. You may still have some lumps of peanut butter, but they will melt during the cooking process. Add the bread cubes, press the bread into the custard, and stir until the liquid is absorbed by the bread. Transfer the mixture to the prepared soufflé dish and drizzle with the melted butter.

3 Pour the water into the pressure cooker and place the trivet in the pot. Using the sling, lower the soufflé dish into the pressure cooker and fold the ends over the pudding to keep them inside the pressure cooker. Lock the lid in place and cook at high pressure for 25 minutes.

4 Release the pressure naturally and remove the lid, tilting the pot away from you to avoid the escaping steam. Using the sling, lift the soufflé dish out of the pot and transfer to a cooling rack to rest for 15 minutes.

5 **To make the sauce:** In a large skillet, melt the butter over medium-high heat. Add the brown sugar and cinnamon and cook, stirring, for 5 minutes, or until the sugar dissolves and begins to turn dark golden brown. Add the bananas to the skillet, stir in the rum, and cook for 2 to 3 minutes, spooning the sauce over the bananas. (Cool any leftover sauce and store in an airtight container in the refrigerator for up to 24 hours.)

6 Serve the bread pudding immediately, warm and topped with the bananas Foster sauce and a dollop of unsweetened whipped cream.

MIXED BERRY BREAD PUDDING WITH ORANGE CUSTARD SAUCE

When berries are at their peak in the summer months, I sometimes feel like making a different sort of dessert, and this one fills the bill. The orange-flavored custard is full of berries, which swirl through the airy croissants. A silky custard sauce adds still another orangey note. You can kick it up a notch by adding a few tablespoons of Grand Marnier.

SERVES 6

....

BREAD PUDDING

6 LARGE EGGS

1½ CUPS HEAVY CREAM

1 CUP WHOLE MILK

½ CUP SUGAR

1 TEASPOON GRATED ORANGE ZEST

1 TEASPOON ORANGE EXTRACT

6 CUPS TORN CROISSANTS OR EGG BREAD (1-INCH CUBES)

1½ CUPS MIXED FRESH BERRIES, SUCH AS BLUEBERRIES, BLACKBERRIES, RASPBERRIES, AND SLICED STRAWBERRIES

2 TABLESPOONS UNSALTED BUTTER, MELTED

2 CUPS WATER

ORANGE CUSTARD SAUCE

⅓ CUP SUGAR

1 TABLESPOON CORNSTARCH

3 CUPS WHOLE MILK

6 LARGE EGG YOLKS

2 TEASPOONS ORANGE EXTRACT

UNSWEETENED WHIPPED CREAM FOR SERVING

1 Coat the inside of a 2-quart soufflé dish with nonstick cooking spray. (Make sure the dish will fit inside your cooker.) Make a sling for the soufflé dish (see Psst on page 391) and place the soufflé dish in the center of the sling.

2 To make the pudding: In a large mixing bowl, whisk together the eggs, cream, milk, sugar, and orange zest and extract. Add the bread cubes and berries, press the bread into the custard, and stir until the liquid is absorbed by the bread. Transfer the mixture to the prepared soufflé dish and drizzle with the melted butter.

3 Pour the water into the pressure cooker and place the trivet in the pot. Using the sling, lower the soufflé dish into the pressure cooker and fold the ends over the bread pudding to keep them inside the pressure cooker. Lock the lid in place and cook at high pressure for 25 minutes.

4 Release the pressure naturally and remove the lid, tilting the pot away from you to avoid the escaping steam. Using the sling, lift the soufflé dish out of the pot and transfer to a cooling rack. Let sit for 15 minutes.

5 To make the sauce: In a 2-quart saucepan, stir together all the ingredients and cook over medium heat until the sauce thickens and comes to a boil. Strain into a heat-proof bowl and cool completely. (Store any leftover sauce in airtight containers in the refrigerator for up to 1 week or in the freezer for up to 2 months.)

6 Serve the bread pudding warm with the orange custard sauce and a dollop of unsweetened whipped cream.

TROPICAL BREAD PUDDING WITH BUTTERSCOTCH MACADAMIA NUT SAUCE

Served for a luxurious breakfast or for dessert, this pudding and sauce are scrumptious.

SERVES 6

BREAD PUDDING
5 LARGE EGGS
1½ CUPS HEAVY CREAM
ONE 14-OUNCE CAN COCONUT MILK
½ CUP GRANULATED SUGAR
1 TEASPOON VANILLA BEAN PASTE OR VANILLA EXTRACT
6 CUPS TORN EGG BREAD (1-INCH CUBES)
1 CUP CHOPPED PINEAPPLE
½ CUP FINELY CHOPPED MANGO
½ CUP FINELY CHOPPED PAPAYA
½ CUP SWEETENED FLAKED COCONUT
2 TABLESPOONS UNSALTED BUTTER, MELTED

2 CUPS WATER

BUTTERSCOTCH MACADAMIA NUT SAUCE
½ CUP (1 STICK) UNSALTED BUTTER
1 CUP CHOPPED ROASTED AND SALTED MACADAMIA NUTS
1 CUP FIRMLY PACKED LIGHT BROWN SUGAR
1½ CUPS HEAVY CREAM

UNSWEETENED WHIPPED CREAM FOR SERVING

1 Coat the inside of a 2-quart soufflé dish with nonstick cooking spray. (Make sure the dish will fit inside your cooker.) Make a sling for the soufflé dish (see Psst on page 391) and place the soufflé dish in the center of the sling.

2 **To make the pudding:** In a large mixing bowl, whisk together the eggs, cream, coconut milk, granulated sugar, and vanilla, whisking until smooth. Add the bread cubes and chopped fruit, press the bread into the custard, and stir until the liquid is absorbed by the bread. Transfer the mixture to the prepared soufflé dish, sprinkle the top with coconut, and drizzle with the melted butter.

3 Pour the water into the pressure cooker and place the trivet in the pot. Using the sling, lower the soufflé dish into the pressure cooker and fold the ends over the pudding to keep them inside the pressure cooker. Lock the lid in place and cook at high pressure for 25 minutes.

4 Release the pressure naturally and remove the lid, tilting the pot away from you to avoid the escaping steam. Using the sling, lift the soufflé dish out of the pot and transfer to a cooling rack to rest for 15 minutes.

5 **To make the sauce:** In a 2-quart saucepan, melt the butter over medium-high heat. Add the macadamia nuts and toast for 2 minutes, or until fragrant. Add the brown sugar and cook, stirring, for another 4 minutes, or until the sauce is a golden brown. Add the cream, bring the sauce to a boil, and cook, stirring, until it is clear. (Refrigerate any cooled leftover sauce in an airtight container for up to 2 weeks.)

6 Serve the bread pudding warm with the warm sauce and a dollop of unsweetened whipped cream.

CORN BREAD PUDDING WITH MIXED BERRIES AND TOASTED ALMOND SAUCE

Corn bread isn't usually used to make bread pudding, but I had this dessert at an Italian restaurant, and it was a delicious way to end a meal.

SERVES 6

....

BREAD PUDDING

6 LARGE EGGS

1½ CUPS HEAVY CREAM

1 CUP WHOLE MILK

½ CUP GRANULATED SUGAR

1 TEASPOON GRATED ORANGE ZEST

1 TEASPOON ORANGE EXTRACT

6 CUPS CRUMBLED CORN BREAD

1½ CUPS ASSORTED BERRIES (IF USING STRAWBERRIES, HULL AND SLICE THEM)

2 TABLESPOONS UNSALTED BUTTER, MELTED

2 CUPS WATER

TOASTED ALMOND SAUCE

½ CUP (1 STICK) UNSALTED BUTTER

1 CUP SLIVERED ALMONDS

1 CUP FIRMLY PACKED LIGHT BROWN SUGAR

1½ CUPS HEAVY CREAM

2 TABLESPOONS AMARETTO DI SARONNO

VANILLA GELATO FOR SERVING

1 Coat the inside of a 2-quart soufflé dish with nonstick cooking spray. (Make sure the dish will fit inside your cooker.) Make a sling for the soufflé dish (see Psst on page 391) and place the soufflé dish in the center of the sling.

2 **To make the pudding:** In a large mixing bowl, whisk together the eggs, cream, milk, granulated sugar, and orange zest and extract. Add the corn bread and berries, press the bread crumbs into the custard, and stir until the liquid is absorbed by the corn bread crumbs. Transfer the mixture to the prepared soufflé dish and drizzle with the melted butter.

3 Pour the water into the pressure cooker and place the trivet in the pot. Using the sling, lower the soufflé dish into the pressure cooker and fold the ends over the bread pudding to keep them inside the pressure cooker. Lock the lid in place and cook at high pressure for 25 minutes.

4 Release the pressure naturally and remove the lid, tilting the pot away from you to avoid the escaping steam. Using the sling, lift the soufflé dish out of the pot and transfer to a cooling rack to rest for 15 minutes.

5 **To make the sauce:** In a 2-quart saucepan, melt the butter over medium-high heat. Add the almonds and toast for 2 minutes, or until fragrant. Add the brown sugar and cook, stirring, for another 4 minutes, or until the sauce is a golden brown. Add the cream and Amaretto, bring the sauce to a boil, and cook, stirring, until it is clear. (Refrigerate any leftover sauce in an airtight container for up to 2 weeks.)

6 Serve the bread pudding warm with a scoop of vanilla gelato and the warm toasted almond sauce.

PUMPKIN PECAN BREAD PUDDING

Fragrant with the aromas of fall, this bread pudding is terrific served as a breakfast dish with vanilla custard sauce (see page 392), or as dessert after Thanksgiving dinner with orange custard sauce (see page 396).

SERVES **6**

6 LARGE EGGS

1½ CUPS HEAVY CREAM

1 CUP WHOLE MILK

½ CUP SUGAR

1 TEASPOON VANILLA BEAN PASTE OR VANILLA EXTRACT

1 CUP CANNED PUMPKIN PURÉE

1 TEASPOON GROUND CINNAMON

½ TEASPOON GROUND GINGER

¼ TEASPOON GROUND CLOVES

6 CUPS TORN EGG BREAD (1-INCH CUBES)

1 CUP CHOPPED TOASTED PECANS (SEE PSST ON PAGE 114)

2 TABLESPOONS UNSALTED BUTTER, MELTED

2 CUPS WATER

UNSWEETENED WHIPPED CREAM FOR SERVING

1 Coat the inside of a 2-quart soufflé dish with nonstick cooking spray. (Make sure the dish will fit inside your cooker.) Make a sling for the soufflé dish (see Psst on page 391) and place the soufflé dish in the center of the sling.

2 In a large mixing bowl, whisk together the eggs, cream, milk, sugar, vanilla, pumpkin, cinnamon, ginger, and cloves, whisking until smooth. Add the bread cubes, press the bread into the custard, and stir until the liquid is absorbed. Transfer the mixture to the prepared soufflé dish, sprinkle the top with the pecans, and drizzle with the melted butter.

3 Pour the water into the pressure cooker and place the trivet in the pot. Using the sling, lower the soufflé dish into the pressure cooker and fold the ends over the bread pudding to keep them inside the pressure cooker. Lock the lid in place and cook at high pressure for 25 minutes.

4 Release the pressure naturally and remove the lid, tilting the pot away from you to avoid the escaping steam. Using the sling, lift the soufflé dish out of the pot and transfer to a cooling rack to cool for 15 minutes.

5 Serve the bread pudding warm with a dollop of unsweetened whipped cream.

LEMON CHEESECAKE

Cheesecakes emerge from the pressure cooker creamy and delicious; no more uneven baking, browned tops, or cracks down the center. This cheesecake has a lemon cream cheese filling swirled with lemon curd for a double burst of lemon flavor. I'm fond of graham crackers for the crust with this cheesecake, but feel free to substitute your favorite cookie crumbs. Homemade lemon curd is delicious, but you can use prepared lemon curd.

You will need a 7-inch springform pan, a pressure cooker that is at least a 6-quart size, and a trivet to hold the pan above the water. You will also need to make a sling from heavy-duty aluminum foil to lower the cheesecake into the pressure cooker.

SERVES **6**

....

CRUST

2 TABLESPOONS UNSALTED BUTTER, MELTED

⅓ CUP GRAHAM CRACKER CRUMBS

1 TABLESPOON SUGAR

CHEESECAKE FILLING

TWO 8-OUNCE PACKAGES CREAM CHEESE, SOFTENED

½ CUP SUGAR

2 LARGE EGGS

1 TABLESPOON FRESH LEMON JUICE

1 TEASPOON LEMON EXTRACT

1 CUP LEMON CURD (RECIPE FOLLOWS)

2 CUPS WATER

1 **To make the crust:** Line the bottom and sides of a 7-inch springform pan with aluminum foil, pressing it down into the bottom. Coat the aluminum foil with nonstick cooking spray. In a small bowl, combine the butter, graham cracker crumbs, and sugar. Pat the mixture into the bottom of the prepared pan.

2 Make a sling for the springform pan (see Psst on page 391) and place the pan in the center of the sling. Set aside.

3 **To make the filling:** In the bowl of an electric mixer, cream together the cream cheese and sugar until smooth. Beat in the eggs, one at a time, and then the lemon juice and extract. Beat the mixture until it is smooth. Transfer the batter to the prepared springform pan, smoothing the top. Dollop the lemon curd over the top of the cheesecake and cut through the batter with an offset spatula to marble the batter. Tightly cover the cheesecake with aluminum foil.

4 Pour the water into the pressure cooker and place the trivet in the pot. Use the sling to lower the cheesecake into the pressure cooker and fold the ends over the pan, being careful not to let them rest on the cheesecake. Lock the lid in place and cook at high pressure for 15 minutes.

5 Release the pressure naturally and remove the lid, tilting the pot away from you to avoid the escaping steam. Use the sling to lift the cheesecake out of the pot. Remove the foil from the top and blot any excess water that may have accumulated on top of the cheesecake. Cool the cheesecake on a rack. Remove the sides of the pan and peel the aluminum foil off the sides of the cheesecake. Slide a cake spatula under the cheesecake and transfer it to a serving platter. Cover with plastic wrap and refrigerate for at least 6 hours or up to 3 days before serving. (Or freeze the cheesecake for up to 3 months.)

6 Bring the cheesecake to room temperature and serve.

PSST

Serve cheesecake at room temperature; this allows the flavors to blossom.

LEMON CURD

Homemade lemon curd is delicious on toast and scones. You can also use it to fill cakes or mix it with mascarpone and dollop it on fresh fruits.

MAKES **3** CUPS

1 CUP SUGAR

6 LARGE EGGS

½ TO ⅔ CUP FRESH LEMON JUICE (2 TO 3 LEMONS)

½ CUP (1 STICK) BUTTER, CUT INTO ½-INCH CUBES

In a 2-quart saucepan, stir together the sugar, eggs, and lemon juice and bring the mixture to a boil over medium heat. Remove from the heat and whisk in the butter, a few pieces at a time. Since some lemons will be sweeter than others, taste the curd, and add more juice to taste. Cool the lemon curd completely, press plastic wrap onto the surface of the lemon curd, and store in the refrigerator for up to 4 days or in the freezer for up to 3 months.

PSST

Substitute an equal amount of fresh lime or fresh orange juice to make lime or orange curd. They are both delicious in this cheesecake.

CHOCOLATE MARBLE CHEESECAKE

This is a reverse marble cake: The chocolate is dominant and the vanilla batter is swirled through the chocolate.

SERVES **6**

....

CRUST

2 TABLESPOONS UNSALTED BUTTER, MELTED

⅓ CUP CHOCOLATE WAFER CRUMBS

1 TABLESPOON SUGAR

CHEESECAKE FILLING

2 OUNCES SEMISWEET CHOCOLATE

TWO 8-OUNCE PACKAGES CREAM CHEESE, SOFTENED

½ CUP SUGAR

2 LARGE EGGS

1 TEASPOON VANILLA BEAN PASTE OR VANILLA EXTRACT

2 CUPS WATER

1 **To make the crust:** Line the bottom and sides of a 7-inch springform pan with aluminum foil, pressing it down into the bottom. Coat the aluminum foil with nonstick cooking spray. In a small bowl, combine the butter, chocolate wafer crumbs, and sugar. Pat the mixture into the bottom of the prepared pan.

2 Make a sling for the springform pan (see Psst on page 391) and place the pan in the center of the sling.

3 **To make the filling:** In a small glass bowl, melt the chocolate in the microwave on high power for 1 minute. Stir to melt the chocolate and set aside to cool. In the bowl of an electric mixer, cream together the cream cheese and sugar, beating until smooth. Beat in the eggs, one at a time, and then the vanilla. Beat the mixture until smooth. Transfer ½ cup of the batter to a small bowl and set aside. Beat the melted chocolate into the remaining batter. Transfer the chocolate batter to the prepared springform pan, smoothing the top. Dollop the reserved vanilla batter over the top of the cheesecake and cut through the batter with an offset spatula to marble the batter. Tightly cover the cheesecake with aluminum foil.

4 Pour the water into the pressure cooker and place the trivet in the bottom. Use the sling to lower the cheesecake into the pressure cooker and fold the ends over the pan, being careful not to let them rest on the cheesecake. Lock the lid in place and cook at high pressure for 15 minutes.

5 Release the pressure naturally and remove the lid, tilting the pot away from you to avoid the escaping steam. Use the sling to lift the cheesecake out of the pot. Remove the foil from the top and blot any excess water that may have accumulated on top of the cheesecake. Cool the cheesecake on a rack. Remove the sides of the pan and peel the foil off the sides of the cheesecake. Slide a cake spatula under the cheesecake and transfer it to a serving platter. Cover with plastic wrap and refrigerate for at least 6 hours or up to 3 days before serving.

6 Bring the cheesecake to room temperature and serve.

PRESSURE-BAKED APPLES WITH CARDAMOM CIDER GLAZE

Baked apples are comfort food. This version, fragrant with cardamom and apple cider, makes a delicious dessert and a beautiful side dish. Or use the apples to garnish roast turkey, game hens, chicken, crown roast of pork or lamb, or baked ham. Make sure you choose firm apples; otherwise, they will disintegrate under pressure.

SERVES **6**

1 CUP APPLE CIDER

½ TEASPOON GROUND CARDAMOM

1 CINNAMON STICK, BROKEN INTO 1-INCH PIECES

1 TEASPOON VANILLA BEAN PASTE OR VANILLA EXTRACT

¾ CUP SUGAR

3 LARGE GRANNY SMITH APPLES, PEELED, CORED, AND HALVED

1 In the pressure cooker, combine the cider, cardamom, cinnamon, vanilla, and sugar, stirring to dissolve the sugar. Add the apples to the pot and spoon some of the sauce over the apples. Lock the lid in place and cook at high pressure for 3 minutes.

2 Quick release the pressure and remove the lid, tilting the pot away from you to avoid the escaping steam. Carefully remove the apples from the cider with a slotted spoon and transfer to a serving bowl or platter.

3 Bring the cider to a boil and continue boiling for 5 minutes to reduce and concentrate the flavor. Fish out the cinnamon sticks and pour some of the syrup over the apples. Serve the remaining syrup on the side. (Store any leftover syrup in an airtight container in the refrigerator up for 4 days or in the freezer for up to 3 months.)

PSST

Use the leftover syrup as a glaze for grilled pork or as a topping for cake, ice cream, or gelato.

POACHED WHOLE PEARS WITH CHOCOLATE GLAZE

Sophisticated and scrumptious, these pears are poached in Prosecco syrup and then enrobed in a luscious fudgy glaze. Serve them with a dollop of whipped cream on the side.

SERVES 4

....

POACHED PEARS

2 CUPS PROSECCO

1 VANILLA BEAN, SPLIT

½ CUP SUGAR

4 FIRM RED PEARS, SUCH AS BARTLETT OR ANJOU

2 TABLESPOONS FRESH LEMON JUICE

GRAND MARNIER CHOCOLATE GLAZE

1 CUP SUGAR

⅓ CUP MILK

5 TABLESPOONS UNSALTED BUTTER

6 OUNCES SEMISWEET OR BITTERSWEET CHOCOLATE, CHOPPED

2 TO 3 TABLESPOONS GRAND MARNIER

4 SPRIGS FRESH MINT FOR GARNISH (OPTIONAL)

2 THIN ROUNDS OF ORANGE, HALVED FOR GARNISH (OPTIONAL)

1 **To make the poached pears:** In the pressure cooker, combine the Prosecco, vanilla bean, and sugar and cook over medium-high heat, stirring to dissolve the sugar. Remove from the heat. Peel and core the pears, sprinkle them with the lemon juice, and place in the pressure cooker. Lock the lid in place and cook at high pressure for 1 minute.

2 Quick release the pressure and remove the lid, tilting the pot away from you to avoid the escaping steam. Using a slotted spoon, carefully remove the pears to a serving platter and cool completely. Refrigerate until cold. Remove the vanilla bean, bring the syrup to a boil, and continue boiling for 5 minutes to reduce and concentrate the flavor. The syrup can be used warm or cold. To store any leftover syrup, cool completely and store in an airtight container in the refrigerator for up to 2 days.

3 **To make the glaze:** In a 2-quart saucepan, combine the sugar, milk, and butter and heat until the butter melts and the milk boils. Continue boiling for 1 minute, stirring constantly. Remove from the heat and add the chocolate and Grand Marnier, stirring to melt the chocolate.

4 Place the cold pears on a rack with a baking sheet underneath to catch any drips. Pour some of the chocolate glaze over each pear, covering it completely. Allow to stand at room temperature until the glaze has set. To serve, pool some of the Prosecco syrup on each plate. Stand a pear in each pool and garnish with a sprig of mint and ½ slice of orange, if desired.

POACHED WHOLE PEARS IN PORT WINE SYRUP

This is one of my favorite pear recipes. The pears poach in port with brown sugar, cinnamon, and cloves, infusing the pears with a red hue and a rich flavor. Warning: The syrup is addictive! Serve the pears with a dollop of goat cheese, Roquefort, or vanilla ice cream. Or, serve them as a side dish or use them to garnish roasted turkey, pork loin, game hens, or chicken.

SERVES **8**

2 CUPS RUBY PORT

1½ CUPS FIRMLY PACKED LIGHT BROWN SUGAR

3 CINNAMON STICKS, BROKEN INTO 1-INCH PIECES

4 WHOLE CLOVES

4 MEDIUM FIRM RED BARTLETT OR ANJOU PEARS, PEELED AND CORED

VANILLA ICE CREAM FOR SERVING

1 In the pressure cooker, combine the port, sugar, cinnamon, and cloves over medium-high heat and cook, stirring, until the sugar is dissolved. Add the pears, spooning the sauce over the pears to coat them. Lock the lid in place and cook at high pressure for 1 minute.

2 Quick release the pressure and remove the lid, tilting the pot away from you to avoid the escaping steam. Using a slotted spoon, remove the pears from the liquid and transfer them to a bowl to cool. Fish out the cinnamon and cloves from the syrup and bring the syrup to a boil. Continue boiling for 10 minutes, or until the syrup is reduced and slightly thickened. Cool a bit before using.

3 When ready to serve, arrange each pear half in a small bowl, pour 1 to 2 tablespoons of warm syrup over the pear, and serve with a scoop of vanilla ice cream and a drizzle of syrup over the ice cream.

POACHED PEACHES WITH GOAT CHEESE IN RED WINE GLAZE

Peaches poached in wine look like a red sunset, and they are a delicious treat when served with fresh goat cheese and a cinnamon-infused red wine syrup.

SERVES 6

1 CUP FULL-BODIED RED WINE, SUCH AS CHIANTI, ZINFANDEL, OR BAROLO

½ CUP PEACH NECTAR

1 CUP FIRMLY PACKED LIGHT BROWN SUGAR

2 CINNAMON STICKS, BROKEN INTO 1-INCH PIECES

5 ALLSPICE BERRIES

3 FIRM PEACHES, HALVED AND PITTED

½ CUP CRUMBLED GOAT CHEESE

1 In the pressure cooker, combine the wine, nectar, and sugar over medium-high heat, stirring to dissolve the sugar. Add the cinnamon sticks, allspice, and peaches, spooning the sauce over the peaches to coat them. Lock the lid in place and cook at high pressure for 1 minute.

2 Quick release the pressure and remove the lid, tilting the pot away from you to avoid the escaping steam. Using a slotted spoon, carefully remove the peaches to a serving platter and let cool until warm or at room temperature. Fish the cinnamon and allspice out of the cooking liquid and bring the liquid to a boil. Continue boiling for 10 minutes to concentrate and reduce the glaze. Remove from the heat and let cool slightly.

3 To serve, pool some of the glaze on each plate, top with a peach half, and sprinkle some goat cheese over the peach. Drizzle with a bit more glaze.

POACHED NECTARINES WITH BLUE CHEESE AND CHAMBORD SYRUP

During the summer, nectarines are often overlooked in favor of peaches or apricots. But I love their sweet yet slightly tart flesh. Poaching them in a raspberry liqueur syrup gives the nectarines a lovely red tint and an intense raspberry flavor. Serve with a sprinkling of blue cheese crumbles and the syrup. It's a delightful way to end any dinner.

SERVES 6

1 CUP PEACH NECTAR
¼ CUP CHAMBORD
1 CUP SUGAR
4 FIRM NECTARINES, HALVED AND PITTED
1 CUP CRUMBLED BLUE CHEESE

1 In the pressure cooker, combine the nectar, Chambord, and sugar over medium-high heat, stirring to dissolve the sugar. Add the nectarines, spooning the syrup over the nectarines to coat them. Lock the lid in place and cook at high pressure for 1 minute.

2 Quick release the pressure and remove the lid, tilting the pot away from you to avoid the escaping steam. Using a slotted spoon, carefully remove the nectarines from the syrup and transfer to a serving platter. Let cool to room temperature.

3 Bring the syrup to a boil and boil for 10 minutes to reduce the syrup and concentrate its flavor. Let the syrup cool to room temperature. Spoon some of the syrup over the nectarines, sprinkle with the blue cheese, and drizzle with a bit more syrup.

PSST

The nectarines are delicious with goat cheese or crème fraîche instead of blue cheese for a different flavor.

SAUCES & CONDIMENTS

Sauces and condiments are the jazz that perks up any weeknight meal. **CHIPOTLE KETCHUP** (page 410) or **APPLE AND ONION COMPOTE** (page 424) will wake up your family's taste buds and have them asking for seconds. Some condiments, such as ketchup or chutney, can take hours on the stove top. A pressure cooker, on the other hand, allows you to support your main dishes with stylish sauces even on weeknights. If you have a garden overrun with fruit or vegetables, this is the place to use that bounty. Most condiments can be refrigerated for a few weeks or frozen for several months, so you can serve them on a night when all you want to do is throw something on the grill.

CHIPOTLE KETCHUP

The chipotle peppers add their smoky and spicy notes to this zesty sauce. Use this in place of your regular bottled ketchup on burgers, meat loaf, or meatballs. It's also terrific to serve alongside grilled chicken and makes a world of difference in baked beans.

MAKES **4** CUPS

2 TABLESPOONS CANOLA OIL

1 LARGE SWEET ONION, SUCH AS VIDALIA, FINELY CHOPPED

2 CHIPOTLE CHILES IN ADOBO SAUCE, FINELY CHOPPED

½ TEASPOON GROUND CLOVES

½ TEASPOON GROUND ALLSPICE

¼ TEASPOON DRY MUSTARD

¼ CUP FIRMLY PACKED LIGHT BROWN SUGAR

TWO 28-OUNCE CANS TOMATO PURÉE

⅓ CUP APPLE CIDER VINEGAR

1 TABLESPOON WORCESTERSHIRE SAUCE

2 TABLESPOONS MAPLE SYRUP

1 In the pressure cooker, heat the oil over medium-high heat. Add the onion, chiles, cloves, allspice, and dry mustard and sauté for 2 minutes, or until the onion begins to soften. Add the sugar, tomato purée, vinegar, Worcestershire, and maple syrup. Lock the lid in place and cook at high pressure for 6 minutes.

2 Release the pressure naturally and remove the lid, tilting the pot away from you to avoid the escaping steam. Cool the ketchup completely and then store in airtight containers in the refrigerator for up to 2 weeks or in the freezer for up to 3 months.

JACK DANIEL'S BARBECUE SAUCE

Smoky and sweet, Jack Daniel's strikes just the right notes to balance the flavors of this Memphis-style red sauce. Serve it with pulled pork, grilled chicken, pork ribs, or beef brisket. It's so mouthwatering, it makes any barbecue dish that much better.

MAKES ABOUT 4 CUPS

2 TABLESPOONS CANOLA OIL

1 LARGE SWEET ONION, SUCH AS VIDALIA, FINELY CHOPPED

2 GARLIC CLOVES, MINCED

⅛ TEASPOON CHILI POWDER

1 TEASPOON SWEET PAPRIKA

ONE 15-OUNCE CAN TOMATO SAUCE

1½ CUPS KETCHUP

2 TABLESPOONS WORCESTERSHIRE SAUCE

1 TEASPOON SOY SAUCE

¼ CUP FIRMLY PACKED LIGHT BROWN SUGAR

¼ CUP JACK DANIEL'S WHISKEY

1 In the pressure cooker, heat the oil over medium-high heat. Add the onion, garlic, chili powder, and paprika and sauté until the onion begins to soften, about 2 minutes. Add the tomato sauce, ketchup, Worcestershire, soy sauce, sugar, and whiskey, stirring to combine the ingredients. Lock the lid in place and cook at high pressure for 5 minutes.

2 Release the pressure naturally and remove the lid, tilting the pot away from you to avoid the escaping steam. If not using immediately, cool the sauce completely and store in airtight containers in the refrigerator for up to 2 weeks or in the freezer for up to 3 months.

MINUTI MARINARA

Marinara is a basic tomato sauce that can be used to make myriad dishes, from pasta to pizza, and it's out of the pressure cooker in four minutes. Freeze the sauce for the days when you need a quick dinner. This sauce is a great way to use up those plum tomatoes in your garden. Be sure to peel and seed them before making the sauce.

MAKES ABOUT **6** CUPS

¼ CUP EXTRA-VIRGIN OLIVE OIL

6 GARLIC CLOVES, SLICED

TWO 28-OUNCE CANS PLUM TOMATOES WITH THEIR JUICE, OR 6 POUNDS FRESH PLUM TOMATOES, PEELED AND SEEDED, WITH THEIR JUICE

2 TEASPOONS SALT, PLUS MORE IF NEEDED

½ TEASPOON FRESHLY GROUND BLACK PEPPER, PLUS MORE IF NEEDED

2 TABLESPOONS SUGAR, PLUS MORE IF NEEDED

¼ CUP FINELY CHOPPED FRESH BASIL

¼ CUP FINELY CHOPPED FRESH FLAT-LEAF PARSLEY

1 Heat the oil in the pressure cooker over medium-high heat. Add the garlic and sauté for 1 minute, or until fragrant. Add the tomatoes, salt, pepper, and sugar. Lock the lid in place and cook at high pressure for 4 minutes.

2 If using fresh tomatoes, release the pressure naturally. If using canned tomatoes, quick release the pressure. Remove the lid, tilting the pot away from you to avoid the escaping steam. Stir in the basil and parsley and taste the sauce for seasoning. Add more salt and pepper if needed, or more sugar if the tomatoes are too acidic. Serve immediately with pasta. Or cool completely and store in airtight containers in the refrigerator for up to 1 week or in the freezer for up to 3 months.

BOLOGNESE SAUCE

Bologna, a jewel of a city in the region of Emilia-Romagna, is famous for this rich sauce. It's traditionally made with ground veal, but you can substitute chicken or turkey. The sauce is often served over pappardelle or tortellini, and you can use it to create a lasagna Bolognese.

MAKES ABOUT **4** CUPS

....

2 TABLESPOONS UNSALTED BUTTER

1 LARGE SWEET ONION, SUCH AS VIDALIA, FINELY CHOPPED

2 MEDIUM CARROTS, FINELY CHOPPED

2 CELERY STALKS, FINELY CHOPPED

1 POUND GROUND VEAL

½ POUND LEAN GROUND PORK

1½ TEASPOONS SALT

½ TEASPOON FRESHLY GROUND BLACK PEPPER

¼ TEASPOON FRESHLY GRATED NUTMEG

½ CUP BEEF STOCK (PAGE 20) OR STORE-BOUGHT BEEF BROTH

ONE 28-OUNCE CAN CRUSHED TOMATOES WITH THEIR JUICE

1 CUP HEAVY CREAM

¼ CUP FINELY CHOPPED FRESH FLAT-LEAF PARSLEY

1 In the pressure cooker, melt the butter over medium-high heat. Add the onion, carrots, and celery and sauté for 2 minutes to soften the onion. Add the veal and pork and sprinkle with the salt, pepper, and nutmeg. Cook until the meat is no longer pink. Stir in the stock, tomatoes, and cream. Lock the lid in place and cook at high pressure for 5 minutes.

2 Release the pressure naturally and remove the lid, tilting the pot away from you to avoid the escaping steam. Skim off any excess fat from the top of the sauce and stir in the parsley. The sauce can be stored in airtight containers in the refrigerator for up to 4 days or frozen for up to 2 months.

PUTTANESCA SAUCE

This is a great pantry sauce, and since I usually have all the ingredients on hand, I can whip this up any night of the week. It takes only two minutes to cook in the pressure cooker, which makes it one of my go-to dinners when I've been writing or out of the house all day. Traditionally, puttanesca sauce contains anchovies, but I've substituted Italian tuna packed in olive oil, which gives the sauce more structure and flavor.

MAKES **3** CUPS

¼ CUP EXTRA-VIRGIN OLIVE OIL

PINCH OF RED PEPPER FLAKES

2 GARLIC CLOVES, MINCED

ONE 28-OUNCE CAN TOMATO PURÉE

ONE 6-OUNCE CAN ITALIAN TUNA PACKED IN OLIVE OIL

½ CUP TINY CAPERS IN BRINE, DRAINED

½ CUP OIL-CURED OLIVES, PITTED

½ CUP CHOPPED FRESH FLAT-LEAF PARSLEY

1 Heat the oil in the pressure cooker over medium-high heat. Add the red pepper flakes and garlic and sauté for 10 seconds, or until fragrant. Add the tomato purée, tuna, capers, and olives. Lock the lid in place and cook at high pressure for 2 minutes.

2 Quick release the pressure and remove the lid, tilting the pot away from you to avoid the escaping steam. Skim off any excess fat from the top of the sauce and stir in the parsley. The sauce will keep in airtight containers in the refrigerator for up to 3 days.

PASTA ALLA PUTTANESCA WITH TOASTED BREAD CRUMBS

Try serving your linguine or spaghetti alla puttanesca with a toasted bread crumb topping. Melt 2 tablespoons of unsalted butter with 2 tablespoons of extra-virgin olive oil over medium-high heat. Add 2 cups of fresh bread crumbs, tossing to coat, and cook until the crumbs are dry and golden brown. Toss the cooked pasta with the sauce and sprinkle the crumbs on top.

VODKA SAUCE

Creamy vodka sauce has just the right amount of heat from the red pepper flakes, and the fresh basil and Parmigiano-Reggiano give it a delicious finish. Your pressure cooker will make quick work of this luxurious sauce.

MAKES ABOUT **4** CUPS

....

½ CUP VODKA

½ TEASPOON RED PEPPER FLAKES

4 TABLESPOONS UNSALTED BUTTER

½ CUP FINELY CHOPPED ONION

1 GARLIC CLOVE, MINCED

2 CUPS HEAVY CREAM

ONE 28-OUNCE CAN CRUSHED TOMATOES

¼ CUP PACKED FRESH BASIL LEAVES, FINELY CHOPPED

½ CUP FRESHLY GRATED PARMIGIANO-REGGIANO CHEESE

SALT AND FRESHLY GROUND BLACK PEPPER (OPTIONAL)

1 In the pressure cooker, heat the vodka over medium heat. Add the red pepper flakes and cook until the vodka evaporates almost completely and a film remains on the bottom of the pot. Add the butter and stir to melt. Add the onion and garlic and sauté for 2 minutes to soften the onion. Add the cream and tomatoes. Lock the lid in place and cook at high pressure for 4 minutes.

2 Quick release the pressure and remove the lid, tilting the pot away from you to avoid the escaping steam. Add the basil and cheese, stirring to blend. Taste the sauce for seasoning and add salt and pepper if necessary. The sauce can be stored in airtight containers in the refrigerator for up to 4 days. Reheat before serving.

PORCINI RED WINE SAUCE

After steeping in red wine, dried porcini come to life in this hearty, rich tomato sauce. The meaty cremini mushrooms add structure to the elegant and tasty sauce, which you can serve on roasted lamb, pork, or beef as well as on pasta.

MAKES ABOUT **5** CUPS

1 CUP FULL-BODIED RED WINE, SUCH AS CHIANTI, ZINFANDEL, OR BAROLO

4 OUNCES DRIED PORCINI MUSHROOMS

2 TABLESPOONS EXTRA-VIRGIN OLIVE OIL

2 GARLIC CLOVES, MINCED

1 LARGE ONION, FINELY CHOPPED

1 POUND CREMINI MUSHROOMS, QUARTERED

ONE 28-OUNCE CAN TOMATO PURÉE

¼ CUP FINELY CHOPPED FRESH FLAT-LEAF PARSLEY

SALT AND FRESHLY GROUND BLACK PEPPER (OPTIONAL)

1 In a small bowl, pour the wine over the porcini and set aside to soften.

2 In the pressure cooker, heat the oil over medium-high heat. Add the garlic and onion and sauté for 2 minutes to soften the onion. Remove the softened porcini from the wine and coarsely chop. Add the porcini and wine, the cremini mushrooms, and the tomato purée to the pot, stirring to blend. Lock the lid in place and cook at high pressure for 4 minutes.

3 Quick release the pressure and remove the lid, tilting the pot away from you to avoid the escaping steam. Stir in the parsley, taste the sauce for seasoning, and add salt and pepper if necessary. The sauce can be stored in airtight containers in the refrigerator for up to 4 days or in the freezer for up to 2 months.

CRANBERRY ORANGE SAUCE

Dried cranberries and juicy oranges make a delicious sauce, which can be served over roast duck, turkey, chicken, or pork loin. It can be used to glaze a ham also. Sweet and tart, it has beautiful color as well as a scrumptious flavor. The sauce makes a nice gift for friends during the holidays.

MAKES ABOUT **2** CUPS

3 LARGE NAVEL ORANGES

2 CUPS DRIED CRANBERRIES

1 CUP FIRMLY PACKED LIGHT BROWN SUGAR

½ TEASPOON GROUND GINGER

1 TEASPOON ALLSPICE BERRIES

¼ CUP GRAND MARNIER

1 Remove the zest from 2 of the oranges and put the zest in the pressure cooker. Juice all 3 oranges into a 2-cup measure and add enough water to measure 1 cup. Pour the juice into the pot and stir in the cranberries, sugar, ginger, and allspice. Lock the lid in place and cook at high pressure for 2 minutes.

2 Release the pressure naturally and remove the lid, tilting the pot away from you to avoid the escaping steam. Fish out the allspice berries and stir in the Grand Marnier. Bring the sauce to a boil and cook, stirring constantly, until thickened, about 3 minutes. Cool completely and store in airtight containers in the refrigerator for up to 2 weeks or in the freezer for up to 2 months.

CHERRY BRANDY SAUCE

Fresh ruby-red, ripe cherries bubbling in a brandy-flavored sauce make a delicious topping for ice cream or cake. The sauce also pairs beautifully with roasted duck, turkey, or pork loin.

MAKES ABOUT **6** CUPS

....

4 TABLESPOONS UNSALTED BUTTER

2 CUPS FIRMLY PACKED LIGHT BROWN SUGAR

1½ CUPS APPLE JUICE

¼ CUP BRANDY

3 CUPS PITTED RIPE CHERRIES, HALVED

1 CUP DRIED CHERRIES

2 TEASPOONS CORNSTARCH

1 Melt the butter in the pressure cooker over medium-high heat. Add the sugar and stir to dissolve. Add the juice, brandy, and cherries. Lock the lid in place and cook at high pressure for 4 minutes.

2 Quick release the pressure and remove the lid, tilting the pot away from you to avoid the escaping steam. In a small bowl, combine the cornstarch and 2 tablespoons of the sauce. Bring the sauce to a boil and stir in the cornstarch mixture. Return the sauce to a boil and cook, stirring constantly, until the sauce is clear and glossy. Cool and store in airtight containers in the refrigerator for up to 2 weeks or in the freezer for up to 2 months.

NECTARINE SAUCE

Nectarines take on an exotic flavor when cooked with cardamom, ginger, and white wine, while brown sugar gives the sauce a caramel note. Serve it as you would applesauce or pear sauce—with grilled fish like halibut or salmon, roasted chicken, or grilled pork chops.

MAKES **4** CUPS

....

1½ CUPS SWEET WHITE WINE, SUCH AS RIESLING OR CHENIN BLANC

1½ CUPS FIRMLY PACKED DARK BROWN SUGAR

1 TEASPOON GROUND CARDAMOM

¼ TEASPOON GROUND GINGER

8 RIPE NECTARINES, PEELED, HALVED, AND PITTED

1 In the pressure cooker, combine the wine, sugar, cardamom, and ginger, stirring to dissolve the sugar. Add the nectarines and spoon the liquid over the fruit. Lock the lid in place and cook at high pressure for 5 minutes.

2 Quick release the pressure and remove the lid, tilting the pot away from you to avoid the escaping steam. Purée the nectarines with an immersion blender or in the food processor. Cool completely before transferring to airtight containers. Store in the refrigerator for up to 1 week or in the freezer for up to 3 months.

STRAWBERRY RHUBARB SAUCE

A little thinner than pie filling, this sauce is delicious spooned over pound cake or vanilla ice cream, layered in a trifle with custard and cake, or made into an English summer pudding. If you add some cornstarch, it becomes a pie filling (see below). The sauce freezes well, allowing you to enjoy the fruits of early summer in the winter.

MAKES ABOUT **6** CUPS

....

1½ POUNDS RHUBARB, CUT INTO 1-INCH PIECES

2 CUPS STRAWBERRIES, HULLED

3 CUPS SUGAR

⅔ CUP WATER

2 TABLESPOONS FRESH LEMON JUICE

1 Put the rhubarb in the pressure cooker and stir in the remaining ingredients. Lock the lid in place and cook at high pressure for 10 minutes.

2 Release the pressure naturally and remove the lid, tilting the pot away from you to avoid the escaping steam. Stir the sauce and cool. Store in airtight containers in the refrigerator for up to 1 week or in the freezer for up to 2 months.

....

STRAWBERRY RHUBARB PIE FILLING

To make a pie from the sauce, when it comes out of the pressure cooker, stir in a slurry of 2 tablespoons of cornstarch mixed with ¼ cup of water. Bring the sauce to a boil and cook until it's clear and thick. Pour into a prebaked 9-inch pie shell and allow to cool.

RED PEAR SAUCE

The combination of juicy red pears, a bit of wine, and fragrant spices makes a colorful alternative to applesauce. The wine turns the pears a delicate shade of pink, and the aromatic cinnamon and allspice flavor the pears while under pressure.

MAKES ABOUT **5** CUPS

½ CUP PEAR NECTAR

½ CUP FULL-BODIED RED WINE, SUCH AS CHIANTI, ZINFANDEL, OR BAROLO

1 CUP SUGAR

2 POUNDS RIPE RED ANJOU OR BARTLETT PEARS, PEELED, CORED, AND COARSELY CHOPPED (ABOUT 4 CUPS)

1 TEASPOON GROUND CINNAMON

⅛ TEASPOON GROUND ALLSPICE

1 In the pressure cooker, combine the pear nectar, wine, and sugar, stirring to dissolve the sugar. Add the pears, cinnamon, and allspice and stir to coat the pears. Lock the lid in place and cook at high pressure for 4 minutes.

2 Quick release the pressure and remove the lid, tilting the pot away from you to avoid the escaping steam. Purée the pear sauce with an immersion blender or in the food processor. Cool the sauce completely and store in airtight containers in the refrigerator for up to 2 weeks or in the freezer for up to 3 months.

SPICY APPLESAUCE

Apples cook quickly in the pressure cooker, so when you get the cooker up to pressure, you will immediately let the pressure drop naturally. The result: perfectly cooked apples that can be puréed with an immersion blender or a food processor. With a nice kick from the cinnamon sticks and apple juice, this applesauce is terrific to serve alongside roasted pork. It's important to use an apple that is specifically for cooking; Cortland, Rome, Jonathan, Granny Smith, McIntosh, and Golden Delicious are usually available in local supermarkets. There may be other varieties in your region; so choose your favorite cooking apple or use several different varieties.

MAKES ABOUT 6 CUPS

....

8 LARGE COOKING APPLES, PEELED, CORED, AND QUARTERED (4 POUNDS)

¾ CUP APPLE JUICE

1½ CUPS SUGAR, PLUS MORE IF NEEDED

2 CINNAMON STICKS

2 TEASPOONS FRESH LEMON JUICE

⅛ TEASPOON FRESHLY GROUND NUTMEG

PINCH OF GROUND CINNAMON (OPTIONAL)

1 Combine all the ingredients except the nutmeg and ground cinnamon in the pressure cooker and stir to blend. Lock the lid in place and bring the cooker to high pressure.

2 When high pressure is reached, remove the pot from the heat and allow the pressure to drop naturally. Remove the lid, tilting the pot away from you to avoid the escaping steam. Remove the cinnamon sticks and use an immersion blender to purée the apples or purée them in a food processor. Stir in the nutmeg, taste the apples, and add more sugar or some ground cinnamon if needed. Cool the sauce and store in airtight containers in the refrigerator for up to 1 week or freeze for up to 2 months.

CINNAMON HOT APPLE PIE SUNDAE SAUCE

There is nothing better than an apple pie, but if you aren't in the mood to bake, and piecrust is your nemesis, this simple sauce can solve all your problems. Sweet, tart, buttery, and laden with brown sugar, it has all the great flavors of an apple pie. It's delicious over vanilla ice cream or cake, served with a dollop of unsweetened whipped cream.

MAKES ABOUT 4 CUPS

½ CUP (1 STICK) UNSALTED BUTTER

⅔ CUP FIRMLY PACKED LIGHT BROWN SUGAR

1 TEASPOON GROUND CINNAMON

⅛ TEASPOON FRESHLY GRATED NUTMEG

½ CUP APPLE CIDER

3 GRANNY SMITH APPLES, PEELED, CORED, AND QUARTERED

1 Melt the butter in the pressure cooker over medium-high heat. Add the sugar, cinnamon, and nutmeg and stir to dissolve the sugar. Add the cider and apples and spoon the sauce over the apples. Lock the lid in place and cook at high pressure for 3 minutes.

2 Quick release the pressure and remove the lid, tilting the pot away from you to avoid the escaping steam. Serve the sauce warm. To store, cool the sauce completely and store in airtight containers in the refrigerator for up to 3 days or in the freezer for up to 3 months.

PSST

The frozen sauce can be microwaved back to bubbling in no time.

APPLE AND ONION COMPOTE

Compotes are little side dishes that add tremendous flavor to ordinary dinners. This recipe, fragrant with orange zest and cinnamon, is terrific served alongside the cranberry sauce at the Thanksgiving table. But don't save it for Thanksgiving. Use it as a relish or as a topping on grilled chicken breasts, roasted game hens, or pan-fried pork chops.

MAKES ABOUT **3** CUPS

1 CUP DRIED APPLES, COARSELY CHOPPED

2 MEDIUM GRANNY SMITH APPLES, PEELED, CORED, AND FINELY CHOPPED

1 CUP FINELY CHOPPED SWEET ONION, SUCH AS VIDALIA

½ CUP APPLE CIDER

2 CINNAMON STICKS, BROKEN INTO 1-INCH PIECES

4 WHOLE CLOVES

1 LARGE NAVEL ORANGE, QUARTERED

1 In the pressure cooker, combine the apples, onion, cider, cinnamon sticks, and cloves, stirring to combine. Squeeze the orange quarters over the pot and toss them in. Lock the lid in place and cook at high pressure for 3 minutes.

2 Release the pressure naturally and remove the lid, tilting the pot away from you to avoid the escaping steam. Remove the orange quarters, cloves, and cinnamon sticks and allow to cool completely. Store in airtight containers in the refrigerator for up to 1 week or in the freezer for up to 2 months.

RHUBARB COMPOTE

When rhubarb and sweet cherries are cooked together, the result is a garnet-colored, richly flavored compote to serve alongside roasted pork tenderloin or chicken. Flavored with ruby port, cinnamon, and cloves, this sauce is also delicious spooned over cream cheese and served with crackers. Or you can give it as a gift during the holidays.

MAKES ABOUT **4** CUPS

1½ POUNDS RHUBARB, CUT INTO 1-INCH PIECES

1 CUP DRIED CHERRIES

2½ CUPS SUGAR

½ CUP RUBY PORT

½ CUP APPLE JUICE

2 CINNAMON STICKS, BROKEN INTO 2-INCH PIECES

4 WHOLE CLOVES

1 Put the rhubarb in the pressure cooker and stir in the remaining ingredients. Lock the lid in place and cook at high pressure for 10 minutes.

2 Release the pressure naturally and remove the lid, tilting the pot away from you to avoid the escaping steam. Remove the cinnamon sticks and cloves and stir the compote. Cool completely. Store in airtight containers in the refrigerator for up to 1 week or in the freezer for up to 2 months.

CRANBERRY RELISH FOR THANKSGIVING

Simple, tart, and sweet, this relish for the traditional feast is also great served at other times of the year, as a glaze for ham or a side dish with roasted chicken or pork.

MAKES ABOUT **7** CUPS

1 LARGE ONION, FINELY CHOPPED

4 CUPS FRESH CRANBERRIES

1 CUP CRANBERRY JUICE

1 CUP SUGAR

4 FIRM PEACHES, PEELED, PITTED, AND COARSELY CHOPPED

1 TEASPOON GROUND CINNAMON

½ TEASPOON GROUND GINGER

1 CUP GOLDEN RAISINS

1 CUP CHOPPED TOASTED WALNUTS (SEE PSST ON PAGE 114)

1 In the pressure cooker, combine the onion, cranberries, juice, sugar, peaches, cinnamon, ginger, and raisins, stirring to dissolve the sugar. Lock the lid in place and cook at high pressure for 4 minutes.

2 Release the pressure naturally and remove the lid, tilting the pot away from you to avoid the escaping steam. Stir in the walnuts and cool completely. Store in airtight containers in the refrigerator for up to 2 weeks or in the freezer for up to 2 months.

CRANBERRY APPLE CHUTNEY

A Thai restaurant here in San Diego sells a sweet, hot cranberry apple chutney that is out of this world. This may not be their exact recipe, but it's close. Serve it with grilled chicken, just as they do in the restaurant.

MAKES ABOUT **4** CUPS

2 CUPS DRIED CRANBERRIES

3 MEDIUM GRANNY SMITH APPLES, PEELED, CORED, AND COARSELY CHOPPED

1 MEDIUM ONION, FINELY CHOPPED

1 CUP APPLE JUICE

1 CUP FIRMLY PACKED LIGHT BROWN SUGAR

1 TABLESPOON FINELY CHOPPED CRYSTALLIZED GINGER

1 TEASPOON TABASCO SAUCE

3 WHOLE CLOVES

1 CINNAMON STICK, BROKEN INTO 1-INCH PIECES

1 In the pressure cooker, combine all the ingredients, stirring to dissolve the sugar. Lock the lid in place and cook at high pressure for 4 minutes.

2 Quick release the pressure and remove the lid, tilting the pot away from you to avoid the escaping steam. Remove the cloves and cinnamon stick from the chutney and cool completely. Store in airtight containers in the refrigerator for up to 2 weeks or in the freezer for up to 2 months.

MANGO CHUTNEY

A standard accompaniment for curried foods, this chutney is also delicious when served on the side with pork chops, roasted pork loin, turkey, chicken, or game hens. When mangoes are plentiful, buy them in quantity, pit and peel them, and cut them up. Store them in airtight containers in the freezer, so you can make this terrific chutney to give to your friends at the holidays.

MAKES 6 CUPS

....

8 RIPE MANGOES, PITTED (SEE PSST ON PAGE 309), PEELED, AND CUT INTO 1-INCH PIECES

2 LARGE ONIONS, FINELY CHOPPED

2 MEDIUM RED BELL PEPPERS, SEEDED, DERIBBED, AND FINELY CHOPPED

2 CUPS PECAN HALVES

1 CUP GOLDEN RAISINS

1 CUP APPLE CIDER VINEGAR

½ CUP HONEY

1 CUP FIRMLY PACKED LIGHT BROWN SUGAR

⅓ CUP FINELY CHOPPED CRYSTALLIZED GINGER

2 TEASPOONS SALT

1 TABLESPOON CELERY SEEDS

1 TEASPOON TABASCO SAUCE

5 WHOLE CLOVES

2 CINNAMON STICKS, BROKEN INTO 1-INCH PIECES

1 Combine all the ingredients in the pressure cooker, stirring to blend. Lock the lid in place and cook at high pressure for 5 minutes.

2 Release the pressure naturally and remove the lid, tilting the pot away from you to avoid the escaping steam. Cool the chutney completely and store in airtight containers in the refrigerator for up to 1 month or in the freezer for up to 2 months.

FIG AND ONION CONFIT

I first had this thick, chunky, sweet and savory sauce one summer when I was teaching at La Combe in Périgord, in the Dordogne region of France. It was served with salty foie gras, along with a sweet wine called Monbazillac. Since then, I have served the confit in the States slathered on goat cheese crostini, as well as with salty cheeses on a cheese platter. And I've baked it into phyllo dough with goat cheese.

MAKES **4** CUPS

....

½ CUP (1 STICK) UNSALTED BUTTER

4 MEDIUM SWEET ONIONS, SUCH AS VIDALIA, FINELY CHOPPED

2 CUPS FIRMLY PACKED LIGHT BROWN SUGAR

20 MEDIUM FIGS, COARSELY CHOPPED

½ CUP DRY WHITE WINE, SUCH AS SAUVIGNON BLANC OR PINOT GRIGIO, OR DRY VERMOUTH

1 CUP GOOD-QUALITY BALSAMIC VINEGAR

1 Melt the butter in the pressure cooker over medium-high heat. Add the onions and sauté for 5 minutes, or until they begin to turn translucent. Add the sugar and stir to dissolve it. Add the figs, wine, and vinegar. Lock the lid in place and cook at high pressure for 5 minutes.

2 Release the pressure naturally and remove the lid, tilting the pot away from you to avoid the escaping steam. Stir the confit and cool completely. Store in airtight containers in the refrigerator for up to 2 weeks or in the freezer for up to 2 months.

AMARETTO PEACH CONSERVE

Dried peaches and apricots create a tangy sweet spread for scones, English muffins, or bagels.

MAKES ABOUT **2** CUPS

1 CUP DRIED PEACHES, COARSELY CHOPPED

½ CUP DRIED APRICOTS, COARSELY CHOPPED

1 CUP PEACH OR APRICOT NECTAR

2 CUPS SUGAR

1 CUP CHOPPED TOASTED WALNUTS (SEE PSST ON PAGE 114)

2 TABLESPOONS AMARETTO DI SARONNO

1 In the pressure cooker, combine the peaches, apricots, nectar, and sugar, stirring to dissolve the sugar. Lock the lid in place and cook at high pressure for 5 minutes.

2 Stir in the walnuts and Amaretto and cool the conserve completely. Store in airtight containers in the refrigerator for up to 2 weeks or in the freezer for up to 3 months.

PEACH BUTTER

Bursting with peachy goodness, this peach butter tastes a bit like a Bellini, that famous drink from Harry's Bar in Venice. The peaches are poached in Prosecco, a sparkling Italian wine that adds sophistication and flavor to this spread. It's delicious on toast or scones.

MAKES ABOUT **6** CUPS

2 CUPS PROSECCO

2 CUPS SUGAR

1 VANILLA BEAN, SPLIT

2 POUNDS RIPE PEACHES, PEELED, PITTED, AND COARSELY CHOPPED (ABOUT 5 CUPS)

1 CUP DRIED PEACHES

1 In the pressure cooker, combine the Prosecco and sugar, stirring to dissolve the sugar. Add the vanilla bean and peaches. Lock the lid in place and cook at high pressure for 10 minutes.

2 Quick release the pressure and remove the lid, tilting the pot away from you to avoid the escaping steam. Remove the vanilla bean and purée the peach butter with an immersion blender or in the food processor until smooth. Simmer the butter for 5 minutes, or until thickened. Cool the butter completely before storing in airtight containers in the refrigerator for up to 1 week or in the freezer for up to 3 months.

PEAR BUTTER

When pears are in season, this cinnamon-and-ginger-flavored spread is simple to prepare, and it makes terrific gifts for teachers or co-workers during the holidays. Keep some on hand for spreading on toast or English muffins or as a substitute for jelly on a PB&J.

MAKES ABOUT **8** CUPS
....

1 CUP PEAR NECTAR

2 TABLESPOONS FRESH LEMON JUICE

1 CUP FIRMLY PACKED LIGHT BROWN SUGAR

1 TEASPOON GROUND CINNAMON

½ TEASPOON GROUND GINGER

4 POUNDS RIPE BARTLETT PEARS, PEELED, CORED, AND COARSELY CHOPPED (ABOUT 8 CUPS)

½ CUP DRIED PEARS, COARSELY CHOPPED

1 In the pressure cooker, stir together the nectar, lemon juice, sugar, cinnamon, and ginger until the sugar is dissolved. Add the fresh and dried pears. Lock the lid in place and cook at high pressure for 4 minutes.

2 Quick release the pressure and remove the lid, tilting the pot away from you to avoid the escaping steam. Using an immersion blender or potato masher, purée the pears in the liquid until fairly smooth. Simmer the pear butter for 10 minutes, or until thickened. Cool completely before transferring to airtight containers. Store in the refrigerator for up to 2 weeks or freeze for up to 4 months.

APRICOT BUTTER

Luxuriously smooth, and with just the right amount of spice and sweetness, this apricot butter can be addictive. There are two steps to the process, but since the apricots cook up in ten minutes, your job will be done in less than half an hour. Enjoy the butter on scones, popovers, toast, English muffins, and pancakes.

MAKES ABOUT 6 CUPS

1 CUP APRICOT NECTAR

3 CUPS SUGAR

2 POUNDS RIPE APRICOTS, HALVED AND PITTED

1 CUP DRIED APRICOTS

1 TABLESPOON VANILLA BEAN PASTE OR VANILLA EXTRACT

⅛ TEASPOON FRESHLY GRATED NUTMEG

1 In the pressure cooker, combine the nectar and 1½ cups of the sugar, stirring to dissolve the sugar. Add the fresh and dried apricots, stirring to coat them with the nectar. Lock the lid in place and cook at high pressure for 10 minutes.

2 Quick release the pressure and remove the lid, tilting the pot away from you to avoid the escaping steam. Press the apricot mixture through a food mill or sieve to remove the skins. Return the apricot mixture and any liquid to the pressure cooker and add the remaining 1½ cups of sugar, the vanilla, and the nutmeg. Cook over medium-high heat for 5 minutes, or until thickened. Cool the butter completely and store in airtight containers in the refrigerator for up to 1 week or in the freezer for up to 3 months.

PSST

Dried apricots help to perk up the flavor of less-than-ripe fresh apricots. I advise you to buy fresh apricots in season and freeze them so you can enjoy this butter year-round.

PUMPKIN BUTTER

Sweet pumpkin gets a caramel note from brown sugar and a flavor boost from dark rum. Scented with the aromas of the fall season, this spread is delicious between cake layers or in an English trifle. Or spread it on scones, English muffins, or toast. It makes a lovely hostess gift during the holidays.

MAKES 6 CUPS

....

1½ CUPS APPLE CIDER

2 CUPS FIRMLY PACKED DARK BROWN SUGAR

1 TEASPOON GROUND CINNAMON

½ TEASPOON GROUND GINGER

⅛ TEASPOON GROUND CLOVES

¼ CUP DARK RUM

6 CUPS CHOPPED SUGAR PUMPKINS (ABOUT 2 SMALL PUMPKINS)

1 In the pressure cooker, combine the cider, sugar, cinnamon, ginger, cloves, and rum, stirring to dissolve the sugar. Add the pumpkin and toss to coat with the spices. Lock the lid in place and cook at high pressure for 6 minutes.

2 Quick release the pressure and remove the lid, tilting the pot away from you to avoid the escaping steam. Purée the pumpkin mixture with an immersion blender or in a food processor. Simmer for 10 minutes, or until thickened. Cool the pumpkin butter completely and store in airtight containers in the refrigerator for up to 2 weeks or in the freezer for up to 3 months.

COOKING FOR BABY

When my daughter, Carrie, announced that she was expecting a baby, we were overjoyed. Now that Princess Poppy has arrived, her parents have been trying to feed her nutritious homemade baby food. The benefits of homemade are clear: no added sugar, salt, starch, or preservatives.

The pressure cooker is the perfect tool for making baby food. The food is ready in a flash, and the cooker does a great job of preserving the nutrients. Homemade baby food can be frozen in ice cube trays or airtight containers for several months. So when fruits and vegetables are in season, cook up several batches and store some for later.

I recommend that you use local organic fruits and vegetables; they have much less residue from pesticides or fertilizers and are fresher. Be sure to wash all unpeeled fruit and vegetables thoroughly before cooking. Honey should never be used when preparing foods for your baby because of the incidence of infant botulism.

The rule for introducing your baby to a new food is simple: Introduce one food at a time, to determine whether your child has any sensitivity to that particular food. If the baby responds well, you can combine it with another food the baby already eats. Try apples with apricots, peaches with blueberries, and lentils with brown rice.

If you have a blender, a food processor, or an immersion blender, you can purée many cooked foods. But unpeeled fruits or vegetables may need to be strained through a fine-mesh strainer or food mill. Once your child has teeth, he or she will be ready for a bit of texture, and you can leave small soft chunks in the baby food. Feeding babies involves trial and error. Each one has his or her own likes and dislikes.

APPLES

Begin with soft apple varieties and then graduate to your favorite cooking apples. Golden Delicious apples are a great way to begin. They fall apart in the pressure cooker, and then it's just a matter of puréeing them in the food processor or blender. Start off using filtered water and then later add apple or other fruit juices as your liquid.

MAKES ABOUT **4** CUPS

6 MEDIUM GOLDEN DELICIOUS APPLES, PEELED, CORED, AND QUARTERED

1 CUP FILTERED WATER

1 Combine the apples and water in the pressure cooker. Lock the lid in place and cook at high pressure for 4 minutes.

2 Quick release the pressure and remove the lid, tilting the pot away from you to avoid the escaping steam. Using a slotted spoon, transfer the apples to a food processor and process the apples, adding some of the cooking liquid to the mixture to thin it. If your baby is just beginning solid foods, the apples should be smooth and loose. Once your baby is used to eating solids, use less of the cooking liquid to thin the apples.

3 Cool the apples completely and store in airtight containers in the refrigerator for up to 3 days or in the freezer for up to 2 months.

GREAT COMBINATIONS

For each of these combinations, quick release the pressure and strain the fruit.

- Combine 4 medium apples, peeled, cored, and quartered; 6 **dried apricots**; and 1 cup of water or juice. Cook at high pressure for 6 minutes.

- Combine 4 medium apples, peeled, cored, and quartered; 1 cup of pitted **cherries**; and 1 cup of water or juice. Cook at high pressure for 6 minutes.

- Combine 4 medium apples, peeled, cored, and quartered; 1 cup of **blueberries**, picked over for stems; and 1 cup of water or juice. Cook at high pressure for 6 minutes.

- Combine 4 medium apples, peeled, cored, and quartered; 2 medium **pears**, peeled, cored, and quartered; and 1 cup of water or juice. Cook at high pressure for 4 minutes.

APRICOTS

Apricots are tart and normally are paired with a sweeter fruit in jarred baby food. But if you are lucky enough to find them at a local farm stand, they will be sweet and juicy. Peeling apricots can be a job in itself, so I recommend pitting the apricots and then cooking them and straining them through a food mill or sieve, which is a lot less labor-intensive.

MAKES ABOUT **4** CUPS

8 LARGE APRICOTS (ABOUT 4 POUNDS), HALVED AND PITTED

1 CUP FILTERED WATER OR APRICOT NECTAR

1 Combine the apricots and water in the pressure cooker. Lock the lid in place and cook at high pressure for 6 minutes.

2 Release the pressure naturally and remove the lid, tilting the pot away from you to avoid the escaping steam. Using a slotted spoon, transfer the apricots to a sieve or a food mill and strain the fruit over a bowl. Cool completely and store in airtight containers in the refrigerator for up to 3 days or in the freezer for up to 3 months.

GREAT COMBINATIONS

For each of these combinations, release the pressure naturally and strain the fruit.

- Combine 6 large apricots, halved and pitted; 2 medium **Golden Delicious apples**, peeled, cored, and quartered; and 1½ cups of water or juice. Cook at high pressure for 6 minutes.

- Combine 6 large apricots, halved and pitted; 2 large **peaches**, halved and pitted; and 1 cup of water or juice. Cook at high pressure for 6 minutes.

- Combine 6 large apricots, halved and pitted; 1 cup of pitted **cherries**; and 1 cup of water or juice. Cook at high pressure for 6 minutes.

- Combine 6 large apricots, halved and pitted; 2 large **plums**, halved and pitted; and 1 cup of water or juice. Cook at high pressure for 6 minutes.

BLUEBERRIES

Blueberries should be introduced to babies only after apples and pears. They need to be cooked with another fruit in order to produce a purée. Blueberries have a tough skin and must be strained through a food mill or sieve.

MAKES ABOUT **4** CUPS

3 CUPS RIPE BLUEBERRIES, PICKED OVER FOR STEMS

3 MEDIUM RIPE GOLDEN DELICIOUS APPLES, PEELED, CORED, AND QUARTERED

1 CUP FILTERED WATER OR FRUIT JUICE

1 Combine the blueberries, apples, and water in the pressure cooker. Lock the lid in place and cook at high pressure for 4 minutes.

2 Quick release the pressure and remove the lid, tilting the pot away from you to avoid the escaping steam. Using a slotted spoon, transfer the mixture to a food mill or sieve set over a bowl and press the mixture through, discarding any solids. Cool completely and store in airtight containers in the refrigerator for up to 3 days or in the freezer for up to 2 months.

GREAT COMBINATION

Combine 3 cups of blueberries, picked over for stems; 2 medium **pears**, peeled, cored, and quartered; and 1 cup of water or juice. Cook at high pressure for 4 minutes. Quick release the pressure and strain the fruit.

CHERRIES

Cherries need to be combined with another fruit to give you a decent purée. I recommend apples, pears, or any of the stone fruits, such as peaches or nectarines.

MAKES ABOUT **4** CUPS

....

2 CUPS PITTED CHERRIES

3 MEDIUM APPLES OR PEARS, PEELED, CORED, AND QUARTERED; OR 3 PEACHES OR NECTARINES, HALVED AND PITTED (ABOUT 2 CUPS OF FRUIT)

1 CUP FILTERED WATER OR JUICE

1 Combine the cherries, apples, and water in the pressure cooker. Lock the lid in place and cook at high pressure for 6 minutes.

2 Release the pressure naturally and remove the lid, tilting the pot away from you to avoid the escaping steam. Using a slotted spoon, transfer the fruit to a food mill or sieve set over a bowl and press the mixture through, discarding any solids. Cool completely and store in airtight containers in the refrigerator for up to 3 days or in the freezer for up to 2 months.

NECTARINES

Nectarines are luscious when fully ripened. I recommend that you try to find nectarines, with either white or orange flesh, at your local farmers' market and serve them to your baby.

MAKES ABOUT 4 CUPS

6 MEDIUM NECTARINES, HALVED AND PITTED

1 CUP FILTERED WATER OR JUICE

1 Combine the nectarines and water in the pressure cooker. Lock the lid in place and cook at high pressure for 6 minutes.

2 Release the pressure naturally and remove the lid, tilting the pot away from you to avoid the escaping steam. Using a slotted spoon, transfer the fruit to a food mill or sieve set over a bowl and press the mixture through. Cool completely and store in airtight containers in the refrigerator for up to 3 days or in the freezer for up to 2 months.

GREAT COMBINATIONS

For each of these combinations, release the pressure naturally and strain the fruit.

- Combine 4 medium nectarines, halved and pitted; 2 large **pears**, peeled, cored, and quartered; and 1 cup of water or juice. Cook at high pressure for 4 minutes.

- Combine 4 medium nectarines, halved and pitted; 2 large **peaches**, halved and pitted; and 1 cup of juice or water. Cook at high pressure for 6 minutes.

- Combine 4 medium nectarines, halved and pitted; 1 cup **blueberries**, picked over for stems; and 1 cup juice or water. Cook at high pressure for 4 minutes.

PEACHES

There is something so right about a fragrant, juicy peach, and your baby should begin to appreciate them from the moment he or she can eat solid foods. Peaches are high in vitamins and minerals and just plain delicious. I prefer making baby food with peaches with orange flesh, but you can certainly use white peaches, donut peaches, or your favorite variety.

MAKES ABOUT **4** CUPS

....

6 MEDIUM PEACHES, HALVED AND PITTED
1 CUP FILTERED WATER OR JUICE

1 Combine the peaches and water in the pressure cooker. Lock the lid in place and cook at high pressure for 6 minutes.

2 Release the pressure naturally and remove the lid, tilting the pot away from you to avoid the escaping steam. Using a slotted spoon, transfer the fruit to a food mill or sieve set over a bowl and press the mixture through. Cool completely and store in airtight containers in the refrigerator for up to 3 days or in the freezer for up to 2 months.

GREAT COMBINATIONS

For each of these combinations, release the pressure naturally and strain the fruit.

- Combine 4 medium peaches, halved and pitted; 2 large **apricots**, halved and pitted; and 1 cup of water or juice. Cook at high pressure for 6 minutes.

- Combine 4 medium peaches, halved and pitted; 1 cup of pitted **cherries**; and 1 cup of water or juice. Cook at high pressure for 6 minutes.

- Combine 4 medium peaches, halved and pitted; 1 cup of **blueberries**, picked over for stems; and 1 cup of water or juice. Cook at high pressure for 6 minutes.

PEARS

Pears cook up quickly, pair well with other fruits, and yield a lot of juice, just like apples. Use any variety of ripe pear for this recipe.

MAKES ABOUT **4** CUPS

6 MEDIUM PEARS, PEELED, CORED, AND QUARTERED

1 CUP FILTERED WATER OR JUICE

1 Combine the pears and water in the pressure cooker. Lock the lid in place and cook at high pressure for 4 minutes.

2 Quick release the pressure and remove the lid, tilting the pot away from you to avoid the escaping steam. Using a slotted spoon, transfer the fruit to a food processor and process the pears, adding some of the cooking liquid to the mixture to thin it. Refrigerate the pears for up to 2 days; you can freeze them for up to 1 month.

GREAT COMBINATIONS

- Combine 4 medium pears, peeled, cored, and quartered; 1 cup of pitted **cherries**; and 1 cup of juice or water. Cook at high pressure for 6 minutes. Release the pressure naturally and strain the fruit.

- Combine 3 medium pears, peeled, cored, and quartered; 3 medium **Golden Delicious apples**, peeled, cored, and quartered; and 1 cup of juice or water. Cook at high pressure for 4 minutes. Quick release the pressure and strain the fruit.

PLUMS

Juicy and sweet, plums are a great fruit to serve to baby either alone or mixed with other fruit.

MAKES ABOUT **4** CUPS

6 LARGE PLUMS, HALVED AND PITTED
1 CUP FILTERED WATER OR JUICE

1 Combine the plums and water in the pressure cooker. Lock the lid in place and cook at high pressure for 6 minutes.

2 Release the pressure naturally and remove the lid, tilting the pot away from you to avoid the escaping steam. Using a slotted spoon, transfer the fruit to a food mill or sieve set over a bowl and press the mixture through. Cool completely and store in airtight containers in the refrigerator for up to 3 days or in the freezer for up to 2 months.

GREAT COMBINATIONS

- Combine 4 large plums, halved and pitted; 2 large **apricots**, halved and pitted; and 1 cup of water or juice. Cook at high pressure for 6 minutes. Release the pressure naturally and strain the fruit.

- Combine 4 large plums, halved and pitted; 1 cup of pitted **cherries**; and 1 cup of juice or water. Cook at high pressure for 6 minutes. Release the pressure naturally and strain the fruit.

Veggies

I recommend that you start your baby off with these vegetables: squash, pumpkin, sweet potatoes, carrots, and beets. They are all high in vitamins and minerals and are sweet enough to be pleasing to your baby. From there, introduce green beans, peas, spinach, and other vegetables. And think about combining lentils with vegetables for added protein. Or, combine vegetables with cooked brown rice for added fiber.

In these recipes, the vegetables are cooked longer than in recipes intended for adults. You want the vegetables to be soft and pliable.

BEETS

Red, golden, pink, and yellow beets are all good choices for baby food. I suggest using medium-size beets, which will cook up faster and taste sweeter than larger ones.

MAKES ABOUT 3 CUPS

1 CUP FILTERED WATER
6 MEDIUM BEETS, SCRUBBED

1 Pour the water into the pressure cooker. Arrange the trivet and steamer basket in the bottom and arrange the beets in the basket. Lock the lid in place and cook at high pressure for 18 minutes.

2 Release the pressure and remove the lid, tilting the pot away from you to avoid the escaping steam. Transfer the beets to a cutting board. When they are cool enough to handle, peel them and cut into small pieces. Purée in the food processor or blender, adding a bit of filtered water to thin the purée. Cool completely. Store in airtight containers in the refrigerator for up to 4 days or in the freezer for up to 3 months.

PSST

When baby is older, add orange or apple juice to flavor the purée.

BROCCOLI

Bright green broccoli is loaded with good-for-baby nutrients and cooks up in a jiffy in the pressure cooker. When babies are older, they often like to eat the cooked small florets or "trees" by picking them up off the high-chair tray.

MAKES ABOUT 4 CUPS

1 CUP FILTERED WATER

4 CUPS BROCCOLI FLORETS
(ABOUT ½ POUND)

1 Pour the water into the pressure cooker. Arrange the trivet and steamer basket in the bottom and arrange the broccoli in the steamer basket. Lock the lid in place and cook at high pressure for 3 minutes.

2 Release the pressure naturally and remove the lid, tilting the pot away from you to avoid the escaping steam. Transfer the broccoli to a food processor or blender and purée, adding a bit of the cooking liquid to thin it. Cool completely. Store in airtight containers in the refrigerator for up to 3 days or in the freezer for up to 2 months.

BUTTERNUT SQUASH

Butternut squash makes a delicious purée for baby. Later on, you can put tiny chunks on the high-chair tray to be picked up by little fingers. My granddaughter, Poppy, loves butternut squash and she eats it with gusto!

MAKES ABOUT **4** CUPS

1 CUP FILTERED WATER

4 CUPS PEELED AND SEEDED BUTTERNUT SQUASH, CUT INTO 1-INCH PIECES

1 Pour the water into the pressure cooker. Arrange the trivet and steamer basket in the bottom and arrange the squash in the basket. Lock the lid in place and cook at high pressure for 12 minutes.

2 Release the pressure naturally and remove the lid, tilting the pot away from you to avoid the escaping steam. Using a slotted spoon, transfer the squash to the food processor or blender. Purée the squash, using some of the cooking liquid to thin the mixture if necessary. Cool the squash completely. Store in airtight containers in the refrigerator for up to 4 days or in the freezer for up to 3 months.

PSST

Substitute filtered apple juice or strained orange juice for the water to add more flavor.

CARROTS

Carrots are a kid-friendly vegetable. From the time children are old enough to eat solids, they all seem to love carrots. I love the speed of cooking them in the pressure cooker and the terrific texture of the purée.

MAKES ABOUT 4 CUPS

1 CUP FILTERED WATER

4 CUPS CUT-UP PEELED CARROTS (1-INCH LENGTHS) OR BABY CARROTS

1 Pour the water into the pressure cooker. Arrange the trivet and steamer basket in the bottom and arrange the carrots in the steamer basket. Lock the lid in place and cook at high pressure for 10 minutes.

2 Release the pressure naturally and remove the lid, tilting the pot away from you to avoid the escaping steam. Transfer the carrots to a food processor or blender and purée, adding a bit of the cooking liquid to thin the purée. Cool completely. Store in airtight containers in the refrigerator for up to 3 days or in the freezer for up to 2 months.

PSST

Carrots can be combined with sweet potatoes, butternut squash, parsnips, or pumpkin for mixed purées.

GREEN BEANS

Tender green beans cook up quickly in the pressure cooker, and they are easily puréed in the food processor or blender.

MAKES ABOUT 2 CUPS

1 CUP FILTERED WATER

2 CUPS GREEN BEANS, STEMMED AND CUT INTO 1-INCH LENGTHS (ABOUT ⅓ POUND)

1 Pour the water into the pressure cooker. Arrange the trivet and steamer basket in the bottom, and arrange the beans in the basket. Lock the lid in place and cook at high pressure for 3 minutes.

2 Release the pressure naturally and remove the lid, tilting the pot away from you to avoid the escaping steam. Transfer the beans to a food processor or blender and purée, adding a bit of the cooking liquid to thin the purée. Cool completely. Store in airtight containers in the refrigerator for up to 2 days or in the freezer for up to 2 months.

PARSNIPS

Parsnips are a great alternative to their cousin, the carrot, with higher levels of calcium, iron, and vitamin E. That's why I urge you to feed them to your baby. The pressure cooker makes fast work of them and they process into a deliciously sweet purée.

MAKES ABOUT **4** CUPS

1 CUP FILTERED WATER

4 CUPS CUT-UP PEELED PARSNIPS
(1-INCH LENGTHS)

1 Pour the water into the pressure cooker. Arrange the trivet and steamer basket in the bottom and arrange the parsnips in the basket. Lock the lid in place and cook at high pressure for 10 minutes.

2 Release the pressure naturally and remove the lid, tilting the pot away from you to avoid the escaping steam. Transfer the parsnips to a food processor or blender and purée, adding a bit of the cooking liquid to thin the purée. Cool completely. Store in airtight containers in the refrigerator for up to 3 days or in the freezer for up to 2 months.

PSST

Try combining parsnips with carrots, sweet potatoes, peas, butternut squash, or pumpkin.

PUMPKIN

Sugar pumpkins are much smaller and sweeter than those you would use to carve for a jack-o'-lantern, and they make a delicious purée for baby to enjoy. Once your baby is eating a variety of foods, I recommend stirring in some cooked lentils or brown rice before processing in the food processor. That way the baby has a complete meal. The beauty of cooking in the pressure cooker is that you will have lots of frozen cooked foods to combine as your baby's diet grows more complex.

MAKES ABOUT **4** CUPS

....

1 CUP FILTERED WATER

ONE 3- TO 4-POUND SUGAR PUMPKIN,
HALVED, SEEDED, AND CUT INTO
2-INCH PIECES

1 Pour the water into the pressure cooker. Arrange the trivet and steamer basket in the bottom and arrange the pumpkin in the basket. Lock the lid in place and cook at high pressure for 15 minutes.

2 Release the pressure naturally and remove the lid, tilting the pot away from you to avoid the escaping steam. When the pumpkin is cool enough to handle, scrape the flesh from the skin and transfer the flesh to a food processor or blender. Purée, adding a bit of filtered water to thin the purée if necessary. Cool completely. Store in airtight containers in the refrigerator for up to 3 days or in the freezer for up to 3 months.

SPINACH

Spinach takes no time to cook in the pressure cooker and it is terrific blended with other foods when your baby is ready. Purée the spinach and blend it with puréed brown rice or lentils for a complete dinner.

MAKES ABOUT **2** CUPS

1 CUP FILTERED WATER
FOUR 10-OUNCE BAGS BABY SPINACH

1 Pour the water into the pressure cooker. Arrange the trivet and steamer basket in the bottom and put the spinach in the basket. Lock the lid in place and cook at high pressure for 1 minute.

2 Quick release the pressure and remove the lid, tilting the pot away from you to avoid the escaping steam. Using a slotted spoon, transfer the spinach to a food processor or blender. Purée the spinach, adding a bit of filtered water to thin the purée if necessary. Cool completely. Store in airtight containers in the refrigerator for up to 3 days or in the freezer for up to 3 months.

SWEET POTATOES

With their smooth texture and pleasing flavor, sweet potatoes are a great first food for babies.

MAKES ABOUT 4 CUPS

....

1 CUP FILTERED WATER

2 LARGE SWEET POTATOES, PEELED AND
CUT INTO 1-INCH CHUNKS

1 Pour the water into the pressure cooker. Arrange the trivet and steamer basket in the bottom and arrange the sweet potatoes in the basket. Lock the lid into place and cook at high pressure for 12 minutes.

2 Release the pressure naturally and remove the lid, tilting the pot away from you to avoid the escaping steam. Using a slotted spoon, transfer the sweet potatoes to the food processor or blender. Purée the sweet potatoes, using some of the cooking liquid to thin the mixture if necessary. Cool the sweet potatoes completely. Store in airtight containers in the refrigerator for up to 4 days or in the freezer for up to 3 months.

Meat

The timing for introducing meat into a baby's diet is purely at the parents' discretion, but most pediatricians recommend waiting until the baby is six to eight months old. At that point, meats should be puréed and mixed with vegetables for a more nutritious dish. One chicken breast half will yield about half a cup of purée. You may want to wait a little longer to introduce beef into your child's diet. Veal and lamb are lean, mild meats, which babies can digest more easily. By the time your child is a year old, he or she should be able to eat table food, as long as it is cooked and mashed into manageable portions.

CHICKEN

Low in fat and calories, chicken will add texture and protein to your child's diet. For baby food, cook chicken longer in the pressure cooker than you normally would, so that it purées easily.

MAKES ABOUT 2 CUPS

4 ORGANIC BONE-IN CHICKEN BREAST HALVES, SKIN REMOVED

1 CUP FILTERED WATER OR SALT-FREE ORGANIC CHICKEN BROTH

1 Combine the chicken and water in the pressure cooker. Lock the lid in place and cook at high pressure for 10 minutes.

2 Quick release the pressure and remove the lid, tilting the pot away from you to avoid the escaping steam. Transfer the meat to a cutting board. Strain the cooking liquid through a fine-mesh sieve and reserve. Cut the meat from the bone, removing any gristle or fat.

3 Put the chicken in a food processor with 2 tablespoons of the cooking liquid and process. With the machine running, add more liquid as needed, until the mixture begins to hold together. Stop the machine and test the consistency. Add more liquid if needed and process again. Cool completely. Store in airtight containers in the refrigerator for up to 2 days or in the freezer for up to 2 months.

TURKEY

Turkey is a lean and flavorful meat and the perfect vehicle to mix with brown rice, lentils, or vegetables for an array of baby foods.

MAKES ABOUT **2** CUPS

....

1 POUND ORGANIC GROUND TURKEY

1 CUP FILTERED WATER OR SALT-FREE ORGANIC CHICKEN BROTH

1 Combine the turkey and water in the pressure cooker, stirring to break up the turkey. Lock the lid in place and cook at high pressure for 5 minutes.

2 Release the pressure naturally and remove the lid, tilting the pot away from you to avoid the escaping steam. Using a slotted spoon, transfer the turkey to a food processor or blender. Strain the cooking liquid through a fine-mesh sieve. Add 2 tablespoons of the cooking liquid to the machine and process for 30 seconds. Scrape down the sides of the bowl and, with the machine running, add more liquid as needed until the mixture begins to hold together. Stop the machine and test the consistency. Add more liquid if needed and process again. Cool completely. Store in airtight containers in the refrigerator for up to 2 days or in the freezer for up to 2 months.

LAMB

Lamb is flavorful and lean, which makes it another great choice for your child. And it cooks up tender in a flash in the pressure cooker, so it's a great choice for you. Try mixing lamb with cooked lentils or any vegetable for a complete baby meal.

MAKES ABOUT **2** CUPS

....

1 POUND ORGANIC GROUND LAMB

1 CUP FILTERED WATER OR SALT-FREE ORGANIC CHICKEN BROTH

1 Combine the lamb and water in the pressure cooker, stirring to break up the lamb. Lock the lid in place and cook at high pressure for 5 minutes.

2 Release the pressure naturally and remove the lid, tilting the pot away from you to avoid the escaping steam. Using a slotted spoon, transfer the meat to a food processor or blender. Strain the cooking liquid through a fine-mesh sieve. Add 2 tablespoons of cooking liquid to the machine and process for 30 seconds. Scrape down the sides of the bowl and, with the machine running, add more liquid as needed until the mixture begins to hold together. Stop the machine and test the consistency. Add more liquid if needed and process again. Cool completely. Store in airtight containers in the refrigerator for up to 2 days or in the freezer for up to 2 months.

VEAL

Lean, mild, and tender, veal is a great meat to start your baby with and to add to baby's favorite vegetables.

MAKES ABOUT **2** CUPS

....

1 POUND ORGANIC GROUND VEAL

1 CUP FILTERED WATER OR SALT-FREE ORGANIC CHICKEN BROTH

1 Combine the veal and water in the pressure cooker, stirring to break up the veal. Lock the lid in place and cook at high pressure for 5 minutes.

2 Release the pressure naturally and remove the lid, tilting the pot away from you to avoid the escaping steam. Using a slotted spoon, transfer the meat to a food processor or blender. Strain the cooking liquid through a fine-mesh sieve. Add 2 tablespoons of cooking liquid to the food processor and process for 30 seconds. Scrape down the sides of the bowl and, with the machine running, add more liquid as needed until the mixture begins to hold together. Stop the machine and test the consistency. Add more liquid if needed and process again. Cool completely. Store in airtight containers in the refrigerator for up to 2 days or in the freezer for up to 2 months.

INDEX

TABLE OF EQUIVALENTS

The exact equivalents in the following tables have been rounded for convenience.

LIQUID/DRY MEASUREMENTS

U.S.	Metric
¼ teaspoon	1.25 milliliters
½ teaspoon	2.5 milliliters
1 teaspoon	5 milliliters
1 tablespoon (3 teaspoons)	15 milliliters
1 fluid ounce (2 tablespoons)	30 milliliters
¼ cup	60 milliliters
⅓ cup	80 milliliters
½ cup	120 milliliters
1 cup	240 milliliters
1 pint (2 cups)	480 milliliters
1 quart (4 cups, 32 ounces)	960 milliliters
1 gallon (4 quarts)	3.84 liters
1 ounce (by weight)	28 grams
1 pound	448 grams
2.2 pounds	1 kilogram

LENGTHS

U.S.	Metric
⅛ inch	3 millimeters
¼ inch	6 millimeters
½ inch	12 millimeters
1 inch	2.5 centimeters

OVEN TEMPERATURE

Fahrenheit	Celsius	Gas
250	120	½
275	140	1
300	150	2
325	160	3
350	180	4
375	190	5
400	200	6
425	220	7
450	230	8
475	240	9
500	260	10